INTERNATIONAL ARBITRATION

IN SWITZERLAND

A HANDBOOK FOR PRACTITIONERS

INTERNATIONAL ARBITRATION IN SWITZERLAND

A HANDBOOK FOR PRACTITIONERS

Edited by:

Gabrielle Kaufmann-Kohler
Blaise Stucki

KLUWER LAW INTERNATIONAL

Schulthess

A C.I.P. Catalogue record for this book is available from the Library of Congress.

ISBN 90 411 2300 8 (Kluwer)
ISBN 3 7255 4797 1 (Schulthess)

Published by Kluwer Law International,
P.O. Box 85889, 2508 CN The Hague, The Netherlands
sales@kluwerlaw.com
http://www.kluwerlaw.com

Sold and distributed in North, Central and South America
by Aspen Publishers, Inc.
7201 McKinney Circle, Frederick, MD 21704, USA

Sold and distributed in all other countries
by Extenza-Turpin Distribution Services,
Stratton Business Park, Pegasus Drive
Biggleswade, Bedfordshire,
SG18 8QB, United Kingdom

Printed on acid-free paper

Printed in the Netherlands.

Table of Contents

Detailed Table of Contents

Authored by Members of the International Arbitration Group of the Law Firm Schellenberg Wittmer, Based in Geneva and Zurich

Zina Abdulla
LL.M, Attorney in Geneva

Martin Bernet
Dr. iur., Attorney in Zurich

Maria Canals Cediel
Dr. iur., LL.M, Attorney in Zurich

Elliott Geisinger
DES, Attorney in Geneva

Christian Girod
LL.M, Attorney in Geneva

Pascale Gola
LL.M, Attorney in Zurich

Alexander Jolles
Attorney in Zurich

Gabrielle Kaufmann-Kohler
Prof., Dr iur., Attorney in Geneva, President of ASA

Corinna Klaus
Attorney in Zurich

Christoph Kurth
LL.M, Attorney in Zurich

Fabrizio La Spada
LL.M, Attorney in Geneva

Manuel Liatowitsch
Dr. iur., Attorney in Zurich

Anna Katharina Müller
Attorney in Zurich

David P. Roney
Barrister and Solicitor, Ontario, Canada and Solicitor, England & Wales

Anne Véronique Schlaepfer
Attorney in Geneva

Georg von Segesser
Dr. iur., Attorney in Zurich

Blaise Stucki
LL.M, Attorney in Geneva

Nathalie Voser
Dr iur., LL.M, Attorney in Zurich

The editors acknowledge the most valuable assistance of **David P. Roney**, who devoted substantial time to ensuring the linguistic accuracy of all contributions.

Selected Bibliography

I. Swiss treaties and monographs

BERTI	S. V. BERTI (ed.), *International Arbitration in Switzerland, an Introduction to and a Commentary on Articles 176 – 194 of the Swiss Private International Law Statute*, Helbing & Lichtenhahn/Kluwer Law International 2000
BUCHER	A. BUCHER, *Le nouvel arbitrage international en Suisse*, Helbing & Lichtenhahn, Basel and Frankfurt-on-the-Main 1988
BUCHER/TSCHANZ	A. BUCHER/P.-Y. TSCHANZ, *International Arbitration in Switzerland*, Helbing & Lichtenhahn, Basle and Frankfurt-on-the-Main 1989
HEINI/KELLER/SIEHR/VISCHER/VOLKEN	A. HEINI/M. KELLER/K. SIEHR/F. VISCHER/P. VOLKEN, *IPRG-Kommentar*, Schulthess, Zurich 1993
HONSELL/VOGT/SCHNYDER	H. HONSELL/N. VOGT/A. SCHNYDER (eds), *Internationales Privatrecht*, Helbing & Lichtenhahn, Basel 1996
LALIVE/POUDRET/REYMOND	P. LALIVE/J.-F. POUDRET/C. REYMOND, *Le droit de l'arbitrage interne et international en Suisse*, Payot, Lausanne 1989

PATOCCHI/GEISINGER — P. M. PATOCCHI/E. GEISINGER, *Internationales Privatrecht*, Orell Füssli, Zurich 2000

POUDRET/BESSON — J.-F. POUDRET/S. BESSON, *Droit comparé de l'arbitrage, international*, Schulthess, Zurich 2002

RÜEDE/HADENFELDT — T. RÜEDE/R. HADENFELDT, *Schweizerisches Schiedsgerichtsrecht,* 2nd edn, Schulthess, Zurich 1993

WALTER/BOSCH/BRÖNNIMANN — G. WALTER/W. BOSCH/J. BRÖNNIMANN, *Internationale Schiedsgerichtsbarkeit in der Schweiz*, Stämpli & Cie AG, Bern 1991

II. General treaties and monographs

BORN — G. BORN, *International Commercial Arbitration*, Kluwer Law International, The Hague 2001

CRAIG/PARK/PAULSSON — W. L. CRAIG/W. W. PARK/J. PAULSSON, *International Chamber of Commerce Arbitration*, 3rd edn, Oceana Publications, Inc., 2000

DERAINS/SCHWARTZ — Y. DERAINS/E. SCHWARTZ, *A guide to the new ICC rules of arbitration*, Kluwer Law International, The Hague 1998

FOUCHARD/GAILLARD/GOLDMAN — E. GAILLARD/J. SAVAGE (eds), *Fouchard Gaillard Goldman on International Commercial Arbitration*, Kluwer Law International, The Hague 1999

LEW/MISTELIS/KRÖLL — J. D. M. LEW/L. MISTELLIS/S. KRÖLL, *Comparative International Commercial Arbitration*, Kluwer Law International, The Hague 2003

RAU/SHERMAN/PEPPET	A. S. RAU/E. F. SHERMAN/S. R. PEPPET, *Process of Dispute Resolution – The Role of Lawyers*, 3rd edn, Foundation Press, New York 2002
REDFERN/HUNTER	D. REDFERN/J. HUNTER, *Law and practice of international commercial arbitration*, Sweet & Maxwell, London 1999

III. Periodicals

Am. Rev. Int'l Arb.	The American Review of International Arbitration
Arb. Int'l	Arbitration International
ASA Bull.	Bulletin of the Swiss Arbitration Association
ASA Special Series	Special Series of the Bulletin of the Swiss Arbitration Association
Bull. CIArb. CCI	Bulletin of the ICC International Court of Arbitration
Int'l Arb. Rep.	Mealey's International Arbitration Report
JDI	Journal du Droit International
JdT	Journal des Tribunaux
J. Int'l Arb.	Journal of International Arbitration
Rev. Arb.	Revue de l'Arbitrage
SJ	Semaine Judiciaire
Yearbook Comm. Arb'n	ICCA Yearbook of Commercial Arbitration

IV. Websites

1. Swiss arbitration links

Basle Chamber of Commerce	<www.hkbb.ch>
Geneva Chamber of Commerce and Industry (CCIG)	<www.ccig.ch>
Swiss Arbitration Association (ASA)	<www.arbitration-ch.org>
Swiss Chambers of Commerce and Industry	<www.cci.ch>
Swiss Rules of International Arbitration	<www.swissarbitration.ch>
Ticino Chamber of Commerce and Industry	<www.cciati.ch>
Zurich Chamber of Commerce (ZCC)	<www.zurichcci.ch>

2. Arbitral institutions

American Arbitration Association (AAA)	<www.adr.org>
Arbitration Institute of the Stockholm Chamber of Commerce	<www.sccinstitute.com/uk/home>
Belgian Center for Arbitration and Mediation (CEPANI)	<www.cepani.be>
Chartered Institute of Arbitrators	<www.arbitrators.org>
China International Economic and Trade Arbitration Commission (CIETAC)	<www.cietac.org.cn>
Court of Arbitration for Sport (CAS)	<www.tas-cas.org>
Deutsche Institution für Schiedsgerichtsbarkeit (DIS)	<www.dis-arb.de>

ICC International Court of Arbitration (ICC)	<www.iccwbo.org/index_court.asp>
International Arbitral Centre of the Austrian Federal Economic Chamber	<www.wko.at/arbitration>
International Center for Dispute Resolution (ICDR)	<www.adr.org/icdr>
International Center for Settlement of Investment Disputes (ICSID)	<www.worldbank.org/icsid/>
London Court of International Arbitration (LCIA)	<www.lcia-arbitration.com>
World Intellectual Property Organization Arbitration and Mediation Center	<www.arbiter.wipo.int>

3. Mediation links

CDR Associates	<www.mediate.org>
Centre for Effective Dispute Resolution (CEDR)	<www.cedr.co.uk>
CPR Institute for Dispute Resolution	<www.cpradr.org>
ICC ADR Rules	<www.iccwbo.org/index_adr.asp>
Mediation Center Zurich	<www.mediation-center.ch>
Mediationsforum Schweiz	<www.mediationsforum.ch>
Swiss Mediation Association	<www.mediation-svm.ch>
WIPO Mediation Rules	<www.arbiter.wipo.int/mediation/rul-es/index.html>

4. *Miscellaneous*

Swiss Federal Tribunal	<www.bger.ch>
International Arbitration Institute (IAI)	<www.iaiparis.com>
International Council for Commercial Arbitration (ICCA)	<www.arbitration-icca.org>
International Institute for the Unification of Private Law (UNIDROIT)	<www.unidroit.org>
United Nations Commission on International Trade Law (UNCITRAL)	<www.uncitral.org>

Abbreviations

AAA	American Arbitration Association
AAA Rules	International Arbitration Rules of the American Arbitration Association effective as of 1 April 1997
ASA	Swiss Arbitration Association
Brussels Convention	Convention on Jurisdiction and the Enforcement of Judgments in Civil and Commercial Matters concluded in Brussels on 27 September 1968
CAS	Court of Arbitration for Sport
CCIG	Geneva Chamber of Commerce and Industry
CCIG Rules	Arbitration Rules of the CCIG effective as of 1 January 1992, amended on 1 May 2000
CEDR	Centre for Effective Dispute Resolution
CISG	United Nations Convention on Contracts for the International Sales of Goods, concluded in Vienna on 11 April 1980
Concordat	Swiss Intercantonal Concordat on Arbitration
CPR	Centre for Public Resources
CRT	Claims Resolution Tribunal
DEBA	Swiss Debt Enforcement and Bankruptcy Act
DFT	Decision of the Swiss Federal Tribunal
GLCP	Geneva Law of Civil Procedure
IBA Rules	IBA Rules on the Taking of Evidence in International Commercial Arbitration adopted on 1 June 1999
ICANN	Internet Corporation for Assigned Names and Numbers

ICC	International Chamber of Commerce
ICC Court	International Court of Arbitration of the International Chamber of Commerce
ICC Rules	Rules of Arbitration of the ICC International Court of Arbitration in force as from 1 January 1998
ICSID	International Center for the Settlement of Investment Disputes
ICSID Convention	Convention on the Settlement of Investment Disputes between States and Nationals of Other States of 18 March 1965
ICSID Rules	ICSID Rules of Procedure for Arbitration proceedings in force as of 1 January 1968, revised on 26 September 1984
JOA	Swiss Judicial Organization Act
LCIA	London Court of International Arbitration
LCIA Rules	Arbitration Rules of the LCIA effective as of 1 January 1998
Lugano Convention	Convention on Jurisdiction and the Enforcement of Judgements in Civil and Commercial Matters concluded in Lugano on 16 September 1988
NY Convention	New York Convention of 10 June 1958 on the Recognition and Enforcement of Foreign Arbitral Awards
OSCE	Organization for Security and Co-operation in Europe
PILA	Swiss Private International Law Act
SCC	Swiss Civil Code
SCO	Swiss Code of Obligations
Swiss Rules	Swiss Rules of International Arbitration in force as of 1 January 2004
UDRP	Uniform Dispute Resolution Policy adopted on 26 August 1999
UNCC	United Nations Compensation Commission
UNCITRAL	United Nations Commission for International Trade Law
UNCITRAL Notes	1996 UNCITRAL Notes on Organizing Arbitral Proceedings
UNCITRAL Rules	UNCITRAL Arbitration Rules adopted on 15 December 1976

WIPO	World Intellectual Property Organization
WTO	World Trade Organization
ZCC	Zurich Chamber of Commerce
ZCCP	Zurich Code of Civil Procedure

Introduction

Gabrielle Kaufmann-Kohler

'*The arbitrators shall meet at Geneva, in Switzerland, at the earliest convenient day after they shall have been named, and shall proceed impartially and carefully to examine all questions that shall be laid before them*'. These are the words of the Washington Treaty of 1871, by which the United States of America and Her Majesty the Queen of the United Kingdom of Great Britain and Ireland chose Geneva, as the seat of arbitration for the famous *Alabama* case. The United States alleged that the United Kingdom had violated its duties as a neutral during the American Civil War, because the Southern States had built and fitted out a large number of vessels in English shipyards, including a vessel named the Alabama. These vessels sank cruisers of the North inflicting substantial loss, for which the United States claimed compensation in the arbitration.

As the then usual practice of resolving such disputes by a mixed commission appeared inadequate, a different type of tribunal was set up, an arbitral tribunal composed of five members, two representatives of the parties, a former Italian minister and senator, a Brazilian diplomat, and a former Swiss federal councillor, all appointed by their governments in accordance with the treaty. The tribunal held a number of hearings between December 1871 and June 1872 and ultimately issued its award in September 1872. By four votes to one, it awarded an amount of 15.5 million gold dollars to the United States, a huge sum at the time. The United Kingdom protested against the award, but nevertheless paid as it was ordered to do.

The hearings were held and the award was made at the City Hall in Geneva, in a room later named the Alabama Hall, the very room in which the First Geneva Convention of the Red Cross was signed in 1864 and which later hosted other well-known arbitrations.

The *Alabama* arbitration is significant for a number of reasons. First, at the time, it averted the acute danger of a war between the United States and the United Kingdom.[1]

---

1 Speech by Judge Gunnar Lagergren in the Rann of Kutch arbitration between India and Pakistan in the Alabama Hall on 15 February 1966, in Gillis Wetter, The International Arbitral Process: Public and Private, Vol. I, New York, 1979, p. 17.

G. Kaufmann-Kohler and B. Stucki (eds), International Arbitration in Switzerland, A Handbook for Practitioners, 1-3.

But its significance for the future was perhaps even greater, as Sir Gerald Fitzmaurice put it when opening the *Beagle Channel* case in the Alabama Hall in 1976: '*Coming when it did, it gave great impetus to the concept of arbitration as a judicial or quasi-judicial method of settling international disputes*'. At the same time, still in Sir Fitzmaurices's words, '*there can be little doubt that it furthered the idea of Geneva as an international city*'. To which he added: '*When I speak of Geneva as an international city,* [...] *I have in mind simply its unsurpassed record in the promotion of the cause of peace and humanity, of good relations between States, and of the settlement of disputes according to justice and law*'.[2]

The *Alabama* case was undoubtedly a milestone in the history of dispute resolution in general, and of dispute resolution in Geneva and Switzerland in particular. Since that time, numerous arbitrations of many different types have taken and are taking place here. A convenient, neutral location, with a long-standing tradition of arbitration, arbitration-friendly legislation, arbitration-supportive courts, and a good infrastructure, are probably the main reasons why parties so often choose Switzerland as a place of arbitration.

Today, the arbitration activity carried out in Switzerland is both intensive and varied. It includes *ad hoc* arbitration, often governed by the UNCITRAL Rules, as well as institutional arbitration. Among the various forms of institutional arbitration in Switzerland, one counts first and foremost ICC arbitration, but there is also a good number of proceedings under other institutional rules, whether they be specialized rules, such as those in the areas of sports and intellectual property, rules administered by foreign associations, or the Swiss Rules of International Arbitration, which the Swiss Chambers of Commerce launched in January 2004.

The scope of arbitration activity also extends well beyond commercial arbitration. It suffices to mention the United Nations Compensation Commission for Claims arising out of the Iraqi invasion of Kuwait, the WTO dispute settlement procedures, the Claims Resolution Tribunal for dormant accounts, and the Property Claims Commission for the compensation of victims of Nazi persecution.

This book is intended to provide insight into one part of this rich field of activity, the part dealing primarily with *commercial arbitration*. It covers the different phases of arbitral proceedings more or less in chronological order, from the drafting of the arbitration clause, including the choice between *ad hoc* or institutional arbitration, to the challenge of the arbitral award. In addition, Chapter 10 provides an overview of the main Swiss and Swiss-based dispute resolution mechanisms, including all of those mentioned above as well as others. Finally, in light of its growing importance as an alternative means of dispute resolution, mediation is also addressed.

This book focuses on *international arbitration* and does not seek to examine domestic proceedings. International and domestic arbitrations are governed by different rules,

2 *Ibid*., p. 19.

Chapter 12 of the PILA for international arbitration and the Concordat for domestic arbitration. It is expected that the Concordat will soon be replaced by Part III of the forthcoming Federal Civil Procedure Act.[3] This dual statutory regime obviously gives rise to the question of what constitutes international arbitration as opposed to domestic arbitration. Article 176(1) of the PILA adopts a 'subjective test' based upon the domicile or habitual residence of the parties. Accordingly, Chapter 12 of the PILA applies to any arbitration if: (i) the seat of the arbitral tribunal is in Switzerland; and (ii) at least one of the parties did not have its domicile or habitual residence in Switzerland at the time of the conclusion of the arbitration agreement.[4]

Focusing on international commercial arbitration, this book adopts a *practice-oriented* approach, adding theoretical support whenever necessary. It primarily aims to provide foreign in-house and external counsel with up-to-date practical information, which will enable them to make the appropriate choices and decisions. The reader will thus find answers to questions such as 'How to draft an arbitration clause?', 'How to choose between *ad hoc* and institutional arbitration?', 'Will the arbitral tribunal grant a specific type of interim measures?', 'How long will setting aside proceedings before the Swiss Federal Tribunal last?' or 'How much will such proceedings cost?'.

With this practice-oriented approach, the authors and editors hope that this book will provide helpful guidance to users and would-be users of international arbitration in Switzerland.

---

3 *Avant-projet de la commission d'expert et rapport accompagnant l'avant-projet de la commission d'expert*, June 2003 available at <www.ejpd.admin.ch/doks/mm/files/030626a_ent-f.pdf>.

4 In a decision of 24 June 2002 (4P.54/2002) in [2003] Bulletin ASA 131, the Swiss Federal Tribunal held that the test is addressed to the domicile (at the time of the arbitration agreement) of persons that are parties to the arbitral proceedings and does not take into consideration the domicile of persons that were parties to the arbitration agreement but are not parties to the arbitral proceedings. For critical comments, see e.g. G. KAUFMANN-KOHLER/A. RIGOZZI, *When is a Swiss arbitration international?*, Jusletter 7 October 2002, available on <www.weblaw.ch/jusletter>.

Chapter 1 - Institutional vs. *ad hoc* Arbitration

Anne Véronique Schlaepfer and Christian Girod

I. Introduction

In Switzerland as elsewhere, there are two basic types of arbitration: *ad hoc* and institutional.

Institutional arbitration plays a dominant role in international arbitration practice, although it is impossible to assess the respective importance of *ad hoc* and institutional arbitration, given that there is no statistical information complied in regard to *ad hoc* arbitration. Nevertheless, during the last twenty years, the well-established arbitral institutions have witnessed a significant growth in activity and numerous new arbitral institutions have opened for business (with more or less success).

The purpose of this chapter is not to assess whether, as a general matter, *ad hoc* or institutional arbitration is a better procedure for parties intending to resort to arbitration. Such a discussion would not be of great interest. Rather, this chapter merely aims to describe the main features of *ad hoc* and institutional arbitration, their advantages and disadvantages (real or supposed), and to assist parties in selecting the form of arbitration they deem appropriate, should a dispute arise in the context of their contractual relationship.

II. *Ad hoc* arbitration

1. *Characteristics*

Ad hoc arbitration is where parties agree upon a form of arbitration that is specific to a particular contract or dispute, without referring to any arbitral institution.[1]

Since *ad hoc* arbitral proceedings are independent of all institutions, the parties have the maximum degree of flexibility to specify different aspects of the arbitral procedure, subject to mandatory law at the seat of the arbitration. For example, the parties may

---

1 LEW/MISTELIS/KRÖLL, N. 3-5, p. 32.

G. Kaufmann-Kohler and B. Stucki (eds), International Arbitration in Switzerland, A Handbook for Practitioners, 5-14.

determine how the arbitrators are to be appointed, how many arbitrators there should be, the procedure to be followed, the timetable for the arbitration and any other special requirements they deem appropriate, having regard to the specific characteristics of the contract in dispute.

In practice, such broad freedom may sometimes prove difficult to manage. Accordingly, parties may choose to subject their *ad hoc* arbitration agreement to existing arbitration rules dealing with all or most of the above issues. For example, the UNCITRAL Rules, which are specifically intended for use in *ad hoc* arbitration, constitute a convenient way for parties to make certain that future arbitral proceedings are adequately regulated, without spending excessive time drafting the arbitration clause and running the risk of creating an arbitration system that proves unworkable once a dispute has arisen.

If parties agree upon *ad hoc* arbitration, they should, however, refrain from referring to institutional arbitration rules in their arbitration agreement. Institutional arbitration rules frequently refer to the role of the concerned institution and, consequently, such an approach is generally unworkable. Similarly, civil procedure rules applicable to proceedings before courts often prove inadequate. Indeed, such rules are not tailored to the needs of international arbitration.

2. *The advantages*

One of the principal advantages of *ad hoc* arbitration is that it can be tailored to the specific needs of the parties and the kind of dispute that may arise under a particular contract.[2]

In certain cases, parties may favour *ad hoc* arbitration in order to avoid being subject to institutional administration or control.

Another advantage sometimes proffered is that *ad hoc* arbitration is faster, since it avoids redundancies and delays supposedly encountered in institutional arbitration. In practice, this is far from being certain. Indeed, in some cases, the assistance of the arbitral institution may facilitate the resolution of difficulties arising during the course of the proceedings, which can prove time-consuming in an *ad hoc* arbitration, particularly when the parties are required to apply to courts. Moreover, the time limits for the early stages of the proceedings (for example, in regard to the appointment of the arbitrators or the determination of the seat of the arbitration) set forth in the rules of the main arbitral institutions ensure that the arbitration is put in motion without unnecessary delay, which is not always the case with *ad hoc* arbitration.

Ad hoc arbitration may be viewed as more confidential.[3] Indeed, since less people are involved (no administrative support by employees of an arbitral institution; no scrutiny

---

2 REDFERN/HUNTER, N. 1-83, p. 47; LEW/MISTELIS/KRÖLL, N. 3-14, p. 35.

3 P. LALIVE, *Avantages et inconvénients de l'arbitrage 'ad hoc'* in *Etudes en faveur de Pierre Bellet*, Litec, Paris 1991, p. 318.

of the award by members of an arbitration court (see Article 27 of the ICC Rules)), the risk of unauthorised disclosure of confidential information should be reduced. In practice, this advantage should not be overestimated. Indeed, breaches of confidentiality obligations are often attributable to the parties themselves (or one of them), not to the institution.

Parties often consider that *ad hoc* arbitration is less expensive.[4] In fact, the cost of arbitral proceedings depends upon several factors, such as the specificity of the case, the method and rate adopted by the arbitral institution or the *ad hoc* arbitral tribunal to charge for its services. Moreover, as already pointed out, the assistance of an arbitral institution may increase the efficiency of the proceedings and lead to significant cost reductions, which may off-set the administrative costs of the institution.

3. The disadvantages

The principal disadvantage of *ad hoc* arbitration is that, in practice, its effectiveness depends upon co-operation between the parties once the dispute has arisen and the assistance that courts at the seat of the arbitration may provide if necessary (particularly in relation to the appointment of arbitrators, the challenge of arbitrators and questions linked to the jurisdiction of the arbitral tribunal).[5] This is particularly true if the arbitration agreement is not well drafted and difficult to interpret and implement. As a result, parties may face unexpected costs and delays to resolve such problems, which may only come to light when one of them seeks to commence the arbitration or during the course of the arbitration. This situation may become even worse if the parties have not determined the seat of the arbitration before the dispute arises (in such a case, it may simply not be possible to implement the arbitration agreement) or when the competent courts are not arbitration friendly. In such circumstances, if a party decides at the outset of the dispute to take advantage of each and every weakness in the arbitration agreement to delay the proceedings, the constitution of the arbitral tribunal may alone take many months (if not prove to be impossible). In Switzerland, parties may apply to the court at the seat of the arbitration to appoint, remove or replace arbitrators, absent an agreement to the contrary (Article 179 of the PILA). More generally, the court at the seat of the arbitration also has jurisdiction to provide further assistance during the course of the arbitral proceedings if necessary (Article 185 of the PILA).

Moreover, the lack of institutional support increases the scope of administrative tasks that must be performed by the arbitral tribunal itself. The appointment of an administrative secretary may to a certain extent mitigate this difficulty.

As a result, the costs that may be saved by not involving an arbitral institution can prove illusory in the light of the additional delays that may be encountered in constituting the

---

4 *Ibid.*, p. 315.

5 REDFERN/HUNTER, N. 1-84, p. 48.

arbitral tribunal, the potential costs of obtaining assistance from courts if faced with a recalcitrant party and the arbitral tribunal's additional administrative burdens.

4. *Drafting the arbitration agreement for ad hoc arbitration: a crucial step*

Due to the lack of support from an arbitral institution, the content of an *ad hoc* arbitration agreement is of crucial importance. Indeed, the parties must make certain that the arbitration system they intend to create will work, even if one of them refuses to co-operate, once a dispute arises. However, in practice, in the context of complex contractual negotiations, parties often do not have the time or the experience to draft a proper arbitration agreement. Moreover, they do not always seek appropriate specialist advice when discussing the content of the arbitration agreement, or seek it too late.

As indicated above, the easiest solution is to adopt arbitration rules specifically developed for *ad hoc* arbitration, such as the UNCITRAL Rules, which provide a universally acceptable *ad hoc* system and have been well received by practitioners. The UNCITRAL Rules contain a model arbitration clause drafted in broad terms,[6] which specifies *inter alia* that the parties may determine the appointing authority in advance (which can be an individual or an institution, as the parties may wish).[7]

In the event that the parties do not wish to refer to any set of pre-established rules for *ad hoc* arbitration, they should set out the framework for the procedure in their arbitration agreement. In this context, the parties should strive to avoid two pitfalls:

- a highly detailed description of the procedure, as the procedure agreed upon may prove to be highly problematic and inappropriate once the dispute arises;
- the absence of key elements, as this may prevent the claimant from enforcing the arbitration agreement if the adverse party refuses to co-operate.

The key elements to include in an *ad hoc* arbitration agreement are the following (see also Appendix 1 *infra*):

---

6 '*MODEL ARBITRATION CLAUSE*
Any dispute, controversy or claim arising out of or relating to this contract, or the breach, termination or invalidity thereof, shall be settled by arbitration in accordance with the UNCITRAL Arbitration Rules as at present in force.
Note – Parties may wish to consider adding:
(a) The appointing authority shall be... (name of institution or person);
(b) The number of arbitrators shall be (one or three);
(c) The place of arbitration shall be... (town or country);
(d) The language(s) to be used in the arbitral proceedings shall be...'

7 If the parties do not agree on an appointing authority, the UNCITRAL Rules provide that the appointing authority shall be designated by the Secretary-General of the Permanent Court of Arbitration at The Hague. Since this system is rather cumbersome, parties would be well advised to specify an appointing authority directly in the arbitration clause.

- the procedure to be followed up to constitution of the arbitral tribunal, including the procedure for commencing the arbitration (for example, by a letter from the claimant to the adverse party);
- the procedure for appointment of the arbitrators;

  Indeed, in *ad hoc* arbitration, the constitution of the arbitral tribunal is the exclusive domain of the parties. They are entirely free to determine the composition of the arbitral tribunal, including the number of arbitrators, the qualifications required of them and the method for appointing them.[8] Most often, the arbitration agreement will stipulate that any dispute arising in the course of the contract shall be resolved by a three-member arbitral tribunal, with each party appointing one arbitrator and the third arbitrator being appointed by agreement of the first two party-appointed arbitrators. In some cases, the parties opt for a sole arbitrator, who shall be appointed upon agreement of the parties. In order to avoid unnecessary delays and costs, the parties should set out time limits in the arbitration agreement for the appointment of the arbitrator(s). In order to ensure the efficiency of the arbitration, the parties should also systematically identify in the arbitration agreement a third party responsible for appointing arbitrators, if a party fails to appoint its arbitrator within the applicable time limit or in the event of a disagreement between the parties on the appointment of the sole arbitrator or between the two arbitrators on the appointment of the chairman. The determination of this appointing authority is of great importance in *ad hoc* arbitration. The parties should make certain that this authority will agree to act when requested to do so. Moreover, the parties would be well advised to designate an appointing authority experienced in arbitration and with sufficient knowledge of individuals who would be qualified to sit as arbitrator or chairman in the context of the specific dispute. As a consequence, the best approach is usually to select one of the major arbitral institutions as appointing authority. Several of these arbitral institutions (for example the ICC, the Swiss Chambers of Commerce, the LCIA) provide a service of this kind.[9]
- the finality of the award;
- if possible, the seat of the arbitration, also known as the place of arbitration.

  The determination of the seat of the arbitration may be a source of disagreement between the parties once a dispute arises and lead to additional costs and delays. Accordingly, it is advisable to specify the seat of the arbitration in the

8 FOUCHARD/GAILLARD/GOLDMANN, N. 957, p. 535.

9 Once the seat of the arbitration has been chosen, the assistance of the local courts may be required to appoint arbitrators (as well as for challenges to and replacement of arbitrators). This may not, however, be the most efficient and practical solution.

arbitration clause and locate the arbitration in a state where the courts and the legislation are arbitration friendly. However, it is not always possible for political or diplomatic reasons for a party to accept a seat of arbitration located abroad in a contract. If the arbitration agreement does not specify the seat of the arbitration, it is essential that the parties specify the appointing authority, in order to ensure that the arbitral tribunal will be constituted. Indeed, if there is no agreement regarding the seat of the arbitration, the claimant will not be in a position to request the assistance of the local court to constitute the arbitral tribunal and commence the arbitration.

The parties may also wish to specify the language of the arbitration and a timetable for an initial exchange of written submissions. Indeed, this would enable the parties and the arbitral tribunal to quickly gain an understanding of the parameters of the dispute.

The inclusion of additional procedural provisions might be counterproductive. Such provisions may make the arbitration agreement more difficult to implement and ultimately prove to be problematic, given the difficulty of foreseeing the specificities of future disputes when entering into an arbitration agreement.

If the parties are able to agree on the above parameters when drafting the arbitration agreement, they will increase the chances of having any future arbitral proceedings run smoothly, notwithstanding the lack of administrative support from an arbitral institution.

III. Institutional arbitration

1. Characteristics

Arbitration is institutional where the parties submit their disputes to an arbitration procedure, which is conducted under the auspices of or administered by an arbitral institution. The role of such arbitral institutions is specifically to provide arbitration services, either exclusively or within the context of other activities and objectives, and assist, in some cases, with the running of the arbitration through the use of its infrastructure.

Most arbitral institutions provide trained staff and a governing body to administer the arbitration and advise users. They often play similar roles during the initial stage of constituting the arbitral tribunal and in resolving subsequent difficulties regarding the composition of the tribunal during the course of the proceedings.[10] Arbitral institutions also establish the basis of remuneration for the arbitrators and ensure that advance payments are made in respect of the fees and expenses of the arbitrators. Moreover, they make certain that time limits applicable prior to the constitution of the arbitral tribunal are observed.

Beyond these common activities, each arbitral institution has its own characteristics. When choosing an arbitral institution, it is thus essential that parties familiarize

10 FOUCHARD/GAILLARD/GOLDMANN, N. 994, p. 552.

themselves with its rules and take these rules into account, since there may be differences *inter alia* regarding the following issues:

- the number of arbitrators: in the absence of an agreement by the parties, some rules favour a sole arbitrator, some three arbitrators;
- the right of the parties to select, nominate, and appoint arbitrators;
- the degree of independence and neutrality required of arbitrators;
- the power of arbitrators to control the proceedings;
- the calculation of the costs of arbitration (arbitrators' fees, administrative fees). The costs of institutional arbitration vary between institutions and may be based upon the amount in dispute (ICC Rules, Swiss Rules) or upon the time spent on a particular matter (LCIA Rules, AAA Rules);
- the possibility for the institution to order the consolidation of arbitral proceedings and the joinder of third parties (Article 4 of the Swiss Rules);
- the possibility for the institution to shorten or extend time-limits (Article 42 of the Swiss Rules applicable in the context of the expedited procedure, Articles 18 and 24 of the ICC Rules);
- the existence of fast-track or expedited procedures (Article 42 of the Swiss Rules);
- the existence of rules on multi-party arbitration, particularly in regard to the constitution of the arbitral tribunal (Article 8 of the Swiss Rules; Article 10 of the ICC Rules).

The level of administrative support may also vary significantly between arbitral institutions. For example, the ICC Rules provide that, in addition to its competence in regard to the appointment, challenge, replacement of arbitrators, the ICC Court is competent:

- to fix the place of arbitration, if there is no agreement between the parties (Article 14);
- to approve the terms of reference, if any of the parties refuses to participate in the drawing up of the terms of reference or to sign them (Article 18);
- to lay down modifications as to the form of the draft award submitted by the arbitral tribunal and draw the arbitral tribunal's attention to points of substance. No award shall be rendered by the arbitral tribunal until it has been approved by the Court as to its form (Article 27);
- to extend time limits set out in the Rules (Articles 18 and 24).

The Swiss Rules provide that, in addition to having competence in regard to the appointment, challenge and replacement of arbitrators, the Chambers (i.e. the Arbitration Committee or the Special Committee) are competent:

- to consolidate arbitral proceedings (Article 4);
- to determine the seat of the arbitration, if there is no agreement between the parties (Article 16);
- to extend the time-limits provided in Section I (Introductory rules) and Section II (Composition of the arbitral tribunal) (Article 2(3)), and to shorten and extend time-limits in the context of Article 42 (Expedited procedure).

Unlike the ICC Rules, the Swiss Rules do not provide for scrutiny of the award.

2. The advantages

The advantages, as well as the disadvantages, of institutional arbitration are in direct contrast to those of *ad hoc* arbitration.

The main advantages of institutional arbitration are the existence of an automatically incorporated set of rules and the availability of a trained staff to ensure that the arbitral tribunal is appointed, advance payments are made and the arbitration runs as smoothly as possible.[11] This is particularly true when the arbitral tribunal has an established track record of successfully administering many cases under its arbitration rules.

As a result, institutional arbitration offers a higher degree of foreseeability and certainty than *ad hoc* arbitration.

Another often perceived advantage of institutional arbitration is the credibility associated with the name of the institution. In certain countries, parties sometimes consider it beneficial, when seeking to enforce an award, to be able to demonstrate that the arbitration was conducted under the auspices of an internationally respected institution.[12]

3. The disadvantages

Institutional arbitration is often viewed as too expensive, with the parties having to finance the administrative support provided by the institution, and too slow, because of the bureaucratic machinery involved.[13]

In reality, these disadvantages vary from one institution to another, depending in part upon the particularities of the dispute. Moreover, as indicated above (see Section II.2 *supra*), if the intervention of the arbitral institution avoids the need for proceedings before courts to resolve procedural difficulties, institutional arbitration may ultimately be less expensive and faster than *ad hoc* arbitration.

---

[11] REDFERN/HUNTER, N. 1-80, p. 45; FOUCHARD/GAILLARD/GOLDMANN, N. 1006, p. 554.
[12] LEW/MISTELIS/KRÖLL, N. 3-20, p. 36.
[13] REDFERN/HUNTER, N. 1-81, p. 46.

Another disadvantage sometimes mentioned is that the greater efficiency of institutional arbitration during the constitution of the arbitral tribunal is gained at the expense of a weaker relationship of trust between the parties and the arbitrators.[14]

4. *The criteria to select an arbitral institution*

Parties wishing to resort to institutional arbitration must select an arbitral institution they deem appropriate for their particular contractual relationship. The choice of the institution may be motivated by the fact that it is well known in a particular geographic or trade area, or simply be made by default.[15]

Parties should, moreover, take into account the following considerations:

- Do the applicable rules correspond to current arbitration practice?[16]
- Do the characteristics of the institution in question and the level of administrative support correspond to the needs and expectations of the parties?
- How are the costs calculated?
- Does the institution have sufficient experience? How long has it been administrating arbitrations? How many cases is it managing every year?
- May one reasonably expect that the institution will continue to exist in the coming years?

5. *Drafting the arbitration agreement in the context of institutional arbitration*

Contrary to *ad hoc* arbitration, drafting a proper arbitration agreement in the context of institutional arbitration is not particularly difficult. Indeed, the best solution is to adopt the standard clause proposed by the relevant arbitral institution[17] and supplement it only

---

14 FOUCHARD/GAILLARD/GOLDMANN, N. 974, p. 540.

15 LEW/MISTELIS/KRÖLL, N. 3-17, p. 35.

16 In the event that the rules have been amended between the conclusion of the contract and the filing of the request for arbitration, one must determine whether the old or the new rules apply (for example, see Article 1 of the Swiss Rules). If the parties do not want the new rules to apply to future disputes, they should specify in the arbitration clause that the rules in force at the time when the contract was entered into shall apply to all disputes.

17 For example, the ICC standard clause:
'*All disputes arising out of or in connection with the present contract shall be finally settled under the Rules of Arbitration of the International Chamber of Commerce by one or more arbitrators appointed in accordance with the said Rules*'.
The Swiss Rules Model Arbitration Clause:
'*Any dispute, controversy or claim arising out of or in relation to this contract, including the validity, invalidity, breach or termination thereof, shall be resolved by arbitration in accordance with the Swiss Rules of International Arbitration of the Swiss Chambers of Commerce in force on the date when the Notice of Arbitration is submitted in accordance with these Rules.*

to the extent appropriate (some institutions suggest parties agree on specific issues to be included in the arbitration agreement), for example, by specifying the seat of the arbitration, the number of arbitrators, the language of the arbitral proceedings and the law governing the merits of the dispute.

It is not advisable to add other specific provisions or to attempt to introduce changes to the provisions of the relevant institutional arbitration rules.

6. *The principal arbitral institutions*

Given the proliferation of international arbitral institutions, there is little point in seeking to list all of them. A more detailed discussion of Swiss and Swiss-based institutional arbitration is set forth in Chapter 10 *infra*.

IV. Conclusion

As emphasized at the beginning of this chapter, it is difficult to draw any general conclusions in regard to the suitability of *ad hoc* or institutional arbitration. It may, however, be advisable to avoid *ad hoc* arbitration if there are significant cultural differences between the parties, or if it is likely that the parties will not cooperate with each other in the event of a dispute. *Ad hoc* arbitration may also prove to be inappropriate when there are state parties involved. Indeed, in such cases, the support provided by an arbitral institution may be essential.

Whatever type of arbitration is chosen, the parties must seek to ensure that it will be possible to constitute an arbitral tribunal and conduct the arbitral proceedings as smoothly as possible, even if one party proves to be recalcitrant once a dispute has arisen. In order to achieve this result, the parties must understand the consequences of their choices when concluding the arbitration agreement. As noted above, the drafting of the arbitration agreement is much more crucial in *ad hoc* arbitration than in institutional arbitration, where the best solution is to adopt the model clause proposed by the selected institution. When opting for institutional arbitration, the parties should focus on choosing the most appropriate institution in order to ensure that the applicable rules will correspond to their expectations in the event of a dispute.

The number of arbitrators shall be... (one or three);
The seat of the arbitration shall be... (city in Switzerland);
The arbitral proceedings shall be conducted in... (insert desired language).'

Chapter 2 – The Arbitration Agreement

Zina Abdulla

I. Definition and purpose

Chapter 12 of the PILA, and in particular Article 178 of the PILA, does not provide a definition of the arbitration agreement. Most legal commentators hold the traditional view that the arbitration agreement may be defined as an agreement whereby two or more parties agree that a dispute, which has arisen or may arise between them in connection with a particular legal relationship, will be finally settled by one or more arbitrators.[1]

Given that arbitration is a consensual dispute resolution method, the touchstone of arbitration is the agreement of the parties. It is a fundamental principle that a valid agreement will exclude the jurisdiction of courts and vest the arbitrators with the necessary power to resolve all the disputes between the parties, which the latter agreed to entrust to arbitrators.[2]

---

1 W. WENGER in HONSELL/VOGT/SCHNYDER, N. 3, p. 1437; POUDRET/BESSON, N. 149 *et seq.*, p. 121.

2 Article 7 of the PILA provides that, where the parties have entered into an arbitration agreement pertaining to an arbitrable dispute, the Swiss court seized with the dispute shall decline jurisdiction, unless either the defendant has proceeded on the merits without reservation, the court finds that the arbitration agreement is null and void, inoperative or cannot be performed, or the arbitral tribunal cannot be appointed for reasons attributable to the defendant. When deciding upon such defence of lack of jurisdiction, the Swiss court will apply the rules under the PILA, provided the seat of the arbitration is in Switzerland. In that case, the Swiss court will decide on a *prima facie* basis (see DFT 122 III 139). On the other hand, when the seat of the arbitration is abroad, the Swiss court will refer to the rules of the NY Convention and will have an unlimited power of review (see DFT 121 III 38).

G. Kaufmann-Kohler and B. Stucki (eds), International Arbitration in Switzerland, A Handbook for Practitioners, 15-31.

II. Requirements for validity

In accordance with Article 178(1) of the PILA, the validity of an arbitration agreement is subject to formal and substantive requirements, which the arbitrators will – if necessary – review when deciding upon their own jurisdiction (Article 186(1) of the PILA).[3]

1. Formal validity

Formally, an arbitration agreement is valid when it is made in writing, by telegram, telex, telecopier or any other means of communication, which enables it to be evidenced by a text (Article 178(1) of the PILA).[4]

As Article 178(1) of the PILA is regarded as a substantive rule of private international law, the parties may not submit the formal requirements of their arbitration agreement to a law other than Swiss law.[5]

The requirement under Article 178(1) of the PILA that the arbitration agreement be in writing or evidenced by writing is mainly intended to ensure legal certainty.[6] To this end, the issue arises as to what the 'written' requirement encompasses under Swiss law. More particularly, must the text bear a signature in order to satisfy the written form requirement under Article 13 of the SCO, or does an unsigned text suffice for the purpose of Article 178(1) of the PILA?

In light of the case law of the Swiss Federal Tribunal,[7] most legal authors now hold the view that Article 178(1) of the PILA does not require a text bearing a signature. A

---

3 The requirements for validity under the NY Convention (Articles II and V(1)(a)) ought to be referred to instead of those set forth under Article 178 of the PILA where the seat of the arbitration is not within Switzerland: W. WENGER in HONSELL/VOGT/SCHNYDER, N. 5, p. 1438; LALIVE/POUDRET/REYMOND, N. 7, p. 316. See also the decision of the Zurich Commercial Court of 25 August 1992 in ZR 1992/93, 72 No. 23.

4 As a general rule, form is governed by Article 178(1) of the PILA when arbitrators sitting in Switzerland are called to rule upon their jurisdiction or when the Swiss Federal Tribunal reviews the arbitration agreement in the context of an application to set aside the arbitral award pursuant to Article 190(2)(b) of the PILA. On the other hand, form is governed by Article II of the NY Convention when Swiss courts are required to rule upon the recognition and enforcement of the arbitral award.

5 LALIVE/POUDRET/REYMOND, N. 8, p. 317.

6 See DFT 119 II 391, 394.

7 See DFT 121 III 38, 45 (*Compagnie de Navigation et Transports SA v. MSC Mediterranean Shipping Company SA*) where the Swiss Federal Tribunal held that in light of the development of modern means of communication, unsigned texts have a growing significance and diffusion and that the requirement for signature has weakened accordingly within international trade. Further, the Tribunal held that specific conduct could be considered as compliance with a formal prerequisite under certain circumstances and pursuant to the principle of good faith. For example, in the case at stake, the Swiss Federal

written text, whether included in a contract or exchanged by telegram, telex, telecopier or any other means of communication allowing the arbitration agreement to be evidenced in writing, is therefore sufficient.

At any rate, the means of communication used must generate a written text that may be kept and produced, if necessary. Therefore, in addition to the means of communication listed in Article 178(1) of the PILA, any document that may be used as evidence – such as order confirmations, notes, minutes, general conditions, articles of association or e-mails – may constitute a 'written' arbitration agreement.[8]

One of the above-noted examples frequently arises as an issue in international commercial practice, namely that of general conditions, which are often incorporated by reference into an agreement. Often, an arbitration clause is not contained in the declarations of the parties as such but in a distinct and separate text, which the parties have incorporated by reference into their contract (so-called 'arbitration clause by reference').[9] The reference to an arbitration clause contained in another document need not be explicit. In other words, the existence of an arbitration clause in the document incorporated by reference need not be expressly mentioned in the wording of the clause setting forth the reference. The formal requirement of Article 178(1) of the PILA is fulfilled provided that both the reference and its object are in writing.[10]

2. *Substantive validity*

With regard to substance, an arbitration agreement is valid provided that it complies either with the law chosen by the parties (specifically to govern the arbitration agreement, which seldom occurs), or with the law governing the subject matter of the dispute - in particular the law governing the main contract - or if it complies with Swiss law (Article 178(2) of the PILA).[11]

Tribunal held that the arbitration agreement was valid as to its form and was binding upon the parties due to their long-term business relationship and the fact that they had always used the same pre-printed bill of lading providing for arbitration.

8 LALIVE/POUDRET/REYMOND, N. 10, p. 318; POUDRET/BESSON, N. 193, p. 161; see also G. KAUFMANN-KOHLER, *Arbitration Agreements in Online Business to Business Transactions*, in BRINER/FORTIER/BERGER/BREDOW, *Law of International Business and Dispute Settlement in the 21st Century*, Liber Amicorum Karl-Heinz Böckstiegel, Munich 2001, p. 355; contrary to Article II of the NY Convention, no exchange of documents is required.

9 See DFT 110 II 54.

10 W. WENGER in HONSELL/VOGT/SCHNYDER, N. 17, p. 1444; LALIVE/POUDRET/REYMOND, N. 13, p. 321.

11 An additional substantive requirement is objective arbitrability pursuant to Article 177(1) of the PILA, which is discussed in Section II.2.b) *infra*.

Article 178(2) of the PILA, which constitutes an *in favorem validatis* conflict of laws provision,[12] does not, however, list the issues to be governed by the applicable substantive law. Such issues may include *inter alia* the conclusion of the arbitration agreement (e.g. offer, acceptance, time and conditions) and the possible lack of assent (e.g. error, duress, misrepresentation), its performance (e.g. delay, impossibility, *exceptio non adimpleti contractus*), as well as its scope, especially with respect to non-signatories or assignees or in general with respect to the parties and disputes.[13]

Where the substantive validity of the arbitration agreement is determined under Swiss law, the parties are required to have expressly or tacitly exchanged mutual declarations of intent with regard to the essential elements of the agreement (i.e. the *essentialia negotii* within the meaning of Articles 1 and 2 of the SCO). The necessary elements of an arbitration agreement are twofold – an agreement between the parties that any dispute between them will be resolved by arbitration, and an indication of the dispute or legal relationship, which will be the subject matter of arbitration.[14]

a) Consent

When examining the substantive validity of the arbitration agreement, the starting point is to determine whether the parties have expressed their consent with respect to the essential elements referred to above. It is thus necessary to make certain that such consent exists, and if so, to assess whom it binds and what it actually encompasses.

aa) Existence

In order to determine the existence of the parties' consent, arbitrators will resort to the general principles of contractual interpretation (e.g. the principle of interpretation in good faith, the principle of effective interpretation, the principle *contra proferentem*, etc.).[15]

Under Swiss law, in ascertaining whether an agreement has been concluded, one must first seek the true and common intent of the parties beyond the wording they actually used (Article 18 of the SCO). Thus, it is necessary to examine not only the wording of the contract but also the whole set of circumstances surrounding the contract, *inter alia*, the context of the conclusion of the contract, the conduct of the parties before and after the conclusion of the contract, the interests at stake, as well as commercial/trade usage.[16]

---

12 The purpose of this provision is to avoid, insofar as possible, any disagreement as to the validity of the arbitration agreement. See DFT 119 II 380, 384.

13 On the other hand, the issue of arbitrability is directly governed by the PILA (Article 177): LALIVE/POUDRET/REYMOND, N. 14, p. 321.

14 POUDRET/BESSON, N. 155-156, p. 125; W. WENGER in HONSELL/VOGT/SCHNYDER, N. 22 *et seq.*, p. 1446.

15 FOUCHARD/GAILLARD/GOLDMAN, N. 648 *et seq.*, p. 394.

16 W. WIEGAND in HONSELL/VOGT/SCHNYDER, N. 26-31, p. 418.

If it is not possible to establish the true and common intent of the parties or should such intent differ, the parties' declarations will be construed pursuant to the principle of confidence. In this second stage of interpretation, the judge or the arbitrators must construe the declarations or behaviour of a party as they would be understood *bona fide* by the addressee in view of all of the circumstances. The principle of confidence thus implies that a party is bound by the objective meaning of its declarations or conduct, even if such meaning is at odds with the actual intent of the party.[17]

In practice, these principles of interpretation prove most valuable with respect to pathological clauses, i.e. incomplete, defective or contradictory arbitration clauses. In light of the principle *in favorem validatis* expressed in Article 178(2) of the PILA, some legal authors hold the view that this tenet should apply when interpreting such pathological clauses.[18] In most cases, arbitrators would prefer to salvage an arbitration clause by construing it as best they can to restore the true intent of the parties, rather than prevent the parties from having recourse to arbitration.

A recurrent example is that of an arbitration clause referring to the ICC 'in Geneva' or 'in Zurich' whereas the ICC has its headquarters is Paris. Most arbitrators will tend to regard such a clause as valid despite this mistake, as it sufficiently reflects the parties' intention to refer disputes to arbitration under the ICC Rules, with the seat of arbitration being in the designated city.[19]

Nevertheless, when entering into an arbitration agreement, the parties should strive to express their consent in an unequivocal manner in regard to the essential elements of such agreement, so as to restrict any room for interpretation and ensure the validity of the arbitration agreement.

In addition, the arbitration agreement should contain other key elements - though not essential within the meaning of Article 2 of the SCO - such as the place of arbitration, the type of arbitration (institutional or *ad hoc*), the number of arbitrators, the composition of the arbitral tribunal, etc.

bb) Scope

Insofar as the existence of the parties' consent has been established, the arbitration agreement is deemed to cover all disputes between the parties, provided that they are arbitrable and arise out of the relationship to which the arbitration agreement refers. Indeed, the Swiss Federal Tribunal held that one must assume that the parties wish the arbitrators to have an all-embracing jurisdiction.[20]

---

17 See unreported decision of the Swiss Federal Tribunal of 9 April 2002 available on the Internet at <www.bger.ch>; DFT 116 Ia 56; DFT 127 III 444; DFT 127 III 279.

18 W. WENGER in HONSELL/VOGT/SCHNYDER, N. 50, p. 1455.

19 See [1991] ASA Bull. 155 and 269.

20 DFT 116 Ia 56.

Further, where consent has been ascertained, the question naturally arises as to whom it is binding upon. Is it binding merely upon the parties, which have entered into the arbitration agreement, or can it be extended to 'non-signatory' parties?

As a general rule, the arbitration clause binds only the parties that have originally agreed to it.[21] However, in practice, the arbitration agreement may be extended to third parties (i.e. non-signatories) under specific circumstances (e.g. assignment, universal succession, corporate articles of association, group of companies).[22]

For instance, in the case of a group of companies - a recurrent topic in practice - the question is whether an arbitration agreement entered into by a company belonging to a group of companies can be extended to include another company of that same group, which has not signed the arbitration agreement.

It is undisputed that the so-called 'group of companies doctrine' may lead to the extension of an arbitration agreement executed by one company within a group to other companies within the same group. However, this does not necessarily entail a piercing of the corporate veil or mean that a company will be bound by an arbitration agreement entered into by another company merely on the ground that both companies are affiliated. The basic rule remains that an arbitration agreement is binding only upon parties that are privy to it. A restrictive view prevails: the group of companies doctrine can justify the extension of an arbitration agreement signed by one company to other companies within the same group only in specific and exceptional circumstances.[23] The

---

21 It should be noted that where the parties are legal entities, the issue as to which entity is empowered to bind other entities is to be examined under the law applicable to the companies at stake (DFT 101 II 168).

22 After completion of this chapter, the Swiss Federal Tribunal ruled that the extension of an arbitration agreement to non-signatories is a substantive issue governed by Article 178(2) of the PILA (see DFT 129 III 727). The fact that the extension of the arbitration agreement is characterized as an issue of substance means that the formal requirement that the agreement to arbitrate "*be made in writing, by telegram, telex, telecopier or any other means of communication which permits it to be evidenced by a text*" (Article 178(1) of the PILA) applies only to the agreement whereby the original parties manifested their intention of resolving disputes by way of arbitration.

23 See the decision of the Swiss Federal Tribunal of 29 January 1996 in [1996] ASA Bull. 496. In this decision, the Swiss Federal Tribunal specifically held that the group of companies doctrine should apply where a party creates a legal appearance engendering the trust of another party, which trust is entitled to protection. The Swiss Federal Tribunal added that it was appropriate to pierce the corporate veil and extend the scope of the arbitration agreement from a subsidiary to its parent in the case at issue because the effect of the contract had largely shifted from the subsidiary to the parent. See also M. BLESSING, *Extension of the Scope of an Arbitration Clause to Non-Signatories*, in (1994) 8 ASA Special Series 151; CRAIG/PARK/PAULSSON, pp. 74-79; M. DE BOISSÉSON, *Le droit français de l'arbitrage interne et international*, Paris 1990, pp. 522-539 ; Y. DERAINS, *L'extension de la clause*

current position under Swiss law is that the extension of an arbitration agreement to a non-signatory party can be contemplated only where: (a) it may be inferred from documents that such party was duly represented by one of the signatories (which does not result from the mere existence of a group); (b) there has been subsequent ratification; or (c) circumventing the arbitration agreement would constitute an abuse justifying a piercing of the corporate veil.[24]

In sum, as confirmed by the arbitral case law,[25] it is not so much the existence of a group that results in companies within the group being bound by an arbitration agreement which they have not signed, but rather the fact that such a result was the true intention of the parties.

b) Arbitrability

The concept of arbitrability, sometimes referred to as 'objective arbitrability', relates to whether or not the subject matter of the dispute may be validly submitted to arbitration. It should be distinguished from the concept of 'subjective arbitrability', which encompasses capacity and broadly refers to whether or not a specific entity or person may be party to an arbitration and is addressed separately in Section II.2.c) *infra*.

Arbitrability is a prerequisite to the validity of the arbitration agreement and, accordingly, to the jurisdiction of the arbitral tribunal.[26]

Article 177(1) of the PILA deals with arbitrability, which an arbitral tribunal is empowered to review *ex officio*, according to some legal authors.[27] This provision is a

---

d'arbitrage aux non-signatories - La doctrine des groupes de sociétés, in (1994) 8 ASA Special Series 241; FOUCHARD/GAILLARD/GOLDMAN, pp. 282-289; C. JARROSSON, *Conventions d'arbitrage et groupes de sociétés*, in (1994) 8 ASA Special Series 209 ; S. JARVIN, *Extending the Scope to Non-signatories: Group of Companies Doctrine*, in (1994) 8 ASA Special Series 181.

24 POUDRET/BESSON, N. 260, p. 236.

25 The following fundamental principle was established in ICC Case No. 4131 (1982) (*Isover Saint-Gobain v. Dow Chemical*): '*Considering, in particular, that the arbitration clause expressly accepted by certain of the companies of the group should bind the other companies which, by virtue of their role in the conclusion, performance, or termination of the contracts containing said clauses, and in accordance with the mutual intention of all parties to the proceedings, appear to have been veritable parties to these contracts or to have been principally concerned by them and the disputes to which they may give rise.*', in S. JARVIN/Y. DERAINS, *Collection of ICC Arbitral Awards 1974-1985*, Deventer 1990, pp. 146 *et seq.* See also ICC Case No. 6519 (1991), in J.-J. ARNALDEZ/Y. DERAINS/D.T. HASCHER, *Collection of ICC Arbitral Awards 1991-1995*, The Hague 1997, pp. 424-425. See also ICC Case No. 10758 (2000) in [2001] 4 JDI 1171, 1177.

26 Swiss Federal Tribunal decision of 23 June 1993 (*Fincantieri – Cantieri Navali Italiani S.p.A. & Oto Melara S.p.A. v. M.*) in DFT 118 II 353. DFT 117 II 94.

substantive rule of private international law. Arbitrability is thus governed by the *lex arbitri*, irrespective of the provisions of the *lex causae* or the parties' respective national laws.[28]

Article 177(1) of the PILA provides that any dispute involving an economic interest may be the subject matter of arbitration. This provision comprises all claims that have a financial value for the parties, whether assets or liabilities, i.e. all rights that, for at least one of the parties, involve some interest which can be assessed in financial terms.[29]

The concept of arbitrability under Article 177(1) of the PILA is to be broadly understood.[30] Moreover, the only bar to arbitrability is public policy within the meaning of Article 190(2)(e) of the PILA.[31]

Although an arbitrator sitting in Switzerland is not required to take into account foreign legal restrictions on arbitrability,[32] it may be argued that the position is different when the foreign restriction is a so-called *loi de police* or *loi d'application immédiate* (mandatory rules) under foreign law.[33] Such a foreign rule of international public policy may, for instance, mandate that certain disputes be brought exclusively before a court.[34]

Arbitrability should not be denied on the grounds that mandatory rules or public policy would result in the nullity of the claim or render it impossible to enforce the claim. Rather, it should only be denied where claims fall within the scope of the exclusive

---

27 F. VISCHER in HEINI/KELLER/SIEHR/VISCHER/VOLKEN, N. 21, p. 1506; B. DUTOIT, *Droit international privé suisse: Commentaire de la Loi fédérale du 18 décembre 1987*, Basel 2001, N. 4, p. 553.

28 DFT 118 II 353 ; LALIVE/POUDRET/REYMOND, N. 1, p. 305.

29 *Ibid.*

30 LALIVE/POUDRET/REYMOND, N. 2, p. 306.

31 R. BRINER in HONSELL/VOGT/SCHNYDER, N. 13, p. 1426. DFT 116 II 634; DFT 117 II 604; DFT 120 II 155. [1998] ASA Bull. 118, 634, 653: the Swiss Federal Tribunal defined public policy as the fundamental principles of law, including the principle *pacta sunt servanda*, the principle of good faith, the prohibition of misuse of law, the prohibition of uncompensated expropriation, the prohibition of discrimination and the protection of the incapacitated.

32 DFT 118 II 353; R. BRINER in HONSELL/VOGT/SCHNYDER, N. 19, p. 1430.

33 Affirmative: A. BUCHER/A. BONOMI, *Droit international privé*, Basel 2001, p. 323. In the *Fincantieri* case, the possibility of a public policy restriction to arbitrability was raised. However, the Swiss Federal Tribunal held that no such restriction applied in that particular case.

34 The mere fact that the dispute bears a connection with public policy is not sufficient *per se* to bar its arbitrability (DFT 118 II 353). This might be so for consumer or employment disputes. On consumer disputes, see G. KAUFMANN-KOHLER/T. SCHULTZ, *Online dispute resolution – new challenges for contemporary justice*, Kluwer Law International, The Hague, forthcoming publication 2004, chapter 3.IV.1.

jurisdiction of courts, pursuant to a rule that is tantamount to international public policy.[35]

In view of the position set forth in Article 177(1) of the PILA, the Swiss Federal Tribunal has held that an arbitral tribunal has no obligation to take into account the public policy requirements of the likely country of enforcement, as the risk of non-enforcement is to be borne by the parties to the arbitration.[36]

By way of example, a growing issue in practice is the arbitrability of competition law claims.

The approach in Switzerland has been rather liberal. In one decision, the Swiss Federal Tribunal held that an arbitral tribunal has jurisdiction to examine the validity of an agreement pursuant to Article 81 of the EC Treaty (formerly Article 85 of the EC Treaty), even though arbitrators do not act as authorities of a EU Member State.[37] It should be noted that this decision related to a matter where the governing law was the law of a EU Member State, which necessarily incorporates EC law as an inherent part.

In a subsequent decision, the Swiss Federal Tribunal held that an arbitral award, which disregarded the application of EU competition law, was not contrary to public policy insofar as the parties had not alleged that the agreement at stake was incompatible with EC competition rules. Indeed, the Swiss Federal Tribunal cast some doubt on whether national or European competition rules were part of the fundamental legal or moral principles recognized in all civilized states, such that a violation of them should be considered as contrary to public policy. On the other hand, where one of the parties has invoked the nullity of the agreement by virtue of Article 81 of the EC Treaty, an arbitral tribunal having its seat in Switzerland must examine the validity of the agreement in light of EC competition law, even if the law chosen by the parties to govern their contract is Swiss law.[38]

In conclusion, an arbitral tribunal having its seat in Switzerland must, insofar as one of the parties raises it, take into consideration EC competition law, whatever the substantive law applicable and irrespective of a choice-of-law clause. However, it should be noted that an arbitral tribunal's duty to apply foreign competition law is not subject to review on an application to set the award aside before the Swiss Federal Tribunal,[39] as opposed to the case of an award rendered by an arbitral tribunal having its seat in an EU Member

---

35 *Ibid.*

36 *Ibid.*

37 See DFT 118 II 193.

38 See the decision of the Swiss Federal Tribunal of 13 November 1998 in [1999] ASA Bull. 529.

39 *Ibid.* See also DFT 120 II 155, 166 *et seq.* (Emirats Arabes Unis et consorts v. Westland Helicopters Limited).

State.[40] Indeed, the Swiss Federal Tribunal does not consider Article 81 of the EC Treaty to be a matter of public policy within the meaning of Article 190(2)(e) of the PILA.[41]

c) Capacity

The concept of capacity is twofold. On one hand, it relates to the capacity of a person or entity to enter into an arbitration agreement on its own behalf and act as a party to arbitral proceedings. On the other hand, it deals with the capacity of a party to enter into an arbitration agreement in the name and on behalf of another person or entity.[42]

According to the Swiss Federal Tribunal, the issue of capacity is to be determined under the law applicable by operation of the general conflict of laws rules governing the capacity of persons and entities (Articles 35-36 and 154-155 of the PILA) and the representation thereof (Articles 126, 155 and 158 of the PILA), as opposed to the special conflict of laws rule of Article 178(2) of the PILA.[43]

Where one of the parties to the arbitration agreement is a state or a state-owned or controlled entity, this issue is expressly addressed under Article 177(2) of the PILA.[44] Under this provision, a state party cannot invoke its own domestic law to contest its capacity to enter into an arbitration agreement. However, Article 177(2) of the PILA merely addresses the capacity to enter into an arbitration agreement, not capacity *stricto sensu*, which is governed by the state's own domestic legislation. Article 177(2) of the PILA also prevents the application of foreign domestic law with respect to the arbitrability of disputes arising out of state contracts, such as rules granting civil or administrative courts jurisdiction over disputes related to state contracts, concessions, administrative contracts, etc. or rules prohibiting arbitration or choice of forum for all contracts in connection with foreign investment on domestic soil.[45]

---

[40] See ECJ Judgment of 1 June 1999 in the Case C-126/97, *Eco Swiss China Time Ltd v. Benetton International NV* in [1999] ASA Bull. 414.

[41] See the decision of the Swiss Federal Tribunal of 13 November 1998 in [1999] ASA Bull. 529, 533 and 534; DFT 120 II 155, 166 *et seq.*; see also A. RIGOZZI, *Arbitrage, ordre public et droit communautaire de la concurrence,* in [1999] ASA Bull. 455.

[42] POUDRET/BESSON, N. 269, p. 244.

[43] See the decisions of the Swiss Federal Tribunal of 22 December 1992 in [1996] ASA Bull. 646, 648.

[44] This provision is a useful codification of a rule of international law developed in the past in a number of awards. Further, with respect to the notion of state-owned or state-controlled entity, such notion should be broadly construed. For instance, in the *Fincantieri* case (note 26 *supra*), the Swiss Federal Tribunal considered that Article 177(2) of the PILA applied to two companies nationalized under Italian law. See also POUDRET/BESSON, N. 234, p. 198.

[45] LALIVE/POUDRET/REYMOND, N. 10-11, p. 311; see also POUDRET/BESSON, N. 234, p. 197.

As a general rule, the issue of arbitrability within the framework of state contracts must only be addressed in light of Article 177(1) of the PILA, irrespective of the rules under the law of the state party.[46]

III. Contents: 'drafting' the arbitration clause

As previously mentioned, the arbitration agreement should set forth two essential elements in order to be substantively valid: the parties' agreement to arbitrate and the definition of the dispute or legal relationship, which will be the subject matter of arbitration (the said *essentialia negotii*).

An arbitration agreement should not, however, enumerate all of the specific claims that might have to be determined by the arbitrator(s). Rather, an arbitration agreement should only refer to 'all disputes', which may 'arise out of or in connection with' a specific contract. These commonly used terms are well defined in practice. They encompass disputes as to the conclusion, the performance, the interpretation, or termination of the contract at issue. Tort claims may also be encompassed within this wording, if they are related to claims arising from an alleged breach of contract or are linked to the contract.[47]

When drafting the arbitration clause, the parties should avoid narrowing down the scope of their arbitration agreement to one or a few of the above-mentioned disputes – for instance, disputes regarding the validity, interpretation and/or performance of the contract – in order to avoid creating any doubt.

In addition to the core elements referred to above, a properly drafted arbitration agreement should indicate:

- **the seat of the arbitration**: this element has significant legal consequences. The seat of the arbitration determines *inter alia* the application of the legal provisions on arbitration of that place, access to the courts for assistance in constituting the arbitral tribunal, and the jurisdiction of the courts to rule upon applications to set aside any arbitral award.[48]

  The designation of the seat of arbitration 'in Switzerland' is not *per se* sufficient. It is necessary to refer to a specific Canton within Switzerland in order to identify the competent court for the purpose of assisting the parties and the future arbitral tribunal, if necessary.[49]

---

46 *Ibid.*

47 W. WENGER in HONSELL/VOGT/SCHNYDER, N. 33, p. 1450; POUDRET/BESSON, N. 307, p. 282.

48 FOUCHARD/GAILLARD/GOLDMANN, N. 1239 *et seq.*, p. 674.

49 LALIVE/POUDRET/REYMOND, N. 9, p. 297.

Designating the seat of the arbitration is primarily a matter for the parties (Article 176(3) of the PILA); they may determine the seat in the arbitration clause or in a subsequent agreement. The agreement of the parties as to the seat may require interpretation, in particular where the seat is determined indirectly. Suffice it to say that the seat need be determinable.[50]

In any event, an arbitration agreement may be valid, even if the seat of the arbitration (i.e. a Swiss Canton) is not expressly designated, as the seat is not an essential element of the arbitration agreement (the said *essentialia negotii*). In fact, the importance of specifying the seat of the arbitration relates not so much to the validity of the arbitration agreement as to the concrete implementation or efficacy thereof.[51]

It is important to recognize that the seat of the arbitration is a legal concept and should not be confused with the place where the proceedings are conducted physically. As such, the arbitral tribunal usually may hold hearings and meetings with the parties at other places, if necessary or convenient, most often with the consent of the parties.

- ***ad hoc* or institutional arbitration**: the choice between these two forms of arbitration belongs to the parties. Under institutional arbitration, an institution (such as a chamber of commerce) provides certain procedural rules, administrative services and quality controls for the arbitration whereas, in *ad hoc* arbitration, the arbitrators operate on their own without assistance of an institution and without reference to institutional rules.

  An important distinction should be drawn between institutional and *ad hoc* arbitration when drafting the arbitration clause. In the case of institutional arbitration, it is advisable to adopt the model clause recommended by the arbitral institution and simply add the number of arbitrators, the seat of the arbitration and, if possible, the language of the arbitration. If these matters cannot be agreed, the institutional arbitration rules may address them.

  On the other hand, one must be more careful in drafting an arbitration clause for *ad hoc* arbitration. In order to achieve greater predictability, it is necessary to ensure that the arbitration clause addresses the following matters at a minimum: the seat of the arbitration, the number of arbitrators, the method of appointment, the appointing authority (preferably knowledgeable about arbitration and arbitrators), the language of the arbitration and possibly the applicable procedure before the arbitral tribunal.

---

50 F. EHRAT in HONSELL/VOGT/SCHNYDER, N. 16 *et seq.*, p. 1416. See also the decision of the Cour de Justice of Geneva of 7 February 1991 in [1991] ASA Bull. 155.

51 POUDRET/BESSON, N. 156, p. 126.

- **composition of the arbitral tribunal**: in accordance with Article 179(1) of the PILA, the parties are free to agree upon the number of arbitrators (sole arbitrator or several arbitrators) and the mode of their appointment (directly or indirectly by reference to the rules of an arbitral institution). Should the parties not reach an agreement in this regard, the competent court may apply the rules of cantonal law, which as a rule are those of the Concordat.[52]
- **applicable law**: the law governing the arbitration agreement *per se* and the arbitration itself must be distinguished from the substantive law governing the contract and the merits of any dispute arising under the contract. The substantive law governing the contract should be specified whenever possible in a separate contractual provision, which is clearly distinguished from the arbitration agreement. On the other hand, there is no need to specify the *lex arbitri*, since it applies by operation of law upon fulfillment of the requirements of Article 176 of the PILA. The choice of arbitration rules is a different matter, as it constitutes the exercise of the parties' freedom to agree upon the procedure before the arbitral tribunal pursuant to Article 182 of the PILA (assuming that the PILA is applicable to the arbitration). Article 182 of the PILA also provides that the parties may submit the arbitral procedure to a national procedural law. This option is not, however, recommended, as such national procedural laws are rarely appropriate for arbitral proceedings.[53]
- **language of the arbitration**: for practical purposes, it is advisable to specify the language of the arbitration, in order to avoid any subsequent dispute regarding this issue and potentially reduce the need to translate documents.

Pursuant to Article 192 of the PILA, the parties may also agree to exclude their right to challenge the award within the meaning of Article 190 of the PILA, either in the arbitration agreement or in a subsequent written agreement, subject to certain conditions. Such exclusion agreements are not, however, generally recommended, as it is usually preferable to retain a minimum degree of judicial control over the arbitration.

In order to avoid ambiguity and the possibility of a so-called pathological clause, parties should therefore contemplate the elements referred to above when negotiating and drafting any arbitration agreement.

If the parties agree upon institutional arbitration, it should be noted that most arbitral institutions recommend a model clause. The majority of such model clauses refer to the core elements (i.e. agreement to arbitrate and indication of the dispute to be resolved by arbitration). Certain model clauses (e.g. UNCITRAL, LCIA, DIS, AAA, Swiss Rules) also contain suggestions as to the additional elements the parties may wish to consider

---

52 DFT 121 I 81, 83.

53 See Chapter 4 *infra*.

inserting into the arbitration clause, namely the seat of the arbitration, the number of arbitrators, the language of the arbitration, etc.[54] One can only endorse such an approach, as it aims at ensuring the effective implementation of the arbitration clause.

An increasingly frequent challenge in practice is the multi-party arbitration clause, which requires particular care in drafting. First, most arbitration clauses and institutional rules are written for two-party arbitrations and significant adaptation is usually required in order to ensure adequate procedural protection for three or more parties, for instance, in terms of selecting arbitrators. Second, one cannot determine in advance when, how many and which of the multiple contracting parties may be involved in a future arbitration. For instance, the claimant may commence arbitral proceedings against only one other contracting party and the respondent may wish to join a third party, or certain contracting parties not joined at the outset may wish to intervene at a later stage of the arbitration. Third, a multi-party arbitration clause must often be quite lengthy in order to take into account all possible scenarios. A variety of drafting mechanisms may be adopted including *inter alia* precise definitions of the parties, the obligation to give notice of any arbitration to all parties, the power to join additional parties to an arbitration, a waiver of the right to participate in or challenge the formation of the arbitral tribunal, etc.

In order to assist in the drafting of arbitration agreements, Appendix 1 sets forth a comprehensive checklist.

IV. Autonomy of the arbitration agreement

Article 178(3) of the PILA provides that the validity of an arbitration agreement may not be challenged on the grounds that the main contract between the parties is not valid or that the arbitration agreement relates to a dispute that has not arisen yet. This provision embodies the principle of the autonomy of the arbitration agreement and constitutes a substantive rule of private international law.

Like a choice-of-forum clause, the arbitration clause is regarded as a procedural agreement. It is autonomous and independent from the main contract in which it is contained. As a result, the arbitration agreement will be valid and apply even where the main agreement is invalid and no longer binding upon the parties.[55]

As a practical consequence of this principle, an arbitral tribunal may be constituted and arbitral proceedings conducted, regardless of the invalidity of the main agreement. The

---

54 If the UNCITRAL Rules are chosen, it is advisable to designate a specific appointing authority, since the Permanent Court of Arbitration at the Hague does not itself appoint the arbitrator(s), but merely selects the appointing authority (see Article 6 of the UNCITRAL Rules).

55 DFT 121 III 495, 499.

arbitral tribunal may then determine the validity of the arbitration agreement and its own jurisdiction, as well as the grounds of nullity, if any, of the main agreement.[56]

The principle of the autonomy of the arbitration agreement does not, however, apply without reservation. There are cases in which the grounds for nullity of the main agreement apply equally to the arbitration agreement, such as cases where one of the parties did not have the requisite capacity to enter into the contract or where the main contract is invalid for lack of consent or vitiated consent (e.g. duress).[57]

The fact that the arbitration agreement is severable from the main contract does not necessarily result in its complete independence from the main contract. For instance, under Swiss law, where a claim or legal relationship is assigned, the arbitration agreement is also transferred - as an accessory clause of a procedural nature - to the assignee, subject to an agreement to the contrary.[58]

V. '*Kompetenz-Kompetenz*'

Article 186(1) of the PILA provides that the arbitral tribunal has the power to decide upon its own jurisdiction. This provision is the embodiment of the widely recognized principle in international arbitration of '*Kompetenz-Kompetenz*'. This principle is also regarded as corollary to the principle of the autonomy of the arbitration agreement.

Article 186(1) of the PILA is not, however, unlimited and does not mean that the arbitral tribunal has the last word on its jurisdiction. Rather, the arbitral tribunal's decision on jurisdiction may be set aside by the Swiss Federal Tribunal pursuant to Article 190(2)(b) of the PILA (subject to Article 192 of the PILA), as well as reviewed at the enforcement stage under Article V(1)(c) of the NY Convention. Moreover, if a Swiss court is first seized instead of an arbitral tribunal, the court will only decline jurisdiction in favor of the arbitral tribunal within the boundaries of Article 7 of the PILA.[59]

When the jurisdiction of the arbitral tribunal is challenged, the arbitrators are usually required to rule on the following types of issues: the existence and/or validity (formal and substantive) of the arbitration agreement, the capacity of the parties to enter into the arbitration agreement, the extension of the arbitration agreement to non-signatory

---

56 [1997] ASA Bull. 291.

57 DFT 119 II 380, 384 (*National Power Corporation v. Westinghouse et al.*): in this case, the Swiss Federal Tribunal was required to determine if the arbitral tribunal was empowered to consider whether the conclusion of the contract had been affected by corruption. In light of Article 178(3) of the PILA, the Swiss Federal Tribunal answered in the affirmative.

58 DFT 128 III 50: in this case, the Swiss Federal Tribunal held that the valid assignment of a claim results in the legal entitlement of the assignee, on the one hand, and the capacity of the assignee to be a party to the arbitral proceedings by virtue of the arbitration agreement, on the other hand.

59 See note 2 *supra*. See also DFT 121 III 495, 502; DFT 120 II 155, 164.

parties, arbitrability and/or the scope of the arbitration clause.[60] With respect to the last issue, the arbitrator(s) may also have to decide whether a counterclaim or a set-off defence falls within the scope of the arbitration agreement.[61]

An arbitral tribunal is only required to examine its jurisdiction where a party has objected thereto in a timely manner.[62] Article 186(2) of the PILA provides that any objection to the arbitral tribunal's jurisdiction must be raised prior to any defense on the merits. This does not mean, however, that if it is raised simultaneously with the defense on the merits, it is out of time (subject to the provisions of different institutional arbitration rules). In that case, the pleadings on the merits are regarded as being made *eventualiter*, in the event the defence of lack of jurisdiction does not succeed. An objection to jurisdiction may not, however, be raised *after* pleadings on the merits have been filed.[63] The arbitral tribunal will generally decide on its jurisdiction by way of a preliminary award, in accordance with Article 186(3) of the PILA.

On occasion, an arbitral tribunal is required to address the issue of jurisdiction in the context of parallel court proceedings. In a recent groundbreaking decision, the Swiss Federal Tribunal held that the principle of *lis pendens* applicable to Swiss courts, as set forth in Article 9 of the PILA,[64] is also applicable to arbitral tribunals, subject to certain conditions.[65] The Swiss Federal Tribunal found that the requirement to stay proceedings in the case of litispendence is a rule of jurisdiction and not simply a procedural rule. The Federal Tribunal emphasized that it would be contrary to public policy for there to be two equally enforceable but contradictory decisions on the same subject matter between the same parties. It was noted that arbitral tribunals are bound by foreign court decisions on jurisdiction under the principle of *res judicata*, provided that such decisions are enforceable in Switzerland. Given that the principles of *res judicata* and *lis pendens* are closely linked and serve the same purpose, the Federal Tribunal found it only logical that an arbitral tribunal faced with previously commenced court proceedings must stay the arbitration until the court first seized renders a decision on jurisdiction, provided that

60 See also DFT 118 II 353, DFT 121 III 495 and DFT 120 II 155.

61 As a general rule, the arbitral tribunal has jurisdiction to rule on a counterclaim, provided that the main claim and the counterclaim arise out of the same legal relationship within the broad meaning of Article 8 of the PILA.

62 On the other hand, an arbitral tribunal is empowered to review objective arbitrability *ex officio* (see Section II.2.b) *supra*).

63 W. WENGER in HONSELL/VOGT/SCHNYDER, N. 38, p. 1582.

64 Article 9(1) of the PILA provides: '*When an action having the same subject matter is already pending between the same parties in a foreign country, the Swiss court shall stay the case if it is to be expected that the foreign court will, within a reasonable time, render a decision capable of being recognized in Switzerland.*'

65 DFT 127 III 279 (*Fomento de Construcciones y Contratas S.A. v. Colon Container Terminal S.A.*).

such decision will be rendered within a reasonable timeframe and will be enforceable in Switzerland.

This decision of the Swiss Federal Tribunal in regard to the principle of *lis pendens* in international arbitration has generated considerable commentary and likely will continue to do so for some time.[66] Moreover, while this decision now represents the state of arbitration law in Switzerland,[67] there are several issues in regard to the applicability of the principle of *lis pendens* in international arbitration which remain unresolved, e.g. the applicability of this principle between two arbitral tribunals, rather than between an arbitral tribunal and a court.[68]

Although *lis pendens* rules for international arbitration are desirable, it is important to recognize that Article 9 of the PILA was not designed for arbitration but rather for court proceedings. As a result, this provision cannot be applied to international arbitration without some adaptation.

In order to make the forecast of whether the foreign court will render a decision within a reasonable time and that will be enforceable in Switzerland as provided under Article 9 of the PILA, an arbitral tribunal sitting in Switzerland will necessarily review the validity of the arbitration agreement. This is so because a foreign court decision made in violation of a valid arbitration agreement under the relevant laws pursuant to Article 178 of the PILA would not be enforceable in Switzerland. As a consequence, the arbitral tribunal will determine either that: (a) the arbitration agreement is valid and that no stay of the arbitration should be granted, in which case the arbitration will proceed; or (b) the arbitration agreement is not valid and, accordingly, the arbitral tribunal has no jurisdiction. A general and mechanical application of the tests in Article 9 of the PILA would not, however, be appropriate within the context of international arbitration.

---

66 POUDRET/BESSON, N. 512, p. 468; L. LÉVY/E. GEISINGER, *Lis Alibi Pendens in International Commercial Arbitration*, in: Complex Arbitrations, 2003 Bull. CIArb. CCI, Special Supplement; L. LÉVY/D. RONEY/E. GEISINGER, *Applying the principle of litispendence*, (2001) Int. A.L.R., Issue 3, N. 28; M. LIATOWITSCH, *Die Anwendung der Litispendenzregel von Art. 9 IPRG durch schweizerische Schiedsgerichte: ein Paradoxon?*, in [2001] ASA Bull. 422; G. KAUFMANN-KOHLER, *Arbitration at the Olympics*, Kluwer Law International, The Hague 2001, p. 33.

67 It should, however, be noted that there is currently a motion pending before the Swiss Federal Parliament to insert a new provision into Chapter 12 of PILA, which would exclude the application of Article 9 of the PILA. The likely outcome of this motion is not known at present.

68 L. LÉVY/E. GEISINGER, *op. cit.*

This does not mean that an arbitral tribunal cannot decide, as a matter of discretion, to stay an arbitration depending on the circumstances.[69] When making such a decision, the arbitral tribunal should consider the interests of each party, as well as the need for speed and efficiency in dispute resolution.[70] The arbitral tribunal should also take into account that a stay should only be granted in exceptional circumstances, given that the granting of a stay runs contrary to the objective of speedy dispute resolution. As a result, the interests of a party opposing such stay override those of the applicant, unless the latter shows it has taken all steps necessary to prevent or limit any delays caused by a stay of the arbitration.[71]

69 The circumstances in the *Fomento* case were such because it turned on a party's waiver of the arbitration agreement by failing to raise the arbitration defence promptly before the foreign court.

70 DFT 119 II 386, 389.

71 DFT 108 Ia 197, 201.

Chapter 3 – The Arbitral Tribunal

Nathalie Voser and Pascale Gola

I. The relationship between the members of the arbitral tribunal and the parties

1. The legal basis

Under Swiss law, the legal relationship between the arbitrators and the parties is deemed to be contractual in nature. Arbitrators and parties are bound by an arbitral contract, the so-called *receptum arbitri*. This contractual relationship arises once the arbitrators have accepted their appointment.[1]

The arbitral contract is a *sui generis* contract. It contains elements of a mandate agreement within the meaning of Articles 394 *et seq.* of the SCO. The statutory provisions governing the law of mandate agreements are, however, subject to and overridden by specific arbitration rules. As a result, it is not permissible to terminate the arbitral contract by simple notice, as provided in Article 404 of the SCO with regard to mandate agreements: the arbitral contract may only be terminated on the grounds set forth in the PILA - in the case of international arbitration - or in the Concordat or the draft Federal Civil Procedure Act - in the case of domestic arbitration. The grounds for termination of the arbitral contract include, most notably, the successful challenge or the replacement of an arbitrator.[2]

Unless the parties agree otherwise, the law applicable to the arbitral contract is the law of the seat of the arbitral tribunal.[3]

2. The obligations of the arbitrators

The arbitrators' obligations are determined by Swiss statutory law, by the applicable arbitration rules and/or by the arbitral contract. In general, the arbitrators are required to

---

1 W. PETER/T. LEGLER in BERTI, N. 55, p. 376; LALIVE/POUDRET/REYMOND, N. 6 to 8, p. 332.

2 W. PETER/T. LEGLER in BERTI, N. 58, p. 377; see also Section V *infra*.

3 LALIVE/POUDRET/REYMOND, N. 3, p. 92 and N. 6, p. 332; RÜEDE/HADENFELDT, p. 152.

G. Kaufmann-Kohler and B. Stucki (eds), International Arbitration in Switzerland, A Handbook for Practitioners, 33-48.

act in good faith, be impartial and treat the parties equally. They are obliged to grant the parties a fair opportunity to present their case,[4] to conduct the arbitration efficiently, with care and in person.[5]

Furthermore, the arbitrators are under a duty to render the award within a reasonable time period, to participate in the hearings and in the deliberations and to carry out their functions until the conclusion of the proceedings.[6] Finally, the arbitrators are bound by the duty of confidentiality.[7]

3. *The rights of the arbitrators*

The arbitrators' rights under the arbitral contract are essentially of a pecuniary nature. In return for the judicial services they provide, the arbitrators are entitled to remuneration. In *ad hoc* arbitration, the arbitrators determine their fees themselves.[8] In institutional arbitration, the position varies depending upon the institution. The fees may either be determined by the arbitrators themselves or by the institution. Institutional arbitration rules usually include a schedule setting forth the parameters for determining the arbitrators' fees.[9]

Apart from pecuniary rights, arbitrators enjoy certain moral rights. Parties cannot challenge arbitrators they have appointed as long as the arbitrators have disclosed all facts and circumstances that may raise doubts as to their independence or impartiality.[10] The arbitrators can only be dismissed with the consent of all parties to the arbitration.[11] Removal upon the application of one party is permissible only if there are valid grounds.[12] Furthermore, the arbitrators enjoy, in principle, immunity from suit.[13]

---

4 FOUCHARD/GAILLARD/GOLDMAN, N. 1129, p. 609.

5 According to RÜEDE/HADENFELDT (pp. 155 *et seq.*), this follows from Article 398 of the SCO.

6 W. PETER/T. LEGLER in BERTI, N. 57, p. 377. An arbitrator must not retire from the arbitral proceedings unless he has a valid ground to do so (DFT 117 Ia 169).

7 RÜEDE/HADENFELDT, pp. 156 *et seq.*

8 Article 182(2) of the PILA. Alternatively, the arbitrators' power to determine their fees may arise from the arbitral contract (F. HOFFET, *Rechtliche Beziehungen zwischen Schiedsrichtern und Parteien*, Schulthess Polygraphischer Verlag, Zurich 1991, p. 151).

9 This is the case, for example, in the Swiss Rules, the ICC Rules and the LCIA Rules.

10 FOUCHARD/GAILLARD/GOLDMAN, N. 1074 *et seq.* pp. 588 *et seq.* and N. 1090, p. 594.

11 Article 22(1) of the Concordat; RÜEDE/HADENFELDT, p. 169; W. PETER/T. LEGLER in BERTI, N. 27, p. 368.

12 It is for the arbitral institution chosen by the parties or for the competent court judge to decide on applications for removal (Article 179(2) of the PILA; Article 3 of the Concordat). A valid ground for removal exists if the circumstances are such that the party applying for removal cannot be expected to remain bound by the arbitral contract. For a more detailed dicussion, see RÜEDE/HADENFELDT, p. 168.

13 See Section I.4 *infra.*

4. *The arbitrators' civil liability*

When arbitrators fail to comply with their duties, the natural target for attack by the parties is the arbitral award, not the arbitrators. Arbitrators enjoy a certain degree of immunity. When acting in their judicial capacity, the arbitrators are, in principle, liable only if they have caused damage as a result of intentional or grossly negligent behaviour. The fact that the award is subsequently set aside by a court is not sufficient to establish the arbitrators' liability.[14] The immunity of arbitrators flows from their status, which is comparable to that of court judges. Arbitrators, like court judges, must be in a position to carry out their judicial function without the fear of being held liable by dissatisfied parties. In this sense, the arbitral contract implicitly provides for a limitation of liability.[15]

On the other hand, arbitrators are liable for damages arising as a result of resignation at an inappropriate time.[16] They are also liable for failure to disclose facts constituting a valid ground for challenging their appointment or for breach of the duty of confidentiality.[17] Under such circumstances, arbitrators may lose their right to remuneration.[18]

II. Composition of the arbitral tribunal

1. *The number of arbitrators*

a) Where the arbitration clause sets forth the number of arbitrators

Arbitration clauses often specify the number of arbitrators required to form the arbitral tribunal. Such clauses usually provide either for a sole arbitrator or a three-member arbitral tribunal. The parties are free to choose another number of arbitrators; however, if five or even more arbitrators are to sit on the panel, the arbitral proceedings will inevitably be more expensive and less efficient. Clauses providing for an even number of arbitrators are valid,[19] but not advisable, since deadlock may occur.[20]

---

14 K. P. BERGER (*Internationale Wirtschaftsschiedsgerichtsbarkeit*, Berlin 1992, pp. 162 *et seq.*) takes the view that the setting aside of the award is, however, a prerequisite for bringing a liability claim against an arbitrator.

15 K. H. SCHWAB/G. WALTER, *Schiedsgerichtsbarkeit*, 4th edn, Verlag C. H. Beck, Munich 2000, N. 9, p. 94; K. P. BERGER, *op. cit.*, pp. 162 *et seq.*; RÜEDE/HADENFELDT, pp. 160 *et seq.* FOUCHARD/GAILLARD/GOLDMAN, N. 1144, p. 619, p. 621 and pp. 1149 *et seq.*

16 DFT 117 Ia 166, 170.

17 K. P. BERGER, *op. cit.*, p. 163; RÜEDE/HADENFELDT, pp. 160 *et seq.*

18 *Ibid.*, p. 162; FOUCHARD/GAILLARD/GOLDMAN, N. 1155, p. 623.

19 DFT 121 I 81.

20 Some authors suggest that if the arbitral tribunal consists of an even number of arbitrators, one of them should be empowered to make a tie-breaking decision in order to ensure that a valid award can be issued (see e.g. W. PETER/T. LEGLER in BERTI, N. 10, p. 364). If the arbitration clause does not provide for such a solution, a party can apply to a court to have a

When determining the number of arbitrators, the parties should keep in mind, among others, the following considerations. On one hand, arbitration with a sole arbitrator saves costs and involves less potential for delay than arbitration involving three or more arbitrators. On the other hand, if the parties agree upon a sole arbitrator, one single individual will decide the parties' dispute without consulting anyone else. This is particularly significant given that the arbitral award is not open to extensive review by the courts, but can only be set aside on very limited grounds.[21] Furthermore, clauses providing for an arbitral tribunal with three or more members allow each party to designate 'its own' arbitrator. This may make the parties feel more comfortable and increase both their confidence in the arbitral tribunal and the likelihood that they will accept the award. The parties may, for example, choose an arbitrator who is familiar with their laws and cultural backgrounds.[22] Furthermore, the complexity of the factual or legal issues of the case, or simply the amount at stake, may make it preferable to opt for an arbitral tribunal equipped with three minds instead of only one.

Since the costs of the arbitration depend in part upon the number of arbitrators, the above-mentioned considerations must be weighed against the amount in dispute. As a rule of thumb, one can say that the advantages of having a three-member arbitral tribunal generally outweigh the increased cost if the amount at stake exceeds USD 2 million.

In this regard, it should be noted that the parties may alter the original arbitration clause by subsequent agreement. The parties may therefore agree upon a sole arbitrator instead of a three-member arbitral tribunal as provided in the arbitration clause (or *vice versa*), after the dispute has arisen and the amount in dispute is known.

b) Where the arbitration clause is silent on the number of arbitrators

If the parties have not agreed on the number of arbitrators in the arbitration clause or once a dispute has arisen, the number of arbitrators depends on the applicable arbitration rules.

Under the ICC Rules, the dispute shall be decided either by a sole arbitrator or by three arbitrators.[23] The wording of Article 8(2) of the ICC Rules seems to suggest a

---

third arbitrator nominated (unreported decision of the Swiss Federal Tribunal of 20 March 1995, quoted by W. PETER/T. LEGLER in BERTI, N. 10, p. 364).

21 See Article 190 of the PILA, which sets forth the grounds for challenge under Swiss law.

22 This is considered important in particular when the dispute involves parties from third world countries (K. P. BERGER, *op. cit.*, p. 141).

23 Article 8(1) of the ICC Rules. The parties are free to agree upon an even or uneven number of arbitrators (see DERAINS/SCHWARTZ, p. 131, who point out that the ICC has nevertheless refused to permit arbitrations with two arbitrators plus an 'umpire' to be appointed to render the award if the two arbitrators initially appointed cannot agree. The umpire system is still commonly used in certain jurisdictions).

presumption in favour of the appointment of a sole arbitrator.[24] In practice, however, the ICC Court is guided by the amount in dispute. Unless the appointment of more than one arbitrator appears uneconomical, the ICC Court will, as a general rule, appoint three arbitrators.[25] The ICC will usually appoint a sole arbitrator whenever the amount in dispute is lower than USD 3 to 5 million, while also taking into account the complexity of the case.

The ICC practice is consistent with prevailing international practice: the UNCITRAL Rules provide for the appointment of three arbitrators unless the parties have agreed on a sole arbitrator.[26]

The Swiss Rules provide for an expedited procedure with a sole arbitrator where the amount in dispute does not exceed CHF 1 million.[27] In cases where the amount in dispute exceeds CHF 1 million, the Chambers may appoint a sole arbitrator or a three-member arbitral tribunal.[28] As a general rule, a sole arbitrator shall be appointed, unless the complexity of the case and/or the amount in dispute justify that the matter be referred to a three-member arbitral tribunal.[29]

In *ad hoc* international arbitration, the Swiss court judge will determine the number of the arbitrators in accordance with the provisions of the Concordat and, in the future, the Federal Civil Procedure Act, based upon the reference by analogy to cantonal law in Article 179(2) of the PILA. According to the provisions of the Concordat, the arbitral tribunal shall consist of three members.[30] The same rule is set forth in the draft Federal Civil Procedure Act.[31]

2. Requirements to act as an arbitrator

Only individuals can be appointed and act as arbitrators. Where the parties have agreed upon a legal entity as arbitrator, it is necessary to interpret the meaning of this agreement. The parties may have intended to appoint a representative of the legal entity mentioned in the arbitration clause.[32]

---

24 Article 8(2) of the ICC Rules provides as follows: '*Where the parties have not agreed upon the number of arbitrators, the Court shall appoint a sole arbitrator, save where it appears to the Court that the dispute is such as to warrant the appointment of three arbitrators.* (…)'.

25 DERAINS/SCHWARTZ, p. 134.

26 Article 5 of the UNCITRAL Rules.

27 Articles 6(4) and 42(2) of the Swiss Rules. See generally Chapter 10 *infra*.

28 Article 6(1) of the Swiss Rules.

29 Article 6(2) of the Swiss Rules.

30 Article 10(1) of the Concordat.

31 Article 351(1) of the draft Federal Civil Procedure Act.

32 DFT 117 III 60; RÜEDE/HADENFELDT, p. 138; W. PETER/T. LEGLER in BERTI, N. 7, p. 364; WALTER/BOSCH/BRÖNNIMANN, p. 99.

Under the PILA, there is no requirement with respect to the professional qualifications of arbitrators.[33] Although knowledge of substantive law is often not determinative, the parties usually endeavour to choose arbitrators who are sufficiently familiar with or even experts on the applicable substantive law and are familiar with the type of transaction or business at stake. If the dispute involves complex technical questions, the parties may be tempted to nominate individuals with technical expertise rather than lawyers. Whether this is advisable is doubtful since it is necessary in all arbitrations to resolve at least some legal questions.[34] Moreover, nothing prevents the arbitral tribunal or the parties from appointing technical experts to assist with technical questions, if necessary. In any event, parties are well advised to choose persons experienced in the efficient management of arbitral proceedings. It is possible to appoint court judges as arbitrators, although there are conflicting views on the wisdom of doing so.[35]

When designating an arbitrator, the parties should take into account the language skills of the candidates. An arbitrator without an adequate working knowledge of the language to be used in the arbitral proceedings will be inefficient and cause delay and additional costs.

Another important factor to consider is availability. An arbitrator with an overloaded agenda may make it difficult to find suitable hearing dates. It is therefore advisable to enquire about the availability of an arbitrator before appointing him or her.

Under Swiss law, there are no legal restrictions as to the nationality of the arbitrators.[36] However, parties from different jurisdictions often attach importance to appointing a chairperson or a sole arbitrator of a different nationality than the parties,[37] while wishing to appoint a co-arbitrator of their own nationality, which may or may not be advisable depending on the circumstances.

To sum up, the parties have considerable freedom in determining the requirements that the arbitrators must fulfil in terms of professional qualifications, language skills, nationality, etc. If they stipulate any requirement in the arbitration clause or at a later stage, they will have a valid ground for challenging any arbitrator who fails to meet such

---

33 W. PETER/T. LEGLER in BERTI, N. 9, p. 364; BUCHER/TSCHANZ, N. 121, p. 67.

34 K. P. BERGER (*op. cit.*, p. 143) takes the view that even in arbitrations involving complex technical transactions, such as contracts for the construction of a plant, the prevailing issues are legal rather than technical in nature; G. KAUFMANN-KOHLER, *Arbitration in Air, Space and Telecommunications Law: Arbitration and the need For Technical or Scientific Expertise*, Proceedings of the International Law Seminar, The Hague February 2001, The Permanent Court of Arbitration/Peace Palace Papers, pp. 285-296.

35 When acting as an arbitrator, a judge may be required by the applicable cantonal law to give notice of such appointment (e.g. high court judges in the canton of Zurich) or ask for permission to accept such appointment (e.g. district court judges in the canton of Zurich).

36 RÜEDE/HADENFELDT, p. 138.

37 K. P. BERGER, *op. cit.*, p. 144. Article 9(5) of the ICC Rules states that the sole arbitrator or the chairperson of the arbitral tribunal shall be of a nationality other than those of the parties. This provision allows for exceptions '*in suitable circumstances*', if neither party objects.

requirement.[38] However, according to the general principle of good faith, a challenge will not be possible if the parties impliedly waived such requirement by appointing an arbitrator knowing that the requirement at issue was not met.

III. Constitution of the arbitral tribunal

1. In general

The constitution of the arbitral tribunal is primarily governed by the arbitration clause or any subsequent agreement between the parties. The parties are free to agree upon each of the arbitrators or to define a mechanism for the appointment of the arbitrators. The parties' freedom is limited only by the fundamental principle of due process. This principle includes, in particular, the parties' right to a fair hearing and the right to equal treatment.[39] Arbitration clauses granting one of the parties an overriding influence on the constitution of the arbitral tribunal are thus invalid.[40]

Under the typical procedure for appointing a three-member arbitral tribunal in a two-party dispute, each party nominates an arbitrator and the two party-appointed arbitrators endeavour to agree upon a chairperson. As explained in the following sections, where the party-appointed arbitrators are unable to reach an agreement, an 'appointing authority' will usually designate the chairperson.[41]

2. Where there is no agreement among the parties

a) *Ad hoc* arbitration

Article 179(2) of the PILA provides that, where the parties have not come to an agreement on the appointment of arbitrators, they may request the court at the seat of the arbitration to act as appointing authority. As explained above, the court will apply by analogy the provisions of cantonal law concerning the appointment of arbitrators, which at present means the Concordat.[42]

Article 11(3) of the Concordat stipulates that, if there is no agreement among the parties on the arbitrators or the method of appointment, each party shall designate an arbitrator. The two party-appointed arbitrators must then appoint a chairperson. If the party-appointed arbitrators cannot agree upon a chairperson, Article 12 of the Concordat sets forth a default mechanism: either party may apply to the competent court of the Canton where the arbitration has its seat to have a chairperson appointed.[43] In Zurich[44] and most other Cantons, the competent court is the High Court; the Cantons are, however, free to

38 Article 180(1)(a) of the PILA.

39 FOUCHARD/GAILLARD/GOLDMAN, N. 750 *et seq.*, p. 452; PATOCCHI/GEISINGER, N. 3, p. 545.

40 DFT 107 Ia 155, 162.

41 BORN, p. 616.

42 M. BLESSING in BÖCKSTIEGEL (ed.), *Die Internationale Schiedsgerichtsbarkeit in der Schweiz*, Band 1/II, Carl Heymanns Verlag KG, 1989, p. 45; RÜEDE/HADENFELDT, p. 122.

43 Article 12 of the Concordat.

44 Article 239(2) of the ZCCP.

designate another court.[45] In the Canton of Geneva, for instance, the Court of First Instance is empowered to appoint arbitrators.[46] The draft Federal Civil Procedure Act similarly provides that the Cantons have the power to determine which court shall make these appointments.[47]

According to the case law and scholarly writings, the parties may seek the assistance of the court in situations not expressly mentioned in Article 12 of the Concordat or Article 179(2) of the PILA. In general, these are situations where an agreed mechanism for appointment has failed. For example, the court's involvement is deemed appropriate where the appointing authority chosen by the parties refuses to appoint a chairperson[48] or where the appointing authority does not exist or has ceased to exist.[49]

In international arbitration, the competent court is under a duty to act,[50] unless a summary examination of the case reveals that there is no valid arbitration agreement between the parties.[51]

Cantonal law may provide for the right to appeal against all decisions taken by the courts.[52] Where the court has *refused* to make an appointment, the matter can also be brought before the Swiss Federal Tribunal.[53] By contrast, there is no right to challenge a court's appointment of an arbitrator before the Swiss Federal Tribunal – such decisions can only be challenged by application to set aside the final award pursuant to Article 190 of the PILA.[54]

b) Institutional arbitration

aa) ICC arbitration

If there is no agreement between the parties on the appointment of a sole arbitrator, the ICC Court will appoint such arbitrator.[55]

In case of a three-member arbitral tribunal, each party nominates one arbitrator. As a general rule, the ICC will confirm the co-arbitrators nominated by the parties, unless the

---

45 Article 3 in connection with Article 45(2) of the Concordat.

46 PATOCCHI/GEISINGER, N. 6, p. 548.

47 Article 346(2)(a) of the draft Federal Civil Procedure Act.

48 DFT 110 Ia 59.

49 LALIVE/POUDRET/REYMOND, N. 4, p. 330.

50 RÜEDE/HADENFELDT, p. 122; W. PETER/T. LEGLER in BERTI, N. 34, p. 370.

51 Article 179(3) of the PILA. No similar provision exists in the Concordat.

52 W. PETER/T. LEGLER in BERTI, N. 53, p. 375; RÜEDE/HADENFELDT, p. 125.

53 DFT 118 Ia 25. Cantonal rights of appeal, if available, must be exhausted for a matter to be admitted before the Swiss Federal Tribunal (DFT 119 Ia 422). The scope of review of the Swiss Federal Tribunal is limited to arbitrariness. For a more detailed examination of this issue, see W. PETER/T. LEGLER in BERTI, N. 50 *et seq.*, p. 49.

54 DFT 115 II 294. For more details, see W. PETER/T. LEGLER in BERTI, N. 48 *et seq.*, pp. 374 *et seq.*

55 Article 8(3) of the ICC Rules.

nominee does not meet one of the requirements for arbitrators under the ICC Rules. If a party fails to nominate 'its' co-arbitrator, the ICC will appoint an arbitrator for such party. Most significantly, it is for the ICC Court to appoint the chairperson, unless the parties have agreed upon another procedure.[56] In multi-party arbitration, the multiple claimants and the multiple respondents will be requested to jointly nominate one arbitrator for each group. In the absence of a joint nomination or where the parties are unable to agree upon another method for the constitution of the arbitral tribunal, the ICC Court will appoint all three arbitrators and designate the chairperson from among them.[57]

The ICC Court ordinarily makes appointments of arbitrators based upon a proposal from a National Committee of the ICC.[58] In most cases, the ICC Court will request a proposal from the National Committee of the country where the party which has failed to make a nomination is based, or, in the case of sole arbitrators or chairpersons, the National Committee of a third country which the ICC Court considers to be appropriate.[59]

bb) The Swiss Rules

Under the Swiss Rules, the parties jointly designate the sole arbitrator, failing which the Chambers proceed with the appointment.

Where the proceedings are referred to a three-member arbitral tribunal, each party designates one arbitrator.[60] The two party-designated arbitrators must then designate a third arbitrator, who shall act as the chairperson of the tribunal.[61] Failing such designation, the Chambers appoint the chairperson.[62]

In multi-party proceedings, the Chambers will invite the group of claimants to designate an arbitrator and then invite the group of respondents to designate an arbitrator. The two party-designated arbitrators must then designate the chairperson.[63] If one group or both groups of parties fail(s) to designate an arbitrator, the Chambers will appoint all three arbitrators and specify which of the arbitrators shall act as the chairperson.[64]

---

56 Article 8(4) of the ICC Rules; FOUCHARD/GAILLARD/GOLDMAN, N. 983, p. 545; DERAINS/SCHWARTZ, p. 139; CRAIG/PARK/PAULSSON, p. 191.

57 Article 10(1) and 10(2) of the ICC Rules.

58 Article 9(3) of the ICC Rules.

59 FOUCHARD/GAILLARD/GOLDMAN, N. 984, p. 546. For details on the selection of the National Committee, see DERAINS/SCHWARTZ, pp. 159 *et seq.*

60 Article 8(1) of the Swiss Rules. The parties' nominations are subject to confirmation by the Chambers (Article 5 of the Swiss Rules).

61 Article 8(2) of the Swiss Rules provides that the party-nominated arbitrators shall appoint the presiding arbitrator within thirty days from the confirmation of the second arbitrator.

62 Article 8(2) of the Swiss Rules.

63 Article 8(3) of the Swiss Rules.

64 Articles 8(3) and 8(4) of the Swiss Rules.

IV. Independence and impartiality of the arbitrators

1. Standard of independence and impartiality

Article 30(1) of the Swiss Federal Constitution expressly guarantees that all legal disputes will be judged by an independent and impartial court. This standard of independence and impartiality is also derived from the constitutional right to a fair hearing under Article 29 of the Swiss Federal Constitution. These constitutional provisions apply not only to courts but also to arbitral tribunals.[65] It is generally accepted that the same rights arise under Article 6 of the European Convention on Human Rights, although the question of the application of this convention to international arbitration is unsettled.[66]

Article 180(1) of the PILA sets forth the grounds for bringing a challenge against arbitrators. Of particular importance, Article 180(1)(c) provides that an arbitrator may be challenged if circumstances exist that give rise to justifiable doubts as to his or her independence.

According to the drafters of Article 180(1)(c) of the PILA, impartiality can be considered to be the corollary of the independence of an arbitrator or, at least, usually results from such independence.[67]

Based upon the fact that the express wording of Article 180(1)(c) of the PILA only refers to independence, some legal commentators have, however, maintained that the standard for the independence and impartiality of a party-appointed arbitrator is less strict than the one applicable to the chairperson or an arbitrator appointed by third parties or a court. The argument seems to be supported by the legal history of Article 180 of the PILA. The fact that this provision only refers to independence and not to impartiality shows the intention of the Swiss Parliament to approach international arbitration with a certain degree of realism and flexibility.[68] An initial decision of the Swiss Federal Tribunal on

65 DFT 117 Ia 166. W. PETER/C. FREYMOND in BERTI, N. 19, p. 384.

66 Although sometimes mentioned in the case law, Article 6 of the European Convention on Human Rights is not directly applicable to arbitral tribunals. However, as the contents of Article 6 of the European Convention on Human Rights form part of Article 29 of the Swiss Federal Constitution, it has an indirect impact on issues relating to the independence and impartiality of arbitral tribunals: decision of the Swiss Federal Tribunal of 11 June 2001 in [2001] ASA Bull. 566; see also C. LIEBSCHER, *The Healthy Award*, The Hague 2003, pp. 74 *et seq.* and p. 104.

67 A. BUCHER, *Die neue internationale Schiedsgerichtsbarkeit in der Schweiz*, Helbing & Lichtenhahn, Basel 1989, N. 169, p. 69; W. PETER/C. FREYMOND in BERTI, N. 12, p. 382. Article 12 of the UNCITRAL Model Law, which refers to the impartiality or independence of the arbitrator, is not applicable to Swiss international arbitration and has not been taken into account in the drafting of the PILA.

68 W. PETER/C. FREYMOND in BERTI, N. 14, p. 383; BUCHER, N. 168, p. 68; BUCHER/TSCHANZ, N. 126, p. 69.

this provision left the issue undecided.[69] However, the views of these legal commentators were confirmed by a subsequent decision, in which the Swiss Federal Tribunal held that the Swiss Parliament intended that party-appointed arbitrators shall not be required to meet the same strict standards of independence as the chairperson.[70] While the co-arbitrators must be neutral and independent, the standard applicable to a co-arbitrator is not as demanding as for the chairperson when assessing the impact of a possible connection between a party and a co-arbitrator.

As a general matter, one can still look to the earlier decisions of the Swiss Federal Tribunal in relation to Articles 58 and 61 of the former Swiss Federal Constitution and Article 19 of the Concordat in interpreting the requirement of independence set forth in Article 180(1)(c) of the PILA.[71] Accordingly, circumstances that give rise to justifiable doubts as to the independence of an arbitrator must be based on concrete facts that can justify, objectively and reasonably, a lack of confidence on the part of a person reacting in a reasonable manner.[72] The criteria of independence must therefore be construed on a case-by-case basis, having regard to the objective circumstances.

Because the standard is based upon objective circumstances, it is not necessary for an arbitrator to actually be biased, but only for there to be circumstances giving rise to the appearance of partiality and risk of bias.[73]

With regard to the standard of independence and impartiality in Swiss domestic arbitration, Article 18 of the Concordat refers to Articles 22 to 25 of the JOA, which contain specific rules about the exclusion and challenge of judges. The draft Federal Civil Procedure Act has adopted the same approach that is set forth in Article 180(1) of the PILA, i.e. it requires that the members of the arbitral tribunal must be independent.[74]

2. *Case law*

An arbitrator may objectively appear to be biased if, for example, he or she has a relationship of subordination with a party (the arbitrator is an executive of a party or member of the law firm representing a party), substantial economic affiliations (the arbitrator is the member of the board of directors of a party or of an affiliated company), ongoing professional connections (the arbitrator is a regular adviser of a party) or promises of additional remuneration exist.[75]

Several Swiss court decisions serve to clarify the objective test applicable to determining independence and impartiality under Article 180(1)(c) of the PILA.

---

69 DFT 118 II 362.

70 Decision of the Swiss Federal Tribunal of 30 June 1994 in [1997] ASA Bull. 104.

71 BUCHER/TSCHANZ, N. 125, p. 69; DFT 118 II 359.

72 DFT 113 Ia 407. DFT 118 II 359; BUCHER/TSCHANZ, N. 124, p. 68.

73 DFT 114 Ia 50, 53; DFT 117 Ia 184; DFT 120 Ia 184.

74 Article 357(1)(c) of the draft Federal Civil Procedure Act.

75 LALIVE/POUDRET/REYMOND, N. 5, p. 340 ; W. PETER/C. FREYMOND in BERTI, N. 15, p. 383.

In the following cases, Swiss courts found that there were not facts or circumstances giving rise to justifiable doubts as to independence and impartiality:

- the arbitrator had acted in the past for a party, but no economic or emotional relationship influencing the arbitrator continued to exist during the arbitral procedure;[76]
- after the resignation of an arbitrator, the two remaining arbitrators refused to repeat the whole proceedings;[77]
- the arbitrator used the German familiar form '*Du*' when addressing the president of the board of directors of the claimant – this fact alone was not sufficient to assume such a strong friendship between them that there would be grounds for challenge;[78]
- the fact that the decision was wrong on the merits and that procedural mistakes were made by the arbitrator.[79]

In the following cases, Swiss courts concluded that there were facts or circumstances giving rise to justifiable doubts as to independence and impartiality:

- a judge communicated *ex parte* with a party, which led to this party to re-apply on the same day for provisional measures with additional supporting explanations, and the judge then granted the provisional measures requested;[80]
- a judge had an ongoing (private) mandate during the course of court proceedings for one of the parties to these court proceedings;[81]
- the wife of a party-appointed arbitrator was an associate in the law firm representing that party.[82]

3. *Institutional arbitration rules*

Pursuant to Article 180(1)(b) of the PILA, an arbitrator may also be challenged if the arbitration rules agreed by the parties provide a ground for challenge.

As with the PILA, Article 7(1) of the ICC Rules employs the single test of independence of the arbitrator. On the other hand, Article 10(1) of the UNCITRAL Rules states that an arbitrator may be challenged if circumstances exist that give rise to justifiable doubts as

---

76 Unreported decision of the Swiss Federal Tribunal of 15 October 2001 in [2002] ASA Bull. 321.

77 DFT 118 II 359.

78 Decision of the Appellate Court of the Canton of Schaffhausen in [1991] ABSH 75.

79 DFT 115 Ia 400.

80 Decision of 11 September 1995 of the Supreme Court of the Canton of Zurich in [1993] SJZ 465.

81 DFT 116 Ia 485.

82 DFT 92 I 271.

to the arbitrator's impartiality or independence. Article 9(1) of the Swiss Rules provides that all arbitrators conducting arbitration under the Swiss Rules shall be and remain impartial and independent of the parties.

Although, as already mentioned, there is no conceptual difference between the ICC Rules and the PILA on the one hand and the UNCITRAL Rules and the Swiss Rules on the other hand, the wording of Article 9(1) of the Swiss Rules can be understood to require that both the chairperson and the party-appointed arbitrators adhere to the same very strict standard of independence and impartiality. This constitutes a stricter approach than is required under present Swiss case law.[83]

4. Duty of disclosure

Although the PILA is silent on this issue, the Swiss Federal Tribunal has held that an arbitrator has a duty to disclose circumstances that may give rise to justifiable doubts as to his or her independence.[84] This duty was considered to be based upon the arbitrator's pre-contractual and, after appointment, ancillary contractual duty to take all necessary steps in order to guarantee an orderly and speedy procedure. Furthermore, it has become widely accepted in international arbitration that an arbitrator must disclose to the arbitral institution and the parties all circumstances which may, on an objective basis, impair his or her independence.

Articles 7(2) and 7(3) of the ICC Rules expressly state that an arbitrator shall disclose all circumstances which may call into question his or her independence in the eyes of the parties at all times before and during the arbitration proceedings. Article 9 of the UNCITRAL Rules contains a similar duty of the arbitrator to disclose such relevant facts. Article 9(2) of the Swiss Rules provides for a duty of disclosure both for prospective arbitrators and arbitrators already chosen or appointed. Under the Swiss Rules, the duty of disclosure extends to circumstances likely to give rise to justifiable doubts as to an arbitrator's impartiality and independence.[85]

Does the very fact that an arbitrator has not disclosed circumstances affecting his or her independence or impartiality itself constitute a reason for challenge? The answer is 'no' – the Swiss Federal Tribunal has held that non-disclosure in and of itself does not provide grounds for a challenge, but only the facts which were not disclosed themselves may provide such grounds.[86]

---

83 See Section IV.1 *supra*.

84 DFT 111 Ia 72.

85 This corresponds to Article 12(1) of the UNCITRAL Model Law.

86 Unreported decision of the Swiss Federal Tribunal of 15 October 2001 in [2002] ASA Bull. 321.

V. Challenge and replacement of an arbitrator

1. Challenge of an arbitrator

a) Procedure

Under Article 180(3) of the PILA, the parties are free to determine the procedure for the challenge of arbitrators. Such an agreement on a challenge procedure may, for example, refer to specific rules established by the parties, the appointing authority under Article 12 of the UNCITRAL Rules or an arbitral institution such as the ICC Court in accordance with the ICC Rules.[87] If the parties have not determined the procedure for the challenge, the court at the seat of the arbitral tribunal shall decide on the challenge (Article 180(3) of the PILA). In such a case, the court must apply, by analogy, the provisions of cantonal law, including the Concordat, regarding the procedure for removal and replacement of an arbitrator.[88] However, the actual grounds for challenge set forth in the Concordat are not applicable by analogy, as the list of grounds for challenge specified in Article 180(1) of the PILA is exhaustive.[89]

Similarly, Article 359 of the draft Federal Civil Procedure Act provides that the parties may agree among themselves on the procedure for the challenge of an arbitrator. If the parties have not provided for such procedure, the same provision stipulates that the challenging party is required to bring its challenge before the competent cantonal court.[90]

b) Time limit for challenge of an arbitrator

The PILA does not provide a specific time limit within which parties must initiate challenge procedures with respect to an arbitrator. However, the principle of good faith requires a party to challenge an arbitrator immediately after becoming aware of a ground for challenge. Furthermore, Article 180(2) of the PILA expressly states that a party may only challenge an arbitrator whom it has appointed, or in whose appointment it has participated, on grounds of which it became aware after such appointment. The challenge must be notified to the arbitral tribunal and the other party without delay. A party is estopped from challenging an arbitrator if the challenge is not undertaken immediately after becoming aware of the ground for challenge.[91]

---

87 BUCHER/TSCHANZ, N. 128, p. 71.

88 RÜEDE/HADENFELDT, N. 25 VI 3 b) aa), p. 187.

89 RÜEDE/HADENFELDT, N. 25 VI 3 b) bb), p. 187. There has been widespread support from legal commentators for the express recognition of agreements between the parties on challenge procedures as set forth in Article 180(3) of the PILA. As a consequence of this provision of the PILA, the Swiss Federal Tribunal's earlier decisions under Article 21 of the Concordat, which ignored such agreements, are no longer applicable to international arbitration: LALIVE/POUDRET/REYMOND, N. 10, p. 343; W. PETER/C. FREYMOND in BERTI, N. 24, p. 385).

90 The competent court is determined by the cantons (Article 346 of the draft Federal Civil Procedure Act).

91 BUCHER/TSCHANZ, N. 133, p. 72; W. PETER/C. FREYMOND in BERTI, N. 21, p. 384.

There is some debate as to whether a distinction should be made in regard to the time limit for challenge based upon the stage of the arbitral proceedings. While some legal commentators do not agree with this approach,[92] the Swiss Federal Tribunal has held that the closer the proceedings are to a final decision, the faster a party must raise the grounds for challenge.[93]

If a party becomes aware of a ground for challenge after the final award has been rendered, it can only raise this ground by filing an application to set aside the final award pursuant to Article 190(2)(a) of the PILA.[94] If the time limit for applying to set aside the final award has expired, no remedy is available, except for an application for revision of the award, provided the relevant requirements are met (see Chapter 8 *infra*).[95]

The Swiss Rules do not stipulate any time limit for challenging an arbitrator. As a consequence, the general considerations applicable under the PILA will govern. Under Article 11(2) of the ICC Rules, a challenge must be raised within 30 days from the notification of the appointment or confirmation of the arbitrator or within 30 days from the date when the party became aware of the ground for challenge. Article 11(2) of the UNCITRAL Rules sets forth a similar approach, although the applicable time limit is only 15 days.

c) Appeal against a challenge decision

In accordance with Article 180(3) of the PILA, the decision of the court at the seat of the arbitration on a challenge to an arbitrator is final. This provision has the effect of excluding a right of appeal either at the cantonal or the federal level against court decisions on challenges to arbitrators.[96] In view of the purposes and approach of the PILA and international arbitration in general, the Swiss Federal Tribunal has also held that that it is not possible to bring a public law appeal, which is an extraordinary remedy with very limited scrutiny for violations of constitutional rights, in respect of court decisions on challenges.[97]

---

92 BUCHER/TSCHANZ, N. 133, p. 72.

93 DFT 111 Ia 72.

94 LALIVE/POUDRET/REYMOND, N. 9, p. 343.

95 BUCHER/TSCHANZ, N. 133, p. 72.

96 W. PETER/C. FREYMOND in BERTI, N. 33, p. 386.

97 DFT 122 I 370; [1998] ASA Bull. 634. This issue remains controversial among scholars. Against the possibility of a public law appeal: LALIVE/POUDRET/REYMOND, N. 12, p. 344; RÜEDE/HADENFELDT, N. 25 VI 3 b) cc), p. 187. In favour of such a possibility: BUCHER/TSCHANZ, N. 132; W. PETER/C. FREYMOND in BERTI, N. 33. For a comparative law analysis see: D.P. RONEY/V. FROSSARD, *How Final is Final: National Court Approaches to Decisions on Challenges by Arbitral Institutions* in Stockholm Arbitration Report, forthcoming in 2004.

2. *Replacement of an arbitrator*

If an arbitrator is successfully challenged, he or she will be replaced in accordance with Article 179 of the PILA and the procedure that led to the arbitrator's appointment.[98] Article 179 of the PILA addresses both the appointment of arbitrators and the replacement of arbitrators in the event of death, resignation, removal following a challenge, or revocation by both parties.[99] The procedure for such replacement is governed by the agreement of the parties, which will often refer to institutional arbitration rules (Article 179(1) of the PILA). In the absence of an agreement between the parties, the court at the seat of the arbitral tribunal will decide on the replacement of the arbitrator, applying by analogy the provisions of cantonal law (Article 179 (2) of the PILA) or the Federal Civil Procedure Act, once it will be enacted.

When an arbitrator is replaced, a number of questions arise in regard to the fate of the arbitral proceedings. Should they be repeated? Should the arbitral proceedings simply continue with the new arbitrator from the stage where they left off at the time of the replacement? In accordance with Article 182 of the PILA, the answer to these questions must be sought in the agreement of the parties, the relevant arbitration rules or the procedural rules established by the arbitrators.[100] If the applicable rules and the agreement of the parties are silent on the steps to be taken in the event that an arbitrator is replaced, it will be for the arbitrators to determine the procedure.[101] In most cases, the arbitral proceedings will continue with the new arbitrator from the stage where they were left off at the time of the replacement. In certain cases, it may, however, be necessary to postpone certain procedural steps in order to allow enough time for the new arbitrator to review the file.

---

98 W. PETER/C. FREYMOND in BERTI, N. 37, p. 387.

99 BUCHER/TSCHANZ, N. 136, p. 74.

100 W. PETER/C. FREYMOND in BERTI, N. 38, p. 387.

101 According to BUCHER/TSCHANZ, N. 135, p. 73, the arbitrators should, however, annul any steps affected by the ground for successful challenge of the removed arbitrator. Other commentators suggest that the court at the seat of the arbitration should decide this issue based upon Article 185 of the PILA (LALIVE/POUDRET/REYMOND, N. 13, p. 334). It is submitted that the newly re-constituted tribunal is in a better position to do so.

Chapter 4 - The Arbitral Procedure

David P. Roney and Anna K. Müller

I. Article 182 of the PILA – a flexible framework for procedure

1. Introduction

Consistent with contemporary best practice in international arbitration,[1] the Swiss legal framework for arbitral procedure is flexible and founded upon the primacy of party autonomy. The fundamental principles of this legal framework are embodied in Article 182 of the PILA, which provides as follows:

	Article 182
VI. Procedure 1. Principle	[1] The parties may, directly or by reference to arbitration rules, determine the arbitral procedure; they may also submit it to a procedural law of their choice. [2] Where the parties have not determined the procedure, the arbitral tribunal shall determine it to the extent necessary, either directly or by reference to a law or to arbitration rules. [3] Whatever procedure is chosen, the arbitral tribunal shall ensure equal treatment of the parties and their right to be heard in an adversary procedure.

Article 182 of the PILA sets forth three guiding principles for the determination of the procedure to be followed before the arbitral tribunal: (i) the parties are generally free to determine the procedure by mutual agreement; (ii) if the parties have not done so, the arbitral tribunal has the power to determine the procedure to the extent necessary; and (iii) the arbitral tribunal has the over-arching duty to ensure that the procedure, however it is determined, complies with minimum standards of procedural fairness or due process.

1 POUDRET/BESSON, N. 525, pp. 484-485; FOUCHARD/GAILLARD/GOLDMAN, N. 120 *et seq.*, pp. 648 *et seq.*; REDFERN/HUNTER, N. 6-03 to 6-05, pp. 278-279.

G. Kaufmann-Kohler and B. Stucki (eds), International Arbitration in Switzerland, A Handbook for Practitioners, 49-68.

The PILA does not contemplate the application of the procedural law of any specific country or Canton, whether directly or by analogy, to international arbitration, unless the parties have expressly agreed upon the application of such a law.[2] For this reason, the law of civil procedure at the seat of the arbitration is usually irrelevant to the conduct of the proceedings before the arbitral tribunal.

It should be noted that the determination of the arbitral procedure under Article 182 of the PILA does not relate to or have any effect upon the determination of the law of the arbitration or '*lex arbitri*'. In Switzerland, the law of the arbitration is the entirety of Chapter 12 of the PILA – it is the overall statutory regime governing the arbitration and applies to questions such as the validity of the arbitration agreement, the availability of court assistance in support of the arbitration, and the grounds for setting aside an arbitral award.[3] By contrast, Article 182 of the PILA relates only to the conduct of the proceedings before the arbitral tribunal, including such matters as the exchange of written submissions, the production of documents, the examination of witnesses, time limits, etc. As a result, the parties' agreement on a specific arbitral procedure under Article 182 of the PILA has no bearing on the applicability of Chapter 12 of the PILA, which is determined solely on the basis of the criteria set forth in Article 176 of the PILA (i.e. the seat of the arbitral tribunal is in Switzerland and at least one party is domiciled abroad).[4]

2. *The parties' freedom to agree upon procedure*

a) General principles

If the seat of an arbitration is in Switzerland, the parties have almost complete freedom to determine the procedure to be followed before the arbitral tribunal, subject only to compliance with the minimum requirements of procedural fairness set forth in Article 182(3) of the PILA. This freedom is in keeping with one the great advantages of international arbitration – the ability of the parties to agree upon a procedure that best meets the unique needs of each specific dispute.

Under Article 182(1) of the PILA, there are no specific requirements as to form that must be fulfilled in order for the parties' agreement on procedure to be valid. Such an agreement can therefore be made implicitly or tacitly.[5] Nevertheless, given the potential for future uncertainty and conflict in regard to procedure, the parties are well advised to agree upon any procedural rules in writing.

---

2 LALIVE/POUDRET/REYMOND, N. 2, p. 350; M. SCHNEIDER in BERTI, N. 2, p. 397.

3 G. KAUFMANN-KOHLER, *Identifying and Applying the Law Governing the Arbitration Procedure – The Role of the Law of the Place of Arbitration*, Improving the Efficiency of Arbitration Agreements and Awards: 40 Years of Application of the New York Convention in (1999) 9 ICCA Congress Series 337; POUDRET/BESSON, N. 523–524, p. 484; CRAIG/PARK/PAULSSON, p. 499; REDFERN/HUNTER, N. 2-06, pp. 79-80.

4 POUDRET/BESSON, N. 523-524, p. 484; see Introduction *supra*, with respect to Article 176 of the PILA.

5 M. SCHNEIDER in BERTI, N. 5, p. 398.

With respect to the substance of the agreement, the parties must intend that the procedural rules will be binding both on themselves and the arbitral tribunal. However, if the parties merely accept procedural rules established by the arbitral tribunal, there is not an agreement on procedure within the meaning of Article 182(1) of the PILA. As a result, the arbitral tribunal would be free to modify any such rules without the consent of the parties, provided that any such modification is consistent with the principles of good faith discussed in Section I.3.a) *infra*.[6]

The Swiss Federal Tribunal has held that the parties' agreement on procedure should be construed in accordance with the general principles of contractual interpretation, in particular the principle of confidence derived from the concept of good faith.[7]

In the event of a dispute between the parties as to whether or not an agreement was concluded on procedure, the arbitral tribunal must determine the issue, usually in the form of a procedural decision.

b) Reference to arbitration rules

Beyond the parties' general freedom to agree upon the arbitral procedure, Article 182(1) of the PILA expressly provides that the parties may determine the arbitral procedure by reference to arbitration rules.

The parties may choose from among two general categories of arbitration rules. Firstly, the parties may agree upon *ad hoc* or independent arbitration rules, which are not connected with any arbitral institution. The most well-known and widely used *ad hoc* arbitration rules are, without doubt, the UNCITRAL Rules. Secondly, the parties may agree upon institutional arbitration rules, which are promulgated and administered by a permanently established arbitral institution such as the ICC Court or the Swiss chambers of commerce and industry. A complete discussion of the features of and differences between *ad hoc* and institutional arbitration is set forth in Chapter 1 *supra*.

Within the scope of Article 182(1) of the PILA, the parties may also agree to adopt only a part of established arbitration rules or to modify specific provisions of such rules.[8] This custom-made approach to arbitral procedure is entirely consistent with the philosophy of *ad hoc* arbitration. However, this approach does not generally function well within the

6 LALIVE/POUDRET/REYMOND, N. 2, p. 350. But see: POUDRET/BESSON, N. 527, p. 485, where it is argued that this position is too categorical and that the parties' acceptance should, unless otherwise demonstrated, be treated as a ratification of the procedural rules, which would consequently be binding on the arbitral tribunal. See also: G. KAUFMANN-KOHLER, *Qui contrôle l'arbitrage? Autonomie des parties, pouvoir des arbitres et principe d'efficacité*, Liber Amicorum Claude Reymond, Éditions du Juris-Classeur, Paris 2004, p. 155, where it is argued that it is often difficult to make fine distinctions in this area and, accordingly, prudence dictates that an agreement of the parties should be deemed to exist in cases of doubt.

7 [1994] ASA Bull. 226, 228; POUDRET/BESSON, N. 526, p. 485.

8 M. SCHNEIDER in BERTI, N. 18, p. 402.

framework of institutional arbitration. Depending upon the nature of the modifications agreed by the parties, the arbitral institution may, in fact, refuse to administer the arbitration, in which case the arbitration would continue on an *ad hoc* basis.[9] In other instances, the parties may agree at the outset to adopt institutional arbitration rules but without any administration by the arbitral institution, usually with a view to reducing costs. Although such an arrangement is possible, it is not usually recommended, given that the arbitral institution often plays an important role within the structure of institutional arbitration rules.

In addition to *ad hoc* and institutional arbitration rules, it should be noted that the parties may agree to apply a set of rules for a specific facet of the arbitral procedure, such as the IBA Rules.

c) Submission to a procedural law

As a final option under Article 182(1) of the PILA, the parties are free to submit the arbitral procedure to any national procedural law, whether such law relates to proceedings before courts or before arbitral tribunals either in Switzerland or abroad.

It is important to recognize once again that an agreement to apply such a national procedural law is only relevant to the procedure before the arbitral tribunal and has no impact whatsoever on the applicability of Chapter 12 of the PILA.[10] Moreover, the mandatory provisions of any national procedural law chosen under Article 182(1) of the PILA are not mandatory in nature for the purposes of the arbitral proceedings.[11]

In the vast majority of cases, it is not advisable for the parties to agree upon the application of a national procedural law. This type of agreement runs contrary to the current trend toward the globalization of arbitral procedure, which will be explored in greater detail in Sections III to V *infra*. Moreover, unless both parties are very familiar with the procedural law in question, this type of agreement can often give rise to unexpected procedural requirements that are overly rigid and entirely inappropriate for the resolution of disputes in an international context.[12]

3. *The arbitral tribunal's power to determine the procedure in the absence of agreement*

a) General principles

Where the parties have not agreed upon the arbitral procedure, Article 182(2) of the PILA provides that the arbitral tribunal shall determine the procedural rules for the arbitration to the extent necessary.

---

9 *Ibid.*

10 LALIVE/POUDRET/REYMOND, N. 1, p. 350; POUDRET/BESSON, N. 523-524, p. 484.

11 M. SCHNEIDER in BERTI, N. 30, p. 406.

12 POUDRET/BESSON, N. 529, pp. 486-487.

In making this determination, the arbitral tribunal has very broad discretion, which is subject only to the minimum requirements of procedural fairness set forth in Article 182(3) of the PILA. Most importantly, it should be emphasized that the arbitral tribunal is not bound by or required to consider any national procedural law, including the law of civil procedure at the seat of the arbitration, either subsidiarily or by analogy.[13]

The arbitral tribunal may establish a complete set of procedural rules at the outset of the arbitration or address individual procedural issues as necessary from time to time during the arbitral proceedings.[14]

Although there is no requirement as to the form of the procedural rules and decisions issued by the arbitral tribunal,[15] it is usual for the arbitral tribunal to issue written documents addressing such procedural matters, either in the form of a simple letter or, more commonly, in the form of a 'procedural order'.

Decisions by the arbitral tribunal regarding the organization of the procedure (e.g. the exchange of written submissions, the production of documents, the examination of witnesses, time limits, the language of the arbitration, etc.) do not constitute 'awards' within the meaning of Articles 188 *et seq.* of the PILA.[16] As a consequence, this type of procedural decision is not subject to being set aside by the Swiss Federal Tribunal.[17] The question of whether or not an arbitral tribunal's decision relates to purely procedural issues or extends to substantive issues, such that it constitutes an award, is not always straightforward and must be determined based upon the content rather than the form of the decision.[18]

It should, however, be noted that, if a procedural decision violates due process or is incompatible with public policy, the aggrieved party may rely upon such a violation or incompatibility as the basis for applying to set aside the final award (Article 190(2)(d) and (e) of the PILA), or as the basis for resisting the recognition and enforcement of the final award (Article V(1)(d) and Article V(2)(b) of the NY Convention).[19]

It is well established that a party must immediately object to any violation of due process when the procedural decision in question is rendered, failing which the party will be

---

13 This was a point of considerable controversy during the legislative debates relating to the enactment of Chapter 12 of the PILA: LALIVE/POUDRET/REYMOND, N. 4, pp. 351-352.

14 [1995] ASA Bull. 198, 203; LALIVE/POUDRET/REYMOND, N. 3, p. 351; POUDRET/BESSON, N. 535, p. 490; FOUCHARD/GAILLARD/GOLDMAN, N. 1197-1198, p. 647.

15 POUDRET/BESSON, N. 544, p. 497; M. SCHNEIDER in BERTI, N. 44, p. 410.

16 LALIVE/POUDRET/REYMOND, N. 10-11, p. 355 and N. 3, p. 405 (regarding Article 188 of the PILA).

17 [1994] ASA Bull. 226, 228; LALIVE/POUDRET/REYMOND, N. 10-11, p. 355 and N. 4, pp. 405-406; M. SCHNEIDER in BERTI, N. 42 and N. 47, pp. 409-410; POUDRET/BESSON, N. 728 *et seq.*, pp. 678-682.

18 LALIVE/POUDRET/REYMOND, N. 11, p. 355; M. SCHNEIDER in BERTI, N. 41, p. 409.

19 See Chapter 9 *infra*.

precluded from raising such defect in any subsequent application to set aside the final award or any enforcement proceedings.[20]

Since a procedural decision does not constitute an 'award', this type of decision does not have *res judicata* effect and may be revisited or modified by the arbitral tribunal, if justified in view of all of the relevant circumstances.[21]

The arbitral tribunal must nevertheless act at all times in accordance with the principles of good faith in deciding upon procedural matters. Accordingly, if the parties have prepared their respective cases in reliance upon a specific procedure, the arbitral tribunal cannot alter this procedure in the midst of the proceedings, unless the parties are given sufficient opportunity to respond to the new procedural arrangements.[22]

b) Practice

Many experienced international arbitrators in Switzerland have recognised that it is good practice for the arbitral tribunal to establish at the outset a case-specific set of procedural rules and a procedural timetable for the conduct of the proceedings.[23]

The arbitral tribunal will often convene a preliminary meeting with the parties upon its constitution for the purpose of settling the contents of these two documents, which thereafter provide the procedural framework for the proceedings.

This type of preliminary meeting has two principal benefits.[24] Firstly, the arbitral tribunal and the parties have the opportunity to openly discuss and come to a common understanding on the best procedures for the resolution of the specific issues in dispute. Secondly, a face-to-face meeting between the parties, their representatives and the arbitral tribunal is often an important confidence building exercise, which can be essential for the efficient conduct and positive tone of international proceedings involving actors from different cultures and legal traditions. Although the parties and their representatives sometimes prefer to dispense with the preliminary meeting, these two benefits often justify holding such a meeting, provided that the associated costs are not disproportionate with the amount in dispute. When the costs of holding such a meeting are disproportionately high, the arbitral tribunal may alternatively organize a telephone conference or videoconference to settle these procedural matters.

---

20 [2000] ASA Bull. 96, 102; DFT 119 II 386; B. CORBOZ, *Le recours au Tribunal Fédéral en matière d'arbitrage international* in [2002] II SJ 21. See Chapter 8 *infra*.

21 LALIVE/POUDRET/REYMOND, N. 10, p. 355; POUDRET/BESSON, N. 542, p. 496.

22 LALIVE/POUDRET/REYMOND, N. 12, p. 356; M. SCHNEIDER in BERTI, N. 48, p. 410; DFT 111 Ia 72, 75.

23 Such a procedural or provisional timetable is mandatory under Article 18(4) of the ICC Rules and Article 15(3) of the Swiss Rules.

24 REDFERN/HUNTER, N. 6-29, pp. 292-293; CRAIG/PARK/PAULSSON, N. 16.04, pp. 302-303; M. SCHNEIDER in BERTI, N. 39, p. 408.

In the case-specific set of procedural rules, the arbitral tribunal will typically address *inter alia* the following issues:[25]

- notifications and communications;
- form of the written submissions;
- documentary evidence, including the form, identification and indexing of documents, translations, authenticity, joint chronological sets of exhibits;
- requests for production of documents, including the form of and basis for determining such requests;
- physical evidence, including arrangements for the submission of such evidence or site visits to view such evidence;
- witnesses, including who may give evidence as a witness, the submission of witness statements, the preparation of witnesses to testify, the procedure for questioning witnesses;
- experts, including the submission of expert reports by party-appointed experts and the procedures in respect of experts appointed by the arbitral tribunal;
- the procedure for setting time limits and granting extensions thereof; and
- confidentiality.

When combined with a procedural timetable setting forth the timing of each procedural step up to the witness hearing, these procedural rules provide the parties with a clear understanding of the future course of the arbitration and thus tend to enhance the parties' overall confidence in the proceedings.

It is important to distinguish between: (i) procedural rules and timetables of the type described above; and (ii) Terms of Reference, which are required under Article 18 of the ICC Rules, and similar documents often entitled Constitution Orders, which are sometimes established at the outset of proceedings under other arbitration rules. Terms of Reference and Constitution Orders are ordinarily signed by the arbitrators and the parties and set forth their agreement on *inter alia* the following matters:

- the issues to be determined, if possible and appropriate;
- the jurisdiction of the arbitral tribunal;
- the seat of the arbitration;
- the applicable substantive law, if not in dispute;

---

25 REDFERN/HUNTER, N. 6-33 to 6-35, pp. 295-297. See also the UNCITRAL Notes.

- the fact that the arbitral procedure shall be governed by Chapter 12 of the PILA, the case-specific procedural rules issued separately by the arbitral tribunal and, if applicable, the relevant institutional or *ad hoc* arbitration rules;
- the language of the arbitration;
- the power of the arbitral tribunal to issue partial and interim awards;
- the appointment of a secretary to the arbitral tribunal; and
- in *ad hoc* arbitration, the arrangements in respect of the payment of the arbitral tribunal's fees and expenses.

When signed by the arbitral tribunal and the parties, Terms of Reference and Constitution Orders constitute agreements on procedure, which are binding on the arbitral tribunal and may not be subsequently modified without the consent of all parties. For this reason, experienced arbitrators usually avoid setting forth detailed procedural provisions in Terms of Reference and Constitution Orders and instead include such provisions in a separate set of procedural rules and a separate procedural timetable, as described above. This ensures that the arbitral tribunal retains the flexibility to modify the procedural rules and timetable as necessary, in order to address any unanticipated developments that may arise during the course of the proceedings.[26]

Notwithstanding the common practices described above, it should be noted that arbitral tribunals sitting in Switzerland adopt a multitude of different approaches to managing the arbitral procedure, depending *inter alia* upon the nature of the dispute, the identity and procedural cultures of the parties and their representatives, and the composition of the arbitral tribunal itself.

II. The right to be heard and the right to equal treatment

Whether the arbitral procedure is agreed by the parties or determined by the arbitral tribunal, it must in all cases comply with the two fundamental principles of procedural fairness set forth in Article 182(3) of the PILA: (i) the right of the parties to be heard in adversarial proceedings; and (ii) the right of the parties to equal treatment. Article 182(3) of the PILA is mandatory in nature and forms a central part of procedural public policy in Switzerland.[27] Moreover, the two principles embodied in this statutory provision reflect a growing international consensus on the minimum procedural standards applicable to arbitral tribunals.[28]

---

26 CRAIG/PARK/PAULSSON, N. 15.02, p. 283, N. 15.05, pp. 286-289 and N. 16.04, pp. 302-303; DERAINS/SCHWARTZ, p. 235.

27 LALIVE/POUDRET/REYMOND, N. 6, p. 352; M. SCHNEIDER in BERTI, N. 49-51, p. 411.

28 POUDRET/BESSON, N. 545 *et seq.*, pp. 498-511; M. SCHNEIDER in BERTI, N. 50, p. 411; FOUCHARD/GAILLARD/GOLDMAN, N. 1194, p. 645; G. KAUFMANN-KOHLER, *Identifying and Applying the Law Governing the Arbitration Procedure – The Role of the Law of the Place of Arbitration*, *op. cit.*, p. 356 and pp. 363-364; G. KAUFMANN-KOHLER, *Globalization of*

The arbitral tribunal has the ultimate responsibility to ensure that the arbitral procedure conforms with the requirements of Article 182(3) of the PILA and, as indicated above, the failure to do so may provide grounds for setting aside the final award (Article 190(2)(d) of the PILA) and for resisting the recognition and enforcement of the final award (Article V(1)(d) of the NY Convention).

1. Right to be heard

The right to be heard in adversarial proceedings under Article 182(3) of the PILA is a fundamental procedural right, which is also recognized in Article 9 of the Swiss Federal Constitution and Article 6(1) of the European Convention on Human Rights.

While the application of Article 6(1) of the European Convention on Human Rights to international arbitration is unsettled,[29] this makes little difference in practice because the Swiss Federal Tribunal has held that its jurisprudence under Article 9 of the Federal Constitution is relevant to the right to be heard in international arbitration.[30] Nevertheless, this jurisprudence should be applied with some care, in order to ensure that the right to be heard is interpreted in a manner consistent with the distinctly international character of arbitral proceedings subject to Chapter 12 of the PILA.[31]

In the context of international arbitration, the Swiss Federal Tribunal has consistently held that the right to be heard guarantees each party's right to submit relevant statements of fact, present legal arguments and request appropriate evidence-taking measures before an award is rendered to its detriment. It has been further held that the right to be heard affords each party the right to participate in the evidentiary proceedings, to rebut the factual allegations of the adverse party, to examine and challenge evidenced adduced by the adverse party and to bring rebuttal evidence of its own.[32] The right to be heard also includes the right of each party to be represented by legal counsel.[33]

It is, however, well established that the right to be heard in adversarial proceedings is not unlimited. There is no violation of this right if the arbitral tribunal refuses to admit evidence that is irrelevant to the determination of the issues in dispute, or refuses to admit evidence relating to facts already established by other evidence on record, or

---

Arbitral Procedure in (2003) 36/4 Vanderbilt Journal of Transnational Law 1313, 1320-1322.

29 G. KAUFMANN-KOHLER, *Identifying and Applying the Law Governing the Arbitration Procedure – The Role of the Law of the Place of Arbitration*, *op. cit.*, pp. 361-363; C. LIEBSCHER, *The Healthy Award*, The Hague 2003, p. 101 and pp. 107-109.

30 DFT 130 III 35, 38; [1999] ASA Bull. 537, 541; DFT 119 II 386, 388.

31 M. SCHNEIDER in BERTI, N. 52-53, pp. 411-412.

32 Decision of the Swiss Federal Tribunal of 31 October 2003 (4P.149/2003), section 3.1; decision of the Swiss Federal Tribunal of 14 July 2003 (4P.114/2003), section 2.2; DFT 130 III 35, 38; [2003] ASA Bull. 601, 624-625; [1999] ASA Bull. 537, 541-542; DFT 119 II 386, 388-390.

33 DFT 117 II 346.

refuses to consider submissions or evidence filed after the expiry of the applicable time limit.[34]

A more detailed analysis of the right to be heard is set forth in Chapter 8 *infra*, which addresses the challenge and revision of the award.

2. Right to equal treatment

As a general principle, the right to equal treatment requires the arbitral tribunal to apply similar procedural rules and requirements for all parties in respect of the exchange of written submissions, the filing of documentary evidence, the questioning of witnesses, etc.

Leading legal commentators agree that the right to equal treatment has both a positive component and a negative component – the arbitral tribunal may not refuse to one party what it has granted to the other and may not grant to one party what it has refused to the other.[35]

The right to equal treatment is not, however, absolute, but rather only requires the arbitral tribunal to treat similar situations in a similar manner. The arbitral tribunal may therefore adopt different measures in regard to one party, if justified by the different situation of such party.[36] In practice, the application of this principle may give rise to difficult questions. Is the granting of a time extension justified in one set of circumstances but not in another? Does the arbitral tribunal's ruling on the language of the proceedings result in an unjustified advantage for one of the parties?[37] Such questions cannot be answered in the abstract, but rather necessitate a case-by-case analysis.

The right to equal treatment does not preclude the arbitral tribunal from conducting default proceedings, provided that the defaulting party is duly notified of the commencement of the proceedings and is given an opportunity to present its case at each stage of the proceedings.[38] However, in default proceedings, the arbitral tribunal may not find in favour of a party without examining the merits of the factual and legal submissions of such party.[39]

---

34 Decision of the Swiss Federal Tribunal of 14 July 2003 (4P.114/2003), section 2.2; [1999] ASA Bull. 537, 541; [1997] ASA Bull. 291, 306; DFT 117 II 346, 348; LALIVE/POUDRET/REYMOND, N. 8, pp. 353-354.

35 LALIVE/POUDRET/REYMOND, N. 7, p. 353; M. SCHNEIDER in BERTI, N. 65, p. 416.

36 [1992] ASA Bull. 381, 396; LALIVE/POUDRET/REYMOND, N. 7, p. 353; M. SCHNEIDER in BERTI, N. 66, p. 416; POUDRET/BESSON, N. 554, p. 507.

37 F. VISCHER, in HEINI/KELLER/SIEHR/VISCHER/VOLKEN, N. 15, p. 1538.

38 POUDRET/BESSON, N. 586 *et seq.*, pp. 535 *et seq.*; F. VISCHER in HEINI/KELLER/SIEHR/VISCHER/VOLKEN, N. 18, p. 1539; FOUCHARD/GAILLARD/GOLDMAN, N. 1224, pp. 662-664.

39 LALIVE/POUDRET/REYMOND, N. 9, pp. 354-355.

III. Evidence

1. Introduction – Article 184 of the PILA

With respect to the procedures for evidence taking in international arbitration, Article 184 of the PILA provides the starting point for analysis:

3. Taking of evidence

Article 184

[1] The arbitral tribunal shall itself take the evidence.

[2] Where the assistance of state authorities is needed for taking evidence, the arbitral tribunal, or a party with the consent of the arbitral tribunal may request the assistance of the court at the seat of the arbitral tribunal; such court shall apply its own law.

Based upon Article 184(1) of the PILA, it is clear that the arbitral tribunal has control over the evidentiary proceedings, within the overall scope of the arbitral procedure agreed by the parties. Accordingly, while the parties may agree upon a variety of different methods for gathering and presenting evidence, it is ultimately for the arbitral tribunal to decide upon the admissibility and relevance of any evidence ultimately offered by the parties.[40]

As a practical matter, the arbitral tribunal's control over the evidentiary proceedings is limited by the fact that, unlike courts, it lacks the coercive powers of *imperium*. In order to address this limitation, Article 184(1) of the PILA entitles the arbitral tribunal to make an application, or authorize a party to make an application, to the Swiss court at the seat of the arbitration for judicial assistance in taking evidence. The Swiss court will apply its own law in disposing of this type of application, although leading legal commentators suggest that the court may also adopt evidentiary procedures foreign to its own law, if justified in the circumstances.[41]

In international arbitration, it is, however, rare that recalcitrant parties or witnesses are domiciled within the territorial jurisdiction of the Swiss court at the seat of the arbitration. As a consequence, arbitral tribunals can make or authorize applications to the Swiss courts under Article 184(2) of the PILA as a first step in obtaining international judicial assistance abroad pursuant to the Hague Convention on the Taking of Evidence Abroad in Civil or Commercial Matters of 18 March 1970. In practice, this type of application is rare because the procedure is slow and cumbersome and witness testimony taken by way of letters rogatory (international judicial assistance) is seldom helpful.

---

40 LALIVE/POUDRET/REYMOND, N. 3, p. 371; M. SCHNEIDER in BERTI, N. 50, p. 449.

41 LALIVE/POUDRET/REYMOND, N. 7, p. 374; M. SCHNEIDER in BERTI, N. 61-62, p. 452. While some Swiss courts insist upon taking the evidence in question themselves in accordance with their usual practice, the Geneva Court of First Instance has ordered a witness to appear before an arbitral tribunal: [1990] ASA Bull. 283.

Arbitral tribunals thus often prefer simply to draw an adverse inference from the failure of a party to secure the attendance of witnesses who are within the control of such party.

Before turning to the different forms of evidence in international arbitration, it should be noted that the overview of evidentiary proceedings in the following sections generally reflects the growing trend towards the globalization of arbitration procedure.[42] The IBA Rules, referred to above, represent one of the best-known manifestations of this trend.

Many Swiss arbitration practitioners have been at the forefront of the globalization of arbitration procedure and, as a consequence, it is no longer accurate to refer to the traditional dichotomy between common law and civil law approaches to evidence taking when considering international arbitration in Switzerland.[43] Notwithstanding this trend towards globalization, arbitral tribunals sitting in Switzerland do not, however, follow any standard form of evidentiary proceedings, but rather adopt a broad range of different approaches, depending *inter alia* upon the nature of the dispute, the identity and procedural cultures of the parties and their representatives, and the composition of the arbitral tribunal itself.

2. Documentary evidence and production of documents

As a general matter, documentary evidence is the most important form of evidence in international arbitration. Although witnesses are usually heard, many arbitral tribunals tend to give greater weight to contemporaneous documents.

The exact procedures as to when and how the parties must produce their documentary evidence are determined either by agreement between the parties or, more commonly, by the procedural rules and timetable established by the arbitral tribunal, in consultation with the parties, at the outset of the proceedings.

Arbitral tribunals sitting in Switzerland ordinarily require the parties to submit all documentary evidence with the written submissions that expressly refer to such evidence. In exceptional cases, the arbitral tribunal may permit a party to submit further documents at a later stage, if appropriate in view of all of the circumstances. The parties are typically required to identify each document with a distinct number, submit each document under a corresponding numbered tab and provide a list of all documents

---

42 G. KAUFMANN-KOHLER, *Globalization of Arbitral Procedure*, *op. cit.*, p. 1333; S.H. ELSING/J.M. TOWNSEND, *Bridging the Common Law-Civil Law Divide in Arbitration* in (2002) 18 Arb. Int'l 59; A. BAUM, *Reconciling Anglo-Saxon and Civil Law Procedure: The Path to a Procedural Lex Arbitrationis*, Law of International Business and Dispute Settlement in the 21st Century, Carl Heymanns Verlag KG, Cologne 2001, pp. 21-30; M. KERR, *Concord and Conflict in International Arbitration* in (1997) 13 Arb. Int'l 121; P. FRIEDLAND, *Combining Civil Law and Common Law Elements in the Presentation of Evidence in International Commercial Arbitration* in (1997) 12 Int'l Arb. Rep. 25; REDFERN/HUNTER, N. 6-61 *et seq.*, pp. 311 *et seq.*

43 *Ibid.*

submitted. There is usually a presumption that all documents submitted are authentic and complete, unless disputed by one of the parties.

With respect to the production of documents from an adverse party, most arbitral tribunals adopt a procedure that is similar or identical to the one set forth in Article 3 of the IBA Rules, although there is no right to documentary production absent an express agreement between the parties.[44]

If a party seeks the production of documents from an adverse party, the arbitral tribunal will typically require the requesting party to submit a 'request for production of documents', which *inter alia*: (i) identifies the requested documents with reasonable specificity; and (ii) establishes how the requested documents relate to facts relevant and material to the outcome of the dispute. Within a given period after receipt of the request for production, the adverse party must then either produce all of the requested documents within its possession, custody or control or object to such production, based upon grounds such as lack of relevance, unreasonable burdensomeness, legal impediment or privilege, technical or commercial confidentiality, protection of sensitive governmental information, etc.[45]

The arbitral tribunal will thereafter issue a procedural order either directing the adverse party to produce the requested documents or denying the request for production as unfounded. If the adverse party refuses to comply with such a procedural order, the arbitral tribunal may either seek the assistance of a court to enforce the procedural order under Article 184(2) of the PILA, which is uncommon, or simply draw an adverse inference against the party.

Documents produced through this procedure will either immediately form part of the evidentiary record or simply be delivered to the requesting party, which will then decide whether to file some or all of these documents as exhibits in the arbitration.

3. *Evidence of fact witnesses*

Although documentary evidence carries substantial weight, the evidence of fact witnesses nevertheless plays an important and sometimes decisive role before arbitral tribunals sitting in Switzerland.

---

44 G. KAUFMANN-KOHLER/P. BÄRTSCH, *Discovery in International Arbitration: How Much is Too Much?*, SchiedsVZ (January 2004) 13; G. KAUFMANN-KOHLER, *Globalization of Arbitral Procedure, op. cit.*, pp. 1325-1328; H. RAESCHKE-KESSLER, *The Production of Documents in International Arbitration – A Commentary on Article 3 of the New IBA Rules of Evidence* in (2002) 18 Arb. Int'l 411; T.H. WEBSTER, *Obtaining Documents from Adverse Parties in International Arbitration* in (2001) 17 Arb. Int'l 41; P.R. GRIFFIN, *Recent Trends in the Conduct of International Arbitration – Discovery Procedures and Witness Hearings* in (2002) 17 J. Int'l Arb. 19.

45 See Article 9(2) of the IBA Rules; R.M. MOSK/T. GINSBERG, *Evidentiary Privileges in International Arbitration*, 50 Int'l & Comp. L.Q. 345 (2001).

It is generally accepted that any person may give evidence as a fact witness, including an officer, employee or representative of a party.[46]

In an effort to reduce the time and costs associated with hearings, it is common practice for arbitral tribunals to require the parties to submit a written witness statement for each of their fact witnesses.[47] These witness statements may take the form of a sworn affidavit made under oath, but more commonly are simply signed declarations. The witness statement is usually intended to take the place of examination-in-chief or direct examination of the witness. Based upon the witness statement, the adverse party and the arbitral tribunal may decide whether or not it is necessary to question a witness and, if so, to prepare for such questioning in advance of the hearing. At the hearing, it is therefore possible, in many cases, to dispense with examination-in-chief entirely and begin with cross-examination of the witness.

Depositions of fact witnesses (i.e. oral examination of witnesses for purposes of discovery prior to the hearing before the arbitral tribunal) and interrogatories (i.e. written questions and answers for purposes of discovery prior to the hearing before the arbitral tribunal) are very rare in international arbitration generally and in Switzerland.[48] Arguably, the usefulness of such procedures is somewhat diminished in international arbitration due to the use of witness statements, which provide advance notice of each witness's evidence.

Although some lawyers are prohibited under rules of professional conduct from meeting with and preparing witnesses to testify in court proceedings, it is clear that few, if any, arbitral tribunals would consider proper witness preparation to be objectionable.[49] Witness preparation is, however, subject to strict ethical limits – nothing in the course of such preparation should compromise the ability of the witness to testify truthfully. Given the overarching need to ensure a level playing field for parties and counsel from different legal traditions, it is good practice for the arbitral tribunal to address the scope for witness preparation in clear terms at the preliminary meeting whenever counsel are likely to have divergent understandings of this matter.[50]

---

46 Article 25(2) of the Swiss Rules; Article 4(2) of the IBA Rules.

47 Article 4 (4) *et seq.* of the IBA Rules; REDFERN/HUNTER, N. 6-78, pp. 321-322; CRAIG/PARK/PAULSSON, pp. 432-434; M. SCHNEIDER in BERTI, N. 24, p. 441; S.H. ELSING/J.M. TOWNSEND, *op. cit.*, p. 63.

48 G. KAUFMANN-KOHLER, *Globalization of Arbitral Procedure*, *op. cit.*, p. 1328; M. SCHNEIDER in BERTI, N. 24, p. 441; S.H. ELSING/J.M. TOWNSEND, *op. cit.*, p. 61.

49 Article 4(3) of the IBA Rules; Article 25(6) of the Swiss Rules; Article 20.6 of the LCIA Rules; D.P. RONEY, *Effective Witness Preparation for International Commercial Arbitration: A Practical Guide for Counsel* in (2003) 20 J. Int'l Arb. 429, 430; G. VON SEGESSER, *Witness Preparation in International Commercial Arbitration* in [2002] ASA Bull. 222, 224; M. SCHNEIDER in BERTI, N. 25, p. 441; CRAIG/PARK/PAULSSON, pp. 441-442.

50 D.P. RONEY, *op. cit.*, p. 430, footnote 5; G. VON SEGESSER, *op. cit.*, p. 223; FOUCHARD/GAILLARD/GOLDMAN, N. 1285, pp. 701-702.

The procedure for the questioning of witnesses at the hearing may vary considerably from one arbitration to the next in Switzerland. Nevertheless, subject to any specific agreement between the parties, arbitral tribunals most commonly direct that: (i) the witness statements stand in place of examination-in-chief (or direct examination) by the party the presenting the witness, although there may be some limited scope for the party or its counsel to put introductory questions to the witness; (ii) after any such introductory questions, the opposing party or its counsel conducts its cross-examination of the witness; (iii) each party or counsel may thereafter be permitted to 're-examine' ('re-direct') or 're-cross' the witness; and (iv) the arbitral tribunal may then put any remaining questions to the witness.[51]

Despite this customary procedure, the arbitral tribunal invariably retains the discretion to put questions to the witness at any stage in the examination and occasionally may even begin by questioning the witness before the parties, particularly where the parties and their counsel are from legal traditions where judges ordinarily put the questions to witnesses. Moreover, in arbitrations involving numerous fact and expert witnesses, arbitral tribunals are occasionally inclined to adopt a procedure known as 'witness conferencing', which consists in the simultaneous joint hearing of all fact and expert witnesses.[52]

Throughout the hearing, the arbitral tribunal generally has control over conduct of the witness examinations and thus may limit or exclude any question to a witness, if it appears that the question is irrelevant, burdensome, duplicative or pertains to matters that are protected by some legal or other privilege.[53]

4. *Evidence of expert witnesses*

In international arbitration, expert evidence is essential for the determination of many different factual issues, ranging from the existence of defects in equipment to the proper valuation of shares in a privately held corporation. The arbitral tribunal may also admit expert evidence on the substantive law applicable to the merits, although there is no requirement for the parties to 'prove' the substantive law before arbitral tribunals sitting in Switzerland.[54]

---

51 G. KAUFMANN-KOHLER, *Globalization of Arbitral Procedure*, *op. cit.*, p. 1329; S.H. ELSING/J.M. TOWNSEND, *op. cit.*, p. 63; P.R. GRIFFIN, *op. cit.*, pp. 28-29; Article 8(2) of the IBA Rules.

52 W. PETER, *Witness 'Conferencing'* in (2002) 18 Arb. Int'l 47; Article 8(2) of the IBA Rules refers to the possibility of arranging the hearing '*in such a manner that witnesses presented by different Parties be questioned at the same time and in confrontation with each other*'.

53 Article 8(1) of the IBA Rules.

54 Under Swiss law, the principle of *iura novit curia* is applicable to international arbitral tribunals, although the proper application of this principle is controversial: DFT 130 III 35, 38-40; DFT 120 II 172; POUDRET/BESSON, N. 55, p. 504 and N. 558, p. 510; G. KAUFMANN-KOHLER, *Globalization of Arbitral Procedure*, *op. cit.*, p. 1333. The following pragmatic formula has been proposed for the application of the principle of *iura novit curia*: (a) the

There are two general approaches to expert evidence, each of which has its advantages and disadvantages.[55] The first and increasingly common approach is for each of the parties to appoint their own expert witnesses, who provide written expert reports setting forth their opinions on specific issues and then are subject to examination at the hearing. The second approach is for the arbitral tribunal to appoint its own expert and define the specific issues to be addressed by such expert. The tribunal-appointed expert then carries out the requisite investigation and reports back to the arbitral tribunal.

While the first approach is most often adopted, the arbitral tribunal ordinarily retains the discretion to appoint its own expert, in order to resolve any issues which remain unclear after assessment of the parties' expert evidence.[56]

It is generally accepted that the arbitral tribunal has the power to appoint a tribunal expert without the express agreement of the parties, provided that the arbitral tribunal does not delegate its responsibility for decision-making to such expert.[57] The arbitral tribunal should consult the parties both in regard to the selection of the tribunal-appointed expert and the definition of the issues to be addressed by the tribunal-appointed expert.[58] In addition, experienced arbitrators often stipulate in the terms of reference for tribunal-appointed experts that the parties should be given advance notice of any site inspections or other investigations carried out by such expert so that they made attend if they so wish, notwithstanding the fact that a failure to do so would not constitute a violation of the right to be heard.[59] Most importantly, the arbitral tribunal

parties allege and establish the applicable substantive law; (b) the arbitral tribunal has the ability, but not the obligation, to make its own enquiries; (c) if such enquiries are made, the arbitral tribunal should provide the parties with an opportunity to comment (whether or not the failure to do so would give rise to recourse); and (d) if the law normally applicable is not established on a specific point, the arbitral tribunal may apply (only in regard to this point) a law close to the law normally applicable or a transnational rule: G. KAUFMANN-KOHLER, *'Iura novit arbiter' – est-ce bien raisonnable? Réflexions sur le statut du droit du fond devant l'arbitre international*', De lege ferenda – Réflexions sur le droit désirable en l'honneur du Professeur Alain Hirsch, Éditions Slatkine, Geneva 2004, p. 78.

55 POUDRET/BESSON, N. 662 *et seq.*, pp. 592 *et seq.*; M. SCHNEIDER in BERTI, N. 29-33, pp. 442-443; G. KAUFMANN-KOHLER, *Globalization of Arbitral Procedure*, *op. cit.*, p. 1330; REDFERN/HUNTER, N. 6-81 *et seq.*, pp. 323 *et seq.*

56 G. KAUFMANN-KOHLER, *Globalization of Arbitral Procedure*, *op. cit.*, p. 1330; M. SCHNEIDER in BERTI, N. 31, p. 443; Article 20(3) and (4) of the ICC Rules; Article 27 of the Swiss Rules.

57 POUDRET/BESSON, N. 663, p. 593; M. SCHNEIDER in BERTI, N. 34, p. 443; REDFERN/HUNTER, N. 6-83, p. 324; FOUCHARD/GAILLARD/GOLDMAN, N. 1224, pp. 662-664.

58 REDFERN/HUNTER, N. 6-84, p. 325; M. SCHNEIDER in BERTI, N. 36-38, pp. 444-445.

59 J.-F. POUDRET, *Expertise et droit d'être entendu dans l'arbitrage international*, Études de droit international en l'honneur de Pierre Lalive, Helbing & Lichtenhahn, Basel 1993, p. 607.

must provide the parties with the report of the tribunal-appointed expert and afford the parties an opportunity to comment on this report before rendering any award.[60]

5. Site inspections

In certain arbitrations, it may be necessary for the arbitral tribunal to inspect the subject matter of the dispute on-site, particularly in cases involving construction projects.

Unless the parties have agreed to the contrary, it is generally accepted that the arbitral tribunal is authorised to undertake such site inspections, even where there is no provision for this procedure in the applicable procedural rules. Ordinarily, the arbitral tribunal will only conduct a site inspection if both parties are present and have the opportunity to make comments. If the parties agree, the arbitral tribunal may, however, conduct a site inspection alone. In either case, it essential for the arbitral tribunal to establish clear ground rules in advance of any such site inspection.[61]

IV. Written submissions

1. Importance of written submissions

Due to the complex nature of the factual and legal issues in many international arbitrations, the parties' written submissions usually play a very important, if not determinative, role in the decision-making processes of the arbitral tribunal. The number, order, contents and timing of the written submissions are determined by the procedural rules agreed upon by the parties or established by the arbitral tribunal.

2. Number, order, contents and amendments

It is difficult to make any generalization about the number and order of written submissions, as this aspect of the arbitral procedure is invariably tailored to the specific issues in dispute.

Nevertheless, the parties will, in most cases, exchange two sets of written submissions before the hearing.[62] The claimant begins by filing a request for arbitration, which may be quite brief or more extensive. The respondent then files an answer to the request for arbitration, as well as a counterclaim, if any. Next, the claimant files a statement of claim, which sets forth a complete statement of its case on the main claims, together with a defence to the counterclaim, if any. Finally, the respondent files a statement of defence, which sets forth a complete statement of its case on the main claims, together with a reply to the defence to the counterclaim. Alternatively, the parties may agree to exchange their written submissions simultaneously rather than successively. Following the hearing, the parties are often given the opportunity to file post-hearing submissions, which address the evidence of the witnesses and set forth each party's closing argument.

---

60 DFT 104 Ia 69, 71.

61 REDFERN/HUNTER, N. 6-91 *et seq.*, pp. 327 *et seq.*; M. SCHNEIDER in BERTI, N. 47-48, p. 447.

62 CRAIG/PARK/PAULSSON, p. 427 and p. 431; REDFERN/HUNTER, N. 6-51 *et seq.*, pp. 305 *et seq.*; FOUCHARD/GAILLARD/GOLDMAN, N. 1261 *et seq.*, pp. 691 *et seq.*

The procedural rules normally specify that each written submission must set forth the parties' factual and legal submissions on the relevant issues in dispute and must be accompanied by all documentary evidence and legal authorities relied upon in the written submission.

Most importantly, the written submissions must include the parties' requests for relief from the arbitral tribunal. It is the parties' requests for relief that determine the scope of the issues submitted to the jurisdiction of the arbitral tribunal.[63]

The parties are usually entitled to amend or modify their requests for relief more freely in international arbitration, as compared with legal proceedings before courts. Nevertheless, the procedural rules applicable to the arbitration may place certain limitations on amendments or modifications to the requests for relief and, in any event, all amendments or modifications must fall within the scope of the arbitration agreement.[64]

V. Hearings

While not always the case, the vast majority of international arbitrations conclude with a hearing, which brings together the arbitral tribunal, the parties, their representatives and the fact witnesses and expert witnesses, if any.[65] The right to be heard does not, however, include the right to an oral hearing, even where the parties have expressly agreed that such a hearing shall be held.[66] Nevertheless, most experienced arbitrators will convene a hearing where the parties have agreed to hold one, given that the failure to respect the parties' agreement on this matter may provide grounds for resisting the recognition and enforcement of the final award (Article V(1)(d) of the NY Convention).

1. Organization of the hearing

The arbitral tribunal ordinarily determines the date of the hearing in consultation with the parties, preferably at an early stage in the proceedings in order to ensure the availability of all persons involved.

The location of the hearing is also ordinarily determined by the arbitral tribunal, in consultation with the parties. Under Swiss law, it well established that the hearing may be held at a location other than the seat of the arbitration, including a location outside of Switzerland.[67]

---

63 See Section I.3(c) of Chapter 8 *infra* and Article 190(2)(c) of the PILA.

64 M. SCHNEIDER in BERTI, N. 82-83, pp. 420-421.

65 REDFERN/HUNTER, N. 6-95, p. 329; M. SCHNEIDER in BERTI, N. 89, p. 424.

66 DFT 117 II 346, 348.

67 POUDRET/BESSON, N. 134, p. 104; F. R. EHRAT in BERTI, N. 18, p. 309; LALIVE/POUDRET/REYMOND, N. 8, p. 297; G. KAUFMANN-KOHLER, *Le lieu de l'arbitrage à l'aune de la mondialisation – Réflexions à propos de deux formes récentes d'arbitrage* in (1998) 3 Rev. Arb. 1998 517, 522-524.

Either the arbitral tribunal or the parties may assume responsibility for making the necessary administrative arrangements for the hearing, e.g. reserving a suitable hearing room, arranging for transcripts and, if necessary, interpreters, etc.

Often, the arbitral tribunal will convene a pre-hearing meeting or telephone conference with the parties and their representatives after all written submissions and evidence have been filed, for the purpose of settling the issues to be addressed at the hearing, the procedure, the schedule, time allocation and any outstanding administrative aspects of the hearing.

In international arbitration, it is generally accepted that hearings are not public and, accordingly, the parties and the arbitral tribunal must mutually agree upon the presence of any non-participants, i.e. anyone other than the arbitral tribunal, its secretary, the parties, counsel and witnesses and experts, if any.[68]

2. Procedure at the hearing

While a wide variety of different formats may be adopted for the procedure at the hearing, there are certain prevailing trends in international arbitration.

Since the parties have most often filed extensive written submissions in advance of the hearing, it usual for the parties to make relatively brief opening statements or, alternatively, to forego opening statements entirely. After any opening statements, the examination of the fact and expert witnesses then proceeds, in accordance with various different procedures as described in Section III.3 *supra*. With respect to closing argument, there are three possible options: (i) each party immediately makes an oral closing argument at the conclusion of the hearing, once all of the fact and expert witnesses have been heard; (ii) each party makes such an oral closing argument at the conclusion of the hearing and then files a post-hearing written submission several days or weeks after the hearing; or (iii) each party foregoes oral closing argument and simply files a post-hearing written submission.

Arbitral tribunals adopt various different methods of time allocation and time management for hearings, invariably in consultation with the parties. One of the best-known methods is the eponymous '*Böckstiegel Method*', which involves allocating a fixed amount of hearing time to each party and then providing the parties with broad freedom to use their allocated time as they wish, as between opening statements, examination-in-chief, cross-examination and closing argument. The time allocated to each party is strictly enforced and the arbitral tribunal must be active in order to suppress any form of disruption by counsel, witnesses, or indeed the arbitrators.[69]

---

68 See Section II of Chapter 6 *infra*.

69 J. PAULSSON, *The Timely Arbitrator: Reflections on the Böckstiegel Method*, Law of International Business and Dispute Settlement in the 21st Century, Carl Heymanns Verlag KG, Cologne 2001, pp. 607-614.

In most international arbitrations, it is customary for a verbatim transcript to be taken of the hearing by a court stenographer. Parties also occasionally request the preparation of real-time transcripts through software such as LiveNote™, in cases where the associated cost is justified. As an alternative to verbatim transcripts where smaller amounts are in dispute, it is sometimes agreed that an audio recording will be made of the hearing, with copies of the audiotapes then being provided directly to the parties for use as they see fit.

It is now relatively common in international arbitration for parties to employ a variety of different aids in presenting their cases at the hearing, including charts, demonstrative exhibits, summaries of key documents on record, etc. Most arbitral tribunals are prepared to grant the parties considerable leeway in employing such aids, provided that the aids accurately reflect the evidence on record.

3. Post-hearing matters

After the hearing, the arbitral tribunal will usually issue a procedural order specifying the final steps to be taken in the arbitration, e.g., the filing of any additional evidence or legal authorities, post-hearing written submissions, statements of costs, etc.

Thereafter, the arbitral tribunal will often formally declare that the proceedings are closed and, in fact, is required to do so under Article 22(1) of the ICC Rules. After the closing of the proceedings or '*clôture des débats*', the parties are not entitled to file any further factual or legal submissions or to file additional evidence, unless the evidence in question only became available for the first time after the closing of the proceedings. In such circumstances, the arbitral tribunal has the discretion to re-open the proceedings upon request of the party, up until the final award is rendered.[70]

---

[70] Craig/Park/Paulsson, pp. 446-447; Redfern/Hunter, N. 6-114, p. 339.

Chapter 5 – Interim Measures

Georg von Segesser and Christoph Kurth*

I. Introduction

When international business relationships derail, time is often of the essence. Although the resolution of disputes through arbitration is often speedier than court proceedings, it nevertheless takes some time for an arbitral tribunal to render a final award. As a consequence, it may be necessary to obtain interim measures in order to stabilize matters on a provisional basis or to regulate the terms of an ongoing relationship for the duration of the arbitral proceedings or to avoid frustration of the final award. Obtaining such interim relief swiftly and effectively is frequently of crucial importance to a party whose interests may be irreparably harmed by the conduct of the adverse party.

This chapter addresses the issues that are of primary importance and interest in such situations: do arbitral tribunals have the authority to grant interim measures? May a party to an arbitration agreement also turn to courts for immediate relief? May a party apply to the arbitral tribunal for a new decision after a court has decided upon interim relief? What are the forms of relief that an arbitral tribunal may grant and what are the prerequisites that must be fulfilled? In particular, may an arbitral tribunal order the freezing of assets in order to secure money claims? In case of non-compliance, how is an arbitral tribunal's order granting interim relief enforced? Will Swiss courts enforce interim measures ordered by arbitral tribunals sitting outside Switzerland? What is the effect of interim measures ordered by foreign courts? What if such foreign interim measures themselves confirm or ratify measures ordered by arbitral tribunals sitting abroad?

When considering these issues, it is important to bear in mind two features typical of interim measures issued by arbitral tribunals in Switzerland. Firstly, international arbitrations conducted in Switzerland often do not have any connection with Switzerland other than the location of the seat of the arbitral tribunal. Consequently, foreign courts

* The authors wish to acknowledge the input and assistance of Blaise Stucki and Benno Strub.

G. Kaufmann-Kohler and B. Stucki (eds), International Arbitration in Switzerland, A Handbook for Practitioners, 69-87.

will often have the power to issue interim measures based upon foreign laws[1] and the enforcement of interim measures ordered by Swiss arbitral tribunals will often be governed by the law at the foreign place of enforcement. Secondly, as modern arbitration procedure has increasingly come to resemble litigation before courts, requests for interim measures have become increasingly frequent in international commercial arbitration both in Switzerland and in other leading venues for international arbitration. While emphasis is often placed on the potential difficulties associated with seeking to enforce interim measures issued by arbitral tribunals, it is important to recognise that many parties tend to comply voluntarily with such measures.

II. The authority of arbitral tribunals to order interim measures

Swiss law affirms the authority of arbitral tribunals to order interim measures. Article 183(1) of the PILA establishes a presumption that the parties have conferred upon the arbitral tribunal unrestricted authority to order such measures: '*Unless the parties have agreed otherwise, the arbitral tribunal may, at the request of a party, grant interim relief and conservatory measures*'.

Except where the parties have agreed to exclude, limit or otherwise qualify this statutory authority, the arbitral tribunal's power to order interim measures is unrestricted. Such an agreement can be entered into before or after the commencement of arbitral proceedings and is not subject to any specific requirements as to form. An agreement to exclude the authority of the arbitrators to order interim measures must, however, be explicit. Thus, reference to a set of procedural rules that does not provide for such authority is not considered sufficient to demonstrate the parties' intent to deprive the arbitral tribunal of the authority presumed under Article 183(1) of the PILA.[2]

III. Interim measures available to arbitral tribunals

1. Applicable law

The question of whether or not an arbitral tribunal has the authority to grant interim relief must be determined under the *lex arbitri*. However, what types of interim measures may be ordered in a specific case is a different question, which is governed either by the relevant procedural rules or by the *lex causae*, depending on whether interim measures are considered to be a matter of procedural law or substantive in nature.[3]

1 In particular, Article 31 of the Brussels Regulation for the European Judicial Space.
2 Rüede/Hadenfeldt, p. 252.
3 POUDRET/BESSON, N. 624, p. 566.

2. *Requirements*

In order to obtain interim relief, the requesting party must generally satisfy the following five requirements:

- *prima facie* jurisdiction of the arbitral tribunal;[4]
- *prima facie* evidence that there is a risk of irreparable harm or injury to the requesting party, i.e. a prejudice that cannot be adequately remedied by a subsequent award of damages;
- reasonable chance of success on the merits;
- urgency of the measure, i.e. with reasonable probability, harm to the requesting party's rights and interests is imminent;[5]
- if ordered by the arbitral tribunal, provision of appropriate security.

Arbitral tribunals generally tend to apply the 'urgency' requirement in a less strict way than courts. In practice, arbitral tribunals may thus grant interim measures notwithstanding the fact that 'urgency' has not been established properly or even alleged. By way of illustration, it is noteworthy that Article 14(2) of the CAS Arbitration Rules for the Olympic Games does not list 'urgency' among the conditions for interim measures: '*When deciding whether to award any preliminary relief the President of the ad hoc Division or the Panel shall consider whether the relief is necessary to protect the applicant from irreparable harm, the likelihood of the success of the claim on the merits, and whether the interests of the applicant outweigh those of the opponent or of other members of the Olympic Community*'.

3. *Types of interim measures*

a) Preliminary comment

Swiss arbitration law does not specify the types of interim measures that may be granted by arbitral tribunals. As a general rule, arbitral tribunals may order whatever measures they deem necessary to: (a) protect the rights of the requesting party from harm that

---

4 A defence of lack of jurisdiction raised by one party does not prevent the arbitral tribunal from ordering interim measures once the file has been transmitted to it, provided that the arbitral tribunal is satisfied that it has *prima facie* jurisdiction. See K.-P. BERGER, *International Economic Arbitration*, The Hague, 1993, pp. 335-336.

5 See e.g. M. WIRTH, Interim or Preventive Measures in Support of International Arbitration in Switzerland, in [2000] ASA Bull. 37; M. BLESSING in BERTI, N. 857, p. 262; A. YESILIRMAK, Interim and Conservatory Measures in ICC Arbitral Practice, in (2000) ICC ICArb. Bull. 31, 34; B. PETER, in A. BÖSCH (ed.), Provisional Remedies in International Commercial Arbitration, de Gruyter, Berlin 1994, pp. 691 et seq.

cannot later be remedied by the final award; or (b) regulate the relationship between the parties during the arbitral proceedings.[6]

Within this permissive framework, arbitral tribunals may consider a number of different sources of law in evaluating the appropriate interim measure to be ordered. They look to the contract that has given rise to the dispute.[7] If the contract provides a mechanism for interim protection, the arbitral tribunal will certainly apply such a contractual mechanism. However, the parties rarely address this type of matter in their agreements. Instead, the parties usually agree upon a particular set of arbitration rules to govern the arbitral proceedings. While these arbitration rules usually do not contain detailed provisions on interim measures,[8] it is sometimes possible to find guidance in previous procedural decisions rendered under such rules.[9]

Arbitral tribunals also regularly turn to the law applicable to the substance of the dispute (the *lex causae*), which may provide for specific measures.[10] Reference to the applicable substantive law may also ensure that any interim measures will be harmonized with the final award on the merits.[11]

b) Measures aimed at ensuring the effectiveness of the arbitral award

Protective measures,[12] which typically require a party to perform or refrain from performing certain specific acts, are designed to ensure the effective enforcement of the final award, i.e. to prevent the final award from becoming irrelevant by the time it is issued. The following are examples of protective measures:

---

6 M. BLESSING, *Introduction to Arbitration – Swiss and International Perspectives*, Helbing & Lichtenhahn, Basel 1999, p. 279; M. WIRTH, *op. cit.*, p. 32.

7 M. WIRTH, *op. cit.*, p. 32.

8 See Article 23 of the ICC Rules and Article 26 of the Swiss Rules. The only two exceptions are: (a) Article 26 of the UNCITRAL Rules, which specifies that 'interim measures' include 'measures for the conservation of the goods' in dispute; and (b) Article 25 of the LCIA Rules, which contains a short list of possible measures, such as the provision of security for the amount in dispute and for legal or other costs. See also M. BLESSING in BERTI, N. 844 *et seq.*, pp. 258-259.

9 F. VISCHER in HEINI/KELLER/SIEHR/VISCHER/VOLKEN, N. 5, p. 1542. With respect to proceedings under the ICC Rules, see A. YESILIRMAK, *Interim and Conservatory Measures in ICC Arbitral Practice* in (2000) ICC ICArb. Bull. pp. 31, 33-34.

10 See, e.g. Article 92 of the SCO, which authorizes the obligor to perform its delivery obligations by depositing the goods when the obligee is in default.

11 POUDRET/BESSON, N. 623, p. 564.

12 Swiss legal commentators usually distinguish between the following two types of interim measures: protective measures ('*Sicherungsmassnahmen*'/'*mesures de protection ou mesures conservatoires*'), regulatory measures ('*Regelungsmassnahmen*'/'*mesures de réglementation*' *ou* '*mesures pacificatrices*') and performance measures ('*Leistungsmassnahmen*'/'*mesures tendant à l'exécution provisoire d'une prétention*'). These classifications are merely for explanatory purposes and do not have any specific legal consequences.

- an order to refrain from disposing of or modifying the object of a proprietary claim;
- an order to deposit the goods in dispute or goods to be delivered with a custodian;
- an order to refrain from drawing on a letter of credit or guarantee;[13]
- an order prohibiting one or both parties from publicizing the evidence or certain aspects of a dispute (while such an order is not directly aimed at ensuring the effectiveness of the final award, it may be necessary to protect the economic interests of a party because a one-sided public account of the dispute may result in significant reputational damage).[14]

c) Measures aimed at regulating the conduct of and the relations between the parties during the arbitral proceedings

In certain circumstances, a party may wish to request measures to regulate the conduct of the parties during the arbitral proceedings. Such regulatory measures are most often requested in disputes involving long-term contracts or disputes arising in corporate settings. The following are examples of regulatory measures:

- an order requiring a contractor to carry on with construction works and/or the owner to continue to make payments (possibly into an escrow account);
- an order requiring a manufacturer to continue supplying a distributor;
- an order requiring a distributor to continue selling a manufacturer's products;
- an order authorizing the suspension of the performance of certain contractual obligations;
- an order suspending the effect of a corporate resolution.

d) Measures aimed at preserving evidence

Arbitral tribunals also have the authority to issue orders aimed at preventing evidence from being altered or destroyed or rendered unavailable. The following are examples of such orders:

- an order authorizing the inspection of a construction site prior to impending changes;
- an order appointing an expert to prepare a report ascertaining the status of facts or events at particular time.[15]

---

13 M. WIRTH, *op. cit.*, p. 33.

14 BUCHER/TSCHANZ, p. 87. See also Chapter 6 *infra*.

15 See POUDRET/BESSON, N. 628, p. 567.

e) Measures aimed at securing the enforceability of money claims

When a party makes a request for measures aimed at securing the enforceability of money claims, two main difficulties arise. The first difficulty stems from the fact that an arbitral tribunal only has jurisdiction over the parties to the arbitration agreement. Yet, in order to be effective, measures securing the enforceability of money claims must often be directed at third parties such as banks, in addition to the parties to the dispute.[16] In such a case, a party will be compelled to request the measures from a competent court.

The second difficulty results from the nature of measures aiming at securing the enforceability of money claims, which are generally considered as measures arising under debt enforcement law, over which courts ordinarily exercise exclusive jurisdiction. Under Swiss law, it is generally accepted that an arbitral tribunal may not grant a freezing order within the meaning of Article 271 of the DEBA.[17] An arbitral tribunal may, however, grant certain alternative measures, such as an order requiring a party to furnish a bank guarantee covering the amount claimed, or provisionally deposit the amount claimed with a custodian, or refrain from disposing of a specific portion of its assets.[18] An arbitral tribunal may also consider ordering a party to pay the amount claimed to the requesting party on a provisional basis.[19] An ICC arbitral tribunal recently considered ordering security for a money claim where the requesting party argued that there was little chance of obtaining recognition and enforcement of an arbitral award against the adverse party under the NY Convention, given a decision on this issue by the highest court of the country where the adverse party was domiciled.[20]

f) Anti-suit injunctions

An anti-suit injunction may be defined as a measure whereby a court orders a party to refrain from commencing or prosecuting proceedings in a foreign court.[21] Originally,

---

16 See M. Blessing, *op. cit.*, N. 837, p. 274.

17 S. Besson, Arbitrage international et mesures provisoires, Schulthess, Zurich 1998, N. 71, p. 63 and further references. Contra, D. Sangiorgio, Vorsorglicher Rechtsschutz in internationalen Schiedsgerichtsverfahren nach Schweizerischem Recht, Aachen 1997, p. 164, who distinguishes between the adjudication of a freezing order and its enforcement, submitting that the former, resulting in an order for the freezing of assets (and not an order for attachment), lies within the authority of the arbitral tribunal. See also M. Wirth in Berti, N. 12, pp. 430-431.

18 S. Besson, *op. cit.*, N. 79, p. 67.

19 See Interim Award in [1994] ASA Bull. 159. See also Article 39 of the Arbitration Act 1996 and Article 25.1(c) of the LCIA Rules.

20 ICC Arbitration No. 8786, Interim Award, published in [2001] ASA Bull. 751: the arbitral tribunal referred to F. Vischer in Heini/Keller/Siehr/Vischer/Volken, N. 6, p. 1542, who considers that arbitral tribunals have the authority to order the deposit of a sum with a third party, a guarantee or surety to serve as a security for a monetary claim.

21 L. Collins (ed.), *Dicey and Morris on the Conflict of Laws*, 12th edn, Sweet & Maxwell, London 1993, p. 408.

anti-suit injunctions were granted exclusively in common law jurisdictions,[22] where the failure to comply with such measures could potentially result in a finding of contempt of court.[23] Although the court granting the injunction has *in personam* jurisdiction over the respondent, who is party to the foreign proceedings, this remedy has been considered to be '*an indirect interference with the process of* [the foreign] *court*'.[24]

In recent years, the use of anti-suit injunctions has become more and more frequent in the context of international commercial arbitration and the scope of such measures has broadened at a similar pace. A party to an arbitration agreement may envisage requesting an anti-suit injunction - from a court or from the arbitral tribunal - *inter alia* in the following circumstances:

- to enjoin the adverse party from commencing proceedings before a court or another arbitral tribunal;
- to order the adverse party to withdraw proceedings pending before another arbitral tribunal or court or to request a stay of such proceedings;
- to resist or support the enforcement of an arbitral award.

Arbitral tribunals often have two reservations of principle when faced with applications for anti-suit injunctions. Firstly, arbitral tribunals may prefer not to issue anti-suit injunctions because such measures may conflict with the principle of *Kompetenz-Kompetenz*, according to which each court and arbitral tribunal has the power to decide upon its own jurisdiction.[25] Secondly, arbitral tribunals are often very cautious when ordering anti-suit injunctions because such measures may interfere with a party's fundamental right to free access to courts and, in certain circumstances, may cause damage to the enjoined party (for instance, where court proceedings are necessary to toll a limitation period).[26]

In practice, arbitral tribunals have adopted a variety of different approaches to anti-suit injunctions. In a recent ICC construction arbitration, the arbitral tribunal denied an application for an order requiring one party to request the stay of parallel arbitral proceedings on the basis that it was not '*empowered to interfere in another arbitration procedure*'.[27] By contrast, two international arbitral tribunals sitting in Switzerland recently issued anti-suit injunctions, which enjoined a party from suing before a court. In

---

22 Civil law jurisdictions rely on the principle of *lis pendens* to deal with parallel proceedings.

23 S. CLAVEL, *Anti-suit injunctions et arbitrage*, in (2001) 4 Rev. Arb. 671.

24 L. COLLINS (ed.), *op. cit.*, p. 408.

25 G. KAUFMANN-KOHLER, Arbitration at the Olympics, Issues of Fast-Track Dispute Resolution and Sport Law, Kluwer Law International, 2001, p. 33.

26 See L. LÉVY, *Les anti-suit injunctions prononcées par les arbitres en droit commun de l'arbitrage*, in the documentation for the 21 November 2003 IAIC conference on 'The Use of Anti-Suit Injunctions in International Arbitration'.

27 Unreported Procedural Order No. 3 of September 2003.

one case, the arbitral tribunal based its order on the arbitration agreement, arguing that it created an obligation to refrain from seeking relief from courts. In the other case, the arbitral tribunal found that such obligation was contained in the contract that gave rise to the arbitration.[28] Finally, an ICSID arbitral tribunal recently held, in a complex case involving a multitude of proceedings, that it was a waste of resources for two arbitral proceedings relating to substantially the same matter to unfold separately and therefore recommended – but did not order – that the other arbitration be stayed.

g) Security for the parties' legal costs

A party, most often the respondent, will sometimes request an order requiring the adverse party to furnish security for costs to be incurred in the arbitral proceedings, including the party's legal fees and other expenses. Under Swiss law, it is generally accepted that arbitral tribunals have the power to order a party to provide such security for costs under Article 183 of the PILA.[29]

Usually, a party will be ordered to provide security for costs where there is a risk of non-recovery by the other party. However, the extent of risk required varies from one decision to another. Thus, in one unreported decision,[30] an arbitral tribunal held that security for costs should only be ordered in exceptional situations, i.e. where there is a clearly documented risk that the assets of a party would not cover a future award of costs. In a decision from 1997, a CCIG arbitral tribunal held that the voluntary liquidation of a party during arbitration is a risk inherent to international trade and that only manoeuvres contrary to good faith could justify an order for security for costs.[31] By contrast, in a decision from 1998, an arbitral tribunal took a less restrictive view and only required the requesting party to demonstrate that there was a potential risk that a future award of costs would not be enforceable.[32] Finally, in 2001, a sole arbitrator ordered security for costs on the basis that the requesting party's interest in obtaining such security prevailed over the adverse party's interest in unimpeded access to arbitral

---

28 These cases are discussed in M. WIRTH, *op. cit.*, pp. 36-37.

29 See M. WIRTH, *op. cit.*, p. 36; M. BLESSING, *op. cit.*, N. 843, p. 274. The provision of security for legal costs must be distinguished from the bond that may be requested from the requesting party (see Section IV.2 *infra*) and the deposit of costs or advance on costs. Such deposits or advances cover the costs of the arbitral proceedings, including the fees of the arbitral tribunal, expenses incurred by the arbitrators and experts, and costs of expert advice, and are provided for in all major arbitration rules (e.g. Article 41 of the Swiss Rules; Article 30 of the ICC Rules; Article 24 of the LCIA Rules). These rules typically provide that, if a party fails to pay its share of the deposit or advance, the other party is free to make the required payment in order for the proceedings to continue (e.g. Article 41(4) of the Swiss Rules; Article 30(3) of the ICC Rules; Article 24.3 of the LCIA Rules).

30 This decision is discussed in M. WIRTH, *op. cit.*, p. 36.

31 Arbitral award of 25 September 1997 in [2001] ASA Bull. 745.

32 Arbitral award of 21 December 1998 in [1999] ASA Bull. 59.

justice, where such adverse party had been the subject of bankruptcy proceedings that were stayed due to lack of assets.[33]

4. *Penalties for non-compliance with measures ordered (Astreintes)*

Do arbitral tribunals have the authority to impose penalties on a party for failure to comply with orders granting interim measures? This issue may have a direct impact on the efficacy of interim measures granted by arbitral tribunals, although penalties are not provisional and any decision providing for them would constitute an award, rather than a decision on interim measures.

Penalties for failure to comply with orders granting interim measures are typically payable to the other party and are characterised as private fines, rather than as a form of compensation for damages sustained.

In French law, such penalties are known as '*astreintes*'. They are also recognised in Dutch and Belgian law.[34] In Switzerland, there is no case law and no consensus on this issue. While there are good arguments in support of the view that arbitral tribunals have the authority to order such penalties,[35] there continues to be considerable debate as to their admissibility. This is particularly true in cases where the parties did not explicitly authorize the arbitral tribunal to impose such penalties[36] and did not agree upon the application of arbitration rules that explicit grant such authority to the arbitral tribunal.[37]

IV. Procedural issues

1. *Ex parte orders*[38]

There are two mains situations in which it may be desirable for a party to obtain interim measures on an *ex parte* basis, i.e. without the adverse party having the opportunity to present its position prior to the order being granted. The first situation arises in cases of extreme urgency, when there is simply no time to hear the adverse party. The second situation is where the very purpose of the interim measure could be defeated if the

---

33 Arbitral decision of 20 November 2001 in [2002] ASA Bull. 467.

34 See S. Besson, *op. cit.*, N. 533, p. 316.

35 See e.g., L. Levy, Les astreintes et l'arbitrage international en Suisse, in [2001] ASA Bull. 21.

36 *Ibid.*, p. 29 (opining that tacit consent of the parties is sufficient); P. Mayer, *Imperium de l'arbitre et mesures provisoires* in J. Haldy/J.-M. Rapp/P. Ferrari (eds), *Etudes de procédures et de l'arbitrage en l'honneur de Jean-Francois Poudret*, 1999, pp. 442-443 (requiring explicit consent of the parties).

37 Although the ICC Rules do not explicitly grant such authority, an arbitral tribunal recently ruled that an injunction coupled with a fine for non-compliance was consistent with the ICC Rules. See A. Yesilirmak, *op. cit.*, p. 33.

38 See generally D. F. Donovan, The Scope and Enforceability of Provisional Measures in International Commercial Arbitration: A Survey of Jurisdictions, The Work of UNCITRAL and Proposals For Moving Forward, in A. J. van den Berg (ed.), ICCA London 2002, pp. 82-149.

adverse party had advance notice of the request, e.g. where there is a risk that the adverse party would dispose of or conceal assets which are the target of the measure.

Whether arbitrators may and/or should order interim measures on an *ex parte* basis is a highly contentious issue in international commercial arbitration.[39] The UNCITRAL Working Group II (Arbitration)[40] is presently redrafting Article 17 of the UNCITRAL Model Law, which relates to interim measures, and has debated this issue at great length. The views expressed within the Working Group have differed considerably, ranging from a recommendation that arbitral tribunals should have no power whatsoever to order *ex parte* measures to a recommendation that arbitral tribunals should be authorised to grant *ex parte* orders, which would then be enforced by courts before the adverse party is given notice. Although it is too early to predict the outcome of this debate, a consensus may well emerge that arbitral tribunals should have some limited power to grant *ex parte* measures, which would appear to be a sensible approach.[41]

Under Swiss law, it is well established that an arbitral tribunal has the power to issue interim measures on an *ex parte* basis.[42] Given that an arbitral tribunal and a court are in an analogous position, there is no reason in principle why arbitrators should not be vested with powers similar to those of a judge in this regard. In order to comply the requirements of due process, an arbitral tribunal should only grant *ex parte* interim measures in situations of utmost urgency. In addition, the adverse party should be notified of the order immediately after it is granted (i.e. prior to enforcement)[43] and given an opportunity to be heard at the first possible opportunity. Furthermore, the interim measure should only continue in force until such time as the arbitral tribunal has heard the adverse party. After having heard all parties, the arbitral tribunal can then decide whether or not to order an extension of the interim measure.

In practice, arbitral tribunals rarely grant interim measures on an *ex parte* basis and only in exceptional circumstances, e.g. where such an order is absolutely necessary in order

---

39 Although *ex parte* measures are regularly ordered both in civil and common law court systems.

40 <www.uncitral.org>.

41 See the Report of the Working Group II, Session held on 23 to 27 February 2004 in New York.

42 See S. V. BERTI in BERTI, N. 8, p. 430; M. WIRTH, *op. cit.*, pp. 31, 38; M. BLESSING, *op. cit.*, N. 866, p. 264; WALTER/BOSCH/BRÖNNIMANN, p. 141; BUCHER/TSCHANZ, p. 90. In court proceedings, *ex parte* orders are often effective when directed at third parties, such as banks having a business relationship with the adverse party. However, arbitral tribunals generally do not have jurisdiction over entities that are not parties to the arbitration agreement. Although on its face Article 183(1) of the PILA vests 'the arbitral tribunal' with the authority to order interim measures, the arbitrators may agree that the chairman shall have the authority to grant *ex parte* interim relief, provided that such delegation is permissible under the applicable procedural rules (Article 182 of the PILA). See BUCHER/TSCHANZ, p. 86.

43 Preferably also of the request when filed.

for the measure to be effective.[44] Generally, arbitral tribunals are reluctant to issue *ex parte* orders for fear that the enjoined party may lose confidence in the arbitration if such an order is granted very early in the proceedings and based upon only one party's version of the facts.[45]

The granting of *ex parte* orders is less rare in CAS arbitrations, where it is sometimes necessary to render an urgent decision on a request to stay the effects of a decision by a sports governing body barring an athlete or team from participating in a competition. Accordingly, Article R37 of the CAS Rules provides that '[i]*n cases of utmost urgency, the President of the relevant Division, prior to the transfer of the filed to the Panel, or thereafter the President of the Panel may issue an order upon mere presentation of the application, provided that the opponent shall be heard subsequently*'.[46]

2. Security

As a condition of granting interim measures, arbitral tribunals often require the requesting party to post security. The purpose of such security is to protect the adverse party by facilitating the recovery of any damages caused by the interim measures, if such measures are ultimately found to be unjustified in the final decision on the merits. Security is only appropriate if the interim measures are capable of causing damage and if the amount of the required security does not exceed the maximum possible loss that could be sustained by the adverse party.[47] The financial situation of the requesting party is irrelevant for the purpose of fixing the amount of the security.[48]

Article 183(3) of the PILA explicitly authorizes the arbitrators (and the courts) to '*make the granting of interim relief or conservatory measures subject to the provision of appropriate security*'. The language of Article 183(3) of the PILA leaves no room for doubt that the arbitral tribunal is empowered to order security for interim measures *ex officio*, without the need for any application by a party. In addition, it is clear that the jurisdiction of the arbitral tribunal extends to claims for damages arising out of interim measures which prove to be unjustified.[49] Most arbitration rules contain provisions to the same effect.[50]

---

44 See M. BLESSING, N. 865, p. 263.

45 See J. E. CASTELLO/Y. DERAINS, *The view against arbitral ex-parte interim relief*, in AAA Dispute Resolution Journal, August - October 2003, pp. 60-69.

46 A similar rule is found in Article 14 of the Rules for the Resolution of Disputes arising during the Olympic Games.

47 Walter/Bosch/Brönnimann, pp. 151-152.

48 M. WIRTH, *op. cit.*, p. 38.

49 S. V. BERTI in BERTI, N. 15, p. 431; F. VISCHER in HEINI/KELLER/SIEHR/VISCHER/VOLKEN, N. 16, p. 1545. *Contra* WALTER/BOSCH/BRÖNNIMANN, p. 152.

50 See Article 26(2) of the Swiss Rules, Article 25(1)(a) of the LCIA Rules (the arbitral tribunal has the power '*to order any respondent party to a claim or counterclaim to provide security for all or part of the amount in dispute*') and Article 26(2) of the UNCITRAL Rules. Article 23(1) of the ICC Rules does not explicitly refer to security for

3. *Form of decisions on interim measures*

The PILA is silent on the form of decisions on interim measures. Most arbitration rules leave it to the arbitral tribunal to determine whether the decision should take the form of an 'order' or an 'award'.[51] The form of the decision as either a procedural order or an arbitral award is relevant to the determination of whether such decision is subject to scrutiny by the ICC Court (Article 27 of the ICC Rules) and may be enforced under the NY Convention.[52]

Generally, the characterization of a decision as an arbitral award or as a procedural order will depend on its substantive contents, not on the title given to it. Whether labelled 'award' or 'order', it is not possible to bring an application to set aside a decision granting or refusing interim measures under Article 190 of the PILA.

V. Enforcement of interim measures

1. *Voluntary compliance*

Most interim measures[53] direct a party to perform or refrain from performing a specific act. Such an order by an arbitral tribunal is '*lex imperfecta*', as arbitral tribunals lack the power to enforce their orders directly against the parties. Despite this fact, there is generally a high incidence of voluntary compliance with interim measures ordered by arbitral tribunals.[54]

---

costs but it is undisputed that such measures are embraced by the broad wording of this provision (see DERAINS/SCHWARTZ, p. 274).

51 See e.g., Article 26(2) of the Swiss Rules and Article 26(2) of the UNCITRAL Rules ('*Such interim measures may be established in the form of an interim award* [...]'); Article 23(1) of the ICC Rules ('*Any such measures shall take the form of an order, giving reasons, or of an Award, as the Arbitral Tribunal considers appropriate*').

52 At its session of 23 to 27 February 2004 in New York, the UNCITRAL Working Group II continued its discussion of a new provision for insertion into the UNCITRAL Model Law (tentatively numbered 17bis), which stipulates that interim measures may, under certain conditions, be enforced abroad upon application to the competent court.

53 Declaratory orders - such as orders authorizing the applicant to call a performance bond or to sell perishable goods - are 'self-executing' and do not need to be enforced.

54 Parties may comply voluntarily because they are conscious of their obligation to mitigate damages and refrain from aggravating the dispute. Non-compliance with an order for interim measures may also have an adverse impact on the arbitral tribunal's assessment of damages in the final award. In addition, the parties' willingness to comply with such orders may be explained by the justified or unjustified concern of antagonizing the arbitrators.

2. *Enforcement of interim measures in connection with arbitration in Switzerland*

a) Assistance by Swiss courts

Pursuant to Article 183(2) of the PILA, the arbitral tribunal may request the assistance of the competent court if a party does not comply with its order.[55] Despite the unambiguous language of Article 183(2) of the PILA, it is generally accepted that the parties themselves may also apply for assistance directly to the court, possibly subject to approval of the arbitral tribunal.[56] As a practical matter, it is necessary to seek assistance from the court at the place where the measure is to be enforced, e.g. at the place where the goods are located or at the domicile or residence of the adverse party,[57] and not at the seat of the arbitral tribunal. Often, the place of enforcement will not be situated in Switzerland and, as a result, Article 183(2) of the PILA will be of little help. In such circumstances, the requesting party is well advised to apply directly to the foreign court for assistance in enforcing the order made by the arbitral tribunal.[58]

In considering applications for assistance in enforcing orders made by arbitral tribunal, Swiss courts focus on two conditions – whether there is a valid arbitration agreement and whether the arbitral tribunal has *prima facie* jurisdiction.[59] If these conditions are satisfied, the Swiss court will not second-guess the substance of the arbitral tribunal's order, but rather restrict itself to a review of the interim measures from the perspective of Swiss public policy.[60]

It should be noted that the Swiss court's order is a decision in and of itself, not merely a decision enforcing the arbitral tribunal's order. As a consequence, the court may only grant measures that are authorized under its own rules of civil procedure applicable at the place where the court is located.[61] If a measure ordered by an arbitral tribunal does

---

55 If the arbitral tribunal anticipates non-compliance based on a party's conduct or other circumstances, it need not to wait for the non-compliance to occur but rather may apply to the court immediately. See BUCHER/TSCHANZ, p. 89.

56 See *e.g.*, S. V. BERTI in BERTI, N. 16, p. 431; P. KARRER/P. STRAUB in F. B. WEIGAND (ed.), *Practitioner's Handbook on International Arbitration*, C. H. Beck/DJOF, Munich/Copenhagen 2002, N. 137, p. 1067 (requiring authorization by the arbitral tribunal); POUDRET/BESSON, N. 637, p. 574 (requiring authorization by the arbitral tribunal). *Contra* S. BESSON, *op. cit.*, N. 511, pp. 303-304 ; BUCHER/TSCHANZ, p. 89; F. VISCHER in HEINI/KELLER/SIEHR/VISCHER/VOLKEN, N. 7, p. 1543.

57 S. BESSON, N. 512, p. 304 (with references).

58 Some maintain that it is possible for a Swiss judge to impose sanctions pursuant to Article 292 of the Swiss Criminal Code for failure to comply with an order both within the territory of Switzerland and extra-territorially. *Contra*, L. LÉVY, *op. cit.*, p. 26 ; *Pro*, M. WIRTH, *op. cit.*, p. 39. However, the case law on this issue is unsettled and, in most cases, it is usually more expedient to seek direct assistance from the foreign court.

59 S. V. BERTI in BERTI, N. 18, pp. 431-432.

60 Walter/Bosch/Brönnimann, p.149; F. Vischer in Heini/Keller/Siehr/Vischer/Volken, N. 14, pp. 1544-1545.

61 LALIVE/POUDRET/REYMOND, N. 10, p. 367.

not correspond to any form of interim relief available under its own rules, the court is required to modify the arbitral tribunal's order so as to make it compatible with such rules. It is only where arbitral tribunal's order of interim measures cannot be adapted to the applicable rules of civil procedure that the court must refuse to enforce them.[62]

b) Assistance by foreign courts

If the place of enforcement is abroad, the question as to whether an arbitral tribunal sitting in Switzerland may apply for assistance directly to a foreign court at that place depends upon the law at the foreign place of enforcement.

c) Enforcement of the Swiss court order

If the Swiss court order is to be enforced in Switzerland, the parties will resort to usual procedures for enforcement of domestic decisions, including recourse to the '*force publique*', and, if applicable, the imposition of criminal sanctions.

If the court order is to be enforced abroad, the party relying on the order may enforce it to the extent provided under the applicable enforcement treaty or the local rules of civil procedure at the place of enforcement. Under the Lugano Convention, which binds Switzerland and the states of the European Union, interim decisions rendered *inter partes* by courts are enforceable.[63]

3. Enforcement of interim measures in connection with arbitration abroad

a) Enforcement of interim measures issued by foreign arbitral tribunals

Article 1(2) of the Lugano Convention expressly excludes arbitration from its scope of application. Accordingly, it is only possible at present to enforce decisions on interim measures made by a foreign arbitral tribunal in Switzerland if such decisions qualify as 'awards' within the meaning of the NY Convention. The situation may change if Switzerland were to adopt regulations along the lines of the forthcoming revision of Article 17 of the UNCITRAL Model Law.

b) Assistance of Swiss courts to foreign arbitral tribunals

While direct enforcement of a foreign arbitral tribunal's order on interim measures is not possible under Swiss law, the majority of Swiss legal commentators[64] maintain that a Swiss court may provide assistance to a foreign arbitral tribunal pursuant to Article 183(2) of the PILA, provided that the Swiss court would have jurisdiction to grant the

---

62 See F. VISCHER in HEINI/KELLER/SIEHR/VISCHER/VOLKEN, N. 14, pp. 1544-1545.

63 Articles 25 and 27; Decision 125/79 of 21 May 1980 of the European Court of Justice.

64 See POUDRET/BESSON, N. 637, p. 574, with further references. This assumes, however, that the foreign arbitration law vests powers in the arbitral tribunal similar to those provided in Article 183(2) of the PILA.

interim measures if such application were made directly to it,[65] i.e. without having recourse to the arbitral tribunal.

c) Enforcement of interim measures ordered by foreign courts

It is generally accepted that interim measures ordered by the courts of a contracting state under the Lugano Convention in connection with a foreign arbitration may be enforced in Switzerland, notwithstanding the fact that arbitration is excluded from the scope of application of such convention.[66]

There are conflicting positions, both in case law and scholarly writings, as to whether interim measures ordered by foreign courts of non-contracting states under the Lugano Convention may be enforced in Switzerland pursuant to the PILA.[67] The debate centres on the interpretation of Article 25 of the PILA, which provides that a foreign court decision will only be recognized in Switzerland if it is final or if it is no longer subject to any ordinary appeal.

The same considerations apply *mutatis mutandis* to the enforcement of interim measures ordered by foreign courts for the purpose of confirming or ratifying interim measures initially ordered by arbitral tribunals.

4. Enforcement of interim measures securing money claims

The enforcement of interim measures securing money claims granted by an arbitral tribunal sitting in Switzerland provides a good illustration of the intricate interplay between private arbitration and public enforcement proceedings, and the balancing of theoretical options and practical needs.

a) Freezing order

Under the DEBA, the remedy provided for securing money claims is the freezing order,[68] which is ordered on an *ex parte* basis by the competent Swiss court and enforced

---

65 Pursuant to Article 24 of the Lugano Convention or Article 10 of the PILA. It is true that one could object that Chapter 12 of the PILA, including Article 183(2), is only applicable when the seat of the arbitral tribunal is in Switzerland, as provided in Article 176 of the PILA.

66 S. Besson, *op. cit.*, N. 659, p. 376, with further references.

67 S. Besson, *op. cit.*, N. 630, pp. 363-364, with further references; P. M. Patocchi/E. Geisinger (eds), *IPRG Internationales Privatrecht – Internationale Übereinkommen – Schiedsgerichtsordnungen*, Orell Füssli, Zurich 2000, N. 2.3, pp. 179-180.

68 Articles 271 *et seq.* of the DEBA. In order to obtain a freezing order, Article 272 of the DEBA requires that the creditor must show on a *prima facie* basis that (i) the creditor has a claim, (ii) there exists a ground for obtaining a freezing order, and (iii) there are assets at hand belonging to the debtor. There are five grounds for obtaining a freezing order against assets located within the territory of Switzerland, but only one of them is of practical importance in the context of international arbitration. If the debtor is not domiciled in Switzerland (even if a Swiss citizen) and none of the other grounds for obtaining a freezing order are fulfilled, Article 271 of the DEBA requires that the claim must have a sufficient

by the competent Swiss debt collection office at the place where the assets are located. As discussed above, there is some controversy as to whether arbitral tribunals have the authority to grant freezing orders. Whatever the ultimate resolution of this controversy, the majority of legal commentators consider that Swiss debt collection offices are not competent to enforce freezing orders granted by arbitral tribunals. Consequently, an arbitral tribunal granting a freezing order must, in any event, seek the assistance of the Swiss courts for the purposes of enforcement, which will of course deprive the measure of its surprise effect.

For this reason, the requesting party's need for a swift and effective measure to secure monetary claims will rarely be met by a freezing order granted by an arbitral tribunal. In most cases, the requesting party is therefore well advised to secure money claims by seeking a freezing order directly from the court at the place where the assets are located.

b) Restraining order

Alternatively, the requesting party seeking to secure money claims could request the arbitral tribunal to grant a restraining order directing the adverse party to refrain from disposing of some or all of its assets (a 'freezing injunction').[69] But again, the arbitral tribunal would be unable to enforce this restraining order if the adverse party failed to comply with it voluntarily.[70] In such an event, both the requesting party and the arbitral tribunal could apply to the competent Swiss court for a similar restraining order.

VI. The authority of courts to order interim measures

1. Concurrent jurisdiction of courts and agreements excluding such jurisdiction

Prior to the commencement of arbitral proceedings and also possibly at a later stage, a party in need of immediate protection may seek interim relief from a court. Under Swiss arbitration law, the arbitral tribunal and the courts have concurrent jurisdiction to grant interim relief.[71] In other words, the parties are free to seek interim relief at any time either from the arbitral tribunal or from a competent Swiss (or foreign) court. Moreover,

---

connection with Switzerland. For an overview of Swiss Debt Enforcement and Bankruptcy law see S. V. BERTI, *Introduction to Swiss Debt Enforcement and Bankruptcy Law*, available on the Internet at <www.schkg.ch/fachliches/betreibungsrecht/swissdebt/tx_swissdebt.htm>.

69 S. V. BERTI in BERTI, N. 12, p. 430.

70 S. V. Berti in Berti, N. 11, p. 430; F. Vischer in Heini/Keller/Siehr/Vischer/Volken, N. 7, p. 1543. *Contra* Walter/Bosch/Brönnimann, p. 137.

71 See S. BESSON, *op. cit.*, N. 231, p. 149 and N. 310, pp. 191-192, with further references; S. V. BERTI in BERTI, N. 5, p. 429; D. SANGIORGIO, *op. cit.*, pp. 128-129. A few authors argue that the courts lose jurisdiction after the constitution of the arbitral tribunal. See RÜEDE/HADENFELDT, p. 252; P. KARRER in [1989] International Business Law Journal 761, 768-769.

the arbitration rules most commonly used do not exclude this concurrent jurisdiction.[72] Under Swiss law, a party's decision to request interim relief from a court does not therefore constitute a waiver of the arbitration agreement.

Obviously, parties who have agreed to exclude the jurisdiction of courts to order interim measures do not have such a choice. Such agreement – the mirror image of an agreement that deprives the arbitral tribunal of its authority to order interim measures – must be explicit and specific. It can be concluded at any time, as part of the arbitration clause, or separately before or after the commencement of arbitral proceedings.[73] Although an agreement to exclude the jurisdiction of the courts over interim relief is not generally advisable, there may be specific reasons that justify such an agreement, e.g. confidentiality, concerns about the risk of parallel proceedings before multiple instances, or an interest in strengthening the mutual obligation to abide by decisions of the arbitral tribunal.

2. *Jurisdiction of the Swiss courts to grant interim measures in the presence of an arbitration agreement*

At the international level, Article 10 of the PILA and Article 24 of the Lugano Convention[74] provide that Swiss courts have jurisdiction to grant interim measures even in cases where they do not have international jurisdiction over the merits of the dispute.

Within Switzerland, federal law governs the jurisdiction of the various courts. The PILA, which applies in international matters, contains very few jurisdictional rules concerning interim measures[75] and, as a result, the jurisdiction *ratione loci* must be determined based upon unwritten federal law.[76] The Swiss Act on Jurisdiction in Civil Matters may provide some additional guidance, but only by analogy, because its scope of application

---

72 See Article 26(3) of the Swiss Rules and Article 26(3) of the UNCITRAL Rules. Article 23(2) of the ICC Rules provides that the parties may apply to a court in '*appropriate circumstances*' once the file has been transmitted to the arbitral tribunal. Article 25.3 of the LCIA Rules provides that the parties may apply to a court only in exceptional circumstances once the arbitral tribunal is formed. By contrast, Article 39 of the ICSID Rules provides that the parties may not apply to a court for interim measures unless '*they have so stipulated in the agreement recording their consent*'.

73 See M. WIRTH, *op. cit.*, pp. 40-41, with further references. A Swiss court faced with a request for interim relief despite the existence of an exclusion agreement should decline jurisdiction. See S. BESSON, *op. cit.*, N. 225, p. 147 and N. 299, p. 184.

74 In *van Uden v. Deco-Line* (C-391/95, ECR 1988, I-7091, N 31-34), the European Court of Justice decided that Article 24 of EU Regulation 44/2001 (the former Brussels Convention) applies in court proceedings even in the presence of an arbitration agreement. See POUDRET/BESSON, N. 612-613, pp. 555-556.

75 See, *e.g.*, Articles 89 (inheritance law) and 153 (company law) of the PILA.

76 See C. LEUENBERGER in K. SPÜHLER/L. TENCHIO/D. INFANGER (eds), *Kommentar zum schweizerischen Zivilprozessrecht, Bundesgesetz über den Gerichtsstand in Zivilsachen (GestG)*, Helbing & Lichtenhahn, Basel 2001, N. 16, p. 324.

does not encompass international matters.[77] Article 33 of the Swiss Act on Jurisdiction in Civil Matters provides that '*the court that has jurisdiction for the main action or the court at the place where the provisional measure must be enforced*' has jurisdiction to grant interim measures. As a consequence, it is clear that the Swiss court at the place of enforcement generally has jurisdiction to grant interim measures even in the presence of an arbitration agreement.

VII. Conflicts between arbitral tribunals and courts

Due to the concurrent jurisdiction of arbitral tribunals and courts over interim measures, there is a risk of conflicts between these two instances: a party may be tempted to file simultaneous applications for interim relief before both the arbitral tribunal and a court; or after failing to obtain interim relief from a court, a party may apply for the same relief from the arbitral tribunal in the hope of securing a more favourable ruling, or vice-versa.

With respect to interim measures, arbitral tribunals and courts are not bound by the doctrines of *lis pendens* and *res judicata*.[78] Nevertheless, in order to prevent conflicting decisions and promote adjudicative efficiency, arbitral tribunals and courts often decide that a party may not apply for interim relief before two instances at the same time and, once a court has dismissed a request for interim relief, a party should not have a second chance to obtain the same interim relief from the arbitral tribunal.

In a recent ICC arbitration in Switzerland, it was held that a party should not be given a second chance to obtain interim measures from the arbitral tribunal where (a) the party had already applied unsuccessfully for identical interim relief before a court, (b) the application for interim relief before the arbitral tribunal was based upon the same facts and evidence as the one brought before the court, (c) the arbitral tribunal would apply the same standards in deciding on the application for interim relief as had the court, and (d) due process had been granted in the court proceedings. The arbitral tribunal held that it would, however, be appropriate to grant a second chance to apply for the interim relief if new facts had arisen since the decision of the court or new evidence had become available.[79]

VIII. Challenge and appeal of interim relief granted by arbitral tribunals

An arbitral tribunal's order on interim measures is not a final decision and therefore is not open to challenge in accordance with Articles 190 and 191 of the PILA. A party may, however, request an arbitral tribunal to reconsider such an order. By contrast, Swiss court orders that enforce decisions on interim measures made by arbitral tribunals are subject to appeal under cantonal and federal laws.

---

77 See C. LEUENBERGER, *op. cit.*, N. 16, p. 324; M. DIETRICH in T. MÜLLER/M. WIRTH (eds), *Gerichtsstandsgesetz: Kommentar zum Bundesgesetz über den Gerichtsstand*, Schulthess, Zurich 2001, N. 104-105, pp. 816-817.

78 See S. V. BERTI/A. K. SCHNYDER in HONSELL/VOGT/SCHNYDER, N. 10-11, pp. 218-219.

79 ICC Procedural Order of 2 April 2002 in [2003] ASA Bull. 810.

Decisions requiring the payment of penalties for non-compliance with interim measures, also known as '*astreintes*', do not constitute provisional measures and must be issued in the form of partial awards. As a result, this type of decision is open to immediate challenge pursuant to Article 190(3) of the PILA, if the ground for setting aside is the improper constitution of the arbitral tribunal or the fact that the arbitral tribunal wrongly accepted or declined jurisdiction. In all other cases, the parties must wait until a final award has been rendered before challenging the award before the Swiss Federal Tribunal.[80]

---

80 See Chapter 8 *infra*.

Chapter 6 - Confidentiality

Alexander Jolles and Maria Canals de Cediel

I. Introduction

When lawyers list the attributes that set international arbitration apart from litigation they mention confidentiality as being one of the significant advantages of arbitration. Often, the desire for confidentiality is, in fact, one of the reasons for resorting to arbitration.[1] Generally, the business community and arbitration practitioners consider that international arbitration is confidential, yet it appears that some of them perceive arbitration as a process shrouded in secrecy. This perception, or expectation, as the case may be, might not be met, as the degree of confidentiality that exists in arbitration is far from being certain.

When the need for confidentiality is a relevant factor in the parties' choice of a dispute resolution method, arbitration is the obvious choice. Many arbitration practitioners will assure clients that, as a general matter, international arbitration offers confidentiality.[2] But how many practitioners have considered exactly what is meant by the oft-mentioned confidential nature of arbitration? Does it mean that arbitration guarantees strict confidentiality, which effectively prevents the disclosure of information? Or is confidentiality in arbitration restricted to some of the participants only, or only to certain kinds of information? If restrictions apply, how can the practitioner secure for his or her client the extent of confidentiality that the particular client expects from arbitration?

This chapter is intended to provide the practitioner with insight into the approach to confidentiality in arbitration in the 'arbitration-friendly' environment of Switzerland. The standard of confidentiality applicable to the various participants in arbitral

---

1 '[I]*n certain classes of transaction, the very existence of a dispute and pending arbitration are themselves strictly confidential to the parties (i.e. patent and know-how licensing, partnership, North Sea Oil etc).*' Editorial, (1995) 11/3 Arb. Int'l. 231.

2 '*Privacy in international commercial arbitration is widely assumed around the world...To a lesser extent, confidentiality is also widely assumed by users of international commercial arbitration.*' Editorial, (1995) 11/3 Arb. Int'l. 231.

G. Kaufmann-Kohler and B. Stucki (eds), International Arbitration in Switzerland, A Handbook for Practitioners, 89-113.

proceedings in Switzerland is examined, as well as the extent to which there is confidentiality in arbitration in other major venues for international arbitration. Finally, certain practical suggestions are proposed for effectively securing confidentiality in arbitration.

II. The common notion of confidentiality

Until the late 1980s confidentiality in arbitration was not debated, it was taken for granted.[3] Today, as a result of the discussion brought about by the 1995 decision of the High Court of Australia in *Esso/BHP v. Plowman*,[4] this is no longer the case. This decision shook the foundations of international arbitration.[5] The debate that ensued led practitioners to take a close look at the notion of confidentiality in arbitration for the first time. A leading journal in the field of international arbitration dedicated a special issue to the question of confidentiality,[6] and one editorial suggested that the foundations of the principle of confidentiality in arbitration needed to be rebuilt.[7] In the wake of this debate, many practitioners were astonished to find that the rule of confidentiality was not as certain as 'it was vaguely supposed to be',[8] and today we know that the private nature of arbitration *per se* does not ensure confidentiality and that confidentiality cannot be assumed in all jurisdictions.[9] The principle of confidentiality and the private nature of arbitration are, in fact, two different things.

Arbitration is a private alternative to litigation. As a consequence, it is ordinarily a process that is governed by a high degree of privacy and party autonomy. Under normal circumstances, only the arbitral institution and the participants know that the arbitration is taking place. Access to hearings is restricted to participants, namely, the arbitral tribunal, its secretary, the parties and counsel, and the witnesses and experts that are called upon in the proceedings. Outsiders can be present at hearings only with the mutual

---

3 H. Bagner, *Confidentiality - A Fundamental Principle in International Commercial Arbitration?* in (2001) 18/2 J. Int'l Arb. 243.

4 See *Esso Australia Resources Ltd and Others v. Plowman (Minister for Energy and Minerals) and Others* in (1995) 128 ALR 391.

5 '*It is a dramatic decision with significance far beyond the shores of Australia. The High Court declares that, contrary to widespread understanding elsewhere* [...], *there is no firm legal basis in contract to support the confidentiality of a commercial arbitration, as distinct from the privacy of the arbitral hearings.*': Editorial, The Decision of the High Court of Australia in *Esso/BHP v. Plowman*, (1995) 11/3 Arb. Int'l. 231.

6 (1995) 11/3 Arb. Int'l.

7 The decision of the High Court of Australia in *Esso/BHP v. Plowman*, Editorial, (1995) 11/3 Arb. Int'l 231; J. Paulsson/N. Rawding, *The Trouble with Confidentiality* in (1995) 11/3 Arb. Int'l 303.

8 J. Paulsson/N. Rawding, *op. cit.*, p. 303.

9 L. E. Trakman, *Confidentiality in International Commercial Arbitration* in (2002) 18/1 Arb. Int'l 1.

consent of the parties and the arbitrators.[10] Public authorities are excluded from arbitral proceedings.

It is the parties who determine the entire framework of their arbitral proceedings by: opting for institutional or *ad hoc* arbitration; selecting the seat of the arbitration and the language of the proceedings; nominating the arbitrators; defining the subject matter. In short, the parties may agree upon a broad range of procedural issues, and, generally, have a say on how the arbitration will be conducted. This explains why international arbitration has gained a reputation for being flexible.

The concept of confidentiality flows from the private character of arbitration and also from the role that party autonomy plays in arbitration. There is broad support for the view that the privacy of the parties should be respected and the subject matter of arbitration should not be made known to the public absent some legitimate reason.[11] Thus, there is an inherent *expectation* that the proceedings will be confidential. Notwithstanding this expectation, an explicit absolute duty of confidentiality binding all participants in the arbitral proceedings does not result simply from the fact that arbitration is private. National law and institutional arbitration rules may, however, provide a *basis* for a duty of confidentiality. The parties, moreover, can - by contract - make their proceedings confidential to a considerable degree. Nevertheless, it should be noted that there is a limitation to confidentiality as a result of duties to disclose which arise out of statute or public policy. In some jurisdictions, the need to protect and pursue a legal right has also been recognised as taking precedence over the duty of confidentiality.[12]

The prudent practitioner must therefore ascertain the standard of confidentiality that applies under the parties' choice of institutional arbitration rules, as well as under the law applicable to the confidentiality of arbitration. Disputes regarding confidentiality arise precisely because it is not always clear to the parties that, even though confidentiality is generally acknowledged in arbitration, the law does not adequately regulate arbitral confidentiality and only a few institutional arbitration rules provide for confidentiality.

---

10 In keeping with the consensual character of arbitration, clearly the parties must consent to the presence of observers at the hearings, yet the arbitrators, who are empowered to conduct the proceedings as they deem appropriate, must also agree. Article 25(4) of the Swiss Rules states that hearings shall be held in camera unless the parties agree otherwise and Article 15(1) empowers the arbitral tribunal to conduct the arbitration in such a manner as it considers appropriate (ensuring equal treatment of the parties and their right to be heard). Articles 25(4) and 15(1) of the UNCITRAL Rules are similar. Article 21 of the ICC Rules explicitly states that persons not involved in the proceedings shall not be admitted to the hearings, except with the approval of the arbitral tribunal and the parties. Article 19(4) of the LCIA Rules also states that meetings and hearings shall be private unless the parties agree otherwise in writing or the arbitral tribunal directs otherwise.

11 DERAINS/SCHWARTZ, p. 264.

12 These limitations are explicitly mentioned in the LCIA Rules under Article 30(1).

Unwanted disclosure is an issue in arbitration. It often comes about as a result of a unilateral act by a party or a third party, or as a result of proceedings to set aside the final award, or to recognize and enforce an award. In such court proceedings, a party may be required to request that the court file be placed under seal or resort to some other procedure sanctioned by the local courts in order to keep information relating to the arbitral proceedings confidential.[13] In order to preserve confidentiality, the Swiss Federal Tribunal does not engage in public deliberation on applications to set aside arbitral awards unless there is some disagreement between the judges on the panel in regard to the proposed decision prepared by the judge in charge of the file.[14] However, the Swiss Federal Tribunal's decisions on challenges to arbitral awards are published because court proceedings are public[15] and because the publication of judgments is held to be in the public interest insofar as judgments address important and precedent-setting questions of law. Notwithstanding this fact, the Swiss Federal Tribunal considers that public interest in the publication of the award is not compromised by the non-publication of the parties' names in the judgment, where such names are not necessary for the comprehension of the judgment and non-publication of them protects a private interest in confidentiality.[16] When judgments are published on the Swiss Federal Tribunal's website,[17] the names of the parties are therefore redacted in a large number of cases.[18]

Although it is now questionable to consider that the private nature of arbitration means that it is also confidential, it is clear that the parties do have the opportunity to provide for confidentiality in arbitration.[19] As noted above, there may be a basis for confidentiality either under the law applicable to the confidentiality of the arbitration (this law will often be the substantive law applicable to the arbitration agreement and/or the procedural law applicable at the seat of arbitration) or the institutional arbitration rules chosen by the parties. Yet, it is nevertheless advisable for the parties to address the issue of confidentiality in an explicit agreement, which will enable them to determine the standard and scope of confidentiality applicable to their arbitral proceedings. Given the growing awareness of the *lacunae* in regard to the legal basis for confidentiality in arbitration, practitioners are increasingly apt to introduce confidentiality clauses in arbitration agreements and to draw up separate agreements for third party participants. In the absence of such measures, it has been suggested that the arbitrators may wish to discuss with the parties the possibility of including a confidentiality clause in the terms

---

13 L. E. TRAKMAN, *op. cit.*, p. 12.

14 F. DESSEMONTET, *Arbitration and Confidentiality* in (1996) 7 Am. Rev. Int'l Arb. 299.

15 Article 30(3) of the Swiss Federal Constitution.

16 The protection of the private sphere of the individual is guaranteed by Article 13 of the Swiss Federal Constitution.

17 <www.bger.ch>.

18 Decision of the Swiss Federal Tribunal of 10 December 2002 (4P.207/2002) in [2003] ASA Bull. 585, 589.

19 DERAINS/SCHWARTZ, p.13.

of reference.[20] Many arbitrators now also favour confidentiality agreements over other measures that were applied in the past[21] when a party is unwilling to produce documents because these contain confidential information.[22]

III. The standard of confidentiality in arbitration in Switzerland

1. The basis for a duty of confidentiality

In Switzerland, it is recognized that users of international arbitration have a common expectation of confidentiality and acknowledged that arbitrators and parties must therefore have an implied obligation of confidentiality. As a consequence, confidentiality is required from the arbitrators and the parties, and it is expected that neither the proceedings nor the award will be publicized. Arbitral proceedings in Switzerland are thus subject to a relatively high degree of confidentiality, even in the absence of an explicit agreement between the parties to that effect.

The Swiss legislator considered arbitration to be inherently contractual[23] and therefore kept statutory interference to a minimum. Accordingly, it is not surprising that the PILA, which applies whenever the seat of the arbitral tribunal is in Switzerland and at least one of the parties is not a resident of Switzerland, does not contain any provision concerning confidentiality.

Institutional arbitration rules are private documents, which bind the parties contractually when the parties opt to have arbitration under a set of these rules. The Swiss Rules contain a provision setting forth the extent of confidentiality that applies in all arbitrations held under those rules.[24] By contrast, under Swiss law, there are no provisions that explicitly lay out applicable standards of confidentiality in arbitration. As a result, such standards must be implied from other rules of Swiss law.

2. The duty of confidentiality of arbitrators

In Switzerland, arbitrators have a strict duty of confidentiality. They have the obligation to keep silent about all facts and circumstances relating to the parties and to the dispute

20 Section 6, § 31 of the UNCITRAL Notes provide as follows: '[…]. *Furthermore, the participants in an arbitration might not have the same understanding as regards the extent of confidentiality that is expected. Therefore, the arbitral tribunal might wish to discuss that with the parties and, if considered appropriate, record any agreed principles on the duty of confidentiality*'.

21 Such measures include asking the party to redact confidential passages or submit confidential documents exclusively to the arbitral tribunal. The latter solution may be problematic in the view of the right to be heard guaranteed in Article 182(3) of the PILA and Article 6 of the European Convention on Human Rights: POUDRET/BESSON, N. 654, p. 588.

22 M. BLESSING in BERTI, N. 913, p. 272.

23 BUCHER/TSCHANZ, N. 115-116, p. 65.

24 Article 43 of the Swiss Rules (similar provisions were previously contained in Article 51 of the ZCC Rules and Article 4 of the CCIG Rules). For a more detailed discussion of the Swiss Rules see Chapter 10 *infra*.

that are not in the public domain and which become known to them in the course of the proceedings.[25] There is, of course, an exception for instances where, for the purpose of properly performing their task, the arbitrators are allowed to divulge information to third parties – such as when instructing an expert.[26] The arbitrators' duty of confidentiality is ongoing and does not end with the conclusion of the arbitration.[27]

Swiss legal commentators derive the arbitrators' duty of confidentiality from the fiduciary relationship that arises from the contract between arbitrators and parties, a contract that is analogous to a contract of ordinary mandate and comes into existence with the arbitrators' acceptance of their appointment.[28]

Arbitrators, in effect, enter into a contract with the parties when they accept the appointment by the parties.[29] When the seat of the arbitral tribunal is in Switzerland, Swiss law governs this contract.[30] All the duties of arbitrators in connection with the conduct of the arbitration flow from this contractual and fiduciary relationship.

Under Swiss law, the main duties of arbitrators are the duty of diligence, the duty to conduct the proceedings in an impartial and independent manner, the duty to inform the parties of any ground for challenge, and the duty to complete the arbitration (subject to an arbitrator's resignation, which is permissible only in very limited circumstances). According to Swiss legal commentators, the duty of confidentiality is classified as a secondary duty of arbitrators,[31] which results from the arbitrators' principal duty of diligence.[32] It follows that arbitrators are under a contractual obligation to refrain from voluntarily disclosing information relating to the arbitration.

The arbitrators' duty of confidentiality exists both *vis-à-vis* the parties and the witnesses. The arbitrators' obligation to keep confidential the testimony of witnesses flows from the direct legal relationship between arbitrator and witness which arises in the framework of arbitral proceedings and is based on private law.[33]

An express release by a party or witness is required to free the arbitrator from his or her duty of confidentiality *vis-à-vis* such party or witness (in practice, notwithstanding that

---

25 H.-H. INDERKUM, *Der Schiedsrichtervertrag*, Dissertation, Fakultät der Universität Freiburg (Schweiz), 1988, p.142.

26 *Ibid.*, p.143.

27 RÜEDE/HADENFELDT, p. 156.; H.-H. INDERKUM, *op. cit.*, p. 203; F. HOFFET, *Rechtliche Beziehungen zwischen Schiedsrichtern und Parteien*, Schulthess, Zurich, 1991, p. 236.

28 BUCHER/TSCHANZ, p.65.

29 This contract is known as *contrat d'arbitre* or *receptum arbitri*, and it need not be in writing (see Chapter 3 *supra*).

30 BUCHER/TSCHANZ, p.65.

31 H.-H. INDERKUM, *op. cit.*, at p. 143.

32 The duty of diligence, in turn, is derived from Article 398(2) of the SCO. S. VOGT, Der *Schiedsrichtervertrag nach Schweizerischem Recht*, Dissertation, Fakultät der Universität Zürich, 1989, p. 130.

33 F. HOFFET, *op. cit.*, N. 879, p. 234.

the witness may release the arbitrator from his or her duty of confidentiality, the parties' right to confidentiality prevails).[34]

The Swiss law basis for the arbitrators' duty of confidentiality is reinforced if the arbitration takes place under the Swiss Rules.[35] When the parties opt for a particular arbitral institution, its rules become part of the arbitration agreement and are thus contractually binding on the parties and on the arbitrators accepting appointments under these rules.

The Swiss Rules stipulate that the arbitrators have a duty to keep confidential all facts, information and materials relating to the dispute, as well as the proceedings, the deliberations of the arbitral tribunal and all orders and awards.[36] The parties also often provide for arbitration in Switzerland under the ICC Rules and under the UNCITRAL Rules. In contrast with the Swiss Rules, neither the ICC nor the UNCITRAL Rules contain a provision that binds arbitrators to a duty of confidentiality.[37] The LCIA Rules, which may also be chosen for international arbitration in Switzerland, are likewise silent on the duty of confidentiality of the arbitrators, save in respect of the arbitrators' obligation to keep confidential the deliberations of the arbitral tribunal.[38]

In Switzerland, arbitrators have an obligation to keep confidential the deliberations and votes of the arbitral tribunal.[39] Swiss legal commentators[40] and case law[41] provide a clear legal foundation for this obligation,[42] even though Article 189 of the PILA (which deals with the making of an award) does not address deliberations and voting confidentiality. The principle of deliberation and voting confidentiality is, however, essential for the independent adjudicative activity of arbitrators, which is why the arbitrators are required to consent explicitly to a waiver of this confidentiality.[43] In fact, some Swiss legal commentators suggest that both the parties *and* the arbitrators must consent to waivers of this confidentiality.[44]

---

34 The duty of confidentiality of the arbitrator is not mandatory law. Therefore, the parties can contractually derogate from its application in the context of their arbitration proceedings.

35 Article 43 of the Swiss Rules.

36 Article 43 of the Swiss Rules (Article 51 of the ZCC Rules and Article 4 of the CCIG Rules also stipulated a strict duty of confidentiality for arbitrators but, unlike the provision of the Swiss Rules, these provisions did not explicitly set forward the arbitrators' obligation to keep the deliberations of the tribunal confidential).

37 DERAINS/SCHWARZ, p. 263.

38 Article 30(2) of the LCIA Rules.

39 Article 43(2) of the Swiss Rules stipulates that the deliberations of the arbitral tribunal are confidential.

40 LALIVE/POUDRET/REYMOND, p. 414. A. HEINI in HEINI/KELLER/SIEHR/VISCHER/VOLKEN, N. 4, p. 1573.

41 Decision of the Swiss Federal Tribunal of 12 November 1991 in [1992] ASA Bull. 265.

42 M. WIRTH in BERTI, p. 545, 551.

43 WALTER/BOSCH/BRÖNNIMANN, p. 201.

44 RÜEDE/HADENFELDT, p. 295.

It follows from the private nature of arbitration that the award is not a matter of public record. Not only is the award private, it is confidential. Arbitrators have an obligation to keep arbitral awards confidential.[45] Nonetheless, if the parties explicitly consent, an award may be made available for publication for scholarly purposes.[46] Increasingly, legal journals are publishing arbitral awards and procedural documents from arbitral proceedings. Court decisions concerning awards are also being published.[47] In most cases, the anonymity of the parties and of the dispute is maintained, although the identity of the arbitrators is sometimes disclosed, a practice that has met with some criticism.[48]

As can be seen, the arbitrators' duty of confidentiality is all encompassing in Switzerland. It stands to reason that the office of arbitrator, like that of judge, cannot be carried out without the exercise of confidentiality. There are situations, however, in which the arbitrators' contractual duty of confidentiality conflicts with a statutory duty to testify. Can and must an arbitrator invoke his or her duty of confidentiality when called to testify about the arbitration? Or rather, given that confidentiality is a prerogative inherent in the judicial function of the arbitrator,[49] are arbitrators exempt from the obligation to testify about facts that have become known to them by reason of their office?[50]

The PILA and the Concordat are silent on this issue. Moreover, the laws exempting civil servants (the concept of civil servant includes the judiciary) from the legal obligation to testify[51] are not applicable to arbitrators.[52] While arbitrators carry out a judicial function comparable to that of judges, they are not vested with the same powers as judges[53] and

---

45 An exception is found in the appeal arbitration proceedings of the CAS (see Chapter 10 *infra*). In appeal proceedings from the decision of a disciplinary tribunal or similar body of a federation, association or sports body, the award or a summary setting forth the results of the proceedings are made public by the CAS, unless both parties agree that they should remain confidential (Article R59 of the CAS Rules). The reason for reversing the confidentiality rule of awards in this particular instance is public interest in the transparency of dispute resolution in sports disciplinary matters.

46 Article 43 of the Swiss Rules (and previously Article 51 of the ZCC Rules and Article 4 of the CCIG Rules), Article 32 of the UNCITRAL Rules and Article 30(3) of the LCIA Rules all require the consent of the parties for the publication of the award (or of any part of the award).

47 [1993] ASA Bull. 294.

48 FOUCHARD/GAILLARD/GOLDMAN, p. 628.

49 *Ibid.*

50 A judgment of 15 May 2003 of the Swedish Court of Appeal judgment illustrates the practical relevance of this issue. In this case, the arbitrators were called to testify before the Swedish Court of Appeal regarding the deliberation process in the arbitration between CME Czech Republic B.V. and the Czech Republic.

51 These legal provisions are found in the Swiss Criminal Code and in the cantonal codes of civil procedure.

52 *Contra* F. WIGET cited in H.-H. INDERKUM, *op. cit.*, p. 174.

53 Due to the fact that the relationship between arbitrators and parties is a matter of private law.

are not considered to be civil servants. As a consequence, the official duty of secrecy applicable to civil servants under criminal and administrative law[54] does not apply to arbitrators. Nor are arbitrators subject to statutory professional secrecy of kind that applies to the professions of lawyer, physician, notary, auditor and clergy.[55] Moreover, since the list of professions subject to secrecy is exhaustive and arbitrators are not listed, it is not possible to argue that those arbitrators who are lawyers admitted to the bar[56] are subject to the statutory attorney-client privilege and therefore exempt from the obligation to testify.[57]

Given that there is no statutory provision expressly enabling arbitrators to refuse to testify on the basis of a duty of confidentiality, some Swiss legal commentators have looked to the cantonal rules on civil procedure for support. Under Article 160(1) of the ZCCP, a judge may excuse a witness from testifying if: (a) the witness exercises a profession which is subject to a secrecy obligation under Article 321(1) of the Swiss Criminal Code and this profession is not listed in Article 159(3) of the ZCCP[58] or (b) if the witness is subject to a particular relationship of trust and confidence, provided that other protective measures are not available and that the interest of the witness in keeping the information confidential prevails over the interest of the party seeking to put the confidential information into evidence.

Although the office of arbitrator is not a profession as such, some Swiss legal commentators submit that arbitrators are subject to a 'particular relationship of trust and confidence', such that it is possible for arbitrators to refrain from testifying based upon Article 160(1) of the ZCCP.

---

54 Article 320 of the Swiss Criminal Code.

55 The laws regulating the practice of the legal profession explicitly set forth the lawyer's obligation to keep secret all information that is not in the public domain that he or she receives and learns of in the course of professional activities, e.g. Article 14 of the Law of the Canton of Zurich regulating the practice of the legal profession of 3 July 1938. See also Article 13 of the Federal Law on the Free Movement of Attorneys, which is federal law. In harmony with this rule of professional conduct, the cantonal codes of criminal procedure (e.g. Article 130 of the Zurich Code of Criminal Procedure) and the cantonal codes of civil procedure (e.g. Article 159 of the ZCCP) exempt lawyers from the obligation to testify.

56 There is no requirement for arbitrators to be lawyers, although arbitrators are most often lawyers. Both the PILA and the Concordat leave the qualifications of arbitrators to the agreement of the parties (Article 11 of the ZCC Rules was one of the few provisions of international arbitration rules requiring that lawyers be appointed as chairpersons of the arbitral tribunals). In the vast majority of cases, arbitrators decide according to law. Article 187(2) of the PILA, however, allows the parties to authorize the arbitral tribunal to decide *ex aequo et bono*.

57 Decision of 7 September 2000 of the Zurich Court of Appeal (Bar Supervisory Board) in [2001] ASA Bull., pp. 322 *et seq*.

58 Article 159(3) of the ZCCP lists only the professional secrecy obligation of clergy, medical doctors and lawyers.

While this position does provide a legal basis for arbitrators to refrain from testifying about the arbitration,[59] it is not altogether satisfactory because: (a) the court continues to have discretion in determining whether or not to excuse the arbitrator from testifying; and (b) not every cantonal code of civil procedure includes a provision similar to Article 160(1) of the ZCCP. Notably, the GLCP does not include such a provision, which leads to the result that arbitrators may not be able to avoid testifying everywhere in Switzerland. It should, however, be emphasized that the draft Federal Civil Procedure Act contains a provision similar to Article 160(1) of the ZCCP, which will provide a legal basis for arbitrators to refrain from testifying everywhere in Switzerland, irrespective of the Canton.[60]

Do arbitrators incur civil liability for violating their duty of confidentiality? The answer is 'yes' in Switzerland.

Swiss legal commentators[61] concur that the liability of arbitrators is analogous to the liability of agents. Accordingly, if arbitrators violate a duty that results from their office, they will face civil liability for failing to perform their mandate with the requisite degree of care (Article 398 of the SCO) and the parties can thus bring an action against them for damages (Article 97 *et seq.* of the SCO).[62] When the arbitral tribunal is composed of more than one arbitrator, the arbitrators are jointly and severally liable (Article 403 of the SCO).

It should be noted that when arbitrators violate one of their primary duties, i.e. those linked to the decision-making process, they are only liable if they have caused damage as a result of intentional or grossly negligent misconduct[63] (in this respect, the arbitrators' immunity is similar to the one of judges).[64] Moreover, under Swiss law, a contractual exclusion of liability for gross negligence or unlawful intent is null and void.[65] If arbitrators did not enjoy a relatively high degree of immunity in respect of the decision-making process (i.e. no liability for simple negligence), their ability to perform their judicial function would be impaired by the risk that dissatisfied parties might bring claims against them for negligence in order to make a collateral attack on the arbitral award before the courts. By contrast, arbitrators are liable even for simple negligence in performing functions unrelated to the decision-making process,[66] i.e. in the carrying out of their secondary duties, which include the duty of confidentiality as previously

59 S. VOGT, *op. cit.*, p. 133.

60 Articles 153 and 157(2) of the draft Federal Civil Procedure Act.

61 BUCHER/TSCHANZ, *op. cit.*, p.65.

62 F. HOFFET, *op. cit.*, p. 294; S. VOGT, *op. cit.*, p. 145; H.-H. INDERKUM, *op. cit.*, p. 163.

63 See Chapter 3 *supra*.

64 H.-H. HINDERKUM, *op. cit.*., p.163; BUCHER/TSCHANZ, p. 66. Judges are only liable for gross negligence in some Cantons, while in others all liability is excluded (e.g. Zurich), which is also the case at the federal level. Article 100(1) of the SCO applies to arbitrators: F. HOFFET, *op. cit.*, at p 305.

65 Article 100(1) of the SCO.

66 H.-H. INDERKUM, *op. cit.*, pp. 170-171.

discussed. It is nevertheless possible for parties to agree upon an enforceable contractual exclusion in respect of liability for simple negligence.[67] According to Swiss legal commentators, a contractual exclusion of liability in relation to the duty of confidentiality must, however, be set forth in unequivocal terms.[68]

If an action for damages is brought against an arbitrator, the judge at the place of the arbitrator's Swiss domicile would have jurisdiction.[69] Where the arbitral tribunal is composed of more than one arbitrator, a party would be required to bring an action in several jurisdictions. If all of the arbitrators are domiciled in countries that have ratified the Lugano Convention, there will be jurisdiction against all the arbitrators jointly at the domicile of any one of them.[70] If certain of the arbitrators are domiciled in jurisdictions not subject to the Lugano Convention, the parties can agree that the judge at the seat of arbitral tribunal shall have exclusive jurisdiction. The judge at the seat of arbitral tribunal also has jurisdiction when the arbitrator does not have a Swiss domicile, as the seat of the arbitral tribunal is the place of performance in respect of the arbitrator's duties.[71] The substantive law governing the liability of the arbitrator would be Swiss law, pursuant to which the general statute of limitation for contractual claims of ten years would be applicable.[72] However, in practice, it is improbable (and unheard of to date) that a party would bring an action for damages against an arbitrator for breach of the duty of confidentiality, as in most cases it would be difficult to prove: (a) the causal relationship between the disclosure of information and specific damages; and (b) the extent and amount of the damages.[73]

In Switzerland, arbitrators are not subject to *criminal liability* for breach of their duty of confidentiality because the provisions of the federal criminal code relating to official secrecy and professional secrecy do not apply to arbitrators, as previously discussed.

To sum up, in international arbitration in Switzerland, there is a contractual basis for the arbitrator's duty of confidentiality. This contractual basis comes into existence with the appointment of the arbitrator, covers all aspects of the arbitrator's judicial function and continues after the arbitral tribunal renders its final award.[74] Moreover, the parties may

---

67 Article 44(1) of the Swiss Rules explicitly stipulates this exclusion in the following terms: '*None of the Chambers or their staff, arbitrators or tribunal-appointed experts shall be liable for any act or omission in connection with an arbitration conducted under these Rules, save where the act or omission is shown to constitute deliberate wrongdoing or extremely serious negligence*'.

68 F. HOFFET, *op. cit.*, p. 308.

69 Article 112 of the PILA; Article 2 of the Lugano Convention.

70 Article 6 (1) of the Lugano Convention.

71 Article 113 of the PILA; Article 5 (1) of the Lugano Convention.

72 Article 127 of the SCO.

73 On the basis of Article 97 of the SCO.

74 Under normal circumstances, the contract with the arbitrator comes to an end when the final award is rendered: BUCHER/TSCHANZ, p. 66.

reinforce this contractual basis by agreeing to the Swiss Rules, which expressly provide that the arbitrator is subject to a clear duty of confidentiality.[75]

3. *The duty of confidentiality of the parties*

In Switzerland, it is not only recognized that the parties expect the arbitral procedure to be confidential,[76] but it is also acknowledged that they are *entitled* to confidentiality because often publicity relating to a dispute may harm a party from a business and commercial point of view.[77]

Based upon these considerations and in view of the fact that there is no provision under Swiss law which explicitly sets out a duty of confidentiality applicable to the parties to the arbitration, some Swiss legal commentators maintain that the parties have an *implied* obligation under the agreement to arbitrate to respect the confidentiality of the arbitration.[78] This implied obligation is said to arise from the expectations of the parties, who agree on arbitration, among other reasons, because they want to dispose of disputes confidentially.

This possible implied obligation of confidentiality under the agreement to arbitrate would be the only basis for the parties' duty of confidentiality in Switzerland. The reliability of this implied obligation is an open issue. There have been no known Swiss court cases as yet confirming this implied obligation. It is, therefore, uncertain to what extent such an implied obligation would be enforceable.

The parties are, however, free to build upon this implied duty of confidentiality by entering into an explicit confidentiality agreement. The parties can also agree upon the application of institutional arbitration rules which expressly provide that the parties have a duty of confidentiality. Both the Swiss Rules and the LCIA Rules impose a duty of confidentiality on the parties (the scope of the duty of confidentiality under these rules is discussed in Section V *infra*).[79]

Notwithstanding the existence of a duty of confidentiality, a party cannot be prevented from disclosing the fact that there is an ongoing arbitration or the arbitral award: (a) where the party has a legal obligation to disclose such matters (for instance, to board members, corporate auditors, shareholders, insurers, banks, tax authorities, etc.); or (b) where the party must divulge this information to protect its legitimate interests in proceedings against third parties; or (c) where the party initiates court proceedings ancillary to the arbitration such as proceedings to appoint or remove an arbitrator, challenge an award or enforce an award. It is undisputed that a statutory obligation to

---

75 Similarly, the ZCC Rules and the CCIG Rules before.

76 M. BLESSING in BERTI, N. 380, p. 153.

77 BUCHER/TSCHANZ, p. 87.

78 *Ibid.*

79 Article 43(1) of the Swiss Rules (also Article 51of the ZCC Rules and Article 4 of the CCIG Rules), Article 30(1) of the LCIA Rules.

make disclosure and a party's need to preserve its legal rights prevail over any contractual duty of confidentiality.[80]

To what extent can the parties' duty of confidentiality be enforced in Switzerland? First, arbitrators will enforce any contractual provisions about confidentiality. When the seat of the arbitral tribunal is in Switzerland, Article 183 of the PILA grants the arbitral tribunal power to order provisional or protective measures (as long as the parties have not agreed to deprive the tribunal of such power). Consequently, where a party is breaching its duty of confidentiality, e.g. by publicising matters relating to the dispute, the arbitral tribunal can order that party to refrain from such conduct.[81] Pursuant to Article 183 of the PILA, an arbitral tribunal can also request the assistance of the competent Swiss court if a party does not comply voluntarily with such an order.[82] In many cases, parties are, however, inclined to comply voluntarily with the orders of the arbitral tribunal in order to avoid the risk of antagonizing the arbitrators and the possibility of being found liable in the award for having violated the obligation to mitigate damages or the obligation not to aggravate the dispute.[83] Where there is an explicit contractual duty confidentiality, a claim for damages could be brought in arbitration, as in any case of breach of contract, and such a claim would likely be covered by the arbitration clause.

With respect to the duty of confidentiality applicable to Swiss counsel, it has previously been noted that lawyers in Switzerland have an obligation of professional secrecy. When considering counsel's duty of confidentiality in an arbitration, it is important to distinguish the situation of counsel *vis-à-vis* his or her client from that of counsel *vis-à-vis* the opposing party.

The lawyer's obligation of professional secrecy relates to information given to the lawyer by the client, which information is protected by the attorney-client privilege. Hence, *vis-à-vis* the client, counsel is bound by professional secrecy and the duration of this obligation of professional secrecy is indefinite. A lawyer's violation of professional secrecy provides grounds for disciplinary measures and penalties under administrative and criminal law. In addition, the client can sue the lawyer for damages for breach of contract.

By contrast, *vis-à-vis* the opposing party, counsel do not have any obligation of professional secrecy or any implied duty of confidentiality arising under the arbitration agreement (as counsel are third parties to the arbitration agreement). As a result, party's counsel would be free to disclose information regarding the opposing party (if the client

---

80 M. WIRTH in BERTI, p. 567.

81 BUCHER/TSCHANZ, p. 87.

82 Article 10 of the PILA provides: '*The Swiss judicial or administrative authorities may order provisional measures even if they do not have jurisdiction to entertain the merits*'.

83 BUCHER/TSCHANZ, *op. cit.*, p. 88.

agrees) *unless* they have a contractual duty of confidentiality flowing from a confidentiality agreement or the applicable rules.[84]

Arbitrators will enforce the contractual duty of confidentiality of counsel no less than that of the parties, and the parties have the legal remedies that are available in cases of breach of contract.

4. *The duty of confidentiality of third parties*

Witnesses and experts are a potential source of unwanted disclosure of information. There is no legal basis in Switzerland for imposing a duty of confidentiality of these persons. Moreover, like counsel, they too are third parties to the arbitration agreement and therefore are not subject to the implied duty of confidentiality that arises from this agreement. Similarly, witnesses and experts are also third parties to any duty of confidentiality arising under institutional arbitration rules. As a result, the only possibility for creating a duty of confidentiality for witnesses and experts is through a confidentiality agreement.

When considering the position of experts, it is important to distinguish between party-appointed experts and experts appointed by the arbitral tribunal. The former are essentially witnesses of the parties and any duty of confidentiality that may bind them would be derived from a confidentiality agreement they have entered into with the parties. By contrast, experts appointed by the arbitral tribunal enter into a contract with the arbitral tribunal when they accept the appointment. They are not, however, bound by a duty of confidentiality as a result of their appointment alone and, accordingly, it is necessary to include an express duty of confidentiality in their terms of appointment.

How can arbitrators protect confidential information that may be disclosed by third parties in their testimony? An arbitral tribunal in Switzerland could draw inspiration from the cantonal procedural rules, for instance from Article 145 of the ZCCP,[85] which provides that the court has discretion to put in place measures to protect the interests of the parties or third parties. Furthermore, if there is a risk that a witness will divulge manufacturing and trade secrets and the arbitral tribunal deems other protective measures to be insufficient, it can choose to excuse the witness from testifying as the Zurich courts can do under Article 160(2) of the ZCCP. Alternatively, the arbitral tribunal may find inspiration in the WIPO Rules, which contain very elaborate provisions for dealing with the potential disclosure of trade secrets and other confidential information in intellectual property arbitrations.[86] The protection of trade secrets and confidential information is addressed separately in Section VII *infra*.

---

84 Formerly, the ZCC Rules provided a duty of confidentiality applicable to *all* participants in the arbitral proceedings.

85 The procedural rules that are applicable to the arbitration are determined in accordance with Article 182 of the PILA.

86 See Chapter 10 *infra*.

IV. The position on confidentiality in other major venues for arbitration

As previously mentioned, the Australian decision in *Esso/BHP v. Plowman* brought the issue of confidentiality in international arbitration to the fore. This decision provoked a lively discussion among legal commentators and created some degree of uncertainty in the world of international arbitration. For comparative purposes, this section sets forth a very brief overview of the position on confidentiality in other major venues for international arbitration, without purporting to provide a complete account.

It appears that most national arbitration laws are silent on the issue of confidentiality, with the notable exception of the Arbitration Act of New Zealand. The UNCITRAL Model Law does not deal with the issue of confidentiality at all.[87] Most countries have adopted the UNCITRAL Model Law without any modification to address confidentiality, with only New Zealand having amended it to introduce a provision on this point.[88]

In the United States, neither the Federal Arbitration Act nor the Uniform Arbitration Act contains a provision regarding confidentiality.[89] Moreover, in *United States v. Panhandle Eastern Corp et al.*,[90] a Delaware District Court ruled that confidentiality does not apply to arbitral proceedings and therefore documents produced in the framework of these proceedings may be obtained by discovery. In the United States, the duty of confidentiality arises from either an express agreement or institutional arbitration rules and is limited to the arbitrators.[91]

In England, the question of the confidentiality of arbitration has long focused on two issues, namely the obstacle posed by confidentiality to the consolidation of proceedings involving more than two parties and the publication of arbitral awards without the consent of the parties. Confidentiality was traditionally taken for granted as a corollary of the fact that arbitration is based upon a private agreement between private parties to

---

87 See the expert report of J. D.M. LEW in (1995) 11/3 Arb. Int'l 289.

88 Section 14 of the New Zealand Arbitration Act provides: '*An arbitral agreement, unless otherwise agreed by the parties, is deemed to provide that the parties shall not publish, disclose or communicate any information relating to arbitral proceedings under the agreement or to an award made in those proceedings*'.

89 Federal Arbitration Act, 9 USC§§1-14; Uniform Arbitration Act, 7 Uniform Laws Annotated I (1978, Supp. 1985).

90 *United States v. Panhandle Eastern Corp et al.*, 118 FDR 346, 10 Fed R Serv 3rd 686 (D. Del. 1988).

91 The AAA Rules provide for the confidentiality of arbitral proceedings (similarly, the AAA Code of Ethics for Arbitrators in Commercial Disputes). Article 34 of the AAA Rules, provides that: '*Confidential information disclosed during the proceedings by the parties or by witnesses shall not be divulged by an arbitrator or by the administrator. Unless otherwise agreed by the parties, or required by applicable law, the members of the tribunal and the administrator shall keep confidential all matters relating to the arbitration or to the award*'. Article 28.4 of the AAA Rules provides: '*An award may be made public only with the consent of all parties or as required by law*'.

withdraw their dispute from public courts and submit it to the decision of a private individual.[92] For this reason, confidentiality in arbitration has been recognised only as an implied duty arising from privacy and privilege. The precise legal basis of this form of privacy was first examined in the decision *Oxford Shipping Co. v. Nippon Yusen Kaisha* ('*The Eastern Saga*').[93] In this decision, the court rejected the argument that the arbitrator had an implied power to override the rights of the parties to a confidential hearing.[94] Legal commentators consider that this decision was founded upon an implied term in the arbitration agreement (subject to an explicit agreement of the parties to the contrary) that each arbitration is private to the parties, requiring strangers to be excluded from the hearing and the conduct of the proceedings.[95] Following the decision in *The Eastern Saga*, it was held in *Dolling-Baker v. Merrett*[96] that both parties have an implied obligation, arising out the very nature of arbitration, not to disclose documents or evidence produced in arbitration. English courts have also considered that the implied duty of confidentiality in relation to arbitration arises out of long-standing custom or the business efficacy of private arbitration.[97] In *Ali Shipping Corporation v. Shipyard Trogir,*[98] the English Court of Appeal implied a duty of confidentiality into an arbitration agreement by operation of law.[99] The Court of Appeal held, however, that the legal duty of confidentiality was not absolute and that exceptions to it were still being defined.[100]

In France, it has been asserted that, even if there is no express written agreement on confidentiality, the tradition of discretion in the private settlement of disputes gives rise to a duty of confidentiality applicable to the arbitrators and the parties (unless the parties have agreed otherwise), which extends to the award. In a widely noted decision, the Paris Court of Appeal addressed the issue of confidentiality in dismissing a party's application to challenge an award, which had been brought before a court that clearly lacked jurisdiction over the application.[101] The Court of Appeal ruled that the very commencement of the proceedings violated the principle of confidentiality because it

---

92 See the expert report of S. BOYD QC in (1995) 11/3 Arb. Int'l 267.

93 See *Oxford Shipping Co. v. Nippon Yusen Kaisha* (The 'Eastern Saga') [1994] 2 LR 373, where the Court addressed the issue of the privacy of the arbitration in the context of hearings, but did not refer to the issue of confidentiality. It appears to have been the first case in which the privacy of arbitral proceedings was in question: expert report of S. BOYD QC, *op. cit.*, p. 267.

94 *Ibid.*, p. 68.

95 LORD JUSTICE STEYN/V.V. VEEDER QC in ICCA International Handbook on Commercial Arbitration, 1988, p. 12, quoting Mr Justice Leggatt, cited by S. BOYD QC, *op. cit.*, p. 268.

96 *Dolling-Baker v. Merrett* [1990] 1 WLR 1205.

97 L. E. TRAKMAN, *op. cit.*, N. 19, p. 9 citing COLEMAN J. in *Hassneh Insurance of Israel v. Mew* [1993] 2 LR 243.

98 [1998] 2 All ER 136.

99 L. E. TRAKMAN, *op. cit.*, p. 9; H. BAGNER, *op. cit.*, p. 244.

100 L. E. TRAKMAN, *op. cit.*, p.9.

101 Decision of the Paris Court of Appeal of 18 February 1986 (*Aita v. Ojjeh*) in [1986] Rev. Arb. 583.

'had caused a public debate of facts which should remain confidential' and that it is in 'the very nature of arbitral proceedings that they ensure the highest degree of discretion in the resolution of private disputes, as the two parties had agreed'.[102] The Court of Appeal ordered the challenging party to pay a substantial penalty to the party that had won the arbitration.

The Swedish Supreme Court has declared that there is no legal duty of confidentiality implied or inherent in an arbitration agreement.[103] The parties normally recognise confidentiality because both parties are interested in restricting the information that becomes available to the public. The parties thus expect that the information revealed in arbitral proceedings will be treated with discretion, and they are obviously free to enter into express confidentiality agreements. But the Supreme Court did not find that an arbitration agreement creates an *implied* legal duty of confidentiality giving rise to legal sanctions, such as damages. The Supreme Court found that the Swedish Arbitration Act is silent on confidentiality and that there is no generally accepted opinion among Swedish lawyers, arbitrators and legal commentators that such a duty of confidentiality exists. The Supreme Court noted that even international opinion on this question was divided.

By contrast, Australian courts[104] have found that confidentiality is not an essential attribute of arbitration and thus that there is no objection to parties to an arbitration disclosing documents or other information. In *Esso/BHP v. Plowman*, the Australian High Court recognised that the public has a legitimate interest in obtaining information about the affairs of public entities, including information that comes to light in arbitrations involving public entities. This is a watershed decision in that the Australian High Court considered that there is a presumption of non-confidentiality in any arbitration in which a state or public entity is a party.

In summary, with one exception, the national arbitration laws reviewed here do not address the issue of confidentiality. Furthermore, the principle of confidentiality in arbitration is subject to different treatment in different jurisdictions. For example, U.S. courts have held that the duty of confidentiality that may only arise from an express agreement between the parties or from arbitration rules. In other jurisdictions such as England, it appears there is a presumption of confidentiality – an implied term – that flows from the private nature of arbitration and from the parties' expectation that the arbitral proceedings and the award will be kept confidential. Legal commentators point out that uncertainties remain regarding the justification and extent of the confidentiality of arbitration, as well as which persons are bound by the duty of confidentiality, although it is generally clear that arbitrators are subject to this duty.[105]

---

102 *Ibid.*

103 Case No. T-6-111-98, *Bulgarian Foreign Trade Bank Ltd v. A.I. Trade Finance Inc.*

104 See *Esso/BHP v. Plowman* ((1995) 128 ALR 391).

105 FOUCHARD/GAILLARD/GOLDMAN, N. 1132, p. 612.

V. The ambit of confidentiality under institutional arbitration rules

Based upon an analysis of a number of institutional arbitration rules from Europe, the United States and Asia contained in an expert report submitted in *Esso/BHP v. Plowman*, it appears that there are considerable differences in the treatment of the duty of confidentiality,[106] although institutional arbitration rules generally provide for some degree of confidentiality. Some rules impose a duty on arbitrators and parties to keep confidential information produced in the proceedings.[107] However, other rules only provide that the arbitrator is bound by a duty of confidentiality.[108] Quite a number of rules make no reference whatsoever to the question of the confidentiality of the arbitration.[109]

The institutional arbitration rules most often chosen for arbitration in Switzerland are the Swiss Rules, the ICC Rules, the LCIA Rules and the UNCITRAL Rules. As discussed below, there is some variation in the degree of confidentiality provided under these different sets of rules.

The Swiss Rules bind the parties, the arbitrators, the Chambers[110] and the Arbitration Committee[111] to a comprehensive duty of confidentiality, unless the parties expressly agree in writing to the contrary.[112] This duty of confidentiality extends to all orders and

---

106 See J. D.M. Lew, *op. cit.*, pp. 287-288.

107 The Swiss Rules (and, previously, the ZCC Rules and the CCIG Rules), the German Arbitration Committee Rules, the London Metal Exchange Rules and the Reinsurance Arbitration Rules of the LCIA (1983).

108 For instance, the AAA and the Code of Ethics for Arbitrators in Commercial Disputes subscribed to by the AAA.

109 For instance, the Euro-Arab Chambers of Commerce, the Hong Kong Arbitration Centre, the CAS, the UNCITRAL Arbitration Rules, the Arbitration Institute of the Stockholm Chamber of Commerce.

110 The Chambers of Commerce and Industry of Basel, Bern, Geneva, Ticino, Vaud and Zurich are referred to collectively in the Swiss Rules as 'the Chambers'; see Introduction (b) of the Swiss Rules and Chapter 10 *infra*.

111 For administration of arbitrations under the Swiss Rules, the Chambers have appointed an Arbitration Committee to exercise the powers vested in the Chambers under the said Rules. Any reference to the Chambers in the Swiss Rules is deemed to refer to the Arbitration Committee; see Introduction (d) and (e) of the Swiss Rules and Chapter 10 *infra*.

112 Article 43 of the Swiss Rules provides: '*(1) Unless the parties expressly agree in writing to the contrary, the parties undertake as a general principle to keep confidential all awards and orders as well as all materials submitted by another party in the framework of the arbitral proceedings not otherwise in the public domain, save and to the extent that a disclosure may be required of a party by a legal duty, to protect or pursue a legal right or to enforce or challenge an award in legal proceedings before a judicial authority. This undertaking also applies to the arbitral tribunal and the Chambers. (2) The deliberations of the arbitral tribunal are confidential. (3) An award may be published, whether in its entirety or in the form of excerpts or a summary, only under the following conditions: (a) A request for publication is addressed to the Chambers; (b) All references to the parties' names are*

awards as well as all materials, as long as they are not in the public domain, that are submitted by a party in the proceedings. A proviso is made that disclosure is permitted to the extent necessitated: (a) by a legal duty to disclose; (b) to protect or pursue a legal right; or (c) to challenge or enforce an award before courts. The duty of confidentiality of the arbitrators under the Swiss Rules also applies to the deliberations of the arbitral tribunal. Finally, the Swiss Rules provide that publication of an award, or a part thereof, is possible, provided that a request is made to the Chambers, the parties do not object and the names of the parties are not revealed.

Article 30 of the LCIA Rules[113] refers to confidentiality in somewhat similar (although narrower) terms as the Swiss Rules.[114] Unless there is an agreement in writing to the contrary, the parties are under the obligation to keep confidential all awards and all materials in the proceedings created for the purpose of the arbitration, as well as all documents produced by another party in the proceedings that are not otherwise in the public domain. The LCIA Rules also carry the proviso that a party is entitled to disclose such documents: (a) if it is under a legal duty to do so; (b) if disclosure is necessary to protect or pursue a legal right; or (c) to enforce or challenge an award in *bona fide* legal proceedings. As for the arbitrators' duty of confidentiality, the LCIA Rules only stipulate that the deliberations of the arbitral tribunal are confidential. The LCIA does not publish awards unless both the parties and the arbitral tribunal consent.

In marked contrast to both the Swiss Rules and the LCIA Rules, the ICC Rules do not deal at all with the confidentiality of the arbitration or of the award and refer only to confidential information. Article 20(7) of the ICC Rules provides that the arbitral tribunal may take measures to protect trade secrets and confidential information. Since no duty of confidentiality is provided under the ICC Rules, arbitrators and parties may, in practice, agree to include a confidentiality provision in the Terms of Reference.

---

deleted; and (c) No party objects to such publication within the time-limit fixed for that purpose by the Chambers'.

113 Article 30 of the LCIA Rules provides: '*(30.1) Unless the parties expressly agree in writing to the contrary, the parties undertake as a general principle to keep confidential all awards in their arbitration, together with all materials in the proceedings created for the purpose of the arbitration and all other documents produced by another party in the proceedings not otherwise in the public domain - save and to the extent that disclosure may be required of a party by legal duty, to protect or pursue a legal right or to enforce or challenge an award in bona fide legal proceedings before a state court or other judicial authority. (30.2) The deliberations of the Arbitral Tribunal are likewise confidential to its members, save and to the extent that disclosure of an arbitrator's refusal to participate in the arbitration is required of the other members of the Arbitral Tribunal under Articles 10, 12 and 26. (30.3) The LCIA Court does not publish any award or any part of an award without the prior written consent of all parties and the Arbitral Tribunal.*'

114 The confidentiality provision in the Swiss Rules greatly resembles that of the LCIA Rules, unlike the previous texts of the ZCC and CCIG Rules.

With respect to arbitration under the ICC Rules, there is, however, a duty of confidentiality applicable to everyone who participates in the work of the ICC Court, i.e. in the administrative bodies of the institution, such as the ICC Court that appoints the arbitrators, the ICC Secretariat and the ICC National Committees (as opposed to the arbitral tribunal deciding the case). This duty of confidentiality is set forth in Article 6 of the Statutes of the ICC Court (Appendix I to the ICC Rules) and in Article 1 of the Internal Rules of the ICC Court (Appendix II of the ICC Rules).

Under the UNCITRAL Rules, there is no explicit mention of confidentiality. However, these rules implicitly acknowledge the confidentiality of the award by stipulating that the award may be made public if both parties consent to it (Article 32(5) of the UNCITRAL Rules).

Undoubtedly, among the institutional arbitration rules, the broad terms of the duty of confidentiality applicable to the parties, the arbitrators and the Chambers under the Swiss Rules provide for the greatest protection in regard to confidentiality.

VI. Providing for confidentiality

Ensuring compliance with the duty of confidentiality is a difficult matter. When confidentiality is an important concern, only an express agreement of the parties concluded *inter se* and with other participants will result in a duty of confidentiality that responds to the parties' expectations and needs. It is important to remember the specific needs of the parties when formulating confidentiality provisions, because legitimate exceptions to confidentiality may apply in the case of one or both parties. Such legitimate exceptions include a party's statutory duty to disclose information, which duty will override any contractual obligations of confidentiality. For this reason, when drafting confidentiality agreements, it is necessary to consider carefully if the parties are under any legal obligations to make disclosure. For example, it may be necessary for a party to disclose the existence and particulars of the dispute, the existence of the arbitration and the award either in due diligence, or to banks, creditors, board members, accountants, auditors, shareholders, insurers, regulatory authorities, etc.

Depending on the parties' objectives in regard to the scope and character of confidentiality to be agreed, the contractual method can be implemented either by an express stipulation in the arbitration agreement itself or a separate confidentiality agreement.[115] If the parties wish that information relating to the arbitration shall remain confidential to the greatest extent possible, a general confidentiality clause in the main contract will be insufficient because it will only bind the parties themselves and will not extend to any third parties who may later become involved in the proceedings and will be potential sources of disclosure.

---

115 L. E. TRAKMAN, *op. cit.*, p.11.

Confidentiality agreements may be prepared in general terms or in specific terms.[116] General confidentiality agreements expressly state that all documents, all pleadings, evidence, the award and the very existence of the arbitration[117] are to be treated as confidential, and that there will only be disclosure of information to the extent required by law or by a competent regulatory body. Specific agreements provide for an obligation of confidentiality that is limited in time, place, space or circumstance, e.g. technical data or a customer list must be kept confidential for a specified number of years. Ideally, both general and specific agreements should expressly stipulate the sanctions for breaching the agreement.[118]

Confidentiality agreements may be adopted before or after the dispute has arisen. Despite growing awareness, it is still rare to find *ex ante* confidentiality agreements, let alone to find elaborate ones. This may well be due to the fact that *ex ante* confidentiality agreements would have to be prepared at a time when the parties are focused on 'positive' factors, i.e. on concluding the contract to implement a transaction, and are therefore unwilling to contemplate 'negative' factors, such as the possibility that the transaction might lead to a dispute.[119]

Ex post agreements can be extended to participants who are not direct parties (and who, as a result, will not be encompassed in a confidentiality agreement between the parties), such as arbitrators (over and above the general duty of confidentiality, if the parties wish to secure additional assurances), counsel (even if legal duties exist between counsel and their clients), witnesses, experts and/or the staff of the arbitral institution. The parties can tailor such agreements to accommodate these special signatories, who often will not all have the same understanding in regard to the extent of confidentiality that is expected in arbitration. Such special signatories may all sign the same agreement or some may require altogether different agreements.[120]

'*Confidentiality has different values to different parties in different contexts*'.[121] This fact is worth remembering when drafting a confidentiality provision or agreement. Confidentiality agreements with specific signatories should be drafted taking into account the circumstances of the signatory in the context of both the dispute and the arbitral proceedings.[122] Likewise, the practitioner should consider the underlying basis of

---

116 J. Paulsson/N. Rawding (*op. cit.*, p. 314) suggest language for confidentiality clauses.

117 Some arbitration specialists are of the opinion that it is unrealistic and undesirable to establish an absolute prohibition against unilateral publication of the mere existence of the arbitration and yet that a legitimate need to divulge such information seldom arises.

118 L. E. Trakman, *op. cit.*, p. 14.

119 H. Bagner, *op. cit.*, p. 248.

120 L. E. Trakman, *op. cit.*, p. 15.

121 *Ibid.*, p. 13.

122 '*In framing specific confidentiality agreements, parties should pay regard to the circumstances surrounding the participants subject to confidentiality, their actual or prospective knowledge about confidential matters, prospective communication with third parties and potential damage arising from such communication*'. *Ibid.*, p. 15.

confidentiality, i.e. the standard of confidentiality that is available at law. One final recommendation – in protracted disputes, confidentiality agreements that were entered into early on in the proceedings should be updated so as to cover new participants.[123]

VII. Confidentiality and trade secrets in Switzerland

Trade secrets require special protection. Article 39 of the TRIPS[124] is a universally accepted provision granting protection to trade secrets.[125]. In those countries that have ratified the TRIPS (such as Switzerland, where it is directly applicable),[126] this multilateral treaty has become the law of trade secrets. Under this law, manufacturing and trade secrets are classified as a right of protected intellectual property and the concept of secrecy is defined, creating a uniform cross-border concept of trade secrecy.

Article 39 of the TRIPS provides that trade secrets must meet the following requirements in order to be entitled to protection: (a) the information must be secret from an objective point of view, i.e. '*it must be secret in the sense that it is not generally known among or readily accessible to persons*' who generally '*deal with the kind of information in question*'; (b) '*it must have a commercial value because it is secret*'; and (c) '*it must have been subject to reasonable steps under the circumstances by the person lawfully in control of the information, to keep it secret*'.[127]

In Switzerland, trade secrets have traditionally enjoyed protection, principally by virtue of provisions of criminal law and the law against unfair competition.[128] Swiss rules of civil procedure also protect the confidentiality of trade secrets.[129]

Moreover, Swiss courts have sought to protect trade secrets *inter alia* by allowing the disclosure of confidential information only to the court.[130] This measure may, however,

---

123 *Ibid.*, p. 13.

124 Agreement on Trade Related Intellectual Property Rights (TRIPS). This agreement resulted from the 1986-94 WTO Uruguay Round trade talks.

125 F. DESSEMONTET, *op. cit.*, p. 11.

126 R. VON BÜREN/L. DAVID, *Schweizerisches Inmaterialgüter- und Wettbewerbsrecht*, Helbing & Lichtenhahn, Basel 2002, p. 52.

127 Article 52(a) of the WIPO Rules has incorporated these requirements: '*For the purposes of this Article, confidential information shall mean any information, regardless of the medium in which it is expressed, which is (i) in the possession of a party, (ii) not accessible to the public, (iii) of commercial, financial or industrial significance, and (iv) treated as confidential by the party possessing it*'.

128 Articles 162, 273 and 321 of the Swiss Criminal Code; Articles 4 and 6 of the Swiss Act Against Unfair Competition; Article 47 of the Swiss Banking Law; O. WENIGER, *La protection des secrets économiques et du savoir-faire (know how)*, thesis, Lausanne 1994, pp. 144-145.

129 Article 203 of the GLCP; Articles 145 and 160 of the ZCCP; F. DESSEMONTET, *op. cit.*, pp. 11-12.

130 [1969-1973] RJN 101; [1975] RSPI 1975 115; DFT 100 Ia 103; DFT 95 I 107; DFT 95 I 445; DFT 92 I 87; DFT 90 II 467; DFT 78 I 88; [1962] BIZR 56; [1985] 51 RSJ 51 269.

be problematic today in view of Article 6 of the European Human Rights Convention[131] and, accordingly, confidentiality agreements or protective orders/confidentiality orders are now preferred.

In Swiss case law, the following types of sensitive information have been identified as deserving protection as trade secrets:[132]

- bids and offers, a pricing policy, terms and conditions for providing goods and services, rebates, an advertising campaign before it is launched, statistical data on turn-over or profitability, loans and borrowings, comments on a balance sheet, taxation schemes, employees' wages;
- compilations of data on service providers and suppliers of raw materials or semi-finished products, as well as their price structure, listings of temporary employees or customers;
- technical tables, blueprints, drawings and designs, software.

When a party objects to a request for production of documents on the grounds that the information is confidential or a trade secret, arbitral tribunals in Switzerland have the power to put in place special measures to protect this information.[133] Arbitrators today deal with a party's objection to produce sensitive documents by issuing a procedural order requiring the requesting party to sign a confidentiality agreement, which would restrict the signatory's use of the confidential documents to the arbitration and limit the number of individuals who will have access to such documents.[134] Alternatively, arbitrators might issue a protective order whereby the arbitral tribunal determines the level of confidentiality of categories of documents, the access to such documents and the restricted use of them in the framework of the proceedings.[135]

In those cases where the parties have agreed upon the application of the IBA Rules, the arbitral tribunal may, on the basis of Article 9(2)(e), exclude from the evidence or refuse to order production of any document, statement, oral testimony or inspection that it determines to be commercially or technically confidential.[136]

---

131 See footnote 21 *supra*.

132 O. WENIGER, *op. cit.*, p. 163.

133 Generally, under Article 183 of the PILA and, in the ICC arbitration, under Article 20(7) of the ICC Rules. The arbitrators may also be inspired by the cantonal procedural rules, such as Article 203 of the GLCP or Article 145 of the ZCCP.

134 FOUCHARD/GAILLARD/GOLDMAN, N. 1265, p. 692; POUDRET/BESSON, N. 654, p. 588.

135 M. BLESSING suggests so-called protective orders with reference to the applicability of the IBA Rules on the Taking of Evidence in International Commercial Arbitration (adopted by the IBA 1 June 1999). M. BLESSING in BERTI, p. 272.

136 Article 9(2)(e) of the IBA Rules provides as follows: '*(2) The Arbitral Tribunal shall, at the request of a Party or on its own motion, exclude from evidence or production any document, statement, oral testimony or inspection for any of the following reasons: (e) grounds of*

In disputes involving intellectual property, the parties may consider opting for arbitration under the WIPO Rules, which contain very comprehensive provisions for confidentiality, a concern which is particularly acute in intellectual property disputes (Articles 52 and 73 to 76 of the WIPO Rules).

Even in non-intellectual property arbitrations, the arbitral tribunal may propose the adoption of arrangements similar to those set forth in Articles 52(d) and (e) of the WIPO Rules, which involve either: (i) designating a 'confidentiality advisor' (who will be required to sign a confidentiality agreement) to determine whether the information rightly deserves to be classified as confidential and, if so, the conditions and persons to whom it may be disclosed in whole or in part; or (ii) appointing such a confidentiality advisor as an expert who shall report to the arbitral tribunal on specific issues contained in the confidential information which the arbitral tribunal considers to be relevant, without disclosing all of the confidential information either to the arbitral tribunal or to the opposing party.[137]

VIII. Conclusion

As a general matter, international arbitration is confidential, but the practitioner should not assume that there is a uniform standard of confidentiality. Compared with many other jurisdictions, the Swiss conception of confidentiality in arbitration is broad. It is widely acknowledged that the duty of confidentiality is founded upon the fiduciary relationship that exists between the arbitrators and the parties and upon the implicit duty of the parties arising from the arbitration agreement. The parties' implicit duty of confidentiality has not, however, been tested before the Swiss courts. Notwithstanding this fact, the Swiss arbitration community accepts, as a matter of practice, that international arbitration is confidential in Switzerland.

If the parties are concerned about confidentiality, they should take steps to reinforce the legal basis of confidentiality existing in Switzerland by making an explicit contractual

---

commercial or technical confidentiality that the Arbitral Tribunal determines to be compelling'.

137 Articles 52(d) and (e) of the WIPO Rules read: '*(d) In exceptional circumstances, in lieu of itself determining whether the information is to be classified as confidential and of such nature that the absence of special measures of protection in the proceedings would be likely to cause serious harm to the party invoking its confidentiality, the Tribunal may, at the request of a party or on its own motion and after consultation with the parties, designate a confidentiality advisor who will determine whether the information is to be so classified, and, if so, decide under which conditions and to whom it may in part or in whole be disclosed. Any such confidentiality advisor shall be required to sign an appropriate confidentiality undertaking; (e) The Tribunal may also, at the request of a party or on its own motion, appoint the confidentiality advisor as an expert in accordance with Article 55 in order to report to it, on the basis of the confidential information, on specific issues designated by the Tribunal without disclosing the confidential information either to the party from whom the confidential information does not originate or to the Tribunal*'.

arrangement or by referring to procedural rules that provide for a strict duty of confidentiality, such as the Swiss Rules. With the proviso that 'confidentiality is never absolute',[138] such explicit provisions for confidentiality, whether contained in a separate contract or the applicable procedural rules, enable the parties to define the scope and extent of confidentiality applicable to the arbitral proceedings in a manner that will be enforced by the arbitrators and by the courts.

138 F. DESSEMONTET, *op. cit.*, p. 9.

Chapter 7 – The Law Governing the Merits of the Dispute and Awards *ex Aequo et Bono*

Fabrizio La Spada

I. Introduction

In arbitration, the parties entrust the arbitral tribunal with the mission of resolving their dispute. In order to resolve the dispute, the arbitral tribunal must determine the facts and apply the law to these facts. The arbitral tribunal may, in certain instances, be empowered to rule *ex aequo et bono.*

This chapter addresses the manner in which the arbitral tribunal determines the rules governing the merits of the dispute. The conflict of laws rules applicable by the arbitral tribunal are reviewed (Section II *infra*), the parties' choice of law is then examined (Section III *infra*), and the determination of the law governing the merits in the absence of a contractual choice is considered (Section IV *infra*). Several additional questions are also examined, including the impact of *lois d'application immédiate* and the status of applicable law in arbitration (Section V *infra*), as well as awards *ex aequo et bono* (Section VI *infra*), before concluding with a consideration of the sanctions for non-compliance with the rules on the determination of the law applicable to the substance of the dispute (Section VII *infra*).

II. Application of the conflict of laws rule of the *lex arbitri*

The jurisdiction of an arbitral tribunal is primarily based on an arbitration agreement entered into by the parties,[1] and is not derived from any connection with a state. It can thus be said that the arbitral tribunal is, in a sense, 'de-nationalized'. As a consequence, arbitral tribunals do not have a '*lex fori*' and, in particular, they are not subject to the private international law applicable to the courts of one country or another.[2]

---

1 See Chapter 2 *supra*.

2 BUCHER, N. 227, pp. 79-80; Y. DERAINS, *L'ordre public et le droit applicable au fond du litige dans l'arbitrage international*, in (1986) 10 Rev. Arb. 380-381.

G. Kaufmann-Kohler and B. Stucki (eds), International Arbitration in Switzerland, A Handbook for Practitioners, 115-134.

However, arbitral tribunals are subject to a '*lex arbitri*', which governs the arbitration and may contain rules on the determination of the substantive law applicable to the dispute. Since the '*lex arbitri*' is generally determined by the seat of the arbitral tribunal, it can be said that the choice of the seat is an indirect choice of the applicable arbitration law.[3] In other words, the arbitral tribunal must determine the applicable substantive law not on the basis of conflict of laws rules contained in any national private international law,[4] but pursuant to methods specific to international arbitration.[5]

Chapter 12 of the PILA contains a specific provision dealing with the determination of the applicable substantive law – Article 187(1) – which establishes the autonomy of the arbitral tribunal with respect to Swiss private international law: '*The arbitral tribunal shall decide the case according to the rules of law chosen by the parties or, in the absence thereof, according to the rules of law with which the case has the closest connection*'.

This provision applies to all international arbitral tribunals having their seat in Switzerland within the meaning of Article 176(2) of the PILA. It confirms that the conflict of laws rules contained in the Swiss private international law are not applicable to the determination of the applicable substantive law in international arbitrations.[6] In other words, Article 187(1) of the PILA constitutes in itself the *entire private international law or conflict of laws system* applicable to arbitral tribunals having their seat in Switzerland.[7]

---

3 P. KARRER in BERTI, N. 52, p. 496; G. KAUFMANN-KOHLER, *Identifying and Applying the Law Governing the Arbitration Procedure – the Role of the Law of the Place of Arbitration* in (1999) 9 ICCA Congress Series, pp. 336-365.

4 In particular, it is generally recognised that there is no legal basis, in Switzerland or most other countries, for imposing upon arbitral tribunals the application of the private international law of the seat of the arbitral tribunal (BUCHER, N. 235, p. 82). At the international level, Article VII(1) of the European Convention on International Commercial Arbitration of 1961 confirms this autonomy of arbitral tribunals in respect of national private international law: '*The parties shall be free to determine, by agreement, the law to be applied by the arbitrators to the substance of the dispute. Failing any indication by the parties as to the applicable law, the arbitrators shall apply the proper law under the rule of conflict that the arbitrators deem applicable. In both cases the arbitrators shall take account of the terms of the contract and trade usages*'.

5 BUCHER, N. 226, p. 80; Y. DERAINS, *op. cit.*, N. 11, p. 381.

6 BUCHER, N. 239, pp. 81-83. See also P. KARRER in BERTI, N. 53, p. 496, who observes that, for an international arbitral tribunal having its seat in Switzerland, no precedence is generally given to Swiss law over foreign law and no precedence is given to Swiss private international law over foreign private international law.

7 P. KARRER in BERTI, N. 37, p. 493 and N. 79, p. 500. See also LALIVE/POUDRET/REYMOND, N. 2, p. 389, who consider that Article 187 of the PILA establishes the independence of Chapter 12 of the PILA from all other parts of Swiss private international law.

This system provides as the *first connecting factor* the choice of law by the parties (see Section III *infra*) and, as a *subsidiary connecting factor*, the concept of the '*closest connection*' with the case (see Section IV *infra*).

III. Rules of law chosen by the parties

1. Preliminary comment

There is a generally applicable principle[8] that directs international arbitral tribunals to the correct choice of law for an international commercial contract: the autonomy of the parties, i.e. the freedom of the parties to choose the law (or the relevant rules)[9] applicable to their contract.[10] Indeed, several legal commentators submit that arbitral tribunals must respect the parties' choice of law as a matter of transnational public policy.[11]

Under Swiss law, Article 187(1) of the PILA codifies this fundamental principle by providing that the first criterion for determining the law applicable to the merits of a dispute is '*the rules of law chosen by the parties*'. This provision, which appears on its face to be straightforward, gives rise to the following main issues:

- What are the requirements as to form and substance that the parties' choice of law must fulfil, i.e. what are the requirements for validity of such choice?
- What are the effects and scope of this choice?
- When do the parties have to make this choice?
- What are the limits of the parties' choice?

---

8 J. D.M. LEW, *Applicable Law in Commercial Arbitration*, Kluwer Law Arbitration, 1978, p. 75: '[...] *despite their differences, common law, civil law and socialist countries have all equally been affected by the movement towards the rule allowing the parties to choose the law to govern their contractual relations. This development has come about independently in every country and without any concerted effort by the nations of the world; it is the result of separate, contemporaneous and pragmatic evolutions, within the various national systems of conflict of laws*'.

9 See Section III.3.b) *infra*.

10 REDFERN/HUNTER, N. 2-24, p. 94; M. BLESSING, *Regulations in Arbitration Rules on Choice of Law* in (1996) 7 ICCA Congress Series 394 and references cited therein.

11 K. P. BERGER, *Internationale Wirtschaftsschiedsgerichtsbarkeit, Verfahrens- und materiellrechtliche Grundprobleme im Spiegel moderner Schiedsgesetze und Schiedspraxis*, W. de Gruyter 1992, pp. 347 *et seq;* P. LALIVE, *Transnational (or Truly International) Public Policy and International Arbitration* in (1987) 3 ICCA Congress Series 257.

2. *Requirements for validity*

According to legal commentators, the validity of the parties' choice of law is governed by the *lex arbitri*.[12] Article 187 of the PILA does not, however, specify any formal or substantive requirements applicable to the choice of the parties.

a) Formal validity

Article 187(1) of the PILA does not contain any requirement as to form. In particular, this provision does not require that the agreement of the parties must be made in writing. In practice, most choice of law clauses are in a written form and are generally contained in the contract, sometimes even in the same contractual provision as the arbitration clause. Nonetheless, Swiss law recognises the validity of a choice of law that is not made in writing.

Moreover, it is generally accepted that the applicable rules of law do not need to be agreed upon expressly. Unlike a number of international conventions on the law applicable to contracts, Swiss arbitration law does not specify that the parties' choice must '*unambiguously result from the provisions of the contract*' or '*be demonstrated with reasonable certainty by the terms of the contract or the circumstances of the case*'.[13] In particular, it must be emphasized that Article 116(2) of the PILA, which contains requirements for the validity of choice of law clauses,[14] is not applicable to the determination of the applicable law by international arbitral tribunals sitting in Switzerland (which are required to apply only Article 187 of the PILA).[15]

As a consequence, an agreement on choice of law can be concluded tacitly, by conduct. This may occur if the parties have made clear references to the provisions or used terminology of a specific national law when performing their contract, or if both parties have presented legal arguments based upon the same substantive law in the course of the arbitral proceedings.[16] On the other hand, the parties' choice of the seat of the arbitral

---

12 POUDRET/BESSON, N. 682, p. 612.

13 See Article 2(2) of the Hague Convention of 15 June 1955 on the Law Applicable to International Sales of Goods and Article 3(1) of the Rome Convention of 19 June 1980 on the Law Applicable to Contractual Obligations. *Contra,* P. KARRER in BERTI, N. 88, p. 503, who submits that, even though the applicable rules of law do not need to be agreed expressly, they must at a minimum result unequivocally from the circumstances '*as they for instance do when the parties did not expressly choose an applicable law but referred to specific provisions of a particular substantive law*'.

14 Article 116(2) of the PILA provides as follows: '*The choice of law must be express or result with certainty from the provisions of the contract or from the circumstances; it is further governed by the chosen law*'.

15 LALIVE/POUDRET/REYMOND, N. 4, p. 390.

16 DFT 102 II 145; LALIVE/POUDRET/REYMOND, N. 4, p. 389; POUDRET/BESSON, N. 682, p. 612 . See also P. BERNARDINI, *L'arbitrato commerciale internazionale*, Giuffrè 2000,

tribunal or reference to the application of a particular procedural law are insufficient grounds, in and of themselves, for finding a tacit choice of substantive law.[17]

b) Substantive validity

Although Article 187(1) of the PILA does not contain any specific requirements for validity and a choice of law can be made tacitly, the arbitral tribunal must nevertheless establish that an *actual choice* has been made by the parties. In other words, there must be *consent* to the applicable substantive law.[18] The arbitral tribunal must be able to determine that the parties intended that the law of one particular country or other specific rules would govern the contract.[19] Once the arbitral tribunal has established the actual intent of the parties, it must enforce their agreement, without examining the merits of the parties' choice or second-guessing whether this choice is legitimate or appropriate.[20] In particular, the arbitral tribunal may not refuse to apply the chosen law because it is incomplete, or surprising in the circumstances of the contractual relationship, or unfair.[21]

If the arbitral tribunal is unable to ascertain the actual and common intent of the parties, it is not entitled to resort to the hypothetical intent[22] of the parties.[23] Rather, in such a case, the arbitral tribunal must conclude that the parties have not agreed upon a choice of law and determine the law applicable to the merits of the dispute on the basis of the closest connection under Article 187(1) of the PILA (*in fine*) (see Section IV *infra*).

A number of legal commentators and arbitral tribunals have expressed the view that, in certain cases, the absence of a choice of law by the parties can be construed as an '*implied negative choice*', i.e. an agreement that no law should be applied to the dispute. In such cases, the absence of a clear choice of law provision in itself is deemed to amount to a negative choice in the sense that the parties agreed not to apply any national law of any country.[24] In ICC Case No. 5953, the parties had negotiated a choice of law

---

p. 197, who submits that a tacit choice of law can also arise out of prior dealings between the parties or the subject matter of the contract, which would be subject to specific legislation.

17 M. BLESSING, *op. cit.*, p. 396.

18 LALIVE/POUDRET/REYMOND, N. 5, p. 390.

19 M. BLESSING, *op. cit.*, p. 396.

20 Y. DERAINS, *L'ordre public et le droit applicable au fond du litige dans l'arbitrage international*, in (1986) 10 Rev. Arb. 380, 381.

21 LEW/MISTELIS/KRÖLL, p. 419.

22 The hypothetical intent of the parties is determined on the basis of what reasonable business people would have agreed if placed in the specific circumstances of the case. It is an objective test. By contrast, Article 187(1) of the PILA (*ab initio*) requires the application of a subjective test.

23 B. DUTOIT, *Droit international privé Suisse: commentaire de la loi fédérale du 18 décembre 1987*, Helbing & Lichtenhahn, N. 3, p. 584 ; P. KARRER in BERTI, N. 88, p. 503; POUDRET/BESSON, N. 682, p. 613.

24 M. BLESSING, *op. cit.*, p. 396.

clause but ultimately failed to come to an agreement on this contractual provision.[25] The arbitral tribunal concluded that the parties had deliberately, albeit tacitly, decided to exclude the application of any national law, in favour of the application of international law.[26]

Under the prevailing view in Switzerland, it is certainly possible for parties to exclude the application of any national law. However, in accordance with the principles set out above, there must be sufficient grounds to establish that the parties *actually agreed* on such exclusion. The mere fact that the parties failed to agree on the applicable law is insufficient.[27]

This view is entirely consistent with Article 187(1) of the PILA – if the parties have not chosen any applicable law, it is the task of the arbitral tribunal to determine the applicable law based upon the objective test of the '*closest connection*' (see Section IV *infra*).

Finally, it should be noted that the parties may also agree indirectly on the applicable substantive law, for example, by referring to a set of arbitration rules. Indeed, many arbitration rules contain provisions dealing with the law that must be applied by the arbitral tribunal to resolve the dispute. For example, Article 17(1) of the ICC Rules provides as follows: '*The parties shall be free to agree upon the rules of law to be applied by the Arbitral Tribunal to the merits of the dispute. In the absence of any such agreement, the Arbitral Tribunal shall apply the rules of law which it determines to be appropriate*'. Similarly, Article 33(1) of the Swiss Rules states the following: '*The arbitral tribunal shall decide the case in accordance with the rules of law agreed upon by the parties or, in the absence of a choice of law, by applying the rules of law with which the dispute has the closest connection*'.[28]

Therefore, if the parties have not specifically agreed upon the applicable substantive law but have made reference to arbitration rules setting forth a method for determining such law, the arbitral tribunal will apply these rules *as the law chosen by the parties*. In these circumstances, the arbitral tribunal will not apply the objective test of Article 187(1) of

---

25 *Primary Coal Inc. (USA) v. Compania Valenciana de Cementos Portland*, Partial Award of 1 September 1988 in ICC Case No. 5953, in [1990] Rev. Arb. 701.

26 *Ibid.*, pp. 710-711. On appeal, the Paris Court of Appeal held that the parties had intended to exclude the application of Spanish, New York and English law and confirmed that the arbitral tribunal is not bound to apply conflict of laws rules arising out of a domestic legal system. On the contrary, the arbitral tribunal can rely on general principles of conflict of laws. For additional references, see M. BLESSING, *op. cit.*, p. 397.

27 P. KARRER in BERTI, N. 89, p. 503; POUDRET/BESSON, N. 682, p. 612.

28 See also, e.g., Article 59 of the WIPO Rules and Article 14 of the LCIA Rules.

the PILA (*in fine*) (see Section IV *infra*).[29] An express choice of law clause will, however, prevail over a reference to arbitration rules.

3. The effects and scope of the parties' choice

According to the wording of Article 187(1) of the PILA, the parties may choose the '*rules of law*' applicable to the case. On this basis,[30] it is generally accepted that the parties' choice is not limited to the designation of a particular national law. Although in practice parties most often agree on a national system of law, they may also agree that their relationship (and any possible dispute arising out of it) will be governed by other rules of law or by transnational rules, such as trade usages or the *lex mercatoria*.

a) National law

In international commercial contracts, the most common choice of law is the choice of a national system of law. Such a choice presents a number of advantages, including the following:[31]

- **Autonomy and comprehensiveness**: a national system of law is not merely a set of general principles or isolated legal rules. It is an interconnected and interdependent collection of rules, designed to address (either directly or through methods of interpretation) all legal situations that may arise.
- **Predictability**: a national system of law clearly exists and is capable of reasonably accurate interpretation, including by reference to case law.
- **Accessibility**: the contents of national laws are organised and easily accessible, thus allowing the parties to ascertain the applicable principles.[32]

The freedom of the parties to choose a national substantive law is almost unlimited. They may, of course, agree upon the national law of one of the parties or another law having an objective connection with the subject matter of their relationship (e.g. the law of the place of performance of contractual obligations). They may also choose a neutral

29 If the parties have chosen the Swiss Rules, the arbitral tribunal will be required to apply a '*closest connection*' test (Article 33(1)). According to certain legal commentators, a reference to arbitration rules should be considered as an agreement on the applicable law only if the parties actually intended it to (also) constitute a choice of law: LALIVE/POUDRET/REYMOND, N. 5, pp. 390-391.

30 It should be noted that the wording of Article 187(1) of the PILA differs in the three Swiss national languages. The French text refers to '*règles de droit*' (i.e., 'rules of law'), whereas the German and Italian texts refer to '*Recht*' and '*diritto*' (i.e., 'law'). However, there is a general consensus that Article 187(1) of the PILA does not limit the parties' choice to national laws.

31 See, e.g., REDFERN/HUNTER, N. 2-29, p. 99.

32 POUDRET/BESSON, N. 681, p. 611.

law, which is unrelated to either party or to the contract.[33] Under Swiss law, there does not need to be any reasonable basis – nor even any reason – for the parties' choice.

Except where specifically provided otherwise, the choice of a specific national law is understood to refer to all of the substantive law provisions of this law,[34] excluding its rules of private international law (conflict of laws rules), so as to avoid any undesired *renvoi.*[35] In particular, the applicable law will include all international conventions forming a part of the national law. In Switzerland, this is notably the case with the CISG.

The parties can include a 'stabilisation' or 'freezing' clause as part of their choice of law, i.e. they may agree that a specific national law at a given moment in time (e.g. the date of execution of their contract) shall govern their relationship, so that any subsequent modifications or new enactments of such law are excluded.[36] This may be particularly useful in contracts with states or state-owned entities, as it protects one party against abuses of the legislative power of its contractual partner.[37] Stabilization clauses may also serve to increase predictability.

b) *'Dépeçage', 'tronc commun',* no rules?

As described above, the choice of the parties is not limited to complete national systems of law. The parties can agree that their relationship will be governed by specific parts of a national system of law or by other rules of law of any kind, including non-state rules of law.[38] Among the possible choices and methods, the following are particularly noteworthy (the *lex mercatoria* is examined separately below):

- ***Dépeçage***: the parties may agree that only certain features of a national legislative system will govern their contract. For example, they may wish to exclude certain mandatory provisions of an otherwise applicable national law.[39]

---

33 FOUCHARD/GAILLARD/GOLDMAN, N. 1435, p. 793.

34 Unless provided otherwise by the parties, it is generally accepted that all substantive rules of law contained in the designated national law are applicable, regardless of their source and regardless of whether they are characterised as private law or public law. On the issue of the applicability of a state's public law, see for example: B. KNAPP, *Le droit Suisse est applicable au présent contrat* in R. PATRY (ed.), *Etudes de Droit International en l'Honneur de Pierre Lalive*, p. 81.

35 M. BLESSING, *op. cit.*, p. 393; P. KARRER in BERTI, N. 91, p. 503; FOUCHARD/GAILLARD/GOLDMAN, N. 1429, p. 790. This view is confirmed by Article 28(1) of the UNCITRAL Model Law: '*Any designation of the law or legal system of a given State shall be construed, unless otherwise expressed, as directly referring to the substantive law of that State and not to its conflict of law rules*'.

36 M. BLESSING, *op. cit.*, p. 395; P. KARRER in BERTI, N. 71, p. 499.

37 FOUCHARD/GAILLARD/GOLDMAN, N. 1437, p. 795.

38 LALIVE/POUDRET/REYMOND, N. 10, p. 393.

39 Y. DERAINS, *op. cit.*, N. 28, p. 390. For example, parties to a mandate contract governed by Swiss law may wish to exclude Article 404 of the SCO, which is mandatory and provides

Similarly, they may wish to choose different laws to apply to different aspects of their relationship or their dispute. Such a *dépeçage* is possible as a result of the autonomy of the parties with respect to the choice of substantive law established under Article 187(1) of the PILA. It should be stressed that, while possible in theory, an agreement to apply components of several different legal systems is most often inappropriate in practice.

- ***Tronc commun***: the doctrine of *tronc commun* is based upon the assumption that, if free to do so, each party would choose its own national law to apply to the relationship. Although this is not possible in practice, the parties can nevertheless go some way toward achieving this objective by agreeing that the contract shall be governed by the common parts of their respective national systems of law.[40] For example: *'This contract shall in all respects be governed by and interpreted in accordance with the principles common to both English law and French law, and in the absence of such common principles by such general principles of international trade law as have been applied by national and international tribunals'*.[41] An arbitral tribunal should enforce such a clause under Article 187(1) of the PILA. However, parties must be aware that a *tronc commun* provision can create significant difficulties and lead to battles of comparative law experts in an effort to determine the extent to which two national laws coincide.[42]

- **No rule at all?** The considerable freedom enjoyed by the parties in regard to choice of law raises the question of whether the parties can go so far as to stipulate that their contract is self-sufficient and is not governed by any rules of law.[43] The purpose of such a choice is to ensure that the examination of the validity and scope of the contract will be performed without any reference to

---

that mandate contracts can be terminated by either party at any time. *Contra* J.-B. RACINE, *L'arbitrage commercial international et l'ordre public*, Librairie générale de droit et de jurisprudence, Paris 1999, N. 410, p. 241.

40 M. RUBINO-SAMMARTANO, *Le "tronc commun" des lois nationales en présence (réflexions sur le droit applicable par l'arbitre international)* in (1987) 4/2 Rev. Arb. 133 ; REDFERN/HUNTER, N. 2-43, pp. 107 *et seq.*

41 Cited in REDFERN/HUNTER, N. 2-43, p. 108.

42 M. BLESSING, *op. cit.*, pp. 398-400; P. RAOUL-DUVAL, *English and French law: The Search for Common Principles* in (1997) 25 International Business Lawyer 182 (on the clause cited above: *'The main reason for the difficulty in applying a clause providing for the application of common principles between English and French law is that although both systems tend to produce the same or very similar results, they fall short of providing the set of common principles which is necessary to cover all contractual disputes')*.

43 This situation is different from the case where parties decide to exclude the applicability of any national law, but still accept that their relationship be governed by rules of law, e.g. by general principles of law or the *lex mercatoria*: see FOUCHARD/GAILLARD/GOLDMAN, N. 1440, p. 799.

rules that would prevail over the contract. It is generally considered that, with the exception of cases involving *amiable composition*, the parties' freedom with respect to choice of law does not extend to the exclusion of any rules. For example, according to FOUCHARD/GAILLARD/GOLDMAN, if faced with a contractual provision excluding the application of all rules of law, the arbitral tribunal will nevertheless be at liberty to apply the rules of law they consider to be appropriate (or, in Switzerland, with which the case has the closest connection).[44]

c) The choice of the *lex mercatoria*

Despite its many advantages, the choice of a national system of law may present difficulties to parties in certain circumstances. Indeed, even well developed and modern commercial law codes are not always well suited to the needs of international commerce. It is thus generally accepted that the parties are free to subject their relationship to transnational law, general principles of law, international trade law, or the *lex mercatoria*.[45] Rather than examining the various possible definitions of the expression '*lex mercatoria*', this term will be used as a generic description of rules of transnational law developed by the international business community to regulate commercial activities within this community.[46] For the parties, the advantage of choosing such rules of law to govern their contract is that they are intended to address business needs and be of uniform application, so as to avoid the vagaries of different national laws.[47] Moreover, the *lex mercatoria* is customary and spontaneous in nature – it is therefore capable of adapting to the changing realities of commerce, with the addition of new principles established by general and constant usage in international trade.[48]

The content of the *lex mercatoria* is – almost by definition – not clearly established. This can, in turn, create problems of predictability, since parties who decide to choose the *lex mercatoria* as the applicable substantive law may not be able to determine with precision which rules will be applied to the dispute by the arbitral tribunal. Compared to national

44 *Ibid.*, p. 801, further mentioning that '*a careful analysis of awards which state that they accept the theory of contracts with no governing law shows that they in fact consider it necessary to apply general principles of law*'.

45 M. BLESSING, *op. cit.*, p. 400; FOUCHARD/GAILLARD/GOLDMAN, N. 1448, p. 807. On the possibility of agreeing upon the *lex mercatoria* as the governing law under Article 187(1) of the PILA, see e.g. LALIVE/POUDRET/REYPOND, N. 10, p. 393.

46 For additional materials on the definition of *lex mercatoria*, see e.g. LEW/MISTELIS/KRÖLL, pp. 451 *et seq.*; FOUCHARD/GAILLARD/GOLDMAN, N. 1446-1447, pp. 805-806 and references cited therein.

47 REDFERN/HUNTER, N. 2-60, p. 118.

48 B. GOLDMAN, *La lex mercatoria dans les contrats et l'arbitrage internationaux, Réalités et perspectives* in (1979) 106 JDI 475.

law, the *lex mercatoria* can be seen as vague and incomplete.[49] However, as GAILLARD has observed, '*the most fundamental answer to the criticism arising from the difficulty of determining the content of transnational rules, is that the recourse to such rules is simply a method, not a list. This method calls upon elements of comparative law, rules of international law (such as model laws and international treaties) and, in particular, arbitration case law*'.[50]

Sources of the *lex mercatoria* can be found, notably, in international conventions which would not be applicable to the dispute, but which are considered to reflect a general consensus (for example, the CISG). Moreover, other rules, contained in internationally accepted principles and standards (such as the UNIDROIT Principles[51] or the Incoterms), can also be considered as part of the *lex mercatoria*.[52] Article 38 of the Statute of the International Court of Justice, which refers to '*international custom, as evidence of a general practice accepted as law*' and to '*the general principles of law recognized by civilized nations*' may also provide guidance when seeking to ascertain the contents of the *lex mercatoria*.

An analysis of the content of the *lex mercatoria* would exceed the scope of this chapter. However, it should be noted that the following main principles are generally considered to be part of transnational law rules: *pacta sunt servanda, clausula rebus sic stantibus*, principle that contracts should be performed in good faith, *exceptio non adimpleti contractus, force majeure*. BERGER has established a useful catalogue of principles, rules, and standards of the *lex mercatoria*.[53]

A choice of law clause designating the *lex mercatoria* does not empower the arbitral tribunal to decide *ex aequo et bono* or as *amiable compositeur*.[54] On the contrary, although the content of this 'law' may be difficult to establish, arbitral tribunals must apply the rules that they determine are part of it.[55] In order to do so, arbitral tribunals will generally first construe the parties' choice of law agreement. Indeed, the generic terms '*lex mercatoria*' or 'general principles of law' may encompass a broad diversity of concepts and it is essential to establish what the parties intended when they referred to them. In this respect, any indications given by the parties as to the method of

---

49 See FOUCHARD/GAILLARD/GOLDMAN, N. 1454, pp. 811-812. For an answer to this criticism, see: A. LOWENFELD, *Lex Mercatoria: An Arbitrator's View* in [1990] Arb. Int'l. 133.

50 E. GAILLARD (ed.), *Transnational Rules in International Commercial Arbitration*, Chambre de Commerce Internationale (CCI), Paris 1993, p. 104.

51 On the UNIDROIT Principles, see e.g. *UNIDROIT Principles of International Commercial Contracts, Reflections on their Use in International Arbitration* in ICC Bulletin, 2002 Special Supplement.

52 See e.g. LEW/MISTELIS/KRÖLL, pp. 461 *et seq.*

53 K. P. BERGER, *The Creeping Codification of the Lex Mercatoria*, The Hague 1999, pp. 279-311.

54 See Section V *infra*; A. LOWENFELD, *op. cit.*, p. 141.

55 M. MUSTILL, *op. cit.*, pp. 102-103.

determining the applicable rules must take precedence. Such indications may include a specified hierarchy between various given sources or instructions to apply only principles common to certain regions of the world.[56] Moreover, the arbitral tribunal should determine the applicable rules by examining comparative law, international instruments and international case law, including arbitral awards.

4. The time of the choice

Based upon the principle of party autonomy, the parties have the right to determine the law applicable to their relationship at the time of contracting as well as thereafter.[57] It is thus accepted that the parties may agree on the applicable substantive law at any time before or after a dispute arises, including at the time when the arbitral tribunal's terms of reference are established or even at a later stage in the arbitral proceedings.[58] If the parties have already included a choice of law clause in their contract, they are free to modify it at any time.

From a practical point of view, it is generally accepted that concurring written submissions by the parties concerning the applicable substantive law are binding on the arbitral tribunal.[59]

5. The limits on the parties' freedom of choice

Although the parties' freedom to determine the applicable substantive law is very broad, it is not without boundaries. On the contrary, arbitral tribunals will, in certain circumstances, apply rules which do not correspond to the parties' choice of law.

a) Scope of the law chosen by the parties

The first limitation on the parties' freedom to choose the applicable law is directly related to the scope of the chosen law. Indeed, a number of specific questions fall outside of the parties' autonomy. For example, the capacity of a party to enter into a contract or the power of a person to represent a company will be governed by the law applicable to that party or company, irrespective of a different choice of law clause applicable to the contract itself. This is due to the fact that a party's capacity and power to contract are questions that arise before the question of the choice of law governing the contract. Consequently, the law governing this type of pre-existing issue must be determined on an objective basis, i.e. by determining the law with the closest connection to this specific issue (Article 187 of the PILA).[60]

---

56 FOUCHARD/GAILLARD/GOLDMAN, N. 1457, p. 815.
57 REDFERN/HUNTER, p. 96.
58 POUDRET/BESSON, N. 683, p. 613.
59 LEW/MISTELIS/KRÖLL, p. 415; FOUCHARD/GAILLARD/GOLDMAN, N. 1430, p. 790.
60 *Ibid.*, N. 1532, p. 860.

b) *Lois de police* or *lois d'application immédiate*

The parties' choice of law may also be defeated by the application of so-called *lois de police* or *lois d'application immédiate.* A *loi de police* or *loi d'application immédiate* is a mandatory rule of national law which governs certain international situations.

In international arbitration, it is necessary to distinguish between two different situations. In the first situation, the *loi d'application immédiate* is part of the law governing the merits. The arbitral tribunal must apply the *loi d'application immédiate* as part of the national system of law governing the dispute. For example, in a 1992 decision, the Swiss Federal Tribunal held that an arbitrator sitting in Switzerland was required to examine the applicability of EU competition law in a matter in which Belgian law applied to the contract.

In the second situation, the *loi d'application immédiate* is part of the legal system of a third country, i.e. a country that is not the one whose law applies to the merits of the dispute. Without entering into the intricacies of this issue, it should be noted that, according to the traditional view, the arbitral tribunal is not bound to apply such a third country *loi d'application immédiate.*[61] This view is often tempered by the consideration that the arbitral tribunal should take into account the mandatory rules of the law of the place of performance of the contract or of the enforcement of the award[62] in order to ensure the effectiveness of the award.

In recent years, there has, however, been a strong emerging opinion that arbitral tribunals must take into account the *lois d'application immédiate* of laws other than the *lex causae.*[63] It is reasonable to maintain that arbitral tribunals sitting in Switzerland should do so by applying by analogy the tests of Article 19 of the PILA.[64] These tests are the following: the *loi d'application immédiate* must be meant to govern international situations such as the one before the arbitral tribunal; it must have a strong connection

---

61 See the description of the different views of Swiss authors in P. KARRER in BERTI, N. 135, p. 513. See also the decision of the Swiss Federal Tribunal of 30 December 1994 in [1997] ASA Bull. 217, 225 and the references cited therein.

62 LALIVE/POUDRET/REYMOND, N. 13, p. 396 ; J.-B. RACINE, *op. cit.*, pp. 273 *et seq.*

63 See, e.g., A. RIGOZZI, *op. cit.*, pp. 461 *et seq.*; BUCHER, N. 257, p. 89; M. BLESSING in BERTI, pp. 228 *et seq.*

64 Article 19 reads as follows: '*(1) When interests that are legitimate and clearly preponderant according to the Swiss conception of law so require, a mandatory provision of another law than the one referred to in this Act may be taken into consideration, provided that the situation dealt with has a close connection with such other law. (2) In deciding whether such provision is to be taken into consideration, one shall consider its aim and the consequences of its application, in order to reach a decision that is appropriate having regard to the Swiss conception of law*'. A. RIGOZZI, *op. cit.*, p. 466. See also M. BLESSING, *Mandatory Rules of Law versus Party Autonomy* in [1997] J. Int'l Arb. 31, 32; M. BLESSING, *Introduction to Arbitration: Swiss and international perspectives*, Helbing & Lichtenhahn, Basle 1999, pp. 260 *et seq.*

with the dispute; and the objectives it seeks to achieve must appear to be worthy of protection in the view of the arbitral tribunal.

The issue of the application of mandatory provisions of 'foreign' law is especially relevant in relation to competition law, in particular EU competition law. In this respect, the Swiss Federal Tribunal has ruled that arbitral tribunals sitting in Switzerland are required to apply Article 85 of the Rome Treaty ('EC Treaty') (now Article 81), even if the parties have agreed on the application of Swiss law to the merits of their dispute.[65]

However, from a practical point of view, an award that does not take into account EU competition law could not be set aside in Switzerland. Indeed, even though Articles 81 and 82 of the EC Treaty are mandatory provisions which must be applied by arbitral tribunals sitting in Switzerland, the Swiss Federal Tribunal has concluded that these provisions are not part of public policy within the meaning of Article 190(2)(e) of the PILA.[66]

The position on this issue is different within the EU. According to the Court of Justice of the European Communities, an award rendered by an arbitral tribunal sitting in the EU which violates Article 81 of the EC Treaty is contrary to public policy and will thus be set aside.[67] In addition, the Court has ruled that Article 81 of the EC Treaty could be considered to be a provision of public policy within the meaning of Article V(2)(b) of the NY Convention.[68]

c) International public policy

It is generally accepted that arbitral tribunals are entitled to disregard the provisions of the substantive law chosen by the parties where they consider these provisions to be contrary to international public policy.[69] In fact, one can argue that arbitral tribunals *must* disregard such provisions, since in most countries, an award may be set aside or refused recognition if it is contrary to international public policy.[70]

It is not an easy task to determine the content of international public policy. Generally speaking, it consists of a narrow range of values widely recognised as fundamental in the international community.[71] However, a rule need not be adopted unanimously in all

---

65 Decision of the Swiss Federal Tribunal of 13 November 1998 in [1999] ASA Bull. 529.

66 *Ibid.*, p. 534. See A. RIGOZZI, *op. cit.*, p. 474.

67 CJCE *Eco Swiss China Time Ltd v. Benetton International NV* of 1 June 1999, C-126/97 in [1999] ASA Bull. 414, 424.

68 *Ibid.*, p. 425.

69 LEW/MISTEL/KRÖLL, p. 422; J.-B. RACINE, *op. cit.*, pp. 355 *et seq.*

70 See in particular Article V(2)(b) of the NY Convention. For the situation in Switzerland, see Chapter 9 *infra*.

71 J. D.M. LEW, *op. cit.*, p. 532 who defines public policy as '*the fundamental economic, legal, moral, political, religious and social standards of every state or extra-national community. Naturally, public policy differs according to the character and structure of the state or*

jurisdictions in order to be considered as reflecting the requirements of a genuinely international public policy.[72] International public policy rules include, for example, the principle *pacta sunt servanda*, observance of good faith, the prohibition of spoliation and discriminatory measures, the prohibition of bribery and corrupt practices and the prohibition of expropriation without compensation.[73]

IV. Absence of choice by the parties – the '*closest connection*' test

If the parties have not chosen the applicable substantive law, either expressly or tacitly, Article 187(1) of the PILA *in fine* provides that the arbitral tribunal shall decide the case '*according to the rules of law with which the case has the closest connection*'.

The power of the arbitral tribunal to determine the applicable law exists only in the absence of a choice of law by the parties. Indeed, if the parties have made such a choice, even tacitly, the arbitral tribunal is bound by it. As one arbitral tribunal has stated, '*the arbitrator has no power to substitute his own choice to that of the parties, as soon as there exists an expressed, clear and unambiguous choice, and no sufficient reason has been put forward to refuse effects to such a choice*'.[74]

On the other hand, in the absence of a choice of law by the parties, Article 187(1) of the PILA empowers the arbitral tribunal to determine the law applicable to the merits of the dispute directly, without the need to resort to conflict of laws rules contained in Swiss private international law.[75] In other words, the arbitral tribunal is bound by a specific conflict of laws rule which constitutes the complete private international law system applicable to the arbitration.[76]

1. Rules of law with which the case has the closest connection

Article 187(1) of the PILA (*in fine*) gives broad discretion to the arbitral tribunal to determine the applicable substantive law. However, this provision nevertheless requires that the applicable law be determined on the basis of an objective criterion – the arbitral tribunal must look for rules of law having the closest connection with the matter in dispute. This choice of law rule precludes the arbitral tribunal from applying other choice of law rules or from exercising greater discretion in its determination of the

---

community to which it appertains, and covers those principles and standards which are so sacrosanct as to require their maintenance at all costs and without exception'.

72 FOUCHARD/GAILLARD/GOLDMAN, N. 1535, p. 863.

73 [1999] RSDIE 603; [1999] ASA Bull. 537, 539; [1999] ASA Bull. 529, 533; [1998] ASA Bull. 118, 130; [1998] ASA Bull. 634, 644; [1998] ASA Bull. 653, 659; [1997] ASA Bull. 291, 304; [1995] ASA Bull. 217, 224; DFT 120 II 155, 166; DFT 117 II 604, 606-607; DFT 116 II 634, 636-637. For additional information on this issue, see Chapter 8 *infra*.

74 Award No. 1512 in (1976) I Yearbook Comm. Arb'n 130.

75 LALIVE/POUDRET/REYMOND, N. 16, p. 397.

76 P. KARRER in BERTI, N. 107, p. 507.

governing law.[77] In particular, the arbitral tribunal cannot determine the applicable law on the basis of a subjective criterion, for example, by deciding to apply the rules of law that it considers to be the 'most appropriate'.[78] The practical effect of this restriction is nevertheless limited, since the arbitral tribunal enjoys considerable freedom in applying the 'closest connection' test.

Generally, the arbitral tribunal will seek to ascertain the 'centre of gravity' of the parties' relationship and apply one single law to the entire case.[79] However, it must be stressed that the arbitral tribunal is not restricted to applying a single national law. On the contrary, if the case is found to have several different facets which each have a closest connection with a different legal system, the arbitral tribunal can decide to apply rules from each of these legal systems.[80] More generally, the arbitral tribunal can (as could the parties) decide to apply any type of '*rules of law*'.[81] In particular, it may be concluded that the closest connection of the case is not with a particular state, but with international commerce in general. In such a case, the arbitral tribunal could decide to apply the *lex mercatoria* to the dispute.

In any event, the arbitrators will need to establish with which sets of rules the dispute has a connection. They will then have to weigh the various connecting factors to identify the legal rules with the closest connection.

2. *The major connecting factors*

The determination of the applicable law on the basis of Article 187(1) of the PILA (*in fine*) is not a mechanical process. It involves an analysis of all the factors bearing on the relationship between the parties. The purpose of this analysis is not merely to find geographical links between countries and the parties' relationship, but rather to establish the legal system with which this relationship has the closest connection.[82] In other words, the arbitral tribunal's task will often be equivalent to determining the parties' expectations in regard to the applicable law.

The following factors have been found to be particularly relevant in applying the '*closest connection*' test:

- the place of business or habitual residence of the parties, particularly of the party which is required to render the 'characteristic performance';[83]

---

77 FOUCHARD/GAILLARD/GOLDMAN, N. 1544, p. 869.
78 P. KARRER in BERTI, N. 110, p. 507.
79 *Ibid.*, N. 114, p. 508.
80 LALIVE/POUDRET/REYMOND, N. 18, p. 399.
81 See Section III.2.b) *supra*.
82 A. HEINI in HEINI/KELLER/SIEHR/VISCHER/VOLKEN, N. 14, p. 1564.
83 With respect to the concept of 'characteristic performance', see: P. M. PATOCCHI, *Characteristic Performance: A New Myth in the Conflict of Laws* in R. PATRY (ed.), *Etudes*

- the place of performance of the contract, particularly of obligations other than the payment of money.

By contrast, the following factors are generally considered irrelevant in applying the 'closest connection' test, because they are fortuitous or only have a connection with the arbitral procedure:[84]

- the place where negotiations were held;
- the place where the contract was signed;
- the language of the contract;
- the nationality of the arbitrators;
- the seat of the arbitral tribunal;
- the likely place of enforcement of the award.

V. The status of the applicable law

The status of the law governing the merits gives rise to two different questions: do the parties have to prove the contents of the applicable substantive law? Is the arbitral tribunal entitled or required to research and establish independently the contents of the applicable law? In order to answer these questions, is it necessary to take into account the rules applicable before courts or the rules specific to arbitration?

The Swiss Federal Tribunal has ruled that the principle *iura novit curia*, according to which the judge is deemed to know the law and entitled to apply it *ex officio*, is also applicable to arbitration.[85] As a consequence, the parties are not required to prove the contents of the applicable law as a fact. Moreover, the arbitral tribunal is not limited by the legal submissions of the parties and may apply other legal principles and provisions to resolve the dispute.[86] The arbitral tribunal must, however, give the parties the opportunity to present their position on the legal issues if it intends to rely upon legal

---

de droit international en l'honneur de Pierre Lalive, pp. 113 *et seq.* See also G. KAUFMANN-KOHLER, *La prestation caractéristique en droit international privé des contrats et l'influence de la Suisse* in Annuaire suisse de droit international, volume anniversaire, 1989, pp. 195-220.

84 See P. KARRER in BERTI, N. 113, p. 508.

85 DFT 135 III 35, 38-39; Unreported decision of the Swiss Federal Tribunal of 19 December 2001 (4P.114/2001); decision of the Swiss Federal Tribunal of 30 December 1994 in [1997] ASA Bull. 217, 219. With respect to the issue of whether the arbitral tribunal must apply *ex officio* mandatory provisions of laws other than the *lex causae* see e.g., A. RIGOZZI, *op. cit.*, p. 467.

86 See G. KAUFMANN-KOHLER, '*Iura novit arbiter' – est-ce bien raisonnable?* in A. HERITIER LACHAT/L. HIRSCH (eds), *De Lege Ferenda – Etudes pour le Professeur Alain Hirsch*, Geneva 2004, pp. 71-78.

theories which were not addressed and could not be foreseen by the parties.[87] Indeed, the application of such legal theories without affording the parties an opportunity to comment upon them may constitute a violation of the parties' right to be heard.

From a practical standpoint, parties must keep in mind that the arbitral tribunal may not be knowledgeable in regard to the applicable law. In addition, access to this law may sometimes be difficult (for reasons of language, unavailability of case law or legal commentary, unreliability of the information available, etc.). For these reasons, it is strongly recommended that the parties establish, present and explain the rules that apply to the merits of the dispute.[88]

VI. Awards *ex aequo et bono*

Article 187(2) of the PILA provides that the parties can authorise the arbitral tribunal to decide *ex aequo et bono*.[89] In such cases, the arbitral tribunal will not resolve the dispute by applying determinate rules of law to the facts, but rather will render a decision according to its perception of justice in the individual case.[90] An arbitral tribunal deciding *ex aequo et bono* is not bound by rules of law and may potentially come to a decision which is incompatible with the rules that would otherwise have been applicable to the case.[91] The only restriction is that the arbitral tribunal must respect international public policy.[92]

The authorisation to decide *ex aequo et bono* does not free the arbitral tribunal from the requirement to give reasons for its decision in the form of a reasoned award. It will therefore still be necessary to apply certain rules to the facts in dispute.[93] In particular, the arbitral tribunal will be required to apply the contractual terms agreed by the parties.[94] However, the arbitral tribunal's methodology will be different – it will seek to achieve justice through an equitable *result*, in view of the specific case at hand.[95]

---

87 Decision of the Swiss Federal Tribunal of 22 February 1999 in [1999] ASA Bull. 537, 544.

88 G. KAUFMANN-KOHLER, *op. cit.*, p. 78, who suggests that the arbitral tribunal should clarify at the start of the proceedings that (i) the parties shall establish the content of the law; (ii) the arbitral tribunal may make its own investigations, without being under an obligation to do so; (iii) if it does make such investigations, it shall consult with the parties about the result thereof.

89 Without entering into the details of the distinction, it should be noted that the concept of a decision *ex aequo et bono* is different from the French concept of *amiable composition*. See: FOUCHARD/GAILLARD/GOLDMAN, N. 1500 *et seq.*, pp. 835 *et seq.*

90 P. KARRER in BERTI, N. 189, p. 5527; LALIVE/POUDRET/REYMOND, N. 20, p. 400.

91 POUDRET/BESSON, N. 710, p. 653.

92 *Ibid.*, N. 717, p. 663; LALIVE/POUDRET/REYMOND, N. 21, p. 401; DFT 107 Ib 63, applying the *ex aequo et bono* provision contained in the Concordat.

93 P. KARRER in BERTI, N. 189, p. 527.

94 LALIVE/POUDRET/REYMOND, N. 21, p. 401.

95 POUDRET/BESSON, N. 714, p. 658.

In order to decide the case *ex aequo et bono*, the arbitral tribunal must be authorised to do so by the parties. Such authorisation does not need to be in writing. It can be express or tacit[96] and can be given at any time, even during the course of arbitral proceedings.[97] However, a clause authorising the arbitral tribunal to decide on the basis of general principles of law must not necessarily be construed as authorising a decision *ex aequo et bono*.[98]

Finally, it should be noted that several authors have expressed the view that a clause providing for *ex aequo et bono* arbitration obliges the arbitral tribunal to decide *ex aequo et bono*.[99]

VII. Sanctions for violation of Article 187 of the PILA

Arbitral tribunals are bound by the above rules regarding the law applicable to the merits of the dispute. Sanctions for non-compliance are, however, limited. Indeed, the failure to decide the case in accordance with the applicable substantive law is not, in principle, a ground to set aside an award,[100] nor a ground to refuse recognition and enforcement of the award.[101]

In connection with the applicable substantive law, a party may seek to set aside an award based upon a violation of public policy, as provided in Article 190(2)(e) of the PILA, if the arbitral tribunal decided *ex aequo et bono* without having been authorized to do so by the parties, or possibly if the arbitral tribunal did not apply the rules of law chosen by the parties.[102]

However, these violations do not, in and of themselves, provide sufficient grounds for setting aside the award.[103] Indeed, in order to set aside an award under Article 190(2)(e) of the PILA, a party must establish that the award is incompatible with public policy. In this respect, the Swiss Federal Tribunal has consistently held that it is not sufficient for the reasons of the award to be incompatible with public policy – an award can only be

---

96 *Contra* A. Heini in Heini/Keller/Siehr/Vischer/Volken, N. 28, p. 1566.

97 Lalive/Poudret/Reymond, N. 22, p. 402 ; B. Dutoit, *op. cit.*, N. 11, p. 586.

98 *Ibid.*, N. 23, p. 402.

99 *Ibid.*, N. 24, p. 403; P. Karrer in Berti, N. 199, p. 529.

100 See Article 190 of the PILA. See also Chapter 8 *infra*.

101 See in particular Article V of the NY Convention, which does not contain any reference to the applicable substantive law; see also Chapter 9 *infra*.

102 The autonomy of the parties' intent is indeed considered to be part of international public policy. See P. Lalive, *Transnational (or Truly International) Public Policy and International Arbitration* in (1987) 3 ICCA Congress Series 257.

103 P. Karrer in Berti, N. 184, pp. 525-526.

set aside if it is shown that the actual and concrete *result* of it is contrary to international public policy,[104] a test that is undoubtedly difficult to meet.

104 Decision of the Swiss Federal Tribunal of 7 March 2003 (4P.250/2002), section 2.1, with references to earlier cases; [1999] RSDIE 603.

Chapter 8 - Challenge and Revision of the Award

Elliott Geisinger and Viviane Frossard

I. Challenge of the award

1. Introduction

Under Swiss law, an application to challenge an arbitral award may only be brought on the extremely narrow grounds listed in Article 190(2) of the PILA. Under this provision, an award may be set aside only:

- if the arbitral tribunal was constituted irregularly (see Section 3.a) *infra*);
- if the arbitral tribunal wrongly accepted or declined jurisdiction (see Section 3.b) *infra*);
- if the arbitral tribunal ruled beyond the claims submitted to it, or failed to decide one of the claims submitted (see Section 3.c) *infra*);
- if the parties' rights of due process were violated (see Section 3.d) *infra*); or
- if the award violates public policy (see Section 3.e) *infra*).

In Swiss case law, it has been held that this list of grounds is exhaustive and that each ground must be interpreted narrowly.[1]

Moreover, awards in international matters are only subject to one level of review before the Swiss courts. Subject to rare exceptions addressed below, an application to challenge an award must be brought directly before the Swiss Federal Tribunal, which is the highest court in Switzerland.

In applications to set aside an award, the Federal Tribunal will not review the facts of the case, nor the law applied by the arbitral tribunal. Broadly speaking, only serious procedural defects or rulings on substance that are contrary to international public policy will be considered. Specifically, it has been consistently held that an award will not be set aside on the grounds that it has been rendered on the basis of obviously wrong

---

1 DFT 116 II 721, 723; DFT 115 II 102, 105.

G. Kaufmann-Kohler and B. Stucki (eds), International Arbitration in Switzerland, A Handbook for Practitioners, 135-165.

findings of fact – even if these findings are contradicted by clear evidence on record – or in clear violation of rules of law or equity.[2] The reason for this very restrictive approach both by the Swiss legislator and by the Federal Tribunal is that parties, having agreed to arbitration, should be held to that agreement and should not be afforded a second opportunity to re-argue the merits of the case in court.[3]

2. Procedural issues

Pursuant to Article 191(1) of the PILA, the procedure for challenging an award is governed by the provisions of the JOA relating to public law appeals, namely Articles 84 *et seq*. of the JOA. The 'public law appeal' is a particular form of judicial recourse under Swiss law, in which the Federal Tribunal examines only certain narrowly defined legal grounds for setting aside decisions rendered by lower courts, administrative bodies or arbitral tribunals. The Federal Tribunal may not review the facts. Moreover, the Federal Tribunal only has the power to confirm or set aside the decisions under review; subject to very limited exceptions, it cannot rule on the merits in a new decision of its own. This form of judicial recourse is intended to be exceptional and the filing of a 'public law appeal' does not stay the enforcement of the decision being challenged. This chapter will provide additional detail regarding these and other procedural matters.

a) Conditions for admissibility of challenges of arbitral awards

aa) Jurisdiction to decide the challenge

Challenges of awards in international matters are brought directly before the Swiss Federal Tribunal (Article 191(1) of the PILA). Under Article 191(2) of the PILA, the parties may, however, agree that the cantonal court at the seat of the arbitral tribunal may have jurisdiction to decide the challenge of the award.

Moreover, the jurisdiction of Swiss courts can be excluded entirely by way of an 'exclusion agreement' made in accordance with and subject to the conditions of Article 192 of the PILA. These 'exclusion agreements' will be discussed in further detail at Section I.4 *infra*.

It should, however, be noted that the fact that Article 192 of the PILA grants the parties the right – subject to restrictive conditions – to exclude the jurisdiction of Swiss courts to set aside awards does not mean that this provision also enables the parties to confer such jurisdiction on the courts of a *foreign* country. If the seat of the arbitral tribunal is in Switzerland, Article 191 of the PILA confers jurisdiction to decide challenges upon Swiss courts, irrespective of whether the parties' agreement to vest the courts of a foreign country with such jurisdiction is valid under the laws of that foreign country. In other words, the effect of Article 192 of the PILA is only to grant the parties the right to

2 [1999] RSDIE 603; [1997] ASA Bull. 291, 307; [1998] ASA Bull. 653, 659; [1995] ASA Bull. 198, 201; DFT 116 II 634, 636; [1992] ASA Bull. 381; DFT 115 II 102, 105.

3 DFT 128 III 50, 58.

make a *negative* choice excluding the jurisdiction of *Swiss* courts that would otherwise be competent to decide the challenge. It does not give the parties a right to make a *positive* choice in favour of *foreign* courts. [4]

bb) Types of awards that can be challenged

In support of an application to challenge a final award, the applicant may invoke any of the grounds exhaustively enumerated in Article 190(2) of the PILA (see Section 3 *infra*). An award is deemed to be final when it completes the mission of the arbitral tribunal.[5] Pursuant to Article 190(1) of the PILA, the award is final, and enforceable, from its notification to the parties.

With respect to partial or interim awards, Article 190(3) of the PILA provides that such awards may be challenged immediately if they dispose of a party's argument that the arbitral tribunal was irregularly constituted (Article 190(2)(a) of the PILA) or wrongly decided for or against its own jurisdiction (Article 190(2)(b) of the PILA).

Under the Swiss Federal Tribunal's practice prior to September 2003, it was also possible to bring an immediate challenge where the partial or interim award created a '*concrete and imminent risk of irreparable harm*' to a party. Although framed broadly, this concept was in fact rather relatively narrow. For instance, the Federal Tribunal had ruled that an immediate application to set aside an interim award on liability is not admissible even if the award contains a finding that the claimant is entitled to damages without quantifying those damages. The rationale for this decision was that an award containing a finding of liability as to its principle but not as to its quantum does not cause any irreparable harm *per se*.[6]

In subsequent cases, the Federal Tribunal ruled that '*irreparable harm*' (and therefore the possibility of bringing an immediate application to set aside the award) could be contemplated if a party was ordered to refrain from or limit ordinary business, if it was ordered to pay monies (for instance costs) where the payment of those monies would

---

4 This results from the fact that the *lex arbitri* determines the judicial bodies having jurisdiction to decide challenges of awards. From a Swiss standpoint, Swiss law applies as the *lex arbitri* by operation of law to all arbitrations falling within the scope of Article 176(1) of the PILA. The parties have no autonomy in this respect (LALIVE/POUDRET/REYMOND, N. 12, p. 299; K. SIEHR, *Das internationale Privatrecht der Schweiz*, Zurich 2002, p. 710). In regard to the determination of the judicial body having jurisdiction to decide challenges, Swiss law grants the parties only limited freedom of choice: they may elect to subject the arbitration to the Concordat (Article 176(2) of the PILA), or they may agree to have challenges decided by a cantonal appellate court (Article 191(2) of the PILA), or they may entirely exclude challenges by way of an exclusion agreement (Article 192 of the PILA). Swiss law does not grant the parties any further choices.

5 REDFERN/HUNTER, N. 8-33, p. 379.

6 DFT 115 II 288, 292-293: the arbitral tribunal had ruled by interim award only on the principle of a party's liability and reserved the calculation of damages for a later award.

jeopardize that party's financial existence, or if a party was ordered to pay monies to the other party and the other party is practically insolvent (so that later recovery of the amounts paid is practically impossible).

In a decision of 18 September 2003, the Federal Tribunal ruled that neither the legislative history of Article 190(3) of the PILA, nor a purposive interpretation of that provision, justified the possibility of setting aside partial or interim awards beyond what is provided in the statutory text. Therefore, partial or interim awards can be set aside only if the arbitral tribunal was irregularly constituted or if the arbitral tribunal wrongly decided on its own jurisdiction. Otherwise, the parties must wait for a final award.[7]

cc) Conditions relating to the party challenging the award

Generally speaking, only a party that is directly affected by an arbitral award and that has a 'personal and concrete interest' in altering the outcome of the arbitration may challenge the award. This will be the case for a party to arbitral proceedings who lost the case, either partially or entirely so that, in practice, this condition rarely causes any difficulties.

However, problems may arise if a person or entity that was not party to the arbitral proceedings seeks to challenge an award. In certain cases involving public law appeals against judicial or administrative decisions, the Federal Tribunal has recognized the existence of a 'personal interest' despite the fact that the applicant was not a party to the proceedings before the lower courts or administrative bodies. Indeed, according to consistent case law of the Federal Tribunal, the fact that the applicant was not a party before the lower instances is not always decisive. The question is rather to determine whether the challenged decision affects the applicant's legal interests in a personal and direct manner and whether all of the other conditions for the admissibility of a public law appeal are met.[8]

To our knowledge, the question of whether this practice is applicable to international arbitration has never been decided. However, the majority of Swiss legal commentators consider that a non-party to the arbitral proceedings may file an application to challenge an award, if that party's legal interests are personally and directly affected and if all other conditions for the admissibility of a public law appeal are met.[9]

dd) Time limits

In accordance with Article 89 of the JOA, an application to challenge an award must be filed within 30 days from the notification of the award.

---

7 DFT 130 III 76.

8 DFT 98 Ia 1, 5; DFT 99 Ia 247, 254-255; DFT 114 Ia 209, 211 and references.

9 C. JERMINI, *Die Anfechtung der Schiedssprüche im internationalen Privatrecht*, Zurich 1997, pp. 323-324; RÜEDE/HADENFELDT, pp. 333-334.

Article 32 of the JOA provides that the day on which the 30 day time limit begins to run is not included in the computation and that, if the expiry date is a holiday[10] or a Sunday, the time limit expires on the next working day. Finally, in accordance with Article 34 of the JOA, time limits do not run:

- from the 7th day before Easter to the 7th day after Easter (inclusively);
- between 15 July and 15 August (inclusively);
- between 18 December and 1 January (inclusively).[11]

ee) Formal requirements relating to the challenge

Pursuant to Article 90 of the JOA, the application to challenge an award must contain the following:

- the designation of the challenged award (and copy thereof, if the applicant has one; if it does not, the Federal Tribunal will set a time limit for submitting a copy of the challenged award. Should the applicant fail to submit it within the given time limit, the application will be dismissed);
- the applicant's prayers for relief;
- a succinct statement of the essential facts; and
- a brief statement of the grounds upon which the applicant relies for setting aside the award.

The application must meet all of these requirements, failing which it will not be considered by the Federal Tribunal. Consequently, the filing of a mere notice of intent to challenge the award, indicating that the specific grounds will be set forth in a later submission, has no legal effect and is not admissible. In particular, such a notice does not toll any time limits and does not validly commence the application to challenge the award.

---

10 The statute refers to legal holidays under the laws of Swiss Cantons. It is an open question as to whether this also applies to holidays at the foreign place of domicile of the applicant, or whether the relevant holidays are those in the Canton of its Swiss counsel (or even of the seat of the arbitral tribunal). As a practical matter, it would be imprudent to rely upon foreign holidays.

11 Article 35 of the JOA gives the Federal Tribunal discretion to set a new time limit, upon a reasoned request showing that the applicant was prevented through no fault of its own from observing a statutory time limit. This is mentioned only *pro memoriam* since, in general, the Federal Tribunal very rarely exercises this discretionary power. To our knowledge, it has never set a new time limit in the field of international arbitration.

b) The proceedings before the Swiss Federal Tribunal

aa) Mains steps and overall duration of the proceedings

In the vast majority of applications to set aside arbitral awards (as in public law appeals in general), the proceedings are entirely written. There is ordinarily one exchange of briefs and no oral argument. There have, however, been cases in which the Federal Tribunal has ordered two exchanges of written briefs; these cases were exceptionally complicated. The Federal Tribunal may also order oral argument where there are 'important reasons' for doing so.[12]

There is no need to obtain leave to file an application to challenge an award. However, the Federal Tribunal will examine all conditions of admissibility *ex officio* and has the power to dismiss the application if it is obviously without merit. If the Federal Tribunal considers that the application is, on its face, inadmissible or devoid of merit, it will declare the application to be inadmissible or dismiss it, without requesting the adverse party to comment. In practice, this procedure achieves a similar result as a requirement to obtain leave.

Usually, the main steps in the proceedings are the following:

- within thirty days of receipt of the award, the party challenging the award must file its written application with the Federal Tribunal, in accordance with Articles 89(1) and 90 of the JOA;
- shortly after receipt of the application, the Federal Tribunal will require the challenging party to provide security for the court costs (not the adverse party's costs) within a time limit of approximately twenty days after the date of filing. This security is posted in the form of a cash deposit made directly with the Federal Tribunal. These costs shall be addressed in greater detail below. If the security is not posted within the prescribed time limit, the application will be declared inadmissible without further ado. The Federal Tribunal is very strict with respect to this time limit;
- after having received security for the court costs, the Federal Tribunal will verify the procedural admissibility of the application and examine whether the application obviously lacks merit on its face. The Federal Tribunal undertakes both of these verifications *ex officio* and, on this basis, may declare the application to be inadmissible or dismiss it outright;
- if, as will usually be the case, the application is admissible and not devoid of merit on its face, the Federal Tribunal will proceed in accordance with Article 93 of the JOA and direct the adverse party or parties to file written submissions, with exhibits if any. The arbitral tribunal is also given the opportunity to comment, but will rarely do so in practice. This order is usually made

12 Articles 91 and 93 of the JOA.

approximately five to six weeks after filing of the application; the time limit for filing the written submissions and comments on the application is 30 days;

- approximately two to four months after receipt of the last written submission, the Federal Tribunal will render its decision, which is communicated in the form of an order without reasons. The reasons are provided approximately four to six weeks later.

Accordingly, the overall duration of the proceedings, from filing of the application to receipt of the decision by the parties, is usually between four to six months, with receipt of the reasons roughly four to six weeks later.

bb) No stay of enforcement of the challenged award, unless otherwise ordered by the Federal Tribunal

Under Swiss law, an award rendered in international arbitral proceedings is enforceable as of the date of notification to the parties (Article 190(1) of the PILA).

The Swiss Federal Tribunal has discretion to stay the enforcement of the award upon request by a party. This request is admissible only once an application to set aside the award has been filed (Article 94 of the JOA). In other words, it is not possible to seek a stay of enforcement prior to the filing of the application (in practice, the request for a stay of enforcement is usually included in the challenging party's brief).

The conditions for a stay are that:

- the party requesting the stay has demonstrated that the immediate enforcement of the award exposes it to serious and irreparable harm in its 'legitimate legal interests'; and
- the challenge itself has very strong *prima facie* chances of success (the Federal Tribunal has become increasingly restrictive in this respect and has recently tended to require that the challenge be almost certain to succeed).[13]

With respect to awards ordering the payment of money, stays of enforcement are very rarely granted (in addition to the conditions listed above, one must show that the party which was successful in the arbitration is either on the verge of bankruptcy or located in a country in which it would be almost impossible to recover amounts paid under the award).

---

13 The Federal Tribunal's ruling on the stay will give a strong indication on the likely outcome of the challenge, particularly if the stay is denied. The ground for denial of a stay that is most often given by the Federal Tribunal is that the challenge has no reasonable prospect of success. In those cases, the final outcome of the proceedings becomes a foregone conclusion (and the most prudent course of action for the party challenging the award is to withdraw its application, in which case the Federal Tribunal will usually be lenient in respect of costs).

Under certain circumstances, the decision to grant a stay of enforcement can be subject to the posting of security. However, this occurs only upon request of the adverse party, which must also show that, failing such security, it would be exposed to irreparable harm. Concretely, such security is posted either in the form of a first-demand bank guarantee from a first-rate Swiss bank, or, more often, of a cash deposit made directly with the Federal Tribunal. The amount of security can be relatively high.

The Federal Tribunal has discretion either to set a time limit for the adverse party and the arbitral tribunal to comment on the request for the stay, or to grant the stay *ex parte* if the conditions for the stay appear to be obviously met on the face of the documents filed by the challenging party (in which case the adverse party and the arbitral tribunal will be invited to comment later and the decision to grant the stay can be reversed).

If the stay is granted *ex parte*, the decision can be expected approximately 5 days after the request is made. If the Federal Tribunal wishes to hear the adverse party, which it usually does, the process will take longer (roughly 20-30 days after the request is made).

cc) Consequences of a successful challenge of the award

If the Federal Tribunal sets aside the award, the matter will be referred back to the same arbitral tribunal for the rendering of a new award.[14] The Federal Tribunal does not issue its own decision on the merits. If it is not possible to re-convene the same arbitral tribunal, a new tribunal will be constituted under the same procedures as those applicable to the initial tribunal.

The Federal Tribunal does not give any instructions to the arbitral tribunal. However, in practice, the arbitral tribunal will render a new award that conforms to the reasons given by the Federal Tribunal.

There is one exception to these principles – in certain cases relating to jurisdiction, the Federal Tribunal will decide the issue finally in order to avoid unnecessary delays.

dd) Costs

The following principles apply to costs:

- the party challenging the award must make a cash deposit in respect of the court costs within the time limit set by the Federal Tribunal (failing which the application will be declared inadmissible without further recourse). In determining the amount of the deposit, the Federal Tribunal will apply its schedule of costs, which is based upon the amount in dispute and capped at CHF 100,000. In proceedings relating to the challenge of arbitral awards, the Federal Tribunal tends to request high deposits on the court costs (often several tens of thousands of francs). The party having filed an unsuccessful application

---

14 C. JERMINI, *op. cit.*, p. 336; LALIVE/POUDRET/REYMOND, N. 3.6, p. 440.

to challenge an award generally loses the entire amount that it deposited in respect of the court costs;

- the Federal Tribunal may order the party challenging the award to provide security for the adverse party's costs, provided that the adverse party makes a request prior to filing its submissions on the substance of the challenge and that the statutory conditions for the posting of such security are met. The time limit for filing submissions on the challenge is suspended pending the ruling on security. If ordered (which only occurs in exceptional cases), the amount of the security for the adverse party's costs can also be significant;
- the losing party bears the court costs and the adverse party's legal costs (if the adverse party filed written submissions). In the event of an unsuccessful challenge, the Federal Tribunal can be very generous in awarding such legal costs, which often reach or exceed CHF 100,000 (the cap on court costs does not apply to legal costs awarded to the successful party; in one particularly complicated case, the party having successfully resisted the challenge was awarded CHF 1 million in legal costs). If there are several adverse parties and they are represented by different counsel, it has become the usual practice to order the losing party to pay amounts in this range to *each* adverse party.

3. *Substantive issues: grounds for challenging awards*

a) Irregular constitution of the arbitral tribunal (Article 190(2)(a) of the PILA)

Article 190(2)(a) of the PILA provides that an award can be set aside if the arbitral tribunal was irregularly constituted. This phrasing is somewhat misleading, for it could be taken to suggest that an award could be challenged whenever the formation or composition of the arbitral tribunal did not comply with the parties' agreement under Article 179 of the PILA (for example, if the arbitral tribunal was not constituted in accordance with institutional rules selected by the parties).

In reality, the ground for setting aside under Article 190(2)(a) of the PILA is much narrower: it guarantees the parties' right to an independent and unbiased judge or arbitrator (this right results from the European Human Rights Convention and from Swiss constitutional law).[15] In other words, the Swiss Federal Tribunal does not consider that its role is to verify whether the constitution of the arbitral tribunal complied in all respects with the procedures agreed by the parties. Based upon Article 190(2)(a) of the PILA, it will set aside an award only if the parties' fundamental right to independent and unbiased justice was violated.[16] Article 190(2)(a) of the PILA thus contains an implicit

---

15 S. V. BERTI/A. K. SCHNYDER in BERTI, N. 25-26, p. 594.

16 [1997] ASA Bull. 99, 103-104. A recent decision of the Federal Tribunal contains *obiter dictum* suggesting that this principle may be unsettled law and merely states that it is 'doubtful' whether requirements agreed by the parties that exceed constitutional guarantees may be raised within the framework of Article 190(2)(a) of the PILA ([2002] ASA Bull.

reference to Article 180(1)(c) of the PILA. A more detailed discussion of this latter provision is contained in Chapter 3 *supra*.

For present purposes, it suffices to add that when a party considers that an arbitrator lacks independence, it must raise the issue immediately,[17] for example, by challenging the arbitrator. Moreover, the Federal Tribunal has stated in *obiter dictum* that a party having incomplete knowledge of circumstances that could potentially raise doubts as to an arbitrator's independence must seek clarification immediately, failing which it may be precluded from relying upon fuller knowledge that may be acquired at a later stage.[18] Whether or not there has been a challenge to the arbitrator, the party considering that an arbitrator lacks independence must apply to set aside the first award rendered by the arbitral tribunal based on Article 190(2)(a) of the PILA, failing which that party will lose its right to rely on this provision with respect to any later awards that the tribunal may render. This results from Article 190(3) of the PILA, pursuant to which immediate challenges to partial or interlocutory awards are admissible – the Federal Tribunal considers that this provision does not confer a simple faculty, but imposes an outright *obligation* upon the parties to act immediately. In any event, a party may not wait for the outcome of the arbitration and, only at that stage, seek to impugn the award based upon the arbitrator's alleged lack of independence.

b) Wrong ruling on jurisdiction (Article 190(2)(b) of the PILA)

In accordance with Article 190(2)(b) of the PILA, an award can be set aside if the arbitral tribunal wrongly accepts or declines jurisdiction. This provision therefore enables a party to challenge the arbitral tribunal's decision on the existence, validity, scope, etc. of the arbitration agreement. These issues are addressed in greater detail in Chapter 2 *supra*. In this chapter, only issues that are specific to applications to challenge arbitral awards, and other particular questions, shall be considered.

To begin, the Federal Tribunal has held that a party disputing the jurisdiction of the arbitral tribunal must raise this argument with respect to the first award rendered by that tribunal, failing which it cannot argue lack of jurisdiction with respect to any subsequent awards. The rule is therefore the same as for challenges based upon an arbitrator's alleged lack of independence: Article 190(3) of the PILA creates an *obligation* to act immediately.

Moreover, in setting aside proceedings, the Federal Tribunal has full power to review legal arguments relating to the jurisdiction of the arbitral tribunal, including preliminary legal issues. For example, if the validity of the arbitration agreement entered into by a

321, 326-327). However, the decision reported at [1997] ASA Bull. 99 is very explicit on this point.

17 B. CORBOZ, *Le recours au Tribunal Fédéral en matière d'arbitrage international*, [2002] II SJ 1, 17.

18 [2002] ASA Bull. 321, 325.

corporation depends on the powers of the person having signed the agreement on that corporation's behalf, the Federal Tribunal may freely examine whether this preliminary issue was decided correctly. Similarly, if the arbitral tribunal was unable to establish the actual and common intent of the parties and thus needed to interpret the parties' presumed intent, the Federal Tribunal has full power to review the arbitral tribunal's application of legal principles governing the determination of the parties' presumed intent. This last example often raises difficulties in practice, since the determination of the parties' actual and common intent is a finding of fact (and thus not subject to review by the Federal Tribunal), whereas the interpretation of the parties' presumed intent is a question of law (that the Federal Tribunal can review freely).

Finally, a particular question arises with respect to arbitral tribunals deciding on the basis of fairness or '*ex æquo et bono*' without having been empowered to do so by the parties and despite a clear choice of law provision in favour of a definite legal system. The question of whether this is a jurisdictional issue is not entirely settled under Swiss law. In a case decided before the PILA entered into force (at that time, possibilities for setting aside arbitral awards were broader), the Federal Tribunal held that an arbitral tribunal which rules *ex æquo et bono* without having received a mandate to do so exceeds its jurisdiction.[19] Certain Swiss legal commentators consider that this precedent remains valid under Article 190(2)(b) of the PILA.[20] However, this approach has been criticized by many legal commentators, who consider that this defect relates to the reasons for the award, not to jurisdiction, and that, accordingly, it can be sanctioned only if the actual and concrete result of the award is contrary to public policy (Article 190(2)(e) of the PILA).[21]

In 1990, the Swiss Federal Tribunal held that an arbitral award based on considerations of fairness (although the parties had selected a specific national law to govern their contract and the arbitral tribunal was not empowered to rule *ex æquo et bono*) was not contrary to public policy, given that the outcome reached by the arbitral tribunal was not fundamentally different from that which would have resulted from the application of the law chosen by the parties *and* that such outcome was not contrary to public policy.[22] This decision would suggest that a party may not challenge an *ex æquo et bono* award on the basis of a jurisdictional defect, but only under Article 190(2)(e) of the PILA, which relates to public policy.

c) *Ultra*, *infra* or *extra petita* (Article 190(2)(c) of the PILA)

Pursuant to Article 190(2)(c) of the PILA, an award can be set aside if the arbitral tribunal has adjudicated beyond the relief sought (*ultra petita*) or granted relief different than what was sought (*extra petita*) or failed to adjudicate certain claims (*infra petita*).

---

19 DFT 110 Ia 56, 57.

20 S. BERTI/A. SCHNYDER in BERTI, N. 39, p. 577; BUCHER, N. 344, p. 117.

21 LALIVE/POUDRET/REYMOND, pp. 424-425, 431; P. KARRER in BERTI, N. 184, p. 525.

22 DFT 116 II 634.

The purpose of this provision is to avoid adjudication of claims upon which a party had no opportunity to present its case and to guarantee each party's right to have its claims addressed by the arbitral tribunal.[23]

It must be stressed that the framework of the relief and claims put to the arbitral tribunal are determined by the parties' *prayers for relief*.[24] With respect to ICC arbitration, this means that this framework is not defined by the '*issues*' listed in the Terms of Reference, but by the prayers for relief or claims.[25] If the prayers for relief are modified in the course of the arbitration, the last version determines the parameters within which the arbitral tribunal must adjudicate.

If the prayers for relief are unclear, the arbitral tribunal may interpret them in accordance with the rule of good faith interpretation, i.e. unclear prayers for relief should be given the meaning that the arbitral tribunal and the adverse party could reasonably ascribe to them in good faith and taking into account all relevant circumstances.[26]

This ground for setting aside does not enable a party to challenge the award:

- when an arbitral tribunal grants relief for legal reasons different from those relied upon by the claimant, because it has been held that the parties' legal characterization of claims does not bind the arbitral tribunal;[27]
- when a party makes a negative prayer for relief (for example, a party may claim a declaration that it did not owe certain amounts) and the arbitral tribunal denies that particular claim not in the form of a statement simply dismissing that prayer for relief, but in the form of a positive declaration to the contrary. The Federal Tribunal held that an award declaring that amounts are owed (without ordering the payment thereof) and an award denying a claim for a declaration that amounts are not owed have the same legal effect;[28]
- when a valid arbitration agreement exists, but the arbitral tribunal adjudicates claims over which it has no jurisdiction, for instance because the claim is not included within the scope of the arbitration agreement.[29] This second hypothesis falls under wrong ruling on jurisdiction within the meaning of Article 190(2)(b) of the PILA.

---

23 [1995] ASA Bull. 217, 219-220.
24 LALIVE/POUDRET/REYMOND, *op. cit.*, N. 5(c), p. 425.
25 *Ibid.*
26 DFT 128 III 50, 59; [1995] ASA Bull. 217, 219.
27 [1995] ASA Bull. 217, 219; DFT 120 II 172, 175.
28 DFT 120 II 172, 176.
29 DFT 116 II 639, 641-642.

d) Violation of due process (Article 190(2)(d) of the PILA)

Pursuant to Article 190(2)(d) of the PILA, an award can be set aside if the parties' right to equal treatment or right to be heard has been violated. Although the statutory provision refers to equal treatment (i.e. the constitutional principle under which similar situations must be treated in a similar manner), in practice Article 190(2)(d) of the PILA relates to cases of gross procedural unfairness.

With respect to the parties' right to be heard, the Swiss Federal Tribunal has found that this principle guarantees each party's right to submit relevant statements of fact, to present its legal arguments and to request appropriate evidence-taking measures before an award is rendered to its detriment. Furthermore, the right to be heard guarantees each party's right to participate in the evidentiary proceedings, to rebut allegations made by the opposite party, to examine and criticize evidence adduced by the opposite party and to bring its own evidence in rebuttal before an award is rendered to its detriment.[30]

Although these general principles are framed in rather broad terms, in practice, the Federal Tribunal interprets this ground for setting aside very restrictively. In particular, it has been held that:

- the parties do not have an unlimited right to adduce evidence, but only such evidence which is material and relevant to adjudicate the case;[31]
- a party may not purport to argue a violation of its right to be heard when, in reality, it is merely criticizing the manner in which the arbitral tribunal applied rules on the burden of proof (i.e. which party has to prove which facts);[32]
- a party may not purport to argue a violation of its right to be heard when in reality it is merely criticizing the weighing of evidence by the arbitral tribunal, provided that each party had the opportunity to present its case on the other's evidence, whether in writing or orally;[33]
- there is no violation of a party's right to be heard merely because the arbitral tribunal relied on the adverse party's otherwise unsupported statements as evidence;[34]

---

30 Decision of the Swiss Federal Tribunal of 31 October 2003 (4P.149/2003), section 3.1; decision of the Swiss Federal Tribunal of 14 July 2003 (4P.114/2003), section 2.2; [2003] ASA Bull. 601, 624-625; [1999] ASA Bull. 537, 541-542; DFT 119 II 386, 388-390.

31 Decision of the Swiss Federal Tribunal of 14 July 2003 (4P.114/2003), section 2.2; [1999] ASA Bull. 537, 541; [1997] ASA Bull. 291, 306; DFT 117 II 346, 348.

32 [1993] ASA Bull. 68.

33 Decision of the Swiss Federal Tribunal of 14 July 2003 (4P.114/2003), section 2.2; [1999] ASA Bull. 537, 542; DFT 116 II 639, 642-643.

34 [1998] ASA Bull. 653, 658.

- the insufficiency (or absence) of reasons is not a violation of the parties' right to be heard.[35] The fact that the applicable procedural rules provide for reasons (which is the case for the ICC rules) is not relevant, as an award can only be set aside on the basis of a disregard of the applicable rules that violates the parties' fundamental procedural right to due process.[36]

Also, the Federal Tribunal has consistently held that a party considering that its right to be heard has been breached must protest immediately, failing which it is deemed to have waived the right to complain at a later stage.[37] If a party became aware of the violation of its right to be heard only once it read the award, it is sufficient for such party to file an application to challenge the award within the statutory time limit.

A further restriction resides in the fact that, if the decision rests on several alternative reasons, only one of which is tainted by a violation of a party's right to be heard, the award will not be set aside. In other words, if there are reasons that are not successfully challenged and that justify the outcome of the award, the application will be dismissed.[38]

That being said, the Federal Tribunal has ruled that the parties are entitled to have relevant arguments properly addressed by the arbitral tribunal. Therefore, if the arbitral tribunal completely fails to consider or fundamentally misconstrues relevant allegations of fact or law made by a party, and if this places the aggrieved party in the same situation as if it had never been given the opportunity to present its position at all, there can be cause for setting aside the award on the basis of Article 190(2)(d) of the PILA.[39] The Federal Tribunal has also ruled that the chances of success of the arguments that were fundamentally neglected or misconstrued are not relevant – this violation of the right to be heard is formal in nature. This ground for setting aside an award is called a 'formal denial of justice'.

In another decision, the Federal Tribunal expressly stated that the application of legal principles different from those argued by the parties is not a 'formal denial of justice'. Therefore, the Federal Tribunal considers that, in accordance with the maxim of *iura novit curia*, an arbitral tribunal may base its findings on legal principles that were not argued by the parties.[40] However, the arbitral tribunal may not take the parties by surprise by applying legal provisions or principles that neither party could reasonably have expected to apply. If the arbitral tribunal considers that the parties have overlooked entirely legal issues that are determinative for the outcome of the case, it must point this

---

35 DFT 116 II 373, 375.

36 [1999] ASA Bull. 537, 541; [1998] ASA Bull. 653, 658; DFT 119 II 386, 388-389.

37 [2002] ASA Bull. 548, 550; [2000] ASA Bull. 96, 102; B. Corboz, *op. cit.*, p. 21.

38 [1993] ASA Bull. 413; [1993] ASA Bull. 525.

39 DFT 121 III 331, 334, later re-affirmed in [1999] ASA Bull. 537, 542; [1997] ASA Bull. 316. In a decision rendered in 2001, the Federal Tribunal re-affirmed the principle again, but narrowed its scope to the formulation set out above (see DFT 127 III 576).

40 DFT 130 III 35, 38-40; [2002] ASA Bull. 548, 550; [1997] ASA Bull. 316, 329.

problem out to the parties and provide them with an opportunity to present their case on these issues (failing which the award may be set aside for violation of the parties' right to be heard).[41]

e) Violation of public policy (Article 190(2)(e) of the PILA)

Pursuant to Article 190(2)(e) of the PILA, an award can be set aside for violation of public policy, which includes 'substantive' public policy and 'procedural' public policy.

aa) 'Substantive' public policy

i) General definition and remarks

'Substantive' public policy is not necessarily limited to Swiss public policy and relates to awards containing a concrete result which is contrary to fundamental legal and moral principles recognized in any civilized state, such as, for example, *pacta sunt servanda* (sanctity of contract), observance of good faith, the prohibition of spoliation and discriminatory measures, the prohibition of bribery and corrupt practices and the prohibition of expropriation without compensation.[42]

The Swiss Federal Tribunal has consistently held that an award can be set aside only if its actual and concrete result is contrary to public policy; it is not sufficient for only the reasons of the award to be incompatible with public policy.[43]

In addition, it is important to stress what is *not* contrary to public policy:

- an award rendered on the basis of obviously wrong – even arbitrary – findings of fact, even if these findings are contradicted by evidence on record, unless the actual outcome of the award is itself incompatible with public policy;[44]
- an award rendered in clear violation of rules of law or equity, even if the award is legally indefensible;[45]
- an award rendered in violation of a contractual provision, unless this itself constitutes a violation of *pacta sunt servanda*;[46]

---

41 DFT 130 III 35, 39-40.

42 Decision of the Swiss Federal Tribunal of 7 March 2003 (4P.250/2002), section 2.1, with references to earlier cases; [2003] ASA Bull. 376, 380-381, with references to earlier cases; [1999] RSDIE 603; B.CORBOZ, *op. cit.*, p. 27.

43 Decision of the Swiss Federal Tribunal of 7 March 2003 (4P.250/2002), section 2.1, with references to earlier cases; [1999] RSDIE 603.

44 Decision of the Swiss Federal Tribunal of 7 March 2003 (4P.250/2002), section 2.1, with references to earlier cases; [2002] ASA Bull. 328, 333, with references to earlier cases; [1999] RSDIE 603.

45 [2002] ASA Bull. 328, 333, with references to earlier cases.

46 [2003] ASA Bull. 384, 389, with references to earlier cases; decision of the Swiss Federal Tribunal of 30 January 2002 (4P.222/2001), section 4, with references to earlier cases.

- an award rendered in violation of clearly established rules on contract interpretation;[47]
- an award based on reasons which are contrary to public policy, provided that the concrete result of the award is not in itself contrary to public policy.[48]

In relation to the recognition and enforcement of foreign judgments, the Swiss Federal Tribunal has further held that there can, in any event, be no violation of public policy when the result of the decision could also have been reached applying Swiss law.[49] Although rendered in a different context (recognition and enforcement of foreign judgments), this precedent presumably also applies to public policy under Article 190(2)(e) of the PILA.

ii) *Pacta sunt servanda* (sanctity of contract)

In the Swiss case law, it has been held that *pacta sunt servanda* is a principle of public policy justifying that an award be set aside when:

- an arbitral tribunal makes a finding that a valid agreement exists but refuses to order its performance on the basis of irrelevant considerations or inapplicable legal provisions; or
- an arbitral tribunal denies the existence of a contract but nevertheless orders the performance of contractual duties; or
- an arbitral tribunal makes a finding that a condition precedent has been fulfilled, but does not order the performance of the contingent obligation; or
- an arbitral tribunal makes a finding that a condition precedent has not been fulfilled, but nevertheless orders the performance of the contingent obligation.[50]

It has also been held that the principle of *pacta sunt servanda* encompasses privity of contract. Consequently, it is possible to set aside an award that imposes contractual obligations on parties that are recognised as not being privy to the contract.[51]

However, the scope of *pacta sunt servanda* has been narrowed in other decisions. For example, the Federal Tribunal has ruled that this principle cannot be relied upon to criticize the manner in which the arbitral tribunal interpreted a contractual provision.[52]

---

47 [2003] ASA Bull. 376, 381, with references to earlier cases; [2002] ASA Bull. 328, 333, with references to earlier cases; [1999] ASA Bull. 537, 539; [1997] ASA Bull. 316.

48 [1999] RSDIE 603; [1999] ASA Bull. 537, 539; DFT 120 II 155, 166; DFT 116 II 634, 636-637.

49 DFT 116 II 625, 631.

50 Decision of the Swiss Federal Tribunal of 24 November 2003 (4P.202/2003), section 5; [1997] ASA Bull. 291, 305; DFT 116 II 634, 638.

51 [1998] ASA Bull. 634, 651.

52 [1997] ASA Bull. 316; [1991] ASA Bull. 169, 170.

More recently, the Federal Tribunal has held in relation to *pacta sunt servanda* that the refusal to order the performance of a contractual obligation must be in contradiction with another part of the award, in which the existence and the enforceable character of the obligation are recognized.[53] Indeed, this is a common denominator of the various situations described above.

To summarise, the precise meaning of *pacta sunt servanda* in the context of public policy is an unsettled matter under Swiss law and depends on the reasons given by the arbitral tribunal.

iii) Observance of good faith

Swiss civil procedure law and arbitration law impose a duty upon all parties to civil or arbitral proceedings to act in good faith. This is a general principle of Swiss federal law.[54] Moreover, good faith is a principle of Swiss public policy in international arbitration and even of transnational public policy.[55]

Good faith imposes upon the parties and their representatives a duty to proceed in a loyal and frank manner in the proceedings. This general rule means that the parties and their representatives:

- have a general duty to refrain from any action which could cause unnecessary delay in the proceedings;[56]
- may not rely on procedural rules contrary to the spirit and purpose of such rules (*abus de droit*) and, in particular, a party must refrain from delaying tactics;[57]
- must be truthful;[58]
- may not use 'surprise tactics';[59] the procedural rules must guarantee the right to be heard and equal treatment and the arbitral tribunal must uphold these rules in order to thwart such surprise tactics;
- must object immediately if they consider that procedural rules have been violated; a party may not wait until an award has been rendered against it and complain only at that stage of alleged violations of its procedural rights;[60]

53 [1999] RSDIE 603, in which the Swiss Federal Tribunal stated that public policy also serves to guarantee a minimum standard of quality in arbitral proceedings.

54 DFT 83 II 345 ; H.-R. SCHÜPBACH, *Traité de procédure civile*, Zurich 1995, pp. 87-89.

55 P. LALIVE, *Transnational (or Truly International) Public Policy and International Arbitration* in P. SANDERS (ed.), *Comparative Arbitration Practice and Public Policy in Arbitration* in (1987) 3 ICCA Congress Series 306; see also Article 15(6) of the Swiss Rules.

56 DFT 111 Ia 259; DFT 109 Ia 81 ; DFT 108 Ia 197.

57 W. J. HABSCHEID, *Droit judiciaire privé suisse*, 2nd edn, Geneva 1981, p. 364.

58 *Ibid.*, pp. 363-364.

59 *Ibid.*, p. 363.

- may not initiate proceedings for the sole purpose of harassing the adverse party.[61]

The good faith principle also imposes upon the arbitral tribunal the duty to actively promote the orderly and expeditious conduct of the proceedings.[62]

iv) Prohibition of confiscation and spoliation

In several decisions, the Swiss Federal Tribunal has recognised the prohibition of confiscation and spoliation as a part of public policy within the meaning of Article 190(2)(e) of the PILA. However, the Federal Tribunal has never elaborated on this particular aspect of public policy. There are no reported decisions in which the Federal Tribunal has set aside an award on this ground and no such decisions are known to the authors.

The prohibition of confiscation and spoliation first appeared in Swiss case law in connection with state-ordered measures such as nationalization; reference was usually made to the generally recognized requirements of public international law relating to nationalizations, including adequate compensation.[63] The Federal Tribunal has also referred to prohibition of confiscation and spoliation in a case involving a state-owned entity that was liquidated after a private company began arbitral proceedings against it.[64] In that case, which was decided many years before the enactment of the PILA, the Federal Tribunal did not intervene on the ground of public policy, despite the fact that the obvious purpose of the successive liquidations of the state-owned entity was to evade the arbitral proceedings. This precedent was criticised very sharply and it is likely that the outcome would be different today.

bb) 'Procedural' public policy

Procedural public policy relates to violations of fundamental procedural principles recognized in Switzerland and which are not already encompassed within due process under Article 190(2)(d) of the PILA.[65] Consequently, this form of public policy covers only those principles that are not included under other provisions of Article 190(2) of the PILA, in particular the right to be heard under sub-article (c).[66] For example, the Swiss Federal Tribunal has ruled that the co-existence in Switzerland of two equally

---

60 DFT 119 II 386; [2000] ASA Bull. 96; LALIVE/POUDRET/REYMOND, *op. cit.*, N. 12, p. 356.

61 W. J. HABSCHEID, *op. cit.*, p. 364.

62 DFT 111 Ia 72.

63 C. JERMINI, *op. cit.*, N. 576, p. 286.

64 DFT 102 Ia 574.

65 [1997] ASA Bull. 316; [1995] ASA Bull. 217, 222.

66 Decision of the Swiss Federal Tribunal of 10 June 2003 (4P.263/2002), section 7.2; [2003] ASA Bull. 829, 840; B. CORBOZ, *op. cit.*, p. 29.

enforceable judgments or awards on the same issue between the same parties would be contrary to (procedural) public policy.[67]

4. *Agreements to exclude challenges of awards*

Article 192(1) of the PILA grants the parties the right to waive, in advance, any rights to challenge an award rendered by an arbitral tribunal sitting in Switzerland before Swiss courts, or to exclude certain grounds for challenging the award. Such 'exclusion agreements' are possible only if neither party had 'its domicile, its habitual residence or a business establishment in Switzerland' when the agreement was made.

With respect to companies, this condition is fulfilled if the company has neither its registered office nor a branch in Switzerland. These are formal criteria, which are considered to be exhaustive (i.e. any other connection is irrelevant). Accordingly, a foreign company having a subsidiary in Switzerland can conclude a valid exclusion agreement since the subsidiary is a distinct legal entity.[68]

There is no case law regarding the question whether the establishment or the branch must have played a role in the underlying contract or in the dispute more generally. For the majority of legal commentators, the very presence of a subsidiary or a business establishment in Switzerland suffices to exclude the right to make an exclusion agreement, even if this subsidiary or business establishment was not involved in the case.

A valid exclusion agreement under Article 192 of the PILA does not necessarily preclude all judicial control over the award. If the parties have made a valid exclusion agreement and the award is enforced in Switzerland, the award is deemed to have been made abroad and the Swiss court seized with the enforcement proceedings may refuse enforcement under the provisions of the NY Convention, which apply by analogy (Article 192(2) of the PILA).

5. *Planned legislative changes regarding proceedings before the Swiss Federal Tribunal*

In 2001, the Swiss federal government presented a bill to the Swiss parliament that aims to simplify proceedings before the Swiss Federal Tribunal.[69]

---

67 DFT 127 III 279, 283.

68 R. BRINER, *Die Anfechtung und Vollstreckung des Schiedsentscheides* in K.-H. BÖCKSTIEGEL (ed), *Die Internationale Schiedsgerichtsbarkeit in der Schweiz (II)*, Carl Heymanns Verlag KG, 1989, p. 102; K. SIEHR in HEINI/KELLER/SIEHR/VISCHER/VOLKEN, N. 11, p. 1603; P. M. PATOCCHI/C. JERMINI in BERTI, N. 8, p. 602.

69 The French-language version of the Swiss Federal government's bill is published in the [2001] V *Feuille fédérale* (official government gazette), pp. 4281 *et seq.* The Federal government's explanatory '*Message*' is published in the [2001] V *Feuille fédérale*, pp. 4000 *et seq.*

The bill drew considerable criticism from arbitration specialists, because it simply subsumed challenges of arbitral awards in international matters under the provisions relating to appeals in civil cases. This was considered to be inappropriate because the bill failed to take into account several specificities of challenges of international arbitral awards, for example, the very limited grounds for setting aside (particularly with respect to findings of fact and law) and the principle that a challenge does not automatically stay the award.[70]

These criticisms were clearly voiced to and presumably understood by the parliamentary commissions that are currently working on the bill. It is expected that the future statute, which had not come before parliament at the time this chapter was completed, will essentially codify the current practice of the Swiss Federal Tribunal. Therefore, the main features of the process described above (namely, very limited grounds for setting aside; no review of findings of fact or law and, more generally, no review of substance except under the very restrictive public policy test; no stay unless granted upon reasoned application; etc.) should continue to be applicable under the future rules.

One change introduced by the bill which was received very positively was the abrogation of Article 191(2) of the PILA, pursuant to which the parties may agree that the court having jurisdiction to hear the challenge is not the Federal Tribunal, but the highest appellate court in the Canton where the arbitral tribunal is seated. Under the future rules, the Federal Tribunal will have exclusive jurisdiction to hear all challenges to international arbitral awards.

II. Revision of the award

1. Legal basis and grounds for 'revision' of international arbitral awards: general overview

In Swiss terminology, 'revision' means the process through which a court or arbitral tribunal is asked to reconsider, for very specific and narrow reasons, a decision that it has previously rendered. This is different from an appeal or an application to challenge an award, mainly because an application for revision is filed with the authority which rendered the decision under review (whereas an appeal or a challenge is brought before a higher court or a different judicial body).

Chapter 12 of the PILA does not contain any express provision on the revision of arbitral awards. However, in a landmark decision dated 11 March 1992, the Swiss Federal Tribunal held that certain provisions of the JOA on the revision of Federal Tribunal decisions were applicable by analogy to 'international' arbitral awards rendered in Switzerland.[71] In this decision, the Federal Tribunal held that the absence of any

---

70 For a general overview of the shortcomings of the 2001 bill see: J.-F. POUDRET, *Le projet de Loi sur le Tribunal fédéral est-il adapté aux recours en matière d'arbitrage international?* in [2002] I JdT 5.

71 DFT 118 II 199.

provision on revision in Chapter 12 of the PILA did not result from a deliberate legislative choice, but rather constituted a lacuna in the PILA, which the Federal Tribunal had the power to fill.

The Federal Tribunal also ruled, in the same decision, that not all grounds for revision provided in the JOA are applicable to international arbitration. The only grounds that can be relied upon in this context are those set out in Article 137 of the JOA.[72] This restriction has been confirmed in several subsequent decisions of the Federal Tribunal.[73]

Article 137 JOA provides as follows:[74]

Art. 137

b. New Facts — A motion for retrial of a Federal Tribunal decision is also possible:[75]

a. when criminal proceedings establish that the decision was influenced to the detriment of the moving party by a felony or a crime, even if no conviction ensued. If criminal prosecution is not possible, proof can be brought in another manner;

b. when the moving party has subsequent knowledge of new and important facts or finds convincing evidence that it had not been able to invoke in the previous proceedings.

In international arbitration, a party may thus seek revision of an award based, in essence, upon two grounds:

- the award was obtained or influenced by a criminal offence (such as forgery of an exhibit, false testimony, intimidation of a witness or bribery); or
- the party seeking revision has discovered new facts or new evidence that existed at the time the award was rendered and the outcome of the proceedings would likely have been different if the arbitral tribunal had known of such facts or evidence.

---

72 DFT 118 II 199, 204.

73 [2000] ASA Bull. 323, 326.

74 Free translation of the JOA.

75 The French version of the statutory text uses the term '*recevable*', which translates into '*admissible*' and which, if taken literally, pertains only to procedure as opposed to substance. However, this is a drafting error in the French text. The provision actually refers to the substantive conditions for a retrial. We have therefore employed the term '*possible*', which better conveys the meaning of the statute.

By restricting the scope of revision to Article 137 of the JOA, the Federal Tribunal excluded the application of Article 136 of the JOA to international arbitral awards. In summary, Article 136 of the JOA provides for the possibility of revision where the court that rendered the decision was improperly constituted (i.e. there was a ground for removal of one of the judges – Article 136(a) of the JOA), or where the court granted relief in excess of what was sought (*ultra petita* – Article 136(b) of the JOA), or where the court failed to rule on a prayer for relief (*infra petita* – Article 136(c) of the JOA), or where the court inadvertently failed to take into account important facts that were apparent on the face of the record (Article 136(d) of the JOA).

The Federal Tribunal excluded the first three of these grounds for revision from the field of international arbitration because Articles 190(2)(a) and 190(2)(b) of the PILA already provide for the challenge of an arbitral award on these grounds and thus exhaustively govern these issues.[76] The Federal Tribunal could not apply the fourth ground under Article 136 of the JOA to international arbitration because it does not even constitute a ground for setting aside an award. There was therefore no reason to open the door to this type of objection in the context of revision.

2. Procedural issues

a) General conditions for admissibility of applications for revision

aa) Jurisdiction to decide the application for revision

As provided in the Swiss Federal Tribunal's decision of 11 March 1992,[77] the judicial authority in Switzerland having jurisdiction to decide applications for revision of arbitral awards is the Federal Tribunal itself. However, the Federal Tribunal ruled that, where the parties have agreed pursuant to Article 191(2) of the PILA that a cantonal court shall decide challenges to the award (in lieu of the Federal Tribunal), such cantonal court shall also have jurisdiction to decide the application for revision.

The rationale for this decision is twofold. First, the Federal Tribunal held that it is preferable to vest such jurisdiction in a court, rather than in the arbitral tribunal having rendered the award, on the ground that courts are permanent, whereas arbitral tribunals will usually cease to exist once they have accomplished their mission. Second, the Federal Tribunal considered that the court having jurisdiction to decide applications to challenge the award should also have jurisdiction to decide applications for revision.

The parallel between jurisdiction for challenges and for revision raises the question of whether exclusion agreements pursuant to Article 192 of the PILA also exclude the possibility of revision. The majority of Swiss legal commentators consider that this is not the case, i.e. Article 192 of the PILA relates *only* to the exclusion of challenges. Up to

76 [1994] ASA Bull. 251, 254.
77 See note 71 *supra*.

the present, the Federal Tribunal has left this question open, but it has expressed similar views in *obiter dictum.*[78]

bb) The award is a decision capable of revision

Revision is possible only for 'arbitral awards'. This condition is obviously not controversial with respect to final awards.

By contrast, the revision of interim or partial awards raises an issue of interpretation. As explained in Section I.2.a)bb) *supra*, interim and partial awards can be challenged immediately based upon Article 190(3) of the PILA (which enables a party to challenge interim awards immediately if the arbitral tribunal was irregularly constituted or erred in ruling on its jurisdiction). Apart from this statutory provision, the Swiss Federal Tribunal has held that challenges to partial or interim awards are possible if a party establishes that such an award will likely cause it to suffer irreparable harm. Given the parallel that the Federal Tribunal generally draws between the challenge and the revision of awards, these rules would also appear to apply to the revision of interim and partial awards.

It should, however, be noted that the irregular constitution of the arbitral tribunal does not constitute a ground for revision. Accordingly, the revision of interim and partial awards should be possible on the basis that the arbitral tribunal erred in ruling on its jurisdiction or in other cases where a party demonstrates a risk of irreparable harm, but not on the basis of the irregular constitution of the arbitral tribunal.

In any event, revision of procedural orders or rulings is not possible, since these are not 'awards'. This applies equally to orders granting provisional interim relief, which can by their very nature be reversed or amended by the arbitral tribunal. A party that wishes to seek reconsideration of such decisions must address its request to the arbitral tribunal.

cc) The party seeking revision was party to the arbitral proceedings

A further condition that is usually mentioned in legal commentary is that the party seeking revision must have been a party to the arbitral proceedings. Third parties (for instance, guarantors of a party that was ordered to pay money) that did not participate in the arbitration may not request revision. It is an entirely open question whether the exceptions relating to the challenge of awards by persons or entities that were not parties to the arbitral proceedings, as described in Section I.2.a)cc) *supra*, are applicable to revision.

dd) Time limits

Pursuant to Article 141(1)(b) of the JOA, an application for revision must be filed within ninety days from the discovery of the ground for revision. The rules relating to the computation of this time limit are identical to those for applications to set aside awards (see Section I.2.a)dd) *supra*).

---

78 [1997] ASA Bull. 494, 497.

Article 141(1)(b) of the JOA also provides that the application for revision may be filed at the *earliest* upon notification of the award, or where the basis of the revision is a criminal offence, upon closing of the criminal proceedings (as explained at Section b) *infra*, revision based on a criminal offence may be sought only if criminal proceedings have been initiated and only once those proceedings have ended, irrespective of whether there was a conviction). An application filed before the end of the criminal proceedings would be declared premature and, consequently, inadmissible. However, the applicant would have the right to re-file the application for revision again once the criminal proceedings have ended.

With respect to important new facts, the starting date is construed as being the time when the applicant had 'sufficient knowledge' of the new facts to decide whether to file an application for revision, even if the applicant was not in a position at that time to prove the relevant facts with conclusive evidence.[79] Moreover, if an auxiliary or agent of the applicant, such as an attorney, becomes aware of the relevant facts or evidence, the ninety-day time limit begins to run at that time.[80] That said, vague knowledge, for example through press reports, is not sufficient to trigger the time limit.[81]

ee) Formal requirements relating to the application for revision

Article 140 of the JOA requires that the application specify the ground for revision that is being invoked. This means, in practice, that a reasoned application for revision must be filed within the statutory time limit. As a result, a simple statement indicating that the applicant intends to seek revision, or a simple declaration without reasons, are inadmissible. The filing of an unreasoned statement thus has no legal effect and, in particular, it does not toll the time limit under Article 141 of the JOA.

Moreover, Article 140 of the JOA also requires that all appropriate evidence in support of the applicant's case be attached to the application. It is not possible to file evidence at a later stage, unless the Federal Tribunal orders a second exchange of written submissions (which, to our knowledge, has never occurred in cases relating to international arbitration).

Article 140 of the JOA also provides that the application for revision must set forth the precise relief sought, i.e. it must specify what change or changes to the award are said to

---

79 J.-F. POUDRET, *Commentaire de la loi fédérale d'organisation judiciaire*, Vol. V, Articles 136-171, Mise à jour du texte légal et du commentaire des articles 1-82, Stämpfli, Bern 1992, N. 1.2, p. 60 ; A. RIGOZZI/M. SCHÖLL, *Die Revision des Schiedssprüchen nach den 12. Kapitel des IPRG*, Bibliothek zur Zeitschrift für schweizerisches Recht, Beiheft 37, Helbing & Lichtenhahn, Basel 2002, p. 27.

80 Unreported decision of the Swiss Federal Tribunal of 8 April 1998, cited by A. RIGOZZI/M. SCHÖLL, *op. cit.*, pp. 27-28.

81 Unreported decision of the Swiss Federal Tribunal decision of 5 July 1994, cited by A. RIGOZZI/M. SCHÖLL, *op. cit.*, p. 27.

be required. In the absence of sufficiently specific request for relief, the application shall be declared inadmissible.

Finally, it should be noted that there is no need to obtain leave to file an application for revision. However, the remarks made above in regard to challenges also apply to the revision of awards – the Federal Tribunal will examine *ex officio* all conditions of admissibility and may declare the application inadmissible in cases where the conditions of admissibility are not met or dismiss the application outright, if it is clearly without any merit. The practical result of such rulings is similar to a refusal to grant leave.

b) Conditions of admissibility that are specific to Article 137(a) of the JOA (award obtained or influenced by a criminal offence)

Pursuant to Article 137(a) of the JOA, an application for revision based upon a criminal offence is admissible only if criminal proceedings have established that the offence was committed. This requirement actually involves three conditions:

- before seeking revision, the party considering that the outcome of the arbitration was influenced by a criminal offence must first initiate criminal proceedings, unless it is impossible to bring such criminal proceedings (see second sentence of Article 137(b) of the JOA);
- Article 141(1)(b) of the JOA expressly states that an application for revision based on Article 137(a) of the JOA cannot be filed before the criminal proceedings have ended.[82] Therefore, considerable time may pass between the moment when the applicant discovers the criminal offence and the date on which revision can be sought on the basis of such offence (and during that time, the award is enforceable);
- the criminal proceedings must establish that the offence was actually committed; whether or not the criminal proceedings resulted in a conviction is immaterial.[83]

To our knowledge, there have been no applications to date for revision of international arbitral awards based on Article 137(a) of the JOA.

---

82 In certain Swiss court decisions and legal commentaries, an exception to this requirement is made for cases in which the criminal proceedings were discontinued due to the death of the accused or for other reasons such as expiry of the limitation period. There is no case law on this point in the field of international arbitration.

83 For instance, the criminal proceedings may result in the finding that a criminal offence was committed, but that the author of the offence was not identifiable or could not be convicted for other reasons (such as mental illness).

c) Conditions of admissibility that are specific to Article 137(b) of the JOA (important new facts or evidence)

Applications for revision based on Article 137(b) of the JOA (important new facts or evidence) are admissible only if the applicant establishes that it has a '*legal interest*' in the revision of the award. In other words, when examining whether the application is admissible from a procedural point of view, the Swiss Federal Tribunal will consider whether the circumstances alleged are capable, *prima facie*, of changing the outcome of the arbitral proceedings in favour of the applicant.

In practice, this condition excludes any application based upon circumstances that would have caused the arbitral tribunal to adopt different reasons, but not to modify the concrete result of the arbitration. It also means that, if the award is based upon several alternative reasons, the important new facts or evidence must be such that they would have led to a different – and more favourable – result on each of the alternative lines of reasoning adopted by the arbitral tribunal.[84]

This condition does not mean that, when verifying the procedural admissibility of the application, the Federal Tribunal will examine in detail whether the applicant has actually established that revision is justified.[85] The Federal Tribunal will simply examine whether, in the abstract, the circumstances alleged by the applicant falls within one of the hypotheses of Article 137(b) of the JOA.

d) The proceedings before the Swiss Federal Tribunal

aa) Mains steps and overall duration of the proceedings

The proceedings for revision follow the same general pattern as proceedings relating to challenges of awards. The main steps are:

- filing of the application in accordance with Articles 140 and 141 of the JOA;
- provision of security for the court costs, within a time limit of approximately three weeks after the date of filing, failing which the application will be declared inadmissible without further ado;
- verification of the procedural admissibility of the application and examination of whether the application obviously lacks merit on its face, both *ex officio* (the application is sometimes declared inadmissible or dismissed at this stage, without requesting the adverse party to comment);

---

84 [2000] ASA Bull. 323, 328.

85 This question relates to the substantive merits of the application, not to its admissibility. The Swiss Federal Tribunal re-affirmed this principle in a decision of 9 July 1997, reported in [1997] ASA Bull. 506, 509 (this decision was not rendered in the context of international arbitration, but the underlying principle is generally applicable); see also J.-F. POUDRET, *op. cit.*, Introductory Remark, p. 21, and N. 1, p. 13; A. RIGOZZI/M. SCHÖLL, *op. cit.*, p. 11.

- if the application is admissible and not devoid of merit on its face, the adverse party will be requested to file written submissions, with exhibits if any, and the arbitral tribunal will be requested to comment (Article 143(2) of the JOA).[86] This order is usually made approximately five to six weeks after filing of the application; the time limit for filing the written submissions and comments on the application is 30 days. In practice, the arbitral tribunal will ordinarily refrain from making any comment;
- approximately two to four months after receipt of the last written submission, the Federal Tribunal will render its decision, which is communicated in the form of an order without reasons. The reasons are provided approximately four to six weeks later.

The overall duration of proceedings for revision is thus the same as for challenges (approximately four and a half to six months from filing of the application to receipt of the decision by the parties).

bb) No stay of enforcement of the award under revision, unless ordered otherwise by the Federal Tribunal

In accordance with Article 142 of the JOA, the filing of an application for revision does not stay the award. However, the Swiss Federal Tribunal has discretion to order a stay upon reasoned request by the party seeking revision (which request is usually made in the same submission as the application for revision).

The conditions for the stay of enforcement in the context of revision are substantially the same as in applications to challenge the award (very strong chance of success; irreparable harm; urgency). Reference is therefore made to Section I.2.b)bb) *supra*.

Article 142 of the JOA expressly states that the Federal Tribunal may grant a stay subject to the provision of security. Such security is aimed at protecting the adverse party from damages that it might suffer if a stay is ordered but the application for revision is ultimately denied.

The proceedings relating to a stay of enforcement run in parallel with the proceedings in regard to the application itself and will be completed before the overall proceedings. As with the challenge of awards, the Federal Tribunal's ruling on the stay will usually foreshadow its decision on the substance of the application – if a stay is requested and denied, it is all but certain that the application for revision will meet the same fate. If a

86 Article 143(3) of the JOA provides that a second exchange of written submissions or oral proceedings are '*exceptional*'. To our knowledge, a second exchange of submissions has never been ordered in connection with the revision of an arbitral award in international matters. Moreover, although a possibility under Article 143(4) of the JOA, the Federal Tribunal has never, to our knowledge, taken evidence in international arbitration matters.

stay is granted, there are strong chances that a revision will be ordered, although this has not yet occurred in practice.

cc) Costs

Costs relating to applications for revision are subject to the same principles as challenges of awards. Reference is therefore made to Section I.2.b)dd) *supra*.

3. Substantive issues

a) Substantive conditions for revision based on a criminal offence (Article 137(a) of the JOA)

In order to justify revision under Article 137(a) of the JOA, the applicant must show:

- that criminal proceedings have established that a criminal offence was committed; and
- that this criminal offence is a serious offence – the statute refers to 'felonies' or 'crimes';[87] and
- that this offence influenced the outcome of the arbitration to the applicant's detriment.

As already mentioned above, this ground for revision presupposes that criminal proceedings have been initiated and completed (subject to narrow exceptions). However, it is not necessary for the criminal proceedings to establish the causal link between the offence and the outcome of the arbitration. This causal link can be established in the revision proceedings themselves.[88]

The criminal offences contemplated by this provision are, generally speaking, perjury (where the arbitral award was influenced by testimony of a person considered to be a sworn witness within the meaning of the applicable criminal law), false testimony (in other cases), bribery (of an arbitrator, a witness or an expert), forgery of evidence or intimidation of witnesses.

The determination of the applicable criminal law is complicated and not settled. For example, it is not clear whether revision can be sought if the facts at issue constitute a criminal offence under a foreign law but not under Swiss law.

Moreover, the determination of jurisdiction and the applicable criminal law can be problematic in cases where the facts occurred outside of Switzerland. For example, if a witness domiciled in London gives false testimony during a hearing in Paris, does the

---

87 Under Swiss law, 'felonies' and 'crimes' are criminal offences that carry a minimum penalty of 'reclusion' or 'imprisonment' (as opposed to misdemeanours, which are punishable by 'jailing'). The minimum duration of the sentence depends upon the characterization of the offence.

88 J.-F. POUDRET, *op. cit.*, N. 1.2, p. 24.

fact that the seat of the arbitral tribunal is in Switzerland confer jurisdiction upon the Swiss penal authorities to prosecute the witness and does it trigger the application of Swiss criminal law? It is submitted that these are questions to be resolved by the criminal authorities within the framework of the criminal proceedings.

As for the causal link between the criminal offence and the outcome of the arbitration, the applicant must show that the criminal offence clearly influenced the arbitral tribunal's rulings on the relief requested by the parties. Conversely, no revision is possible if the criminal offence serves as the basis for a finding of fact that was not relevant to the outcome of the dispute (for example, the arbitral tribunal considered that the testimony of a perjured witness was irrelevant for the outcome of the arbitration).

b) Substantive conditions for revision based on new and important facts or evidence (Article 137(b) of the JOA)

Under Article 137(b) of the JOA, revision based on the discovery of new and important facts or evidence is possible if the cumulative conditions described below are met.

The application must be based upon 'facts' or evidence relating to 'facts'. This condition precludes reliance on changes to the law that may occur after the award has been rendered.[89]

In addition, the facts relied upon by the applicant must have existed at the time the award was rendered (or the new evidence must relate to facts that existed at that time). Circumstances that arose after the rendering of the award do not constitute grounds for revision.[90]

Furthermore, the facts or evidence must have been discovered after the award was rendered (see the term '*subsequent knowledge*' in Article 137(b) of the JOA). In this regard, the applicant must establish that, through no fault of its own, it was prevented from or otherwise unable to adduce the relevant facts or evidence in the course of the arbitral proceedings. This means that the applicant must show that it acted diligently in the arbitral proceedings and that it did everything it could to elucidate the facts that it deemed relevant to its case.[91] In international arbitration matters, the Swiss Federal Tribunal has adopted a rather strict approach in regard to this condition.[92]

Finally, the new facts (or the facts to which the newly discovered evidence relate) must be 'important', i.e. relevant to the outcome of the dispute. This is a crucial condition. The applicant must establish that the arbitral tribunal would *likely* have ruled differently *and in the applicant's favour* if it had known of the new facts (or the newly discovered

---

89 J.-F. POUDRET, *op. cit.*, N. 2.2.1, pp. 26-27.

90 J.-F. POUDRET, *op. cit.*, N. 2.2.3, pp. 27-28.

91 This condition flows from the final words of Article 137(b) of the JOA. See also J.-F. POUDRET, *op. cit.*, N. 2.2.5, 29-30pp; A. RIGOZZI/M. SCHÖLL, *op. cit.*, pp. 44-45 (with references to unreported decisions).

92 [2000] ASA Bull. 323, 329 (relating to new evidence).

evidence) when rendering its award.[93] A distinction must be drawn here in regard to the standard of proof. The application for revision must establish the objective *existence* of the facts relied upon by the applicant. However, the application must only establish the *likelihood* of a more favourable award based upon those facts. In other words, although it puts the applicant to a strict standard of proof with respect to the accuracy of the new facts alleged, the Swiss Federal Tribunal will only examine the relevance of those facts to the outcome of the arbitration on a *hypothetical* basis. If the Federal Tribunal is satisfied that the 'new' facts or evidence *could* lead the arbitral tribunal to a different ruling in the favour of the applicant, it will order revision of the award. The question of whether the outcome of the arbitration will actually be different in practice is left to the arbitral tribunal. That said, the Federal Tribunal sets a relatively high threshold in this regard – to date and to our knowledge, it has never found that an application for revision has satisfied this test.

4. Consequences of a successful application for revision

If the Swiss Federal Tribunal decides that the application for revision is valid on the merits, it will set aside the award and refer the matter back to the arbitral tribunal for a new decision.[94] If possible, the arbitral tribunal should be constituted of the same arbitrators as the original tribunal. If this is not possible, a new tribunal must be constituted.

In proceedings relating to revision, the Federal Tribunal only examines whether the conditions for revision are met. It does not re-try the case itself. Therefore, the Federal Tribunal will not set out what it considers to be the proper outcome of the new arbitral proceedings. This is the task of the arbitral tribunal in the new proceedings.[95]

If revision is ordered based upon a criminal offence, the arbitral tribunal is bound by the Federal Tribunal's findings on the existence of a criminal offence and on the influence that the offence had on the outcome of the original arbitral proceedings. However, depending on the facts of each case, the arbitral tribunal continues to have the power to weigh the concrete impact of the criminal offence on the outcome of the new arbitral proceedings and other factors may enter into consideration, which were not relevant in the original proceedings.

---

93 See note 71 *supra* (decision of Swiss Federal Tribunal of 11 March 1992); see also J.-F. POUDRET, *op. cit.* N. 2.2.2, p. 27; A. RIGOZZI/M. SCHÖLL, *op. cit.*, pp. 47-48 (with reference to an unreported Swiss Federal Tribunal decision).

94 Article 144(1) of the JOA, first sentence.

95 The distinction between the decision ordering revision and the new ruling in the subsequent arbitral proceedings corresponds to the distinction between the '*rescindant*' phase (which determines whether or not to set aside the decision and to subject the case to a fresh review) and the '*rescisoire*' phase (in which a new decision is made on the substance of the case). The distinction between '*rescindant*' and '*rescisoire*' is well known in civil law jurisdictions.

If revision is ordered based upon new facts or evidence, the arbitral tribunal is bound by the Federal Tribunal's findings on the existence of those facts or evidence. However, since the Federal Tribunal only makes a hypothetical assessment of the relevance of those facts (or evidence) on the outcome of the arbitration, the arbitral tribunal retains full power to determine the *concrete relevance* of them.

As a consequence, a successful application for revision will not necessarily result in a new award that is different from the original award.[96]

Nevertheless, considering the Swiss Federal Tribunal's openly stated policy of upholding arbitral awards unless there is a very serious deficiency, one can assume in practice that, if and when the Federal Tribunal sets aside an award and orders revision, the circumstances of the case will be such that the outcome of the new arbitral proceedings will be different from the original award.

5. Planned legislative changes regarding proceedings before the Swiss Federal Tribunal

The 2001 bill on proceedings before the Swiss Federal Tribunal mentioned above also contains provisions on revision of decisions by the Federal Tribunal. As with the current rules of the JOA, these provisions do not apply directly to the revision of arbitral awards, and will therefore remain applicable to international arbitration only by analogy.

The bill did not make any substantive changes to the rules of the JOA that are relevant for the revision of international arbitral awards and the main features of the proceedings are the same. Therefore, subject to changes that may yet be proposed during the legislative process, the principles set out above should continue to apply under the future statute in regard to the revision of international arbitral awards in Switzerland.

---

96 For example, in the original award, the arbitral tribunal may have denied a claim for damages based on a finding that there was no breach (so that the arbitral tribunal did not take evidence on quantum). It later transpires that the arbitral tribunal's finding on the breach rested on a forged document (revision based on a criminal offence), or a party subsequently discovers evidence establishing the breach (revision based on new facts or evidence). In the new proceedings, the arbitral tribunal may accept that there was a breach, but decline to award the damages claimed (or only reduced damages) on the ground that the claimant did not prove quantum.

Chapter 9 - Recognition and Enforcement of Foreign Arbitral Awards

Martin Bernet and Anna K. Müller

I. Introduction

1. Article 194 of the PILA and the NY Convention

The recognition and enforcement of foreign arbitral awards in Switzerland is governed by Article 194 of the PILA and by the NY Convention. Switzerland ratified the NY Convention on 1 June 1965 and it entered into force on 30 August 1965. Originally, Switzerland applied the NY Convention under the reciprocity reservation, i.e. the requirement that the award to be recognised and enforced in Switzerland must be issued in a contracting state. This situation changed with the entry into force of the PILA on 1 January 1989. Article 194 of the PILA provides that the NY Convention shall be applicable to the recognition and enforcement of all foreign arbitral awards. Consequently, the NY Convention is applied *erga omnes*, i.e. to all foreign awards rendered after 1 January 1989, irrespective of whether or not the award was made in a contracting state.[1]

Despite the reference in Article 194 of the PILA to the NY Convention, the latter is not applied in Switzerland as national law but as an international treaty. As a consequence, in order to ensure internationally uniform application, Swiss courts are required to take into account not only Swiss but also foreign decisions interpreting the NY Convention.[2]

---

1 As a consequence, Switzerland formally withdrew its reciprocity reservation with effect as of 23 April 1993.

2 P. M. PATOCCHI, *The New York Convention - The Swiss Practice*, in (1996) 9 ASA Special Series 151.

G. Kaufmann-Kohler and B. Stucki (eds), International Arbitration in Switzerland, A Handbook for Practitioners, 167-179.

2. *Bilateral treaties*

Article VII of the NY Convention provides that the NY Convention shall not affect the application of other bi- or multilateral treaties entered into by the contracting states concerning the recognition and enforcement of arbitral awards.

Switzerland is a party to various bilateral treaties concerning the recognition and enforcement of arbitral awards.[3] A party applying for the recognition and enforcement of an award rendered in a contracting state to a bilateral treaty may therefore rely upon the NY Convention or the bilateral treaty, whichever is more favourable.[4]

3. *The recognition and enforcement of ICSID awards*

The ICSID Convention[5] provides for institutional arbitration in respect of investment disputes between a contracting state and a person or legal entity of another contracting state, if the parties have stipulated in writing that the ICSID Convention is applicable. Pursuant to Article 54 of the ICSID Convention, the contracting states must recognize an award rendered pursuant to the ICSID Convention as binding and enforce the pecuniary obligations[6] imposed by that award as if it were a final judgment of a court in that state. Therefore, neither the NY Convention nor Article 194 of the PILA are applicable with respect to ICSID awards. Rather, ICSID awards are enforced pursuant to the domestic law on enforcement of domestic judicial decisions, which excludes, in particular, the application of public policy rules.[7]

4. *The notion of 'foreign arbitral award' for purposes of recognition and enforcement*

a) Arbitral awards

An arbitral award is a decision made by an arbitral tribunal (be it an *ad hoc* arbitral tribunal or a permanent arbitral body; see Article I(2) of the NY Convention). Expert determinations do not qualify as arbitral awards;[8] they cannot be enforced immediately, but only indirectly through a claim based upon the contractual provision giving rise to such determination. While foreign partial awards and awards of costs can be recognised

---

3 Switzerland has concluded bilateral treaties with Belgium, Germany, Italy, Liechtenstein, Austria, Sweden and Spain. Some of these conventions deal not only with the recognition and enforcement of arbitral awards but also with other issues, such as the recognition and enforcement of judicial decisions in family matters or inheritance law.

4 DFT 110 Ib 194; K. SIEHR in HEINI/KELLER/SIEHR/VISCHER/VOLKEN, N. 5, p. 1622.

5 The ICSID Convention entered into force in Switzerland on 14 June 1968.

6 The obligation to enforce does not extend to other forms of relief such as specific performance (see C. H. SCHREUER, *The ICSID Convetion: a Commentary*, Cambridge University Press, Cambridge 2001, N. 69 to 74, pp. 1124-1126).

7 F. SATMER, *Verweigerung der Anerkennung ausländischer Schiedssprüche wegen Verfahrensmängeln*, Diss. Zürich 1994, p. 20.

8 DFT 117 I 365.

and enforced under the NY Convention, foreign court decisions recognising an award or declaring it enforceable and procedural orders cannot.[9]

b) Foreign arbitral awards

The NY Convention only applies to the recognition and enforcement of foreign arbitral awards. An arbitral award is considered to be foreign if it was rendered by an arbitral tribunal whose seat was *not* in Switzerland. The seat of an arbitral tribunal is at the place stipulated by the parties in the arbitration agreement, or, if the arbitration agreement does not provide for a seat, at the place determined by the arbitral tribunal.

Usually, the arbitral award explicitly indicates where the seat of the arbitral tribunal is located, and if there is such an indication, the Swiss court is bound by it.[10] The seat of the arbitral tribunal is not necessarily at the place where the hearings were conducted or where all or some of the arbitrators signed the award.[11] Also, the fact that the parties have chosen Swiss law to apply to the arbitral procedure or to the merits of the dispute does not *per se* imply that the arbitral tribunal has its seat in Switzerland.[12]

There is one situation where the NY Convention applies to the recognition and enforcement of an award made by an arbitral tribunal with its seat in Switzerland. This is where none of the parties has its domicile, habitual residence, or business establishment in Switzerland and the parties have by express agreement, fully or partially waived the right to challenge the award before the Swiss courts. In such an event, the NY Convention applies by analogy to recognition and enforcement in Switzerland (Article 192(2) of the PILA).

5. Recognition and enforcement

Recognition of a foreign award means that the award is given the same effect in Switzerland as in its country of origin. Hence, the award will carry the effect of *res judicata*. The Swiss courts will thus be bound by it and the parties barred from re-litigating the same matter. If matters already decided in a foreign award are raised in a

---

9 P. M. PATOCCHI/C. JERMINI in BERTI, N. 7 p. 634.

10 P. M. PATOCCHI, *op. cit.*, N. 2, p. 153.

11 G. KAUFMANN-KOHLER, *Arbitration Procedure: Identifying and Applying the Law Governing the Arbitration Procedure – The Role of the Law of the Place of Arbitration in Improving the Efficiency of Arbitration Agreements and Awards: 40 Years of Application of the New York Convention*, in (1999) 9 ICCA Congress Series 356 and *Le lieu de l'arbitrage à l'aune de la mondialisation – Réflexions à propos de deux formes récentes d'arbitrage*, in [1998] Rev. Arb. 517.

12 P. M. PATOCCHI/C. JERMINI in BERTI, N. 13, p. 635. Conversely, an award by an arbitral tribunal with its seat in Switzerland does not qualify as a foreign award even if the tribunal applies foreign law. Arbitral awards rendered by an arbitral tribunal with seat in Switzerland must be declared enforceable by the competent court at the place where the arbitral tribunal has its seat and are then enforced as a Swiss judicial decision.

court proceeding in Switzerland, the court may recognize the award as a preliminary matter without separate recognition proceedings being required.

Enforcement of a foreign award means that its terms are 'physically' enforced by coercive measures, i.e. that debt collection or other enforcement proceedings can be commenced and execution carried out in Switzerland.

The difference between recognition and enforcement is of particular importance when it comes to declaratory awards. Declaratory awards cannot be 'enforced', but only recognised in Switzerland.[13]

II. Enforcement proceedings

Swiss court proceedings for the enforcement of a foreign arbitral award are, in principle, the same as those for foreign judicial decisions.[14] The enforcement procedure depends on the nature of the relief awarded. Where an amount of money has been awarded, the arbitral award is enforced on the basis of the DEBA, whereas for other awards (e.g. injunctions), the procedural provisions of each Canton apply (see Section II.*2 infra*). Awards that contain both the award of a sum of money and other awards must therefore be enforced in two separate proceedings.[15] Normally, the *exequatur*, i.e. the question whether or not the foreign award can be recognised and/or enforced in Switzerland, is decided as a preliminary question by the enforcing court, but the party seeking enforcement may also institute separate proceedings limited to *exequatur* (see Section II.*3 infra*).

1. Awards of a sum of money

a) Commencement of debt collection

Pursuant to the provisions of the DEBA, the creditor (i.e. the party which has been awarded a sum of money) commences enforcement proceedings by a request for debt collection[16] to the debt collection office, normally, at the place of the debtor's domicile (Article 46 of the DEBA). The request for debt collection can be submitted by using the official form issued by the debt collection authorities, or in any other written form, or orally at the debt collection office. The creditor must pay a modest fee, which depends on the amount of the claim.[17]

---

13 Decision of the Cour de Cassation of the Canton of Neuchâtel of 15 January 1996 in [1996] RJN 60.

14 DFT 101 Ia 521.

15 P. M. PATOCCHI/C. JERMINI in BERTI, N. 35, p. 643.

16 *Betreibungsbegehren/Réquisition de poursuite*.

17 The fees for issuing and serving the payment order range between CHF 7 and CHF 400 as set out in the Federal Order to the DEBA on Fees (*Gebührenverordnung/ Ordonnance sur les émoluments perçus en application de la loi fédérale sur la poursuite pour dettes et faillite*.

b) Opposition and summary court proceedings

Upon receipt of the request for debt collection, the debt collection office issues a payment order[18] and serves it on the debtor. The payment order requires the debtor either to pay the debt within twenty days or file an objection (known as an 'opposition')[19] within ten days. If the debtor fails to take either step, the creditor may request that debt collection proceedings be continued at any time within one year after the debtor was served with the payment order.

If the debtor objects to the payment order within ten days, the creditor can commence summary court proceedings for an order setting aside the opposition.[20] The time limit for commencing such proceedings is also one year after service of the payment order on the debtor.

If the creditor does not act within one year after service of the payment order, he is free to commence fresh debt collection proceedings, starting with a new request for debt collection.

In such summary court proceedings, the court ordinarily examines two issues:

- whether the prerequisites for the recognition and enforcement of the foreign award stated in the NY Convention are met (Articles IV and V of the NY Convention); and
- (if raised by the debtor) whether the debt under the award has been paid, deferred, or become time-barred. The defences of redemption or deferred payment terms are entertained only if supported by documents.

The court will normally render its decision within a few weeks. The time required primarily depends upon the court's workload and the complexity of the case. Court costs and attorneys' fees vary between a few hundred and several thousand Swiss francs, depending upon the amount of the award and the complexity of the case.

The court's decision is subject to appeal within the court system of the Canton where enforcement proceedings were commenced and a final appeal lies to the Swiss Federal Tribunal. If the defendant avails itself of all possibilities of appeal, the court proceedings for setting aside the opposition may last several months. In one reported case, it took more than two years for the foreign award to be declared enforceable.[21]

18 *Zahlungsbefehl* (*Commandement de payer*).

19 *Rechtsvorschlag/Opposition*.

20 *Rechtsöffnung/Mainlevée*.

21 D. HOCHSTRASSER, *A Case Study: Switzerland* in (1996) 9 ASA Special Series, pp. 208 *et seq*. In other published cases, the proceedings took between two and eight months before the first instance, three to five months before the second instance, and between three and fourteen months before the Swiss Federal Tribunal (DFT 101 Ib 191, DFT 108 Ib 85, JdT

c) Continuation of debt-collection proceedings

Only once the court decision setting aside the debtor's opposition is final, may the creditor request that debt collection proceedings be continued.[22] These proceedings are reasonably expeditious, although certain decisions on the way to the realisation of the debtor's assets may again be challenged in the courts.

2. *Non-monetary awards*

These awards can be declaratory awards, orders for specific performance or restitution of a chattel, awards of rights in real property, or orders requiring a party to refrain from or perform a specified act (e.g. restraining orders or orders requiring a party to make a specific declaration).[23]

As civil procedure is not currently unified in Switzerland (i.e. each of Switzerland's 26 Cantons still has its own Code of Civil Procedure), non-monetary awards are enforced pursuant to the procedural rules of each Canton. Typically, these rules provide for summary proceedings, similar to those applicable to the enforcement of awards for a sum of money.[24]

3. *Proceedings limited to the question of exequatur*

Rather than commencing enforcement proceedings, a party may elect to seek first a court declaration on the recognition and enforceability of the foreign award in separate *exequatur* proceedings.[25] This may, for example, be the case where the party ordered to pay a sum of money is expected to comply with the award once the enforceability of the award in Switzerland is confirmed by the Swiss courts.

1992 II 115, (1997) SJZ 17, [1991] BJM 144 and unreported decision of the Swiss Federal Tribunal of 31 May 2002 (4P.102/2001)).

22 *Fortsetzungsbegehren/ Requisition de continuer la poursuite*. If the debtor is registered in the Swiss Commercial Register, the debt collection will take the form of bankruptcy proceedings. If the debtor is a private individual, it will take the form of a proceeding for the seizure of specific assets. If sufficient security was given, the proceeding will be limited to the realisation of that security.

23 P. M. PATOCCHI/C. JERMINI in BERTI, N. 47, p. 646.

24 Following an amendment to the Swiss Federal Constitution, which gives the federal state the power to legislate in the area of civil procedural law and which was accepted by the majority of the Swiss people and all 26 cantons in a popular vote in the year 2000, a group of experts appointed by the Federal Justice Department prepared a draft Federal Civil Procedure Act which will replace the existing cantonal codes. The draft is presently going through a consultation process that will be completed during the course of 2004. The new Federal Civil Procedure Act is not expected to enter into force for a few years. Under the draft (Articles 325 *et seq.*), the enforcement of awards other than for a sum of money will continue to be carried out through summary proceedings.

25 DFT 116 Ia 394.

Separate *exequatur* proceedings are typically summary proceedings and are governed by the rules of the civil procedure of the Canton concerned.[26]

While the Swiss Federal Tribunal has never positively confirmed that a decision on the *exequatur* of a foreign award obtained in separate proceedings is binding in subsequent enforcement proceedings,[27] it is highly likely that this is the case, given that the Swiss Federal Tribunal has come to this conclusion in regard to foreign court judgments.[28]

4. Protective measures

Neither the foreign award as such nor the declaration of enforceability in Switzerland (the '*exequatur*' decision; see Section II.*3 supra*) *per se* give a party the right to obtain protective measures aimed at securing the enforcement of the award.[29] Rather, the general rules for obtaining protective measures apply.

The enforcement of awards of a sum of money can be secured by way of a civil attachment, i.e. an order freezing assets of the debtor. With respect to debtors domiciled outside Switzerland, a civil attachment can be obtained quite easily, in reliance on an enforceable award, and the order will be granted *ex parte*. In order to obtain a civil attachment against persons domiciled in Switzerland, it is necessary to establish on a *prima facie* basis that certain additional conditions are fulfilled (e.g. that the debtor is removing his assets with the intent to evade his obligations).[30]

With regard to non-monetary awards, a protective measure can only be obtained if the creditor can make a *prima facie* showing that the prerequisites under the civil procedure of the Canton concerned are met. Although such requirements may vary slightly from Canton to Canton, the applicant must typically show that there is an imminent risk that the enforcement of his claim would be jeopardized without a protective measure. The judge has wide discretion in deciding whether or not to grant a protective order *ex parte* or only after hearing both parties.[31]

---

26 These rules will soon be replaced by the new Federal Civil Procedure Act (see footnote 24 *supra*).

27 DFT 116 Ia 394.

28 DFT 118 Ia 118, § 6, as cited in (1997) 96 ZR 110 and JDT 1994 II 148. With particular regard to judgments rendered in a state with which Switzerland has concluded a treaty on the enforcement of judgments, the Swiss Federal Tribunal had found in an earlier decision (DFT 115 III 28) that the *exequatur* decision is binding in subsequent enforcement proceedings.

29 This is different with regard to judgments emanating from courts in Western European states where, according to Article 39 of the Lugano Convention, the judgment creditor has the right to obtain *ex parte* protective measures from the Swiss enforcement judge simultaneously with the declaration of enforceability.

30 See Articles 271 and 272 of the DEBA.

31 The existing cantonal rules will soon be replaced by the new Federal Civil Procedure Act (see footnote 24 *supra*). The Federal Civil Procedure Act will not change the conditions for obtaining protective measures (see draft Articles 275 *et seq.*).

An application for a civil attachment or a protective measure under cantonal civil procedure law can be made before or after the commencement of enforcement proceedings. If the application is made prior to the commencement of enforcement proceedings, i.e. at a stage where no Swiss judge has yet decided on the enforceability of the foreign award, the judge seized with the request for a civil attachment or for protective measures will be required to make a decision on this question, applying a *prima facie* test to determine whether the conditions of the NY Convention are met.[32]

III. Requirements for recognition and enforcement (Article IV of the NY Convention)

Article IV(1) of the NY Convention provides that the party applying for recognition and enforcement of a foreign arbitral award must submit the following documents:

- the original duly authenticated award or a duly certified copy thereof;
- the original or a duly certified copy of the arbitration agreement.

Furthermore, pursuant to Article IV(2) of the NY Convention, the party seeking enforcement must provide a translation in German, French, or Italian of the award and the arbitration agreement, depending upon where in Switzerland the award is sought to be enforced. The translation must be certified by an official or sworn translator or by a diplomatic or consular agent.

The term 'authenticated', as used in Article IV(1) of the NY Convention, means that the arbitral award must be signed and that the signature(s) must be legalised by a competent authority. A certified copy is a copy on which a notary public certifies that the copy and the original are identical. The NY Convention does not stipulate which law is applicable to determine the validity of the authentication and/or certification. The general view is that it is sufficient if the authentication/certification fulfils the requirements of the law under which it was executed or the law of the country in which enforcement of the award is sought.[33] Arguably, this means *inter alia* that if, under one of those laws, the signature of the chairperson alone (as opposed to the signatures of all members of the arbitral tribunal) is sufficient, this should satisfy the requirement for due authentication. It does not, however, appear that this question has arisen before the Swiss courts up to the present. Swiss embassies and consulates are authorised to authenticate the signatures of the arbitrators. Certified translations can be done either in Switzerland or abroad.

In recent Swiss case law, there has been growing flexibility regarding the formal requirements set forth in Article IV of the NY Convention.[34] Before certain cantonal

---

32 W. STOFFEL in STAEHELIN/BAUER/STAEHELIN (eds), *Kommentar zum Bundesgesetz über Schuldbetreibung und Konkurs unter Einbezug der Nebenerlasse*, Basel 1998, N. 78, p. 2510.

33 P. M. PATOCCHI/C. JERMINI in BERTI, N. 50, p. 646.

34 See the summary of the case law in the decision of the Cour de Justice of Geneva of 15 April 1999 in (2000) 4 SZIER 605.

courts, it is not necessary to submit translations if the judges understand the original language,[35] while others examine whether or not the formal prerequisites are met only if the defending party disputes this fact,[36] or allow the party seeking enforcement to file additional documents at later stage in the proceeding.[37]

IV. Grounds for refusing recognition and enforcement (Article V of the NY Convention)

1. Overview

Under Article V(1) of the NY Convention, the debtor may raise the following objections to recognition and enforcement of a foreign arbitral award:

- invalidity of the agreement to arbitrate (with respect to the terms 'agreement in writing', set out in Article II(2) of the NY Convention);
- lack of proper service of process or any other reason which prevented the debtor from presenting its case;
- relief was granted on matters beyond the scope of the arbitration agreement;
- irregular constitution of the arbitral tribunal, or the procedure was not in accordance with the arbitration agreement or the applicable law;
- the award has not yet become binding, has been set aside, or its enforcement has been stayed in the state where it was rendered or in the state under the laws of which it was rendered.

Under Article V(2) of the NY Convention, enforcement may be denied if the debtor shows, or if the court establishes on its own motion, either that:

- the subject matter of the dispute was not capable of being submitted to arbitration under Swiss law; or
- the enforcement of the award is contrary to Swiss international public policy.

From a procedural perspective, the main difference between the two paragraphs of Article V of the NY Convention is that the court will examine *ex officio* the issues of arbitrability (Article V(2)(a)) and public policy (Article V(2)(b)), whereas the grounds for refusal set forth in Article V(1) are only taken into consideration upon request of the debtor.

The grounds for refusal of recognition and enforcement listed in Article V of the NY Convention are exhaustive. Therefore, the request for recognition and enforcement of a foreign award may not be denied on any other grounds (e.g. on one provided by cantonal

---

35 P. M. PATOCCHI, *op. cit.*, p. 160.
36 *Ibid.*, p. 162.
37 (1985) 84 ZR, Decision No. 51.

law)[38] and a review of the arbitral award on the merits is excluded in any event, except to a very limited extent in the context of Swiss international public policy.

2. *Article V(1) of the NY Convention*

a) Article V(1)(a): incapacity of one party/invalidity of the arbitration agreement

Under Article V(1)(a) of the NY Convention, recognition and enforcement is denied if the responding party shows that it lacked capacity to enter into the agreement to arbitrate under the law applicable to that party's personal status. This provision includes the incapacity to be a party, the incapacity to act (both of natural persons and legal entities), or the lack of the power of representation (e.g. *ultra vires* acts). In examining the question of incapacity, the court will apply its conflict of laws rules to determine which law applies to the question of capacity.[39] If one of the parties is a state or a state-owned body, it may not invoke its incapacity under its own national law, unless the other party knew about this fact (Article 177 of the PILA, applied by analogy).[40]

The other grounds for finding that the arbitration agreement is invalid relate to formal or substantive defects. Article V(1) of the NY Convention refers to Article II of the NY Convention, which lists the formal and substantive requirements for the validity of an arbitration agreement and excludes the application of other provisions governing the validity of the arbitration agreement. Pursuant to Article II(2) of the NY Convention, an arbitration agreement is formally valid if it was signed by all parties or if it is contained in an exchange of letters or telegrams. The Swiss courts have become increasingly liberal in this regard and have even considered arbitration agreements that did not meet the literal requirements of this provision to be valid.[41] However, an exchange of documents remains necessary and, thus, an arbitration agreement stipulated in a confirmation letter is not valid, unless the confirmation letter is signed and returned to the confirming party.[42] Arbitration agreements entered into by e-mail or web-based communication should be deemed valid, provided they are accessible for later consultation.[43]

---

38 P. M. PATOCCHI/C. JERMINI in BERTI, N. 56, p. 648.

39 K. SIEHR in HEINI/KELLER/SIEHR/VISCHER/VOLKEN, N. 16, p. 1625.

40 P. M. PATOCCHI/C. JERMINI in BERTI, N. 63, p. 649.

41 See DFT 121 III 38, in which the Swiss Federal Tribunal examined the validity of an arbitration clause contained in a bill of lading. It was found that, even though the strict requirements of Article II(2) of the NY Convention were not met, the consignor who did not sign the bill of lading, was bound by the arbitration clause because he knew of the clause due to his long-standing business relation with the charterer and his experience in the maritime business.

42 P. M. PATOCCHI/C. JERMINI in BERTI, N. 72, p. 655.

43 G. KAUFMANN-KOHLER, *Arbitration Agreements in Online Business to Business Transactions*, in BRINER/FORTIER/BERGER/BREDOW, *Law of International Business and Dispute Settlement in the 21st Century, Liber Amicorum Karl-Heinz Böckstiegel*, Munich 2001, pp. 355-369, especially 358-362 and references.

b) Article V(1)(b): breach of due process

Pursuant to Article V(1)(b) of the NY Convention, recognition and enforcement of a foreign arbitral award may be refused if the party against whom the award is to be enforced was not given proper notice of the appointment of the arbitrator or of the arbitral proceedings, or was otherwise unable to present its case. These grounds are an expression of the general principle of due process or the right to be heard and represent minimum standards with which all arbitral proceedings must comply. Although Article V(1)(b) of the NY Convention only mentions proper notice and a party's right to present its case, it includes all aspects of due process.

However, if a party refused to participate in the arbitral proceedings, it cannot invoke a breach of due process in the subsequent enforcement proceedings relating to the award, unless fundamental elements of the right to be heard were disregarded.[44]

c) Article V(1)(c): relief granted on matters beyond the scope of the arbitration agreement

The enforcement of an arbitral award may be refused if it determines matters that do not fall within the scope of the arbitration agreement. The parties may, however, expand the arbitral tribunal's competence upon mutual agreement. Such an award will be enforced despite the narrower scope of the arbitration agreement. In any case, those parts of an award that remain within the reference to arbitration remain untainted and are capable of enforcement, if they can be separated from the *ultra petita* parts of the award.[45]

d) Article V(1)(d): constitution of the arbitral tribunal and arbitral procedure

Under Article V(1)(d) of the NY Convention, recognition and enforcement of an award may be denied if the arbitral tribunal was not properly constituted or if the agreed arbitral procedure was not followed. The party opposing enforcement of the award must prove that the arbitral tribunal violated the procedural rules agreed by the parties or, those applicable in the country in which the arbitral tribunal had its seat. The procedural rules also determine whether or not a breach of procedure may be cured or if the parties have waived their application. In any case, the party relying on Article V(1)(d) of the NY Convention must have objected to the breach of the procedural rules at the time when it occurred, failing which the party may not invoke such breach in subsequent enforcement proceedings.[46] From a Swiss point of view, it is to be regretted that, in providing for the non-enforcement of a foreign arbitral award for violation of agreed procedural rules, the NY Convention allows greater scope for opposing enforcement than the PILA. In Switzerland, an award could not be annulled on this basis, unless the violation also amounts to a breach of due process (Articles 182^3 and 190^2 of the PILA). Although this ground seems to leave substantial room for non-enforcement, practice

44 P. M. Patocchi/C. Jermini in Berti, N. 82, p. 657.

45 K. Siehr in Heini/Keller/Siehr/Vischer/Volken, N. 24, p. 1627.

46 DFT 113 Ia 67 and [1980] SJ 75.

shows that parties are very rarely successful in resisting enforcement on this ground.[47] In particular, Swiss case law contains no example to our knowledge of enforcement being refused for violation of the agreed arbitral procedure.

e) Article V(1)(e): award not yet binding

If the arbitral award to be enforced is not yet binding between the parties or has been set aside or suspended by a competent court, its recognition and enforcement may be refused under Article V(1)(e) of the NY Convention. It is not necessary for the arbitral award to be declared enforceable in the country where it was rendered. However, if the period for bringing an application to set aside the award is still running or if the award has already been set aside or suspended by a court at the seat of the arbitral tribunal or by a court of the country under the laws of which the award was rendered, the enforcement of the award may be refused.[48] Furthermore, pursuant to Article VI of the NY Convention, if proceedings have been brought to stay or set aside the award, Swiss courts have discretion to stay the enforcement proceedings or to order the party seeking enforcement to provide security.

3. Article V(2) of the NY Convention

a) Lack of arbitrability

Pursuant to Article V(2)(a) of the NY Convention, the court seized with the application for recognition and/or enforcement must determine *ex officio*, and according to the laws of the country in which the award is to be enforced, whether the award deals with a subject matter that is capable of being settled by arbitration. Article 177(1) of the PILA, which deals with the notion of arbitrability and is also applicable in recognition and enforcement proceedings in Switzerland, provides that '*any dispute involving an economic interest may be the subject of an arbitration*'. This is a rather broad conception of arbitrability, as compared to those prevailing in many other jurisdictions.

Consequently, it is only in very exceptional cases that an award may be refused recognition and enforcement in Switzerland based upon Article V(2)(a) of the NY Convention.

b) Violation of Swiss international public policy

A foreign arbitral award cannot be recognised and enforced in Switzerland if its enforcement would violate public policy. In this context, the relevant concept is Swiss international public policy and not domestic public policy. Generally speaking, the Swiss courts have always given a narrow interpretation to public policy. An arbitral award will only be denied recognition and enforcement in Switzerland if it is irreconcilable with fundamental notions of justice, as they are perceived in Switzerland. It is not relevant

---

47 G. KAUFMANN-KOHLER/H. PETER, *Formula 1 Racing and Arbitration: the FIA Tailor-made System for Fast-Track Dispute Resolution* in [2001] Arb. Int'l, pp. 187-188.

48 P. M. PATOCCHI/C. JERMINI in BERTI, N. 117, p. 667.

whether the substantive law was applied correctly to the dispute on the merits, but only whether the enforcement of the award in Switzerland would lead to a practical result which, taking into account all of the relevant circumstances of the particular case, would offend Swiss fundamental conceptions of justice. International public policy addresses violations of both procedural and substantive principles of justice.[49]

With respect to the procedural public policy, it is not just any breach of procedural rules that justifies a refusal of recognition and enforcement, but only a breach of fundamental principles of procedure. This includes, in particular, the requirement that the arbitral tribunal must be impartial and independent.[50]

---

49 DFT 101 Ia 521.

50 An extreme example is described in decision of the district court of Affoltern a. A. of 26 May 1994 ((1997) 11 SJZ 227), in which the judge refused the enforcement of an arbitral award on the grounds of public policy where the arbitration agreement provided for the appointment of Dr. X as sole arbitrator, who had previously counselled one of the parties and drafted the contract containing the arbitration clause. The arbitration clause, furthermore, provided that the arbitrator could not be removed or replaced, and that a breach of the arbitration clause (e.g. replacement of the arbitrator) would give rise to contractual damages in the amount of CHF 1 million.

Chapter 10 – Swiss and Swiss-based Arbitral Institutions

Blaise Stucki and Elliott Geisinger

I. Commercial arbitration

1. The Swiss Rules

a) Overview

aa) History

The Swiss Rules entered into force on 1 January 2004. They were adopted by six Swiss chambers of commerce and industry providing arbitration services in Switzerland, namely, Basel, Bern, Geneva, Ticino, Vaud and Zurich and replace these chambers' previously existing rules for international matters.

These chambers of commerce and industry each had their own rules of arbitration in the past. Seen from abroad, institutional arbitration in Switzerland therefore tended to present a somewhat fragmented picture. This led these chambers of commerce and industry to unify their rules and provide for harmonised administration of arbitrations. The process that led to the adoption of the Swiss Rules began in the mid-1990s. It took a decisive turn in the year 2001, when the chambers of commerce of Basel, Bern, Geneva, Ticino and Vaud (later to be joined by Zurich) formed a working group for the drafting of the new rules. This working group included not only representatives of the various chambers of commerce, but also of the Swiss arbitration community, in particular from ASA. The new Swiss Rules were formally adopted on 30 September 2003.[1]

bb) General features

The Swiss Rules are based on the UNCITRAL Rules, to which two main types of changes were made.

First, since the UNCITRAL Rules were designed for *ad hoc* arbitral proceedings, it was necessary to adapt them to institutional arbitration. This is reflected *inter alia* by the

---

1 A 'Special Series' of the [2004] Bull. ASA is devoted to these new Swiss Rules.

G. Kaufmann-Kohler and B. Stucki (eds), International Arbitration in Switzerland, A Handbook for Practitioners, 181-221.

provisions governing the bringing of arbitral proceedings (Article 3), the constitution of the arbitral tribunal (Articles 5 to 14) and the arbitration costs (Articles 38 and 39 and Appendices B and C).

Second, the Swiss Rules make changes and additions to the UNCITRAL Rules to reflect the modern practice of international arbitration. For example, the Swiss Rules contain provisions on multiparty arbitrations (Article 8), on the joinder of proceedings and the participation of third parties (Article 4), on jurisdiction for set-off defences (Article 21(5)), on confidentiality (Article 43), etc. One particular innovation is the provision on Expedited Procedure (Article 42), which the parties may elect in their arbitration clause and which apply in principle to all cases in which the amount in dispute does not exceed CHF 1 million.

The Swiss Rules are reproduced below in Appendix 2. A comparative version of the Swiss Rules, in which the changes to the UNCITRAL Rules are italicised, is available on the Internet at <www.swissarbitration.ch>.

b) Institutional structures

The adoption of the Swiss Rules was implemented by each of the six participating chambers of commerce modifying their existing rules. In other words, the entry into force of the Swiss Rules was not concomitant with the creation of a new arbitral institution in Switzerland. Instead, the participating chambers of commerce (the 'Chambers') created an 'Arbitration Committee' formed of experienced arbitration practitioners from all of the Chambers (paragraph (d) of the '*Introduction*' to the Swiss Rules). This Arbitration Committee is entrusted with the majority of the administrative services that the Chambers will provide to the users of the Swiss Rules. For example, it is the Arbitration Committee that receives the Notice for Arbitration, forwards it to the Respondent and, if necessary, constitutes the arbitral tribunal. The Arbitration Committee is also the contact point for the parties and the arbitrators in their dealing with the Chambers. To this extent, the Arbitration Committee exercises functions that can be compared to those of the Secretariat of the ICC Court.

The Swiss Rules also provide for a 'Special Committee', formed of members of the Arbitration Committee whose experience in international commercial arbitration is particularly extensive (paragraph (e) of the '*Introduction*' to the Swiss Rules). The Special Committee rules on particularly important matters under the rules such as challenges of arbitrators. Its role is also to provide advice to the Arbitration Committee whenever required.

c) Application of the Swiss Rules and seat of the arbitration

In accordance with Article 1, the Swiss Rules apply to all international arbitrations commenced on or after 1 January 2004. This includes arbitrations where the arbitration clause refers to the previously existing rules of any of the six participating Chambers.

However, in such cases, the parties may agree to arbitrate under the previously existing rules.

Moreover, the Swiss Rules specify that the seat of the arbitration is in Switzerland (Article 1(2)),[2] so that the *lex arbitri* will be Swiss law (Article 176(1) of the PILA). This explains why Article 32(7) of the UNCITRAL Rules, which makes reference to arbitration legislation requiring the filing or the registration of the award, was simply deleted from the Swiss Rules (Swiss law contains no such requirements).

It is uncertain whether the parties can provide for a seat abroad. In the spring of 2004, the Chambers were discussing a possible amendment to the Rules, with a view to enable the parties expressly to choose a seat abroad. These discussions were still ongoing as this chapter was being completed.

Finally, the Swiss Rules are extremely valuable in cases where the arbitration agreement is pathological. For example, parties all too frequently provide for institutional arbitration having its seat in Switzerland, but designate a non-existing institution such as the 'Swiss Chamber of Commerce' or the like. Given that the parties' intent is to arbitrate in Switzerland under the arbitration rules of a Swiss chamber of commerce, the Swiss Rules can apply and cure the defective drafting of the arbitration agreement. Moreover, Swiss practitioners are often faced with arbitration clauses that do not specify the place in Switzerland in which the arbitration is to be seated. Given Switzerland's federal structure, such clauses often raise considerable practical problems, although they are not invalid as such. The Swiss Rules overcome this difficulty. Indeed, if a clause does not specify the place in Switzerland where the arbitration has its seat, the Special Committee determines the seat of the arbitration (Article 16(1)).

d) Main steps in the arbitral proceedings under the Swiss Rules

aa) Bringing arbitral proceedings under the Swiss Rules

A party wishing to commence arbitration under the Swiss Rules may submit its notice of arbitration with any of the six Chambers. The addresses of each of the Chambers are found in Appendix A of the rules. It is, however, recommended that the notice of arbitration be submitted to the Chamber of the city in which the arbitration is seated.

The formal requirements for the notice of arbitration are set out in Article 3(3) of the Swiss Rules. As with the UNCITRAL Rules, the notice of arbitration need not be a complete statement of claim, with all particulars and exhibits. Pursuant to Article 3(4) and Article 18 of the Swiss Rules, the claimant may, however, submit a more complete notice of arbitration if it so chooses (i.e. containing the statement of claim). The notice of arbitration must be submitted either in English, French, German or Italian, failing which a translation can be requested.

---

2 The same rule was set out in the ZCC Rules (Article 6), in the Arbitration Rules of the Chamber of Commerce of Basel (Article 3) and in the Lugano Arbitration Rules (Article 4.1).

Upon receipt of a non-refundable registration fee, the Arbitration Committee forwards the notice of arbitration to the respondent, which is then required to submit an answer that may be in summary form or contain the complete statement of defence; at the same time, the respondent is required to submit any counterclaim and should also indicate whether it has any objections in regard to jurisdiction (Articles 3(7) to 3(10) of the Swiss Rules). In this respect, the Swiss Rules are very similar to most major institutional regimes.

Article 4(1) of the Swiss Rules represents one important innovation as compared to the UNCITRAL Rules. This provision enables the Arbitration Committee to consolidate several proceedings between identical parties; under certain circumstances, such consolidation may even be ordered when the parties to the various proceedings are not strictly identical (there is an indirect precedent for this in CCIG arbitration). Where a new case is consolidated with pending arbitral proceedings, the parties to the new case are deemed to have waived their right to appoint an arbitrator.

Under Article 4(2) of the Swiss Rules, a party may also seek to intervene in pending arbitral proceedings (or the parties to those proceedings may seek to cause a third party to participate). Jurisdiction to rule on such issues lies with the arbitral tribunal. Strictly speaking, this does not relate to the bringing of proceedings. However, for the intervening party or the third party whose participation is ordered, the proceedings begin at this stage.

bb) Constitution and composition of the arbitral tribunal

Articles 5 to 14 of the Swiss Rules relate to the constitution and composition of the arbitral tribunal. These provisions are similar to those found in other major institutional rules, such as the ICC or LCIA Rules, and to most of the previous Swiss institutional rules. Compared to the ZCC Rules, there is a major change: the list system has been abandoned and the parties are entirely free to agree upon the sole arbitrator or chairperson.

The Swiss Rules have incorporated certain mechanisms designed to prevent delaying tactics during the constitution phase. Under Article 5(2), the Chambers have the power to appoint an arbitrator if a party persists in designating persons that do not meet the standards of independence and impartiality required under Article 9. Moreover, Article 13 enables the Chambers to appoint a replacement arbitrator if a party fails to replace a panel member who has ceased to perform his or her duties, or was challenged successfully or has resigned. This provision considerably limits the risk and impact of 'truncated' tribunals.

With regard to the number of arbitrators, the Swiss Rules leave the choice to the parties. If the parties have not agreed on the number of arbitrators, Article 6 provides that the case will usually be referred to a sole arbitrator, unless the overall circumstances, including the amount in dispute, justify the constitution of a three-member panel. In past experience, clauses sometimes provided for three arbitrators although the dispute was clearly best suited for resolution by a sole arbitrator. In such cases, Article 6(3) provides that the Chambers shall invite the parties to consider the possibility of agreeing to refer the dispute to a sole arbitrator.

In cases where the amount in dispute does not exceed CHF 1 million, the provisions on Expedited Procedure apply, so that the case will in principle be referred to a sole arbitrator (see Articles 6(4) and 42(2)).

The Swiss Rules also contain detailed provisions on the constitution of the arbitral tribunal in multi-party cases (Article 8).

The challenge, removal and replacement of arbitrators are governed by Articles 9 to 14.

cc) Proceedings before the arbitral tribunal and the award

The arbitral procedure itself is governed by Articles 15 to 30. These provisions are broadly based on the UNCITRAL Rules. The usual sequence is therefore one or two exchanges of briefs, followed by simultaneous exchange(s) of witness statements and/or expert reports, followed by the evidentiary hearing, followed by post-hearing memorials. Of course, this is only a 'typical' sequence, which will vary from case to case. In this regard, the UNCITRAL Notes can be helpful.

Compared to the UNCITRAL Rules, the main novelties and changes are:

- the respondent files an answer before the arbitral tribunal is constituted (Articles 3(7) to 3(10));
- broad jurisdiction for set-off defences (Article 21(5));
- express 'abolition' of the distinction between witnesses and party representatives or employees (Article 25(2));
- specific references to expert witnesses (Article 25);
- power of the arbitral tribunal to award costs in connection with interim measures (Article 26(4)).

Articles 31 to 41 govern the award and contain few changes to the UNCITRAL Rules. The main changes and additions are:

- the authority of the chairman to render the award alone where there is no majority, which amounts in practice to the abolition of the majority rule (Article 31(1));
- the possibility for the arbitral tribunal to award costs in non-final awards (Article 32(1));

- the determination of the law applicable to substance in accordance with Article 187(1) of the PILA. Article 33(1) of the Swiss Rules adopts this statutory provision *verbatim* (including the slight mistranslation in the German text).[3]

There is no provision for the scrutiny of the award by the arbitral institution. Article 40(4) states only that the arbitral tribunal must submit its draft award to the Chambers for consultation on the costs. In practice, this provision also enables the Chambers to draw the attention of the arbitral tribunal to obvious issues that may affect other aspects of the award. For instance, past practice in CCIG arbitration (which included a similar mechanism regarding the costs and no provision on scrutiny) has shown that the institution will sometimes spot unclear or incomplete operative parts of the award and provide the arbitral tribunal with the opportunity to rectify this type of problem before the award is notified.

dd) Expedited Procedure

Article 42(1) of the Swiss Rules enables the parties to agree[4] to an 'Expedited Procedure', the main features of which are:

- the phase for constitution of the arbitral tribunal can be shortened;
- there is normally only one exchange of written submissions after the arbitral tribunal is constituted;
- there is normally only one evidentiary hearing;
- the reasons of the award are provided in summary form.

The overall purpose of this simplification is to enable the arbitral tribunal to render its award within six months from the date that it received the file from the Chambers (Article 42(1)(d) of the Swiss Rules). This time limit may be extended, but only in exceptional cases. Based on past experiences in Geneva and Lugano, where the former rules also provided for expedited proceedings, extensions are given only for short periods. As a result, the overall duration of cases conducted under the Expedited Procedure will be short.

Article 42(2) of the Swiss Rules provides that the Expedited Procedure of Article 42(1) applies to all cases in which the amount in dispute does not exceed CHF 1 million,[5] i.e. even where the parties have not agreed to the Expedited Procedure. Moreover, this provision states that the case will be referred to a sole arbitrator. If the arbitration agreement provides for a three-member tribunal, the parties shall be invited to agree to

---

3 For a commentary on Article 187 of the PILA, see Chapter 7 *supra*.

4 Such agreement can be made either in the initial arbitration agreement, or in a submission agreement, or at the outset of proceedings arising out of an arbitration agreement which does not provide for an expedited procedure.

5 The amount in dispute within the meaning of this provision is the aggregate of the claim and counterclaim or any set-off defence.

refer the case to a sole arbitrator. If the parties do not agree to do so, the three-member arbitral tribunal shall be paid a minimum hourly rate (currently CHF 350 per hour; see Section 2.8 of Appendix B to the Swiss Rules).

This provision aims at providing high-quality arbitration in cases where the amount in dispute is relatively modest. In fact, the very idea of submitting such cases to the Expedited Procedure of Article 42(1) of the Swiss Rules arose when the drafters were discussing the Schedule of Costs. In that context, it was difficult to strike a balance between a level of costs that remains reasonable compared to the amount in dispute and adequate remuneration for the arbitral tribunal. The best solution was to provide for a mechanism that compels the parties and the arbitral tribunal to proceed expeditiously and efficiently.

That said, the amount in dispute is not the only factor that will determine whether a case should be conducted under the Expedited Procedure. For this reason, Article 42(2) enables the Chambers to decide that the arbitration will be governed by the 'ordinary' procedures set out elsewhere if this is justified by the circumstances of the case (for example, foreseeable and complicated technical issues).

e) Costs

Articles 30 to 41 of the Swiss Rules relate to the costs of the arbitration. These provisions were deliberately kept as close as possible to the UNCITRAL Rules. As a result, the general definition of the costs (Article 38) is essentially identical to that of the UNICTRAL Rules, with the only material change being the addition of administrative costs in certain cases. Also, it is the arbitral tribunal, not the Chambers, which determines the costs, including the initial deposit, and requests payment thereof from the parties. However, the Chambers are always kept informed of all decisions relating to costs. In addition, the maximum costs resulting from the Schedule found at Appendix B of the Swiss Rules cannot be exceeded without prior approval of the Chambers. Therefore, the parties benefit from monitoring by the Chambers of all decisions relating to costs.

As for the arbitrators' fees, Article 39(1) provides that they '*shall be reasonable in amount, taking into account the amount in dispute, the complexity of the subject-matter, the time spent by the arbitrators and any other relevant circumstances of the case, including, but not limited to, the discontinuation of the arbitral proceedings in case of settlement or other reasons*'. Moreover, this provision continues: '*In the event of such discontinuation, the fees of the arbitral tribunal may be less than the minimum amount resulting from Appendix B (Schedule of the Costs of Arbitration)*'.

Appendix B to the Swiss Rules includes a scale of costs and additional provisions on this issue. The website of the Chambers (<www.swissarbitration.ch>) features a calculator enabling users to obtain the range of fees and administrative costs that would be charged based upon a given amount in dispute.

As a general matter, the scale of costs adopted by the Chambers is similar to that of most major arbitral institutions. The administrative costs remain relatively modest because they reflect the general structure of the Swiss Rules, i.e. the administrative role of the Chambers is less significant than in many other institutions.

2. ICC arbitration

Although this chapter deals exclusively with Swiss and Swiss-based arbitral institutions, it would not be complete without mentioning ICC arbitration. As a matter of fact, over the years, ICC arbitration has become the most significant source of arbitrations in Switzerland. According to the ICC 2002 Statistical Report,[6] 111 arbitrations had their seat in Switzerland in 2002, i.e. about one out of five arbitrations. By contrast, the parties or the ICC Court chose a seat in the UK 53 times, 88 times in France and 50 times in the US. Arbitrators from Switzerland were appointed in 152 arbitrations, either as sole arbitrators, co-arbitrators or presiding arbitrators. There were 95 French arbitrators, 109 UK arbitrators and 140 US arbitrators. Finally, Swiss law was the second most popular applicable substantive law, immediately after English law.

These statistics reflect Switzerland's predominant role as a leading venue for international arbitration, which has resulted from the recognition over time of Switzerland as a neutral venue with a modern infrastructure, the Swiss legal system as neutral and developed, the Swiss *lex arbitri* as well suited to international disputes, and the high professional standards of the Swiss legal profession.

II. IP/IT arbitration

1. WIPO Domain Name Dispute Resolution

a) Overview

aa) Definitions

A domain name is the human-friendly form of an Internet address. It corresponds to a series of numbers – the IP address[7] - comparable to a telephone number. An IP address is unique and serves to connect users to a specific Internet location. Domain names have several parts (at least two), separated by dots.

In a domain name, the part following the last dot is called the Top Level Domain (TLD). The TLD serves to broadly categorize the name as to its type or purpose. Generic TLDs (gTLDs) include notably '*.com*', '*.net*' and '*.org*'. There are also hundreds of country TLDs (ccTLDs) such as '*.ch*' (Switzerland), '*.uk*' (United Kingdom), '*.us*' (United States), '*.fr*' (France), etc. The second part (reading from the right) is the Second Level Domain (SLD). It is the 'readable' part of the domain name, and may be the name of its owner, a generic word or sentence, or any sequence of letters or numbers.

---

6 See (2003) 14/1 ICC ICArb. Bull.

7 IP address is an abbreviation of Internet Protocol address. The IP address corresponds to a domain name in human language.

The Domain Name System (DNS) is an Internet protocol that provides mapping between a computer's IP address and a domain name in human-friendly form.

The Internet Corporation for Assigned Names and Numbers (ICANN) is the body responsible for managing and coordinating the DNS to ensure that each IP address is unique and that all Internet users can find all valid addresses. It does this by overseeing the distribution of unique IP addresses and domain names and by ensuring that each domain name maps the correct IP address.

bb) The genesis of the UDRP and the UDRP Rules for Uniform Domain Name Dispute Resolution

In 1998, upon request of the US government, WIPO undertook a consultation process aimed at making recommendations to ICANN on issues arising out of the interface between Internet domain names and intellectual property rights. In its 'Final Report of the WIPO Internet Domain Name Process' of 30 April 1999 (the 'Final Report'), WIPO pointed out that disputes over domain names and intellectual property rights presented a number of special characteristics, *inter alia* that domain names give rise to global presence, that such global presence may give rise to infringements of intellectual property rights in several jurisdictions, that the need to resolve a domain name dispute was urgent in view of the ease and speed with which an Internet registration may be obtained and that there was a considerable disparity between the low cost of obtaining an Internet domain name and the high cost incurred by the intellectual property owner in seeking to remedy an infringement through litigation.

On 26 August 1999, on the basis of the recommendations provided in the Final Report, ICANN adopted the UDRP[8] setting forth the general principles governing domain name dispute resolution. Simultaneously, ICANN issued the UDRP Rules.[9] Both of these texts entered into force on 1 December 1999. Between the end of 1999 and early 2000, ICANN accredited four dispute resolution centers to administer domain name disputes, including the WIPO Arbitration Center (the 'Center').[10] The Center has issued its own set of rules, the WIPO Supplemental Rules for Uniform Domain Name Dispute Resolution Policy (the 'Supplemental Rules'),[11] effective as of 1 December 1999.

---

8 <www.icann.org/dndr/udrp/policy.htm>.

9 <www.icann.org/dndr/udrp/uniform-rules.htm>.

10 In addition to the Center, the National Arbitration Forum, eResolution and CPR have been accredited as dispute resolution centers. In December 2001, eResolution ceased to handle UDRP disputes and the Asian Domain Name Dispute Resolution Centre was accredited by ICANN.

11 <www.arbiter.wipo.int/domains/rules/supplemental/index.html>.

The first complaint was filed electronically with the Center on 2 December 1999 and decided on 14 January 2000.[12] Through 31 December 2003, no less than 5,658 cases have been filed with the Center.[13]

b) Salient procedural features

aa) Applicable rules

The UDRP is incorporated by reference into the registration agreement entered into between each domain name holder and the entity with which such domain name is registered (the 'Registrar').[14] The UDRP provides that proceedings before one of the administrative dispute resolution service providers (the 'Provider') in relation to a dispute over the registration and use of an Internet domain name are mandatory and will be conducted according to the UDRP Rules and the Supplemental Rules of the selected Provider.

bb) Commencing the proceedings

Any domain name holder must defer to the mandatory administrative proceeding in the event that a third party (the 'complainant') asserts that the domain name holder was not entitled to the registration of the domain name and that the domain name must be transferred or deleted.

As a first step, the complainant must select the Provider from among those approved by ICANN by submitting its complaint to such Provider (Article 4(d) of the UDRP).[15] The selected Provider will then administer the proceeding.

The complaint must be submitted in hard copy and in electronic form.[16] In accordance with Article 3(b) of the UDRP Rules, the complaint must specify *inter alia* that the complaint is submitted for decision in accordance with the UDRP and the UDRP Rules, the e-mail address and contact details of the complainant (or of any authorized representative)[17] and of the respondent (or of any authorized representative), whether the complainant elects to have the dispute settled by a single-member or a three-member Panel and, in the event that the complainant elects a three-member Panel, the names and contact details of three potential panelists, the domain name that is the subject of the

12 See the Administrative Panel Decision of 14 January 2000 in the case No. D99-0001 at <www.arbiter.wipo.int/domains/decisions/1999/d0000-0199.html>.

13 Out of which 1,036 were filed in 2003.

14 Article 1 of the UDRP.

15 A complaint submitted to the Center must be sent at the following address: <www.domain.disputes@wipo.int>. An Online Complaint Filing Form for complaints under the UDRP is available at the following address: <www.arbiter.wipo.int/domains/filing/udrp/complaint.html>.

16 Under the Supplemental Rules, any submission may be made, if both parties agree, through the Center's Internet-based case filing and administration system (Article 3(a)(iii)).

17 A complaint may be filed by the licensee of a trademark.

dispute, the Registrar with which such domain name is registered, the trademark or service mark upon which the complaint is based (including a description of the goods or services with which the mark is used), and the grounds upon which the complaint is made and the remedies are sought.[18] In addition, the complaint must provide that the complainant will submit to the jurisdiction of the courts at the location of the principal office of the Registrar or the domain name holder's address in the event of any challenge to a decision rendered in the UDRP proceeding and cancelling of transferring the domain name.[19]

If the complaint complies with the UDRP and the UDRP Rules, it is forwarded to the respondent within three days from receipt of the fee to be paid by the complainant. According to Article 4(b) of the UDRP Rules, a deficient complaint is deemed withdrawn unless remedied within 5 days from the notification by the Provider.

The respondent[20] must submit its response to the complaint within 20 days from the date of commencement of the proceedings, i.e. from the date the complaint is forwarded to the respondent (Article 4(c) of the UDRP Rules). The response must be submitted in hard copy *and* in electronic form and must *inter alia* specify - in addition to the respondent's defence - the e-mail address and contact details of the respondent, whether the respondent elects to have the dispute decided by a three-member Panel (in the event that the complainant has elected a single-member Panel) and the names and contact details of three candidates to serve as one of the panelists (Article 5(b)).

cc) The panelists

If neither of the parties has elected a three-member Panel, the Provider must appoint a single-member Panel from its list of panelists (Article 6(b) of the UDRP Rules).[21] If either of the parties elects to have the dispute decided by a three-member Panel, the Provider *must* appoint three panelists (Article 6(c) of the UDRP Rules). In so doing, the Provider must endeavour to appoint one panelist from the list of candidates submitted by each of the parties. The third panelist will be appointed from a list of five candidates submitted by the Provider to the parties in a manner that balances the preferences of both parties, as they may specify to the Provider.[22]

---

18 Under the Supplemental Rules, the description of the grounds upon which the complaint is made may not exceed 5,000 words (Article 10(a)).

19 Article 3(b)(xiii) of the UDRP Rules.

20 Only the person legitimated by the WHOIS, i.e. the database containing the name of the holder of each domain name, may submit a response.

21 In accordance with Article 6(a) of the UDRP Rules, each Provider must maintain and publish a list of panelists and their qualifications. Currently, the Center's list contains 329 panelists from 46 countries (<www.arbiter.wipo.int/domains/panel/panelists.html>).

22 Article 6(e) of the UDRP Rules. Under the Supplemental Rules, a party must submit the names of its three candidates in order of preference and the Center must, subject to availability, respect such order (Article 7(a)).

The UDRP Rules do not provide for a challenge procedure and merely require that a panelist promptly disclose to the Provider circumstances giving rise to justifiable doubts as to his or her impartiality or independence. In such a case, the Provider may, *in its discretion*, appoint a substitute panelist (Article 7 of the UDRP Rules).

dd) The procedure

The UDRP Rules provides that there will be no in-person hearings – including hearings by telephone conference, video conference or web conference – unless otherwise decided by the Panel in its discretion and as an exception (Article 13 of the UDRP Rules).

Article 15(a) of the UDRP Rules provides that the Panel may decide a dispute in accordance with any rules and principles of law it deems appropriate. The UDRP Rules thus incorporate the so-called '*voie-directe*' principle under which arbitrators enjoy considerable freedom in the choice of rules of substantive law. Where all parties are domiciled in the same country, UDRP Panels regularly apply the law of that country.[23] Often panelists merely apply the test set out in Article 4(a) of the UDRP, i.e. whether the domain name is identical or confusingly similar to a trademark or service mark in which the complainant has rights, whether the domain name holder has rights or legitimate interests in respect of the domain name and whether the domain name has been registered and is being used in bad faith.

ee) The Panel's decision

According to the UDRP, the only remedies available before an administrative Panel are the cancellation of the domain name or the transfer of the domain name registration to the complainant (Article 4(i)). Therefore, no damages can be awarded under the UDRP. The Panel's reasoned decision, made in writing, can be made by a majority. It must be forwarded to the Provider for notification to the parties within 14 days of the Panel's appointment (Article 15 of the UDRP Rules). In accordance with Article 16(a) of the UDRP Rules, the Provider must communicate the decision to the parties and the relevant Registrar within three days from its receipt.

ff) Implementation of the Panel's decision

Upon receipt of the Panel's decision, the Registrar must immediately communicate to the parties, the Provider and ICANN the date for implementation of the decision in accordance with the UDRP (Article 16(a) of the UDRP Rules). The Registrar will implement the decision unless informed by the domain name holder that legal proceedings have been initiated against the complainant (Article 4(k) of the UDRP). In such a case, the Registrar will take no further action until receipt of evidence that the

---

23 See, e.g., Case No. D1999-0001 (*World Wrestling Federation Entertainment Inc. v. Michael Bosman*); Case No. D2000-0053 (*Microsoft Corporation v. Amit Mehrotra*).

dispute between the parties has been resolved, e.g. by the dismissal or withdrawal of the domain name holder's legal proceedings.

Unless the Panel decides otherwise, the full text of each decision must be published by the Provider on a publicly accessible web site.[24] The portion of any decision holding that a complaint was made in bad faith must be published in any event (Article 16(b) of the UDRP Rules).

gg) Effect of court proceedings before, during or after mandatory administrative proceedings

The mandatory administrative proceedings do not prevent the parties from submitting their dispute to a court, either before, during or after a mandatory proceeding (Article 4(k) of the UDRP). In the event of legal proceedings commenced before or during an administrative proceeding in respect of a domain name dispute subject to a complaint, the Panel must decide, as a matter of discretion, whether to suspend or terminate the proceeding or to continue up to a decision. A party wishing to commence legal proceedings pending an administrative proceeding with respect to a domain name dispute must promptly notify the Panel and the Provider (Article 18(b) of the UDRP Rules).

2. WIPO Arbitration Center (WIPO Arbitration Rules and WIPO Expedited Arbitration Rules)

a) Overview

The 'Convention Establishing the World Intellectual Property Organization' was signed in Stockholm on 14 July 1967. With headquarters in Geneva, Switzerland, WIPO is dedicated to promoting the use and protection of works of the human mind. As of 15 July 2003, WIPO was comprised of 179 member states and administered 23 international treaties dealing with different aspects of intellectual property.

The establishment of the WIPO Arbitration and Mediation Center (the 'Center') was approved in September 1993 by the General Assembly of WIPO. Based in Geneva, the Center has offered arbitration and mediation services for the resolution of international commercial disputes involving intellectual property since 1994.

The Center has issued three distinct sets of rules, namely the WIPO Arbitration Rules (the 'WIPO Rules'), the WIPO Expedited Arbitration Rules (the 'WIPO Expedited Rules') and the WIPO Mediation Rules. Under these rules, the Center offers the following dispute-resolution procedures:

- mediation;
- mediation-arbitration;

24 The decisions issued by WIPO Panels are available on the Internet at <www.arbiter.wipo.int/domains/cases/index.html>.

- arbitration;
- expedited arbitration.

Mediation under the WIPO Mediation Rules is a non-binding procedure in which a mediator appointed by the Center after consultation with the parties (unless the parties have agreed upon a mediator) assists the parties to settle their dispute. The mediation-arbitration procedure is an hybrid procedure combining mediation and, where the dispute is not settled through mediation within an agreed period of time, binding arbitration, with the WIPO Mediation Rules and the WIPO Rules applying sequentially. The Center has drafted a recommended submission agreement for parties willing to follow the mediation-arbitration procedure. The WIPO Expedited Rules ensure that the procedure can be conducted in a shortened timeframe and at a reduced cost.[25] This section will focus on the salient procedural features of the WIPO Rules and the WIPO Expedited Rules, to the extent that they differ from the standard rules.[26]

b) Salient procedural features

aa) Application of the WIPO Rules

The WIPO Rules apply whenever an arbitration agreement provides for arbitration under the WIPO Rules (Article 2) or where the parties agree to submit existing disputes to WIPO arbitration. The mandatory provisions of the law applicable to the arbitration are expressly reserved (Article 3), i.e. Swiss law if the seat of the arbitration is in Switzerland.

The parties that wish the arbitral procedure to be conducted under the WIPO Expedited Rules must specify this fact in their arbitration agreement or, with respect to existing disputes, in a submission agreement.

bb) Commencing the arbitration

Unlike the Swiss Rules and ICC Rules, the request for arbitration in WIPO arbitration must be addressed both to the Center *and* to the respondent (Article 6).[27] In addition to the usual contents of a request for arbitration (e.g. a description of the nature and circumstances of the dispute, the relief sought, etc.), the request for arbitration may, at the choice of the claimant, be accompanied by a 'statement of claim', i.e., a comprehensive statement of the facts and legal argument supporting the claim, with a statement of the relief sought and, to the extent possible, the documentary evidence

---

25 For a consolidated version of the WIPO Expedited Rules, effective as of 1 October 2002, see <www.arbiter.wipo.int/arbitration/expedited-rules/rules.html#1>.

26 The mediation-arbitration procedure also leads to the issuance of a binding award where the dispute is not settled through mediation. In such a case, the WIPO Arbitration Rules apply to the arbitration part of the procedure, which does not differ from a procedure conducted under the WIPO Rules from the outset.

27 However, the receipt of the request for arbitration by the Center is decisive for determining the date of commencement of the arbitration (Article 7 of the WIPO Rules).

relied upon (Article 10 of the WIPO Rules). In practice, the claimant will often need time to prepare its case and will generally wait to file a statement of claim until the arbitral tribunal has been constituted.

The respondent must send its answer to the request for arbitration to the Center *and* the claimant within 30 days from receipt of the request for arbitration (Article 11 of the WIPO Rules). The answer may include a counterclaim. If the claimant has filed a statement of claim, the respondent may in turn file a statement of defence together with its answer.[28]

Under the WIPO Expedited Rules, the statement of claim must be filed with the request for arbitration (Article 10 of the WIPO Expedited Rules). The answer to the request for arbitration must be filed within 20 days from receipt of the request for arbitration or the date of the appointment of the arbitral tribunal, whichever event occurs later and must be accompanied by the statement of defence (Articles 11 and 12).

cc) The arbitral tribunal

Absent an agreement between the parties on the number of arbitrators – and unless the Center determines that a three-member tribunal would be more appropriate – the arbitral tribunal will be composed of a sole arbitrator (Article 14(b) of the WIPO Rules). In practice, a sole arbitrator is appointed in approximately 80% of all arbitrations.

Under the WIPO Expedited Rules, the arbitral tribunal is always composed of a sole arbitrator appointed jointly by the parties or, failing agreement between the parties, by the Center (Article 14).

If the parties fail to constitute the arbitral tribunal within the agreed period of time or, in the absence of such an agreed period of time, within 45 days from the commencement of the arbitration, i.e. the date on which the request for arbitration is received by the Center, the Center will constitute the arbitral tribunal (Article 15(b) of the WIPO Rules). The Center's default appointment of the sole or presiding arbitrator takes place under an novel and efficient procedure. In accordance with Article 19(b) of the WIPO Rules, the Center suggests to the parties at least three candidates appearing on the Center's list of arbitrators.[29] Each party may then delete the name of one candidate out of the three and number the remaining candidates in order of preference. If the returned lists do not result in an acceptable candidate or if a candidate is not able or willing to act as sole or presiding arbitrator, the Center will appoint the sole or presiding arbitrator.

---

28 Article 12 and 42 of the WIPO Rules. In accordance with Article 42(a) of the WIPO Rules, the statement of defence must in any event be filed within 30 days from receipt of the statement of claim.

29 The WIPO list of arbitrators comprises over 1,000 arbitrators and mediators from 70 countries.

Arbitrators may only be challenged on the ground that there are circumstances giving rise to justifiable doubts as to their impartiality or independence (Article 24(a)).[30]

dd) Interim measures and security for the claim, counterclaim and costs

The arbitral tribunal has the power to issue provisional orders or take other interim measures it deems necessary (Article 46(a) of the WIPO Rules).[31] This is consistent with Article 183(1) of the PILA, which acknowledges the power of the arbitral tribunal to order precautionary or conservatory measures but not with Article 26(1) of the Concordat, which confers exclusive jurisdiction to grant interim measures upon the courts. Article 46(b) of the WIPO Rules enables the arbitral tribunal to order a party to provide security for the claim or counterclaim, as well as for the costs of the arbitration.

ee) Protection of confidential information

The WIPO Rules deal with confidential information in a comprehensive manner to ensure that, through the intervention of the arbitral tribunal, trade secrets and secret know-how is protected from improper disclosure (Article 52 of the WIPO Rules).[32] Indeed, this can be a particularly important issue in IP cases. In accordance with Article 52(a) of the WIPO Rules, the protection of confidentiality applies to information in the possession of a party, not accessible to the public, which is of commercial, financial or industrial significance and is treated as confidential by the party possessing it. Protection may be secured by order of the arbitral tribunal – the party invoking the confidentiality of any information it wishes or is required to submit must make a reasoned application to the arbitral tribunal detailing the information it seeks to have classified as confidential. In accordance with Article 52(c) of the WIPO Rules, the test is whether disclosure would be likely to cause serious harm to the party invoking its confidentiality. Special protection should be granted as soon as the person seeking the protection demonstrates a reasonable interest in obtaining it and that it would suffer serious harm if such protection were not granted.[33] A truly innovative feature of the WIPO Rules is the ability of the arbitral tribunal to designate, at the request of a party or on its own motion, a 'confidentiality advisor' who will determine whether or not information should be classified as confidential (Article 52(d) of the WIPO Rules).

The WIPO Rules also deal with the protection of information that has been disclosed in the arbitration. In accordance with Article 73, a party is prohibited from disclosing the

---

30 By contrast, Article 11(1) of the ICC Rules provides that a challenge may be made '*whether for an alleged lack of independence or otherwise* […]' thus opening the way to a challenge based on other grounds than a lack of impartiality or independence, e.g., a lack of qualification of an arbitrator.

31 Article 46(a) of the WIPO Rules. In accordance with Article 56(d) of the WIPO Rules, courts have concurrent jurisdiction to order interim measures.

32 H. SMIT, *Disclosure of Trade Secrets and other Confidential Information* in (1998) 9 Am. Rev. Int'l Arb. 177.

33 H. SMIT, *op. cit.*, p. 179.

existence of *the arbitration*, unless it is required to do so by law or by a competent regulatory body or to the extent necessary in connection with a court challenge or an action for enforcement of an award. Even in such cases, a party may disclose no more than what is legally required and must provide the arbitral tribunal and the other party – provided the disclosure takes place during the arbitral proceedings – or the other party alone, with details of the disclosure and an explanation of the reason for it (Article 73(a)(ii) of the WIPO Rules).[34] The WIPO Rules also prohibit disclosure to a third party of any documentary or other evidence given by a party or witness in the arbitration, to the extent that such evidence describes information not in the public domain, without the consent of the parties or a court order (Article 74(a) of the WIPO Rules).[35] Finally, Articles 75 and 76 of the WIPO Rules deal with the disclosure of the award by the parties, the arbitral tribunal or the Center.

ff) The law applicable to the merits and the arbitration law

The WIPO Rules recognize the freedom of the parties to choose the law or rules of law applicable to the substance of their dispute (Article 59(a) of the WIPO Rules). Failing such a choice, the WIPO Rules incorporate the so-called '*voie-direct*' principle under which the arbitral tribunal enjoys considerable freedom in determining the applicable rules of substantive law in view of the facts of the case.

The WIPO Rules also recognize the power of the parties to agree upon the application of an arbitration law other than the law of the seat of arbitration, provided such a choice is permitted by the law of the seat of arbitration (Article 59(b) of the WIPO Rules).[36]

gg) Fees and costs

The request for arbitration must be accompanied by the payment of a non-refundable registration fee (Article 67(a) of the WIPO Rules).[37] According to the new Schedule of Fees and Costs, which applies to all procedures commenced after 1 December 2002, the registration fee is USD 2,000, irrespective of the amount in dispute. In addition to the registration fee, an administration fee is payable by the claimant and by the respondent in the case of a counterclaim.[38] The real change brought by the new Schedule of Fees and Costs is that the fees of the arbitrators will be fixed by the Center after consultation

34 Article 73(a)(ii) of the WIPO Rules.

35 Article 74(a) solely applies to a party whose access to information arises exclusively as a result of its participation in the arbitration. A witness is not to be considered as a third party for the purpose of that provision (Article 74(b)).

36 Swiss law does not permit the 'opting out' of the statutory framework provided by chapter 12 of the PILA. Hence, Article 59(b) of the WIPO Rules is deprived of any effect where the place of the arbitration is located in Switzerland.

37 Article 67(a) of the WIPO Rules. A similar registration fee applies to any counterclaim (Article 67(b)).

38 Article 68(a) and (b) of the WIPO Rules.

with the parties and the arbitrators. The indicative hourly rate for the arbitrators ranges from USD 300 to USD 600.

Under the WIPO Expedited Rules, the registration fee is of USD 1,000, irrespective of the amount in dispute. Unlike under the WIPO Rules, the arbitrators' fees are fixed according to the Schedule of Fees and Costs, except where the amount in dispute exceeds USD 10 million. For lesser amounts, the arbitrators' fees range from a fixed fee of USD 20,000 to a fixed fee of USD 40,000.

hh) The WIPO Emergency Relief Rules

Following the example of the ICC Pre-arbitral referee, the Center is currently developing the WIPO Emergency Relief Rules, which establish a standby Panel of arbitrators available on 24-hours notice to decide applications for emergency interim relief *before* the arbitral tribunal has been constituted. It is envisaged that two forms of application may be brought under the WIPO Emergency Relief Rules, namely *ex parte* and *inter partes* applications. An *ex parte* procedure is considered to be essential for those cases in which there is evidence of bad faith on the part of the adverse party or an indication that notice would entail the risk that evidence might be destroyed or other irreparable damage incurred. The main concern is that an order made *ex parte* by the emergency arbitrator would not be enforceable under the NY Convention. The *inter partes* form of application in the proposed WIPO Emergency Relief Rules envisages a very quick procedure conducted within strict and very short time limits. The draft WIPO Emergency Relief Rules are still under consideration.

III. The Court of Arbitration for Sport

1. Overview

a) The purpose of the Court of Arbitration for Sport

The Court of Arbitration for Sport (the 'CAS') was created at the instance of the International Olympic Committee (the 'IOC') and became operational on 30 June 1984. The purpose of the CAS is to provide for the resolution of sports-related disputes through arbitration or mediation.

b) The nature of the CAS awards

In a decision of 15 March 1993,[39] the Swiss Federal Tribunal addressed the nature of decisions rendered by the CAS. The applicant was a professional horseman, licensed by the International Equestrian Federation (the 'FEI'). As such, he was subject to the rules of the FEI according to which a competitor may appeal against a decision of the FEI to the CAS. The horseman, who had been suspended and fined by the FEI, brought an appeal to the CAS, which partially confirmed the FEI decision. The horseman then brought an application to set aside the CAS decision before the Swiss Federal Tribunal.

39 DFT 119 II 271.

The Swiss Federal Tribunal found that it would have jurisdiction if the CAS decision were an arbitral award, as opposed to an internal decision of a sports body. The Swiss Federal Tribunal defined an arbitral award as a judgment rendered on the basis of an arbitration agreement by a private tribunal to which the parties have entrusted the resolution of a dispute involving an economic interest. A decision by an internal body of a sports federation is not usually considered to be an arbitral award because such an internal body is seen to be a mere emanation of the sports federation, rather than an independent judicial authority. On this basis, the Swiss Federal Tribunal held that, where the IOC was not a party to the proceedings, the CAS is an independent judicial body and that its decisions are thus arbitral awards.

In the aftermath of this decision, major reforms were undertaken to detach the CAS from the IOC. First, the International Council for Arbitration for Sport (the 'ICAS') was established to act as the supervisory authority of the CAS. Second, in order to make a clear distinction between cases where the CAS acts as a sole instance and cases where it hears appeals against internal decisions of a sports body, two arbitration divisions were created, the Ordinary Arbitration Division and the Appeals Arbitration Division. Finally, the CAS rules of procedure were amended. The Code of Sports-related Arbitration (the CAS Rules) – which enshrined these reforms – was enacted on 22 November 1994.

The independence of the CAS vis-à-vis the IOC was recently questioned in the context of the IOC's exclusion of two Nordic skiers from the 2002 Olympic Games in Salt Lake City. Doping controls carried out during the Games revealed that the two skiers had made use of a prohibited doping substance. On 24 February 2002, the IOC excluded the two skiers from the Olympic Games. The IOC decision was transmitted to the International Ski Federation (the 'FIS'), which suspended the two athletes from all competition for a period of two years. The skiers challenged the IOC and FIS decisions before the CAS, which, by four awards of 29 November 2002, confirmed the decisions of the IOC and the FIS. The skiers applied to set aside the CAS decisions before the Swiss Federal Tribunal, on the grounds *inter alia* that the CAS does not constitute an independent tribunal in proceedings where the IOC is a party. In its decision of 27 May 2003, the Federal Tribunal held that the CAS was sufficiently independent from the IOC for the CAS decisions to be considered as true awards, similar to courts judgments.[40]

c) The *ad hoc* Division of the CAS at the 1996 Atlanta Olympic Games and thereafter

One of the major achievements of the ICAS was the creation of a special body for the resolution of all disputes arising during the course of and in connection with the Olympic Games. An *ad hoc* Division of the CAS was set up for the first time in connection with the 1996 Olympic Games in Atlanta. The objective was to provide athletes and other

[40] DFT 129 III 445.

participants with a body able to resolve disputes occurring during the Games in a final manner within time limits corresponding to the pace of the competition.[41]

The jurisdiction of the *ad hoc* Division stemmed from Article 74 of the Olympic Charter, which provides that '[a]*ny dispute arising on the occasion of or in connection with the Olympic Games shall be submitted exclusively to the Court of Arbitration for Sport, in accordance with the Code of Sports-related Arbitration*'. The entry forms signed by all athletes, judges, trainers, medical staff, etc. included an express acceptance of the jurisdiction of the CAS.[42] In addition, a party was deemed to have consented to arbitration by filing an application with the *ad hoc* Division or by participating in the proceedings without raising an objection to the jurisdiction of the *ad hoc* Division.

The procedure before the *ad hoc* Division was governed by a specific set of rules adopted by ICAS for this purpose. One of the striking features of the rules was that the seat of the *ad hoc* Division and of each panel of arbitrators would be set by the President of the *ad hoc* Division. Lausanne, Switzerland, was chosen as the seat. As a consequence, Chapter 12 of the PILA applied to all arbitrations of the *ad hoc* Division and it would have been necessary to bring any challenge before the Swiss Federal Tribunal in accordance with Article 191 of the PILA.

Ad hoc Divisions of the CAS were subsequently set up in connection with the 1998 Olympic Games in Nagano, the 2000 Olympic Games in Sydney and the 2002 Olympic Games in Salt Lake City.

d) The CAS and anti-doping

In 1998, it was noted that doping disputes accounted for a large majority of the disputes submitted to the Appeals Arbitration Division of the CAS.[43] This is likely to become even more true following the recent adoption of the World Anti-Doping Code and the USADA Protocol for Olympic Movement Testing.

aa) The World Anti-Doping Code

In March 2003, all major sports federations participating in the Copenhagen World Conference on Doping in Sport and several governments signed the Copenhagen Declaration on Anti-Doping in Sport established under the auspices of the World Anti-Doping Agency (the 'WADA'), thereby recognising the role of the World Anti-Doping Code (the 'Code') as the foundation for the world wide fight against doping and committing to implement it. As of 22 March 2004, 103 governments have signed the Copenhagen Declaration.

---

41 G. KAUFMANN-KOHLER, *Arbitration at the Olympics – Issues of Fast-Track Dispute Resolution and Sports Law*, Kluwer Law International, The Hague 2001, p. 106.

42 *Ibid.*, p. 107.

43 J.-P. ROCHAT, *Tribunal Arbitral du Sport: quelle procédure pour quel litige?* in [1998] 11 ASA Special Series, p. 19.

In accordance with Article 13.2 of the Code, the CAS has jurisdiction to hear appeals lodged by athletes against decisions regarding violations of anti-doping rules, the consequences thereof and provisional suspensions in cases arising from competition in an *International Event*[44] or in cases involving *International-Level Athletes*.[45] These proceedings before the CAS are governed by the CAS Rules (Article 13.2.1 of the Code).

bb) The USADA Protocol for Olympic Movement Testing

The United States Anti-Doping Agency (the 'USADA'),[46] a non-profit corporation, was established as a result of recommendations issued by the Unites States Olympic Committee's Select Task Force on Drug Externalization and began operations on 1 October 2000.[47] USADA is responsible for managing the testing and adjudication process for athletes on behalf of the United States Olympic Committee. On 7 January 2003, the USADA was recognized by the US Congress as the '*official anti-doping agency for Olympic, Pan American, and Paralympic sport in the United States*'.[48]

The conduct of drug testing and results management is governed by the USADA Protocol for Olympic Movement Testing (the 'USADA Protocol'), effective as of 7 October 2000.[49] Dispute resolution is governed by Article 9(b) of the USADA Protocol, which provides for a two-level mechanism. Upon receipt of the USADA notice setting forth the charges and the sanction sought by the USADA, the athlete may contest the sanction before an arbitration panel of the AAA under the AAA Supplementary Procedures for Arbitration initiated in the United States Anti-Doping Agency (Articles 9(b)(i) and 9(b)(ii) of the USADA Protocol).[50] Both the athlete and the relevant

---

44 According to Appendix 1 to the Code [Definitions], an International Event is '[a]*n event where the International Olympic Committee, the International Paralyimpic Committee, an International Federation, a Major Event Organizer, or another international sport organization is the ruling body for the Event or appoint the technical officials for the Event*'.

45 International-Level Athletes are those '[a]*thletes designated by one or more International Federations as being within the Registered Testing Proof for an International Federation*', i.e. a pool of top level athletes established by each International Federation and national anti-doping organization who are subject to testing as part of the test distribution plan of that International Federation or National Organization.

46 <www.usantidoping.org>.

47 The United States Olympic Committee (the 'USOC') set up the Select Task Force on Drug Externalization after some criticism had been expressed in regard to its policy in the field of anti-doping, in particular that the USOC was not doing everything within its power to eliminate doping by US athletes. The Select Task Force concluded that in order to address this perception, an independent organization should be created to conduct a comprehensive anti-doping program in the US on behalf of the USOC.

48 See Section 636 of the Joint Resolution of the 108th Congress of the United States (<www.cfo.doe.gov/budget/billrept/fy03/omni_enrolled_hjres_2_doe.pdf>).

49 <www.usantidoping.org/files/USADA_Protocol.pdf>.

50 See Annex D to the USADA Protocol.

International Federation may challenge the AAA decision before the CAS (Article 9(b)(iii) of the USADA Protocol). The USADA Protocol requires that the hearing be conducted in the US[51] and that the CAS conduct a *de novo* review of the matter on appeal (Article 9(b)(iii) of the USADA Protocol). Finally, the USADA Protocol provides that the CAS decision is final and binding on all parties and is not subject to further review or appeal.[52]

On 7 February 2002, the CAS issued its first award in its capacity as the appeal body of AAA decisions on sanctions imposed by the USADA.

2. Salient procedural features

a) Introductory remark

The scope of the following section will be limited to a description of the salient features of the procedure before the Appeals Arbitration Division of the CAS, i.e. cases where the CAS is called upon to resolve disputes generally arising out of decisions rendered by a disciplinary tribunal or a similar body of a federation or a sports body.

b) Applicable rules

In accordance with Article R27, the CAS Rules apply whenever the parties have agreed to refer a sports-related dispute to the CAS. Such agreement may result from a contract containing an arbitration clause providing for the jurisdiction of the CAS or a submission agreement entered into after a dispute has arisen. In practice, the agreement to submit a dispute to the jurisdiction of the CAS often results from an arbitration clause found in articles of association of a corporate sports body that a licensee has accepted by adhering to such sports body.[53] Under Swiss law,[54] such an arbitration clause is binding upon the members of the corporate body, including upon those who do not consent to the relevant provision when it is introduced after they have joined the body.[55] Difficulties may arise

51 In accordance with Article R28 of the CAS Rules, the seat of the CAS is nevertheless located in Lausanne, Switzerland.

52 Article R28 of the CAS Rules provides that the seat of each CAS arbitration panel is located in Lausanne, Switzerland. Accordingly, CAS/USADA arbitrations will be conducted under the PILA, notwithstanding the requirement of the USADA Protocol that the CAS hearing take place in the US. For more details on the effect of the application of the PILA to CAS/USADA arbitrations, in particular with respect to the challenge and enforcement of the CAS decision, see A. RIGOZZI, *Les nouvelles compétences du Tribunal Arbitral du Sport en matière de dopage, premiers commentaires sur le nouveau système de résolution des litiges aux Etats-Unis*, Jusletter of 15 April 2002 (www.weblaw.ch).

53 See e.g. Article 62(1) of the General Statutes of the Fédération Internationale de Basket Association ('FIBA').

54 According to Article R28 of the CAS Rules, the seat of the CAS and of each Panel is in Lausanne, Switzerland. The effect of this provision is that arbitrations before the CAS are always governed by Chapter 12 of the PILA.

55 W. WENGER in BERTI, N. 63, p. 352.

when the adverse party is not a member of the corporate sports body. For the present purposes, it suffices to note that the sports body itself is bound by the arbitration agreement included in its articles of association. As set out above in relation to the *ad hoc* Division of the CAS, it is equally clear that an appellant voluntary submits to CAS arbitration by commencing proceedings before the CAS, as does a respondent that does not object to such jurisdiction at the outset of the arbitration.

The procedure before the Appeals Arbitration Division is governed by the *General Provision*, i.e. Articles R27 to R37 of the CAS Rules, and by the *Special Provisions Applicable to the Appeal Arbitration Proceedings*, i.e. Articles R47 to R59 of the CAS Rules.

c) Admissibility

In accordance with Article R47 of the CAS Rules, an appeal lodged with the Appeals Arbitration Division is admissible only if so provided in the statutes or regulations of the body which rendered the decision under appeal or in a specific submission agreement and only insofar as the legal remedies available to the appellant under such statutes or regulations have been exhausted prior to the appeal.

d) Time-limit to file the Statement of Appeal

The Statement of Appeal must be filed with the CAS within 21 days from the communication of the decision under appeal (Article R49 of the CAS Rules). The appellant has then 10 days to file an appeal brief stating the facts and legal arguments giving rise to the appeal and the exhibits relied upon (Article R51).

e) Application to stay the enforcement of a decision under appeal and application for provisional and conservatory measures

The Statement of Appeal may be accompanied by an application to stay the enforcement of a decision under appeal (Article R48 of the CAS Rules). Once the Statement of Appeal has been filed, the President of the Appeals Arbitration Division – before the file has been transmitted to the Panel – or the Panel, thereafter, may make an order for provisional or conservatory measures upon application by a party (Article R37). In cases of utmost urgency, the President of the Appeals Arbitration Division may issue an *ex parte* order upon '*mere presentation*' of the application (Article R37(3)).

f) Constitution of the Panel

Unless the appellant establishes in the Statement of Appeal that the parties have agreed to a Panel composed of a sole arbitrator or that a sole arbitrator would be more appropriate due to an emergency, appeals are submitted to a Panel composed of three arbitrators (Article R50) appointed in accordance with Article R40 of the CAS Rules.

g) Applicable substantive law

The Panel must apply the applicable regulations and the rules of law chosen by the parties. In the absence of such a choice, the applicable substantive law is that of the country in which the federation, association or sports body having issued the decision under appeal is domiciled (Article R58 of the CAS Rules).

h) Waiver of the right to challenge the award before the Swiss Federal Tribunal

According to Article R59(3) of the CAS Rules, an award of the Appeals Arbitration Division may not be challenged by way of an application to set aside if the parties have no domicile, habitual residence, or business establishment in Switzerland and they have expressly excluded all setting aside proceedings in their arbitration agreement or in their submission agreement. This provision is a restatement of Article 192(1) of the PILA, which authorizes the parties to waive the right to file an application to set aside an award provided that neither of the parties has its domicile, habitual residence or place of business in Switzerland.[56] However, and according to Swiss case law, the requirement of an express waiver is not satisfied if the parties refer in general terms to a set of arbitration rules which contain a provision to the effect that the award shall be final.[57] Nevertheless, certain legal commentators maintain that there is a valid waiver where the parties specifically refer to the provision of a set of arbitration rules, which stipulates that the parties waive all setting aside proceedings.[58]

IV. Arbitration between states

1. WTO Understanding on Rules and Procedures Governing the Settlement of Disputes (the 'DSU')

a) Overview

aa) Dispute settlement procedure under the GATT

At the end of World War II, the United States and the United Kingdom submitted a proposal regarding the establishment of an international trade body, the International Trade Organization (ITO). While the Preparatory Committee responsible for drafting the ITO Charter was still working, a first round of negotiations on tariffs took place from April to October 1947, which resulted in the General Agreement on Tariffs and Trade (the 'GATT'). Pending the entry into force of the ITO Charter, a mechanism was needed to implement the tariff concessions negotiated in 1947. In order to bring the GATT into force, a Protocol of Provisional Application ('PAP') was developed and the GATT entered into force as of 1 January 1948.

With respect to dispute resolution, the GATT only provided for limited rules, namely Articles XXII ('*Consultation*') and XXIII ('*Nullification or Impairment*'). In fact, more

56 See note 54 *supra*.
57 DFT 116 II 639.
58 P. M. PATOCCHI/C. JERMINI in BERTI, N. 14, p. 604.

detailed provisions on the settlement of disputes were to be incorporated in the ITO Charter.[59] The Charter was eventually completed and adopted at a conference held in March 1948 in Havana, Cuba. However, for various reasons, including the United States' failure to ratify it, the Charter never came into force. As a result, Articles XXII and XXIII of the GATT were the only rules dealing with the settlement of disputes. During the 47 years of the GATT's provisional existence, the dispute settlement procedure evolved and was 'codified' in the '*Understanding on Notification, Consultation, Dispute Settlement and Surveillance*' (the 'Understanding'), a document adopted on 28 November 1979 by the contracting states and setting forth in its annex an '*Agreed Description of the Customary Practice of the GATT in the Field of Dispute Settlement (Article XXIII:2)*' (the 'Agreed Description').[60]

However, the GATT dispute resolution procedure had a significant weakness – a consensus in favour of a report was required for its adoption. In practice, this meant that '*the losing party in a dispute settlement proceeding not only could refuse to agree, and therefore "block" the adoption of an adverse report, it even could refuse to agree to the very establishment of a Panel, thereby avoiding the embarrassment of an adopted adverse report altogether*'.[61]

bb) Dispute settlement under the WTO

On 15 April 1994, most of the 125 states participating in a meeting in Marrakech signed the Marrakech Agreement Establishing the World Trade Organization (the 'WTO Agreement'), thereby concluding the Uruguay Round of trade negotiations. The WTO has its headquarters in Geneva, Switzerland.

One of the major achievements of the Uruguay Round was the adoption of the DSU.[62] The DSU provides for the Dispute Settlement Body (the 'DSB') – a permanent and independent body for resolving disputes that may arise between WTO members in the course of performance of the various WTO agreements – and the Appellate Body, a standing body of seven persons that decides appeals from reports issued by Panels established under the DSB. Under the DSU, reports are adopted unless there is a consensus not to adopt them.[63]

To date, 305 disputes have been submitted for resolution under the auspices of the DSU. On 24 November 2003, the United States announced that it would comply with the Appellate Body report of 10 November 2003, which upheld a 11 July 2003 Panel report ruling that safeguard measures on imports of steel products imposed by the United States

---

59 See Chapter VIII of the ITO Charter ('*Settlement of Differences*'). D. PALMETER/P. C. MAVROIDIS, *Dispute Settlement in the World Trade Organization – Practice and Procedure*, Kluwer Law International 1999, pp. 7-8.

60 Available at <www.wto.org/english/docs_e/legal_e/tokyo_notif_e.pdf>.

61 D. Palmeter/P. C. Mavroidis, *op. cit.*, pp. 9-10.

62 Annex 2 to the WTO Agreement.

63 Article 16(4) of the DSU. See also D. PALMETER/P. C. MAVROIDIS, *op. cit.*, p. 153.

were inconsistent with the Safeguards Agreement and the GATT 1994 following complaints brought by Brazil, China, the European Communities, Japan, South Korea, New Zealand, Norway and Switzerland.

b) Salient procedural features of the DSU

aa) Scope of application

In accordance with Article 1(1), the DSU applies to any dispute brought pursuant to the settlement mechanisms of the agreements listed in Appendix 1, i.e. the WTO Agreement, the 13 individual multilateral agreements on trade in goods (e.g. the GATT 1994), the GATS,[64] the TRIPS[65] and four plurilateral agreements (together, the 'covered agreements'). The DSU does not preclude the application of special or additional dispute settlement procedures contained in the covered agreements. Those special or additional procedures are identified in Appendix 2 to the DSU and Article 1(2) of the DSU expressly provides that they will prevail in the event of a conflict between them and provisions of the DSU.

bb) The DSB

The DSB is composed of representatives of every WTO member and has the authority to administer the DSU, as well as the consultation or dispute settlement provisions of the covered agreements. In this capacity, the DSB has the authority to establish Panels, adopt Panel and Appellate Body reports, monitor the implementation of rulings and recommendations and authorize suspension of concessions and other obligations under the covered agreements (Article 2(1) of the DSU). In accordance with Article 2(4) of the DSU, the DSB takes its decisions by consensus.[66]

cc) The Consultation period

The first stage of a DSU procedure is a consultation period of at least 60 days (Article 4 of the DSU). The request for consultation must be submitted in writing and must set forth the reasons for the request, including an identification of the measures at issue and an indication of the legal basis of the complaint, i.e. the provisions of one or more of the covered agreements that are allegedly violated (Article 4(4)). Although the DSU is silent on this point, some legal commentators maintain that the establishment of a Panel without prior consultation is permissible in certain circumstances.[67]

---

64 The abbreviation for 'General Agreement on Trade in Services'.

65 Standing for 'Agreement on Trade-Related Aspects of Intellectual Property Rights'.

66 According to Article 2(4) of the DSU and footnote, a consensus is deemed to exist if no Member present at a deliberation formally objects to a proposed decision ('negative consensus').

67 N. Komuro, *The WTO Dispute Settlement Mechanism, Coverage and Procedures of the WTO Understanding* in (1995) 12/3 J. Int'l Arb. 122.

dd) Establishment of the Panels

The dispute settlement procedure begins with the filing of a written request for the establishment of a Panel with the DSB, which sets forth a brief summary of the legal basis of the complaint (Article 6(2) of the DSU). Unless the DSB decides by consensus not to establish a Panel, a Panel will be established at the latest at the DSB meeting following that at which the request first appears on the DSB's agenda (Article 6(1)).

ee) Composition of the Panels

Unless the parties to the dispute agree upon a Panel composed of five members, Panels are composed of three persons, with one of them serving as chairperson (Article 8 of the DSU). The Secretariat proposes nominations for the Panel to the parties.[68] Failing an agreement on the Panel members, the Director-General of the WTO will determine the composition of the Panel.

ff) Terms of Reference

Unless the parties to the dispute agree otherwise, the Panels have standard terms of reference, namely to '*examine, in the light of the relevant provisions in (name of the covered agreement(s) cited by the parties to the dispute), the matter referred to the SB by (name of party) in document ... and to make such findings as will assist the DSB in making the recommendations or in giving the rulings provided for in that/those agreement(s)*' (Article 7(1) of the DSU).

gg) Written submissions

The parties' written submissions must set forth the facts of the case and their arguments (Appendix 3 to the DSU, Article 4). In this respect, the Appellate Body has ruled that there is no requirement in the DSU that all claims relating to the matter referred to the DSB be set forth in the complaining party's first written submission to the Panel.[69] The DSU does not provide for counterclaims. Accordingly, where the responding party files its own complaint against the complaining party, such complaint will be heard separately.[70]

hh) Interim reports

Interim reports are issued at two stages of the procedure. A first interim report is issued after the Panel has considered the rebuttal written submissions and oral arguments and contains the factual and argument sections of the draft final report (Article 15(1) of the DSU). The Panel issues a second interim report after expiration of the time limit it has set for the parties to comment on the first interim report. The second interim report

68 The parties to the dispute may not oppose nominations except for compelling reasons (Article 8(6) of the DSU).

69 Case No. AB-1997-3, WT/DS27/R of 9 September 1997 available at <www.wto.org/english/tratop_e/dispu_e/ab_reports_e.htm>.

70 D. PALMETER/P. C MAVROIDIS, *op. cit.*, N. 4.10, p. 75.

contains – in addition to the factual and argument sections - the Panel's findings and conclusions.

ii) Final report

In the event that the parties fail to reach an agreement, the Panel will submit to the DSB a final report setting out its findings of fact, the applicability of the relevant provisions, the basic rationale for any findings and its recommendations (Article 12(7) of the DSU). If the parties do not comment on the interim reports, such reports will be considered to be the final report and will be circulated to the members (Article 15(2) of the DSU).

jj) Adoption of the final report

A final report will be automatically adopted by the DSB within 60 days after its circulation to the members, unless a party to the dispute indicates to the DSB that it intend to appeal against such report or the DSB decides by consensus not to adopt it (Article 16(4) of the DSU).

kk) The Appellate Body

The DSU provides for the establishment of a permanent Appellate Body to review the Panel rulings (Article 17(1) of the DSU). The Appellate Body is a permanent body composed of seven members. On 15 February 1996, it adopted the Working Procedures for Appellate Review (the 'Working Procedures') governing the appeal process.[71]

ll) Appeal

An appeal is commenced by a notification in writing to the DSB and the simultaneous filing of a notice of appeal with the Appellate Body (Article XX(1) of the Working Procedures). The notice of appeal must contain *inter alia* the title of the Panel report under appeal and a brief statement of the nature of the appeal, including the allegations of errors in the issues of law covered in the Panel report and in the legal interpretations developed by the Panel.

mm) Scope of review

As indicated above, the appeal is limited to issues of law covered in the Panel report and legal interpretations developed by the Panel (Article 17(6) of the DSU).

nn) Adoption of the Appellate Body report

Once issued, the Appellate Body report will be automatically adopted by the DSB unless the DSB decides by consensus to reject it within 30 days following its circulation to the members (Article 17(14) of the DSU).

71 Available at <www.wto.org/english/news_e/pres96_e/ab3.htm>.

2. *OSCE Court of Conciliation and Arbitration (Rules of the Court of Conciliation and Arbitration within the OSCE)*

a) Overview

On 15 December 1992, the Ministerial Council for Security and Co-operation in Europe (CSCE) – the governing body of the Organisation for Security and Co-operation in Europe (OSCE)[72] – adopted and declared open for signature by interested participating states the text of a 'Convention on Conciliation and Arbitration within the CSCE' (the 'Convention') providing for the establishment of a Court of Conciliation and Arbitration (the 'Court') to settle disputes between contracting parties. On the same date, the CSCE also approved the text of the Rules of the Court of Conciliation and Arbitration within the OSCE (the 'OSCE Rules'). The Convention entered into force on 5 December 1994, after the deposit of the twelfth instrument of ratification.[73]

The Court is composed of the Bureau and the Registrar. The Bureau is the permanent executive body of the Court and is responsible *inter alia* for the appointment of conciliators and arbitrators. The Bureau consists of the President, the Vice-President and three other members of the Court. The Registrar supervises the Court's officials under the authority and control of the Bureau and principally serves as secretary of the Court, the Bureau and the conciliation commissions and arbitral tribunals established within the Court.

The Court members convened for the first time on 29 May 1995. On this occasion, they elected the first President of the Court, appointed its Registrar and adopted the OSCE Rules. The OSCE Rules have been in effect since 1 February 1997, the date of their approval by the state parties to the Convention.

To date, no dispute has been brought before the Court.

b) Salient procedural features

aa) The seat of the Court and the arbitral tribunals

The seat of the Court and of the arbitral tribunals established within the Court is located in Geneva, Switzerland (Article 10(1) of the Convention).[74]

---

72 The OSCE decision-making and governing power lies with the CSCE during periods between OSCE summits. The CSCE, composed of the Foreign Ministers of the OSCE participating States, meets once a year.

73 For the status of the ratifications of the Convention, see <www.osce.org/cca/documents/ratification.pdf>.

74 In accordance with Article 10(2) of the Convention, this does not prevent an arbitral tribunal from meeting at another location.

bb) The request for arbitration

In accordance with Articles 26(1) of the Convention and 23(2) of the OSCE Rules, the request for arbitration may be made by means of an agreement between two or more contracting states or between one or more contracting states and one or more other CSCE participating states. Where a contracting state has made the declaration that it will recognize the jurisdiction of an arbitral tribunal as compulsory, *ipso facto* and without special agreement, subject to reciprocity, the request for arbitration may also be made by means of an application filed with the Registrar. The request for arbitration must indicate the subject matter of the dispute. If it is made pursuant to an agreement and no such agreement has been reached with respect to the described dispute, each party may set out its own position (Articles 27(1) of the Convention and 23(2) of the OSCE Rules). Where the request for arbitration is made by means of an application, it must indicate, in addition to the subject matter of the dispute, the means of settlement previously used and the main legal arguments invoked (Articles 27(2) of the Convention and 23(3) of the OSCE Rules).

cc) The arbitral tribunal

The arbitral tribunal is *ex officio* composed of the arbitrator or alternate appointed by each state party after entry into force of the Convention. In addition to the arbitrators, the Bureau will appoint a number of members to sit on the arbitral tribunal (Article 28(3) of the Convention). The chairperson will be appointed by the Bureau from among the members (Article 28(6) of the Convention).

dd) Interim measures

The arbitral tribunal has the power to recommend *non-binding* interim measures that should be taken by the parties to avoid an aggravation of the dispute, greater difficulty in reaching a resolution or the possibility of a future award becoming unenforceable due to the conduct of one or more of the parties to the dispute. The arbitral tribunal may do so on its own motion or upon request by one or all the parties (Article 26(4) of the Convention).

ee) The award

In accordance with Article 28(1) of the OSCE Rules, the award must be reasoned. It is final and binding and not subject to appeal (Article 31(3) of the Convention). However, a party may request that the arbitral tribunal interpret the meaning or scope of its award. Unless agreed otherwise by the parties, the time limit for filing a request for interpretation is six months from the communication of the award (Article 31(3) of the Convention).

ff) Revision of the award

A party may apply for revision of the award within six months from discovery of new elements of facts which are decisive for the outcome of the dispute and were unknown to the arbitral tribunal at the time the award was rendered (Article 31(4) of the Convention). No application for revision may be filed after the expiry of a 10-year cut-off period from the date of the award (Article 31(4) of the Convention).

V. Other institutions

1. UNCC Provisional Rules for Claims Procedure

a) Overview

aa) Genesis of the UNCC

In the early hours of 2 August 1990, more than 100,000 Iraqi soldiers, backed up by 700 tanks, invaded Kuwait. The UN Security Council condemned the invasion in Resolution 660 of the same day. In Resolution 678 of 29 November 1990, the UN Security Council authorized the member states to use all necessary means to restore international peace unless Iraq implemented Resolution 660 and subsequent resolutions on or before 15 January 1991. On 17 January 1991, coalition forces launched Operation Desert Storm, which led to the restoration of Kuwait's sovereignty.

At its meeting of 3 April 1991, the UN Security Council adopted Resolution 687 (1991)[75] whereby it affirmed that '*Iraq,* [...] *is liable under international law for any direct loss, damage, including environmental damage and the depletion of natural resources, or injury to foreign Governments, nationals and corporations, as a result of Iraq's unlawful invasion and occupation of Kuwait*'. Resolution 687 also imposed a formal cease-fire, subject to Iraq's acceptance of the provisions of the Resolution and, in particular, the creation of a fund to pay compensation for claims resulting from loss and damage incurred following Iraq's invasion of Kuwait.[76]

On 20 May 1991, the UN Security Council adopted Resolution 692 establishing the United Nations Compensation Commission (the 'UNCC') and locating it in Geneva, Switzerland, at the offices of the UN.[77] On 26 June 1992, the UN Security Council approved the UNCC's Provisional Rules for Claims Procedure (the 'UNCC Rules').

bb) The UNCC's structure

The UNCC is composed of the Governing Council, the Secretariat and the Commissioners. The Governing Council is the executive body of the UNCC. It meets periodically and sets out the UNCC's policy, establishes the criteria for the compensability of claims, the procedures for processing the claims, the guidelines for the administration and financing of the Compensation Fund and the procedures for the payment of compensation. The Secretariat, headed by the Executive Secretary, provides administrative, technical and legal support to the Governing Council and the Panels of Commissioners. It also administers the Compensation Fund. The Commissioners are the

---

75 <www.unog.ch/uncc/resolutio/res0687.pdf>.

76 See §18 and 19 of Resolution 687 (1991).

77 <www.unog.ch/uncc/resolutio/res0692.pdf>.

experts appointed by the Governing Council for verification and evaluation of the claims.

b) Salient procedural features

aa) A decision on the quantum

In Resolution 687, the UN Security Council reaffirmed the principle of Iraq's liability, which was expressly accepted by Iraq. The procedure before the UNCC is therefore similar to any arbitral procedure where the liability of the parties has been determined and it remains necessary to render a decision on the *quantum*.

bb) Filing of claims

One of the peculiarities of the UNCC procedure is that only governments and international organizations, to the exclusion of individuals, are entitled to file claims with the UNCC (Article 5 of the UNCC Rules). Governments may file claims on behalf of their nationals or, in their discretion, on behalf of other persons resident in their territory, or on behalf of corporations or other entities that were incorporated or organized under their laws on the date on which the claim arose (Article 5(a) and (b) of the UNCC Rules). International organizations may only submit claims on their own behalf (Article 5(c) of the UNCC Rules).

cc) Preliminary assessment of the claims

In accordance with Article 14 of the UNCC Rules, a claim is subject to an initial 'screening' by the Secretariat upon its receipt. The Secretariat determines whether it meets the formal requirements established by the Governing Council, such as the use of the appropriate claim forms, the required number of copies, etc.[78] A claim is considered as not having been filed if any formal defect is not cured within a 60-day time limit set by the Secretariat (Article 15 of the UNCC Rules).

dd) Categories of claims

In order to facilitate the work of the Commissioners, the Secretariat categorizes the claims in one of six categories devised by the Governing Council according to *inter alia* the type or size of the claim and the similarity of legal and factual issues raised (Article 17 of the UNCC Rules). The six categories include four categories relating to claims of individuals, one to claims of corporations and one to claims of governments and international organizations:

- '*A claims*' are claims submitted by individuals who were forced to leave Iraq or Kuwait. Compensation for successful claims in this category is set at a fixed lump sum of USD 2,500 for individual claimants and USD 5,000 for families.

78 Article 14 of the UNCC Rules.

An individual claimant that only submits an '*A claim*' is eligible to maximum compensation of USD 4,000 (USD 8,000 for a family);[79]

- '*B claims*' are claims submitted by individuals who suffered serious personal injury or whose spouse, child or parent died as a result of Iraq's invasion and occupation of Kuwait. Compensation for successful claims in this category is set at USD 2,500 for individuals and up to USD 10,000 for a family;[80]
- '*C claims*' are individual claims for damages in excess of USD 2,500 and up to USD 100,000 for different types of losses ranging from departure from Kuwait or Iraq to mental pain and anguish or loss of bank accounts;[81]
- '*D claims*' are individual claims for damages in excess of USD 100,000 for types of losses identical to those claimed under '*C claims*' but relating the most frequently to loss of personal property, loss of income or business losses;[82]
- '*E claims*' are claims of corporations or other entities;[83]
- '*F claims*' are claims of governments or international organisations.[84]

ee) Appointment of the Commissioners

The Commissioners are appointed for fixed terms by the Governing Council. They sit in three-member panels, with each of the members of a panel being of a different nationality (Article 28 of the UNCC Rules). Each panel is established to review a specific category of claims. The Executive Secretary transmits to the Governing Council the nominations for Commissioners proposed by the Secretary General, with an indication of which Commissioners are to serve on each panel and who will act as chairperson. The panels normally meet in Geneva, at the UNCC's headquarters (Article 33(2) of the UNCC Rules).

---

79 The UNCC received approximately 920,000 '*A claims*' seeking a total of approximately USD 3.6 billion in compensation.

80 The UNCC received approximately 6,000 '*B claims*' seeking a total of approximately USD 21 million in compensation.

81 The UNCC received approximately 420,000 '*C claims*' seeking a total of approximately USD 9 billion in compensation. On top of that, the Central Bank of Egypt submitted a consolidated '*C claim*' on behalf of over 800,000 workers in Iraq for the non-transfer of remittances by Iraqi banks to beneficiaries in Egypt. This claim comprised 1,240,000 individual claims with an asserted value of approximately USD 491 million.

82 The UNCC received approximately 10,500 '*D claims*' seeking a total of approximately USD 10 billion in compensation.

83 The UNCC received approximately 5,800 '*E claims*' seeking a total of approximately USD 80 billion in compensation.

84 The UNCC received approximately 300 '*F claims*' seeking a total of approximately USD 210 billion in compensation.

ff) Privileges and immunities

The Commissioners have the status of 'experts on mission' within the meaning of Article VI of the Convention on the Privileges and Immunities of the United Nations of 13 February 1946 while serving for the UNCC (Article 26 of the UNCC Rules). As such, they are immune *inter alia* from legal proceedings of every kind with respect their words – spoken or written – and their acts.[85]

gg) Applicable law

In accordance with Article 31 of the UNCC Rules, the Commissioners must apply the resolutions of the UN Security Council, in particular Resolution 687 of 1991, the criteria established by the Governing Council and, where necessary, other relevant rules of international law.

hh) The Governing Council's approval

Under Article 40 of the UNCC Rules, the amounts recommended by the Commissioners are subject to the Governing Council's approval. The Governing Council may increase or reduce such amounts and even return a particular claim to the Commissioners for further review.

ii) Waiver of appeal

The decisions taken by the Commissioners and approved by the Governing Council are final and are not subject to appeal or review on procedural, substantive or other grounds (Article 40(4) of the UNCC Rules).

2. CRT Rules of Procedure for the Claims Resolution Process

a) Overview

aa) The CRT I

On 2 May 1996, the World Jewish Restitution Organization, the World Jewish Congress and the Swiss Bankers Association (the 'SBA') entered into a settlement agreement (the 'Memorandum of Understanding') establishing the Independent Committee of Eminent Persons (the 'ICEP') to conduct an investigative audit to determine whether there were any dormant accounts of the victims of Nazi persecution deposited in Swiss banks.

On 23 July 1997, the SBA published the names of holders of 1,756 accounts opened by non-Swiss nationals and residents prior to the end of World War II (8 May 1945) and that had been dormant since that time, inviting any person believing to be the rightful owner of a published dormant account, or an heir thereof, to file a claim within six months after the publication.

---

85 Article 12(22)(b) of the United Nations Convention on the Privileges and Immunities of 13 February 1946.

In September 1997, the Independent Claims Resolution Foundation (the 'Foundation') was established for the purpose of adjudicating claims to the above accounts. In order to do so, the Foundation, supervised by the ICEP and the Swiss Federal Banking Commission, created an independent arbitral institution, the Claims Resolution Tribunal for Dormant Accounts in Switzerland (the 'CRT'). On 15 October 1997, the Board of Trustees of the Foundation adopted the Rules of Procedure for the Claims Resolution Process (the 'CRT Rules') under which the CRT 1 operated until 2001.

In October 1997, the names of holders of 14,000 dormant accounts were published.[86]

bb) The CRT 2

In late 1996 and early 1997, a series of class actions were filed with the US District Court for the Eastern District of New York against UBS and Crédit Suisse Group. In August 1998, the parties agreed to settle such actions for USD 1,25 billion. The settlement agreement was signed on 26 January 1999 and approved on 9 August 2000 by Judge E. R. Korman.

Thereafter, on 22 November 2000, Judge E. R. Korman ratified a Plan of Allocation and Distribution according to which up to USD 800 million out of the USD 1.25 billion settlement payment were set aside for awards to claimants.

On 8 December 2000, Judge E. R. Korman appointed Mr. P. Volcker, former chairman of the US Federal Reserve, and Mr. M. Bradfield as Special Masters to establish, organize and supervise the claims resolution process using the CRT as the forum for the adjudication of the claims. In this process, the CRT makes determinations regarding the rights of claimants to accounts in Swiss banks. Awards resulting from this process are then certified to the US District Court for payment by the Special Masters, subject to court approval. The banks are not parties to the proceedings but are cooperating by providing information for the claims resolution process.

After a comprehensive ICEP investigation of Swiss bank records, certain accounts were identified by the ICEP auditors as being either possibly or probably owned by victims of Nazi persecution. In connection with the settlement agreement, the Swiss Federal Banking Commission mandated that the SBA bring about the publication of those accounts. On 5 February 2001, the SBA published an official list of names of account holders of 21,000 dormant accounts.

This section will exclusively focus on the CRT Rules under which the CRT 1 operated.

b) Salient procedural features

aa) Scope of application

The CRT Rules govern all claims to accounts[87] opened by non-Swiss nationals or residents that were dormant since 9 May 1945 and were published by the SBA on 23

86 Overall, 10,753 Swiss and 5,570 foreign dormant accounts were published by the SBA.

July 1997 or after (Article 1(1)(i) of the CRT Rules). According to the definition proposed by the Swiss Federal Banking Commission, a 'dormant' account is an account opened before or during World War II and that has not moved since 8 May 1945. Claims to accounts opened by Swiss nationals may also be filed with the CRT, provided that the Swiss national acted as an intermediary for a victim of Nazi persecution (Article 1(1)(2)).

bb) Filing of claims

Claims are submitted to the CRT by the filing of a signed claims resolution agreement, either directly with the CRT or through one of the five contact offices set up in New York, Tel Aviv, Budapest, Sydney and Basle (Article 2(1) of the CRT Rules).[88]

cc) Number and appointment of arbitrators

Claims submitted to the CRT are decided by a single-member panel or by a three-member panel appointed by the Chairman of the CRT (Article 3 of the CRT Rules). A sole arbitrator has jurisdiction over all claims processed under the fast track procedure (see Section *ee) infra*) or relating to accounts with a balance of CHF 3,000 or less. Panels of three arbitrators have jurisdiction over all cases that do not fall within one of the above categories (Article 5).

dd) Initial screenings of the claims

The first step of the claims resolution process is the assessment made by the concerned bank as to whether a particular claim should proceed further to arbitration. If the bank considers that the claim appears plausible, it must disclose to the Central Contact Office (the 'CCO') its name, complete bank records and the balance of the claimed account within 20 days from receipt of the claim. If the bank refuses to disclose its name and the balance of the account, the CCO will submit the claim to the CRT for an initial screening by a sole arbitrator (Article 10 of the CRT Rules). The sole arbitrator will determine whether or not sufficient information has been submitted by a particular claimant to justify the release of the name of the bank and the balance of the claimed account. The sole arbitrator must order disclosure of the name of the bank and the amount in the claimed account unless the claimant has not submitted any information as to its entitlement or unless it is apparent that the claimant is not entitled to such account. In the event that the sole arbitrator decides not to order disclosure, the claim may not proceed further to arbitration. However, the claimant may, within 30 days from receipt of the sole arbitrator's determination, re-submit the claim for decision by a panel of three arbitrators. In the event that the sole arbitrator decides to order disclosure, the claim may

---

87 'Account' includes all types of bank accounts (current account, savings and securities accounts, etc.) as well as any other form of dormant bank liability such as cheques, bonds, etc. (Article 1(2) of the CRT Rules).

88 Cf. T. BAUER, *The Search for Dormant Accounts – Publication – Filing of Claims – Third Party Information* in (2000) 13 ASA Special Series 4.

proceed further under the fast track (see Section *ee) infra*) or the ordinary procedure (see Section *ff) infra*). In discharging its screening function, the CRT has taken a broad and flexible approach of the concept of plausibility and used a relaxed standard of proof applying in the resolution procedure.[89]

ee) Fast track procedure

Unlike initial screening, the fast track procedure is an arbitral procedure. However, it should not be confused with an expedited procedure whereby an award must be rendered within a shorter time limit.[90] Fast track review under the CRT Rules takes place where the bank has identified a claimant as being entitled to an account and offered to pay a certain amount. Accordingly, the purpose of the fast track review is not only to accelerate the adjudication process, but also to ensure that a bank will not pay favoured clients or persons who may have questionable entitlements.[91] In order to make an award under the fast track procedure, a sole arbitrator must reach the conclusion that the claimant has a valid claim (provided that such conclusion is possible by simple legal and factual enquiries, taking into account any sworn written or oral statement), that the payment offer made by the bank complies with the guidelines on interest and fees and that the claim does not have to be referred to a panel of three arbitrators (Article 12 of the CRT Rules). A claim initially submitted to the fast track procedure will be referred to a panel of arbitrators if the sole arbitrator has reason to believe that the named account holder may have acted as an intermediary for a victim of Nazi persecution, may have submitted a fraudulent claim or that the assets deposited may have been looted from such victims (Article 13).

ff) Ordinary procedure

A claim that is not submitted under the fast track procedure will be processed through the ordinary procedure. The ordinary procedure involves a full review of the claim and all available evidence (i.e. not limited to '*simple legal and factual enquiry taking into account the oral or written statement of the claimant*') (Article 14 of the CRT Rules). Nevertheless, a relaxed standard of proof applies in the ordinary procedure (Article 22 of the CRT Rules).

gg) Applicable substantive law

When deciding matters in regard to the relationship between the published account holder and the claimant, a panel must apply the law with which the matter in dispute has the closest connection (Article 16(1) of the CRT Rules). In the context of inheritance matters, legal commentators maintain that the closest connection is almost always with the state with which the account holder had the closest connection at the time of his or

---

89 A. RAMASASTRY, *Initial Screening of Claims* in (2000) 13 ASA Special Series 30.

90 Although Article 11 of the CRT Rules provides that a claim submitted to a fast track review should be resolved within 30 days from such submission.

91 A. JOLLES, *Fast Track Procedure* in (2000) 13 ASA Special Series 37.

her death.[92] The relationship between the Swiss bank and the claimant will be governed by Swiss law, except as otherwise provided by the CRT Rules (Article 16(2)). The Interest Guideline applies to issues of interest, fees and charges.

hh) Applicable procedural rules

Part VII of the CRT Rules (the 'Procedural Rules') specifies the procedure to be followed by the arbitrators. To some extent, the CRT procedure is based upon the inquisitorial principle applied by civil courts in specific procedures, whereby the court must conduct on its own the factual and legal enquiries in order to assess the claims as comprehensively as possible (Article 17(ii) of the CRT Rules). Another feature typical of a procedure designed to simplify matters for the claimant is that all time limits must be set by indicating the specific date of expiry, as opposed to a fixed number of days (Article 19 of the CRT Rules).

ii) Evidence

The claimant must show that it is plausible that he or she is entitled, in whole or in part, to the claimed account (Article 22(1) of the CRT Rules). A finding of plausibility requires *inter alia* that all documents and information that can reasonably be expected to be produced in view of the particular circumstances surrounding the relationship between the claimant and the account holder have been submitted, that there is no basis to conclude that fraud or forgery affect the claim or the evidence submitted or that other persons may have an identical or better claim to the dormant account (Article 22(2)(ii)).

jj) The award

The award must be made in writing and signed by the sole arbitrator or by the chairperson and at least one other member for a three-member panel (Article 33 of the CRT Rules).[93] The award must contain the name of the arbitrators, the designation of the parties, a description of the factual findings and the applicable law, the arbitral tribunal's decision and the date of the award.

kk) The seat of the CRT

The seat of the CRT is in Zurich, Switzerland. However, the CRT Rules authorise a panel to hold hearings wherever it deems appropriate (Article 34).

3. The German Forced Labour Compensation Program

a) Overview

In 1999, a class action was commenced in the US District Court for the Eastern District of New York against German industry for its use of slave and forced labour.

---

92 N. VOSER, *Arbitrability and the Applicable Law in the Claims Resolution Process for Dormant Accounts in Switzerland* in (2000) 13 ASA Special Series 50.

93 In accordance with Article 31 of the CRT Rules, a panel of arbitrators must decide by a simple majority of all its members and the arbitrators may not abstain from voting.

On 17 July 2000, Belarus, the Czech Republic, Poland, Russia, Ukraine, Israel, Germany, the United States and German industry, as well as victims of Nazi persecution, entered into a settlement agreement to compensate these victims for their suffering during World War II.

On the same day, Germany and the United States entered into an agreement whereby Germany approved the creation of a foundation dedicated to overseeing the compensation process of former forced labourers and other persons affected by Nazi persecutions (the 'Foundation'). The statute creating the Foundation 'Remembrance, Responsibility and Future' (the 'Statute') was enacted on 2 August 2000 and entered into force on 12 August 2000.

The Foundation operates two different programs. Article 11 of the Statute, which defines the eligible persons, distinguishes between claims for payment relating to slave labour, forced labour, personal injury or death of a child lodged in a home for children of slave or forced labourers and claims for property losses suffered under the Nazi regime as a result of direct participation of German companies (the 'property claims').

In accordance with Article 10 of the Statute, the Foundation's resources must be made available to claimants through partner organizations for processing. The Foundation has appointed the International Organization for Migration (the 'IOM') as the official entity to process all property claims.

Article 9(6) of the Statute provides that a commission formed within the IOM would have the task of ruling upon the claims submitted. The IOM thus established the Property Claims Commission (the 'PCC') to decide on claims submitted under the Statute. On 5 June 2001, the PCC issued its Supplemental Principles and Rules of Procedure (the 'PCC Rules'). The PCC has its seat in Geneva, Switzerland.

To date, the PCC has processed approximately 9,100 property claims out of more than 30,000 claims received. Approximately 1,900 claims have been accepted and 7,200 claims denied.

b) Salient procedural features

aa) Eligibility to file a claim

Article 3.1 of the PCC Rules provides that only the individual who suffered the loss, or, as the case may be, his surviving spouse and children, grandchildren or siblings may submit a claim. If none of the above files a claim, beneficiaries named in an individual's will may submit a claim.

bb) Costs

The processing of claims before the PCC is free of charge. However, expenses incurred by claimants, in particular for representation, are not reimbursed (Article 5 of the PCC Rules).

cc) Waiver of claims against German enterprises and against Germany

As part of the agreement providing for the creation of the Foundation, Germany and the United States have agreed that it would be in their interests for the Foundation to serve as the exclusive remedy and forum for the resolution of all claims that may be asserted against German companies.[94] Accordingly, the United States has undertaken to inform its courts, each time a claim covered by the settlement agreement has been asserted, that it would be in the foreign policy interests of the United States that the Foundation be the exclusive remedy and forum for resolving such claims.[95] Article 6 of the PCC Rules restates the above condition by providing that claimants may only receive payments on the condition that they have signed a waiver of all Nazi claims against German enterprises as well as Germany.

dd) Filing of claims

In accordance with Articles 9(1) and 13(1) of the PCC Rules, the claims must be filed with the IOM in one original and one copy using the claim form devised by the IOM.[96] The claimant's signature must be notarized (Article 8).

ee) The statement of claim

Pursuant to Article 10 of the PCC Rules, the claim must state the circumstances of the loss, who caused the loss and why it should be considered as resulting from Nazi persecution. If the claim is for a persecution-related property loss, the statement of claim must indicate why no claim was made under the previous German restitution or indemnification laws.

ff) Evidence

Under Article 11(1) of the PCC Rules, the claims must be supported by written evidence. Where no such written evidence is available, the claim must state why. The heirs of the person who suffered the loss must provide proof of their relationship with such person.

According to Article 22 of the PCC Rules, the PCC must apply a relaxed standard of proof, taking into account the lapse of time between the date the loss occurred and the submission of the claim, the circumstances in which the specific loss or types of losses occurred, the information available from other cases and the background information available to the Commission regarding the circumstances prevailing during the Nazi era and World War II and the participation of German enterprises in the commitment of Nazi wrongs. In practice, the PCC applied the relaxed standard of proof and a number of presumptions based upon historical research.

---

94 See Article 1 of the Agreement of 17 July 2000.

95 *Ibid.*, Article 2(1).

96 The deadline set for the filing of claims expired on 31 December 2001.

gg) The PCC

In accordance with the Article 9(6) of the Statute, the PCC must consist of '*one member each to be named by the Ministry of Finance of the Federal Republic of Germany and the Department of State of the United States of America and a chairperson to be chosen by those two members*'.

hh) Decisions of the PCC

Decisions of the PCC must be made by a majority of the members, unless a member is unable to attend a meeting, in which case the remaining members may provisionally decide with the Chairman having a preponderant vote. Decisions must be made in writing and include reasons (Article 23 of the PCC Rules).

ii) Appeal process

In accordance with Article 34 of the PCC Rules, claimants may lodge an appeal against a decision of the PCC with respect to the *quantum* only. On 7 February 2003, the IOM established the IOM Appeals Body for Forced Labour Claims and enacted corresponding Principles and Rules of Appeals Procedure. The appeal process for property loss claims has not been determined yet.

Chapter 11 - Mediation

Corinna Klaus and Manuel Liatowitsch*

I. Introduction

Mediation is becoming an increasingly important tool for conflict resolution in Switzerland. This chapter outlines the essential features of mediation, the typical stages of mediation and certain related legal issues. Some of Switzerland's mediation organisations and institutions are also described.

II. What is mediation?

1. Definition

a) Essential features

Although there is no universally accepted definition, mediation has been defined as '*the non-binding intervention by a neutral third party who helps the disputants negotiate an agreement*'.[1]

Mediation is a form of assisted negotiation. A neutral third person - the mediator - helps the parties themselves find a legally binding agreement for the solution of their dispute. The mediator has no authority to impose a solution on the parties.

Mediation is an alternative, non-judicial dispute resolution procedure. It is based on the free will of the parties and is purely contractual in nature. The parties are free to terminate the mediation process at any time. The parties retain full authority and responsibility to decide on the solution of the matter in dispute and on how the mediation is conducted. Though the mediator may and will often put forward various proposals, the parties have the final word on whether or not to accept them. The mediator has no decisional power. The mediator's role is to establish the procedure, create a favourable

---

* The authors wish to acknowledge the input and assistance of Blaise Stucki.

1 C. BÜHRING-UHLE, *Arbitration and Mediation in International Business*, Kluwer Law International, 1996, p. 273.

G. Kaufmann-Kohler and B. Stucki (eds), International Arbitration in Switzerland, A Handbook for Practitioners, 223-237.

negotiation atmosphere and encourage and facilitate communication between the parties. These principles of self-determination and responsibility of the parties are the foundation of mediation.[2]

b) The aim of mediation

The aim of mediation is to find a solution that is acceptable to each of the parties. Mediation focuses on finding convergence in the parties' interests, rather than on recognising the parties' legal rights.[3] The final objective of mediation is to find a 'win-win' solution.

As a consequence, mediation often leads to 'dynamic solutions': by resolving an existing dispute through mediation, the parties are, at the same time, creating a new basis for a future relationship. Contrary to judicial or arbitral proceedings, mediation does not focus on the past, but on the future.[4]

2. Mediation distinguished from arbitration and conciliation

The essential differences between mediation and arbitration are the role of the intervening third person, the method for reaching a solution, the nature of the solution reached and the applicable statutory regime:

- an arbitrator has the power to issue a binding decision whereas a mediator has no such decisional power, but merely assists the parties in finding a solution on their own;
- in arbitration, the solution is primarily based on legal considerations whereas mediation aims at finding a convergence of the parties' interests. Therefore, in mediation, the dispute is not translated into legal issues.[5] Legal considerations do, however, play a role: the mediated solution is intended to be legally binding and, therefore, should not violate mandatory provisions of any laws;

---

2 D. BROWN-BERSET, *La médiation commerciale: le géant s'éveille*, in (2002) 4 SJV 319, 347. P. LIATOWITSCH, *Anhang 'Mediation'*, in I. Schwenzer (ed.), *Scheidungsrecht*, Basel 2000, N. 34, p. 995 (referring to M. GALLI-WIDMER, *Vom Anwalt zum Mediator*, in Der Schweizerische Beobachter (edn), *Mediation in der Schweiz*, Zurich 1994, p. 39). W. J. HABSCHEID, *Die aussergerichtliche Vermittlung (Mediation) als Rechtsverhältnis*, in [2001] AJP 938, 940.

3 D. BROWN-BERSET, *op. cit.*, p. 331.

4 *Ibid.*, p. 324; A.-C. SALBERG, *Médiation, de la rupture au lien*, in [2002] AJP 1401, 1405.

5 According to RAU/SHERMAN/PEPPET, the parties' lawyers are more likely to translate the dispute into legal issues. Therefore, where lawyers participate in the negotiation, mediators often ask the parties to make an additional statement of their own (RAU/SHERMAN/PEPPET, p. 345).

- arbitral awards are binding on the parties like court judgments whereas mediation, if successful, leads to a settlement agreement binding on the parties as a matter of contract;
- contrary to arbitration, the mediation procedure is not subject to any particular statutory rules.

The difference between mediation and conciliation is much less clear-cut and both terms tend to be used interchangeably to designate the same concept.[6] Article 1(3) of the UNCITRAL Model Law on International Commercial Conciliation illustrates this by defining conciliation as '*a process, whether referred to by the expression conciliation, mediation or an expression of similar import, whereby parties request a third person or persons ("the conciliator") to assist them in their attempt to reach an amicable settlement of their dispute arising out of or relating to a contractual or other legal relationship. The conciliator does not have the authority to impose upon the parties a solution to the dispute*'.[7] In Switzerland, there is a long tradition of judicial conciliation and most court proceedings start with an optional or mandatory conciliation procedure before a justice of the peace or other magistrate. Some Cantons also provide for conciliation hearings during the course of the court proceedings.

3. *Mediation's fields of application*

a) Commercial mediation

Commercial mediation primarily serves an important role in the following conflict situations:

- conflicts involving social and personal factors, e.g. internal business conflicts within a company, such as conflicts between employees and the employer, between shareholders and the board of directors, etc.;
- conflicts involving a variety of interacting business parties, e.g. in construction and information technology projects;
- conflicts where a quick solution is needed and it is difficult for a third person to resolve the dispute in an acceptable manner, e.g. in the context of long-term supply agreements of goods, energy or services, particularly in information technology;
- conflicts where one of the parties' priorities is to preserve their existing business relationship;
- conflicts where the parties would suffer considerable loss of reputation in the public due to the publicity of judicial proceedings.

---

6 RAU/SHERMAN/PEPPET, p. 328.

7 Article 1(3) of the UNCITRAL Model Law on International Commercial Conciliation.

Mediation may help to create a basis for future relations and is therefore particularly suited to situations where the parties are willing to resolve an existing dispute in such a way that future cooperation remains possible. However, mediation may also be an appropriate means for resolving one-time conflicts. Parties regularly resort to mediation to resolve claims arising out of past projects, even where there is no longer any on-going relationship or any prospect of a future relationship.[8]

b) Other fields of application

In Switzerland, mediation is currently most often used in the context of family matters, as well as criminal offences.[9]

Mediation is also used in several other areas, e.g. in the context of projects with a major environmental impact, disputes between different administrative authorities, neighbourhood conflicts, etc.

4. When is mediation inappropriate?

Mediation is based upon the sincere willingness of the parties to come to a fair solution by finding a convergence of their interests. Thus, as a minimum requirement, the parties must be committed to seeking an amicable solution through mediation.[10]

Mediation is therefore not appropriate:

- if one of the parties is not willing to find an amicable solution;
- if the interests of the parties differ in such a way that a convergence is simply not conceivable or the matter in dispute is not under their control;[11]
- if the parties' legal positions are so extreme that it is not possible to come to a fair solution;
- if one of the parties wants to send a message to the public.[12]

---

8 See T. WÄLDE, *Pro-Active Mediation of International Business & Investment Disputes Involving Long-Term Contracts: From Zero-Sum Litigation to Efficient Dispute Management*, available on the Internet at <www.gasandoil.com/ogel>, according to whom the settlement reached through mediation may be '*a "velvet divorce", i.e. a peaceful liquidation of* [the parties'] *relationship*'.

9 The Canton of Geneva has institutionalised the penal mediator by providing for specific rules in the Geneva Judicial Organisation Act (Articles 156 *et seq*).

10 P. LIATOWITSCH, *op. cit.*, N. 35, p. 995.

11 *Ibid.*, N. 102, p. 1021.

12 For example, a car manufacturer facing a high profile lawsuit for defects in a series of cars may prefer to establish that the allegation of defects is unfounded in court proceedings that are public, rather than reach a private settlement through mediation.

III. Role and duties of the participants

1. Role and duties of the parties

One of the main obstacles to mediation is the failure of the parties' managers to take the necessary time to focus on the dispute. As a matter of fact, it may appear easier and faster to delegate the handling of a dispute to in-house counsel, who will in turn instruct outside counsel to commence court proceedings or arbitration. It is therefore essential that each of the parties voluntarily engages in the process of mediation and is willing to find an amicable solution. This may require that the individuals having power to decide on the final resolution of the dispute (including, in certain cases, banks or insurers) be present during the mediation or delegate their authority to representatives who will be present.

2. Role of the law and the lawyer

As noted above, legal considerations are not the main focus of mediation. However, as mediation aims at achieving a legally binding solution, the agreement ultimately reached must comply with the law. Non-mandatory legal provisions are the tools the parties can work with to find an acceptable solution. Mandatory provisions of law represent the limit of the parties' contractual freedom. In international matters, rules of international public policy also constitute a limit on the parties' contractual freedom.

Therefore, although the role of the parties' lawyers may be less significant in mediation than in some other forms of dispute resolution, the assistance of lawyers may be required at different stages of the mediation procedure:

- lawyers, whether in-house or outside counsel, may assist their clients in assessing whether a particular case would be appropriate for mediation, as an effective and less expensive form of business dispute management;[13]
- lawyers may assist their clients in preparing for mediation, in particular by gathering all relevant information and documents;
- during the mediation, lawyers may either play a passive role (e.g. intervening only when the parties need legal advice) or a more active role (e.g. helping to re-focus discussions, suggesting solutions and advising the parties on legal issues). There are also mediation models where the parties' lawyers are the only participants, either attending without any clients or attending with clients, who do not take any active part in the mediation procedure;[14]

---

13 D. BROWN-BERSET, *op. cit.*, p. 358.

14 RAU/SHERMAN/PEPPET, p. 439.

- at the end of a successful mediation, lawyers may help in drafting a settlement agreement and/or reviewing the agreement reached for fairness, completeness and compliance with the law.[15]

3. *Role and duties of the mediator*

The mediator's initial role is to establish the mediation procedure. This may include drafting the mediation agreement to be signed by the participants, issuing rules setting forth the calendar of the mediation procedure as well as the rules to be followed (unless the parties' agreement to mediate incorporates existing rules of procedure), the provision of a confidentiality agreement, etc.

Once the mediation procedure is under way, the mediator's role is to help the parties in finding a settlement. The exact nature of this role may vary, depending in particular on whether the parties wish to engage in *facilitative* or *evaluative* mediation. In the first case, the mediator's role is limited to guiding the parties' discussions in order to help them decide what to do.[17] In evaluative mediation, the parties themselves negotiate the settlement, but the mediator may express his or her views on the merits of issues in dispute.[18]

Similar to an arbitrator, a mediator is required to be 'neutral'.[19] However, the mediator's 'neutrality' or 'independence' has a slightly different meaning than in arbitration or court proceedings. Unlike an arbitrator or a judge who stands in judgment over the dispute, the mediator is in the centre of the process and actively assists the parties in finding a solution. In view of this specific role, the concept of 'neutrality' requires that the mediator support each of the parties without favouring either of them. The mediator should balance the parties' positions and should ensure that the parties are in a position to negotiate freely, without undue pressure, whether as a result of violence, coercion or threat.[20] Due process standards apply to the mediation process, although to a much lesser extent than in court or arbitral proceedings. For instance, the mediator must be independent and must treat the parties equally. However, mediators often choose to meet in private with one party, without the adverse party being privy to the information

---

15 P. LIATOWITSCH, *op. cit.*, N. 62, p. 1004.

16 *Ibid.*

17 L. L. RISKIN, *Mediator Orientations, Strategies and Techniques*, reproduced in RAU/SHERMAN/PEPPET, p. 416.

18 H. BROWN/A. MARRIOTT, *ADR Principles and Practice*, Sweet & Maxwell, London 1999, p. 353.

19 I. MEIER, *Mediation und Schlichtung in der Schweiz*, in *Veröffentlichungen des Schweizerischen Instituts für Rechtsvergleichung*, 44/I, Zürich/Basel/Genf 2002, <www.ifm-suisse.ch/PDF/mediation_CH.pdf>, p. 8. Compare with D. BROWN-BERSET, *op. cit.*, p. 347.

20 A.-C. SALBERG, *op. cit.*, p. 1407.

conveyed during this meeting (a so-called 'caucus'). In arbitration, such conduct would constitute a breach of the adverse party's right to be heard.[21]

Under Swiss law, the legal relationship between the parties and the mediator contains elements of the mandate contract.[22] Hence, the mediator is under a duty of diligence, which implies *inter alia* that the mediator should only serve in cases where he or she has substantive knowledge of the subject matter of the dispute.

Generally, the parties will agree at the outset that the mediator will be under a duty to refrain from disclosing all information obtained during the mediation procedure.

IV. The mediation procedure

1. The procedural steps

In Switzerland, the procedure for mediation is not regulated by law. Several mediation organisations have, however, adopted procedural rules that the parties may incorporate into their mediation agreements.[23] Moreover, nothing prevents the parties from mediating under the rules of organisations located abroad such as the ICC ADR Rules, the CEDR Model Mediation Procedure and Agreement and the CPR Mediation Procedure or under the rules of international organisations located in Switzerland, e.g., the WIPO Mediation Rules.

Mediation typically involves four different stages:

a) Preparation phase: the mediation agreement between the parties and the contract with the mediator

The parties can agree to mediation either by including a mediation clause in their contract or by entering into a separate mediation agreement. The mediation clause or agreement may set forth detailed procedural rules or simply provide for the obligation or option to mediate.

Mediation rules often provide a procedure for the selection and appointment of the mediator.[24] Where the parties' agreement to mediate does not incorporate such rules and the mediation clause does not make provisions regarding the appointment of the mediator, the parties will be required to agree on the appointment process.

The next step is drafting a 'mediation contract' between the parties and the mediator. The mediation contract defines the mediation procedure and the duties and roles of the participants, including *inter alia*:

---

21 G. KAUFMANN-KOHLER/T. SCHULTZ, *Online Dispute Resolution – New Challenges for Contemporary Justice*, Kluwer, The Hague, publication forthcoming 2004, Chapter 3.V.

22 Article 394 *et seq*. of the SCO.

23 E.g. the Procedural Rules of the Mediation Center Zurich.

24 See, e.g., Article 2 of the CPR Mediation Rules and Article 3 of the ICC ADR Rules.

- organizational issues (types of meetings, their frequency and duration, etc.);
- submission of relevant information;
- the costs of the mediation and apportionment of them among the parties;
- the mediator's obligation of neutrality;
- waiver of the right to call the mediator as a witness in subsequent court or arbitral proceedings;
- the duty of confidentiality of all participants;
- whether and under what conditions, the mediator may disclose in joint meetings information obtained during caucuses;[25]
- a recommendation for a final fairness control;
- the parties' and/or the mediator's right to terminate the mediation contract at any time.[26]

Through the process of negotiating the mediation contract, the participants will be able to assess whether the necessary conditions for mediation exist, i.e. whether the parties have the willingness and availability necessary to reach a constructive solution.[27]

b) Scope of mediation

Once the mediation contract has been concluded, the mediator must identify the relevant issues in dispute, with the assistance of the parties. As a first step, it is necessary for the parties to identify all information required for a proper understanding of the dispute. The parties may seek the assistance of their respective lawyers to focus on the most relevant information. This process should be performed in the spirit of mediation and, therefore, may include information that would not be communicated in court proceedings, e.g. because it may be seen as damaging to a party's case. Relevant information may be submitted through written statements filed by the parties or simply by oral submissions made at the initial meeting.

c) Understanding the conflict and developing solutions

When the relevant information has been gathered and the issues identified, the mediator will help the parties to identify and focus on their common interests, as opposed to pursing their respective rights-based positions.

---

25 See section IV.1.c) *infra* for further details.

26 P. LIATOWITSCH, *op. cit.*, N. 72, p. 1045; C. BONO-HÖRLER, *op. cit.*, p. 557.

27 P. LIATOWITSCH, *op. cit.*, N. 70, p. 1008.

Techniques generally used by mediators include *inter alia* caucusing, brainstorming, substantive proposals and, where the parties have agreed upon it from the outset, co-mediation.

Caucusing (or 'shuttle mediation') involves the mediator holding separate meetings with each party, either by moving between the parties in different rooms or by remaining in the same room and having the parties move in and out. Caucusing often enables the mediator to gather critical information that the parties would not otherwise disclose, usually because they consider that such information may damage their case. This information may, however, assist the mediator in identifying common interests between the parties, which may provide a foundation for the resolution of the dispute. As such, many consider caucusing to be an essential element for successful mediation.[28] Confidentiality is a central issue where separate meetings are held. In particular, an agreement must be reached on whether and under what conditions information obtained by the mediator from one party in caucuses may be disclosed to the other party in a subsequent joint meeting. While the parties may agree that matters discussed in separate meetings will be fully disclosed in joint meetings, it is more often agreed that the mediator will not disclose information obtained in a separate meeting unless specifically authorized to do so.[29]

During a brainstorming session, the mediator will ask the parties to submit as many options as possible, without limiting themselves to those they consider acceptable. The various options put forward by the parties may then be written down and developed in greater detail.

Although the mediator's role is usually limited to helping the parties to negotiate an agreement, any substantive proposals put forward by the mediator may be decisive where he or she enjoys a high degree of authority with the parties. As a consequence, most mediators are reluctant to make any substantive proposals until rather late in the mediation procedure. In this way, the parties will have had an opportunity to actively participate in the process and the mediator's proposal will likely better reflect their positions. This in turn increases the prospects that the parties will be prepared to accept the mediator's proposal.[30] In an evaluative mediation, the mediator will express his or her opinion about the strengths and weaknesses of the parties' positions and the likely outcome of litigation.[31]

---

28 H. BROWN/A. MARRIOTT, *op. cit.*, p. 175; C. BÜHRING-UHLE, *op. cit.*, p. 285.

29 H. BROWN/A. MARRIOTT, *op. cit.*, p. 489.

30 *Ibid.*, p. 300.

31 L. L. RISKIN, *Mediator Orientations, Strategies and Techniques*, reproduced in RAU/SHERMAN/PEPPET, p. 416.

Co-mediation involves the use of two mediators. This technique may be useful in large and complex cases, where it may be helpful to combine the expertise and skills of two persons with different qualifications or backgrounds.[32]

Once several possible solutions have been considered, parties sometimes encounter difficulties in agreeing upon an overall resolution of the dispute because they continually focus on one specific and divisive issue, rather than adopting a global approach. In such cases, the mediator can play a central role in assisting the parties to reach a final and workable solution.

d) Agreement and end of the mediation process

Once the parties have agreed upon a solution of the dispute, the parties and/or their lawyers will then draft a written agreement to implement it. If disagreements arise in regard to the drafting of this agreement, the mediator may assist the parties in finding an acceptable text. Depending upon the case, it may be appropriate to review the agreed solution after a certain period (e.g. 6 months from its adoption), particularly if it involves an on-going relationship between the parties.

2. Termination of the mediation procedure

In addition to the case where the parties enter into a settlement agreement, the mediation procedure may terminate at any time in the following circumstances:

- one of the parties decides to unilaterally terminate the mediation;
- the parties agree to terminate the mediation, leaving some or all of the issues unresolved; or
- the mediator considers that the mediation will not resolve the dispute and decides to terminate it.[33]

3. Costs and duration of mediation

a) Costs of mediation

The costs of mediation depend primarily on the investment of time made by the parties and the mediator preparing for and engaging in the mediation. Mediation is by definition less expensive than court proceedings or arbitration.[34]

---

32 C. BÜHRING UHLE, *op. cit.*, p. 299.

33 See, e.g., Article 6(1)(d) of the ICC ADR Rules.

34 A recent study conducted by an independent firm and sponsored by the AAA ('*Dispute-Wise Management, Improving Economic And Non-Economic Outcomes in Managing Business Conflicts*') shows that companies which resolve disputes through mediation and other forms of ADR (the 'dispute-wise companies') surpass other companies in controlling costs and preserving their business relationships. The study is available on the Internet at <www.adr.org>.

Since mediator's fees are not regulated by law in Switzerland, fees in commercial mediations are often based upon the hourly fees of lawyers.

b) Duration of mediation

The parties are free to agree on the time frame for mediation of their dispute and they often do so. The mediation period should be long enough to allow for the emergence of a realistic and lasting convergence of interests and, at the same time, short enough to maintain a certain constructive pressure.[35] In commercial mediation, it is common to set up several consecutive meetings within a limited period of time.

The duration of mediation also depends upon the availability of the different actors, the number of parties involved and the complexity of the dispute. Since mediation is based on the parties' willingness to put an end to the dispute and restore a foundation for co-operation, the parties are, however, generally interested coming to agreement as fast as possible. Moreover, the absence of procedural formalities allows for an accelerated process. For these reasons, mediation is almost always significantly shorter than arbitral or court proceedings.

V. Selected legal issues

1. The enforceability of the mediation clause

The mediation clause is contractual in nature and, therefore, binding upon both parties like any other contract. But is it enforceable?

According to some legal commentators and Swiss case law, a mediation clause - contrary to an arbitration or choice of forum clause - has no procedural consequences. Its effects are purely contractual. As a result, a party's breach of its contractual obligation to mediate before submitting a dispute to the court would not constitute an impediment to that court's jurisdiction.[36] However, the French Cour de Cassation in *Poiré v. Tripier*[37] and an English High Court in *Cable and Wireless v. IBM*[38] both held that courts must give effect to mediation clauses if one of the parties relies on it and therefore declare inadmissible or stay court proceedings brought in breach of such a clause.

Given the divergent treatment of mediation clauses in different jurisdictions, it is clear that practitioners engaged in drafting mediation clauses must carefully consider what jurisdictions may become relevant if a dispute arises between the parties.

---

35 P. LIATOWITSCH, *op. cit.*, N. 71, p. 1008.

36 Decision of 23 August 1999 of the Swiss Federal Tribunal in (2000) 99 ZR 29; D. BROWN-BERSET, *op. cit.*, p. 368.

37 Decision of 14 February 2003 of the French Cour de Cassation in [2003] Rev. Arb. 403.

38 Decision of 11 October 2002 of the High Court (Queen's Bench Division) in [2003] Arb. Int'l 352.

In order to avoid any difficulties in this regard, the mediation clause should clearly define whether: (a) the parties have an obligation to mediate before having recourse to the arbitration or court proceedings; or (b) mediation is merely an optional form of dispute resolution. If the parties agree that they will have an obligation to mediate, the mediation clause should specify when and under what conditions the parties may terminate the mediation process and resort to either arbitration or court proceedings. It will then be necessary for a party to terminate the mediation process in accordance with the mediation clause in order to avoid the risk that a court will declare the legal proceedings to be inadmissible or that an arbitral tribunal will decline jurisdiction over the dispute.

Parties to a mediation agreement may also provide for a penalty for violating the obligation to mediate. There have not been any court decisions dealing with the enforceability of such penalty clauses up to the present. Moreover, while a penalty clause may indeed dissuade some parties from refusing to mediate, it cannot prevent this from occurring.[39] The success of mediation ultimately depends upon the willingness of the parties to find an amicable solution and, as a consequence, it is virtually impossible to compel a party to participate in mediation as a practical matter.

2. *Confidentiality*

In Switzerland, the question whether confidentiality clauses are valid and enforceable by the courts in subsequent legal proceedings is not settled.[40] German legal commentators tend to consider that confidentiality clauses whereby the parties waive their right to use evidence obtained in mediation are valid and enforceable.[41] In the United States, Rule 408 of the Federal Court Rules of Evidence provides that '[e]*vidence of (1) furnishing or offering or promising to furnish, or (2) accepting or offering or promising to accept, a valuable consideration in compromising or attempting to compromise a claim which was disputed as to either validity or amount, is not admissible to prove liability for or invalidity of the claim or its amount*' and that '[e]*vidence of conduct or statements made in compromise negotiations is likewise not admissible*'. Mediation seems to be regarded as simply another form of settlement discussions and legal commentators consider that the above provision should apply to the mediation process.[42]

---

39 D. BROWN-BERSET, *op. cit.*, p. 369.

40 A majority of Swiss legal commentators appear to deny that confidentiality clauses have any effect in court proceedings (see I. MEIER, *op. cit.*, footnote No. 20, p. 30; P. LIATOWITSCH, *op. cit.*, N. 54, p. 1001). They consider that the parties have a procedural right to benefit from all available evidence and that a waiver of such right may infringe a party's right to be heard and the principle of free assessment of evidence by the court (see I. MEIER, *op. cit.*, p. 12; (1990) 89 ZR 118).

41 I. MEIER, *op. cit.*, p. 12.

42 RAU/ SHERMAN/ PEPPET, p. 464.

The question of the mediator's right or obligation to refuse testify in subsequent court proceedings is a matter of evidence. In Switzerland, civil procedure falls within the authority of the Cantons. The cantonal codes of civil procedure do not yet include any specific rules concerning the rights and obligations of mediators in discovery.[43] However, Article 157(1)(c) of the draft Federal Civil Procedure Act provides that a mediator may refuse to testify in regard to facts learned while serving in the capacity of mediator. The rationale underlying this provision is that parties involved in mediation would be much less forthcoming if they knew that information disclosed in this context could be subsequently used in court proceedings. Another issue is whether a lawyer's professional secrecy extends to his or her functions as mediator and thus entitles him or her to refuse to testify in subsequent court proceedings. Although this question is not settled under Swiss law, it appears that a lawyer's professional secrecy only relates to the core activity of a practising lawyer and would not therefore extend to a lawyer's activity as a mediator. In this regard, the Swiss Federal Tribunal has held that commercial correspondence exchanged between a company and its lawyer was not protected by the lawyer's professional secrecy where the lawyer was a member of the company's board of directors, as well as being a practising lawyer.[44] Similarly, the Swiss Federal Tribunal has distinguished between a practising lawyer's core activity and his additional business activities, in respect of which a lawyer cannot refuse to testify.[45] The Zurich Court of Appeal also recently held that a lawyer's professional secrecy does not extend to his or her activity as arbitrator.[46]

Because of the uncertainty as to the validity and enforceability of confidentiality agreements, experienced mediators produce as few working papers as possible.[47] It is even advisable for the parties to include a provision in the mediation agreement authorizing the mediator to destroy all working papers upon termination of the mediation procedure.

3. *Statute of limitation*

Since mediation is a purely contractual dispute resolution mechanism, a statutory limitation period is neither stayed nor tolled by the commencement of a mediation procedure. It is therefore possible for a claim to become time-barred during mediation. Accordingly, the parties should, where possible, waive the right to rely upon the statute

---

43 However, some minimal protection already exists. Pursuant to Article 139 of the SCC, a mediator who acted in a family matter may not testify as a witness in subsequent divorce proceedings. Articles 160 and 161 of the Geneva Judicial Organisation Act provide that penal mediators have an obligation to keep confidential the information obtained in the context of mediations.

44 DFT 114 III 105.

45 DFT 115 I 197.

46 Decision of 7 September 2000 of the Zurich Court of Appeal (Bar Supervisory Board), published in [2001] ASA Bull. 322.

47 D. BROWN-BERSET, *op. cit.*, p. 349.

of limitation for the duration of mediation or take all other appropriate legal steps to preserve their rights while the mediation is ongoing.[48] The mediator should encourage the parties to address this matter with their lawyers at the outset.

Even if the parties do not agree to a waiver, it is possible that a party's reliance upon a statute of limitation in court proceedings following a failed mediation may, under certain circumstances, constitute an abuse of rights within the meaning of Article 2(2) of the SCC.[49]

VI. Mediation organisations and training institutes

1. Swiss mediation organisations

There are quite a number of mediation institutions in Switzerland, e.g. the Mediation Center Zurich, the Institute for Mediation ('*Institut für Mediation*'), the Swiss Mediation Forum FH ('*Mediationsforum Schweiz FH*'), the Swiss Mediation Association ('*Schweizerischer Verein für Mediation*'/'*Association Suisse pour la Médiation*'), etc. These institutions promote mediation and seek to maintain high training standards and respect for the professional duties of mediators.[50] In particular, the Mediation Center Zurich is a network of well-trained mediators with different professional backgrounds. Mediators who are members of the Mediation Center Zurich are committed to high quality standards and professional rules of ethics.[51] There is also a Swiss 'umbrella association' ('*Schweizerischer Dachverband für Mediation*'/'*Association Faîtière pour la Médiation Suisse*') that aims to facilitate the cooperation between mediation institutions.[52]

2. Training possibilities

Switzerland offers a broad range of mediation training at various levels. The number of conferences and workshops on mediation is increasing each year. Introductory courses typically last three to five days and focus on the objectives and practical importance of mediation. These courses are particularly useful for professionals who often come in contact with mediation, but do not participate in mediation themselves.

Some institutions offer comprehensive training programs, e.g. the University of St. Gallen and the WIPO Arbitration and Mediation Center. For more focused training, the Faculty of Law at the University of Geneva organizes a mediation workshop given by a U.S. law professor and mediator every year or second year.[53]

---

48 D. BROWN-BERSET, *op. cit.*, p. 350.

49 D. BROWN-BERSET, *op. cit.*, p. 351; W. J. HABSCHEID, *op. cit.*, p. 943.

50 I. MEIER, *op. cit.*, p. 7.

51 <www.mediation-center.ch>.

52 I. MEIER, *op. cit.*, p. 7.

53 Information at Geneva University Law School, Private International Law Department; Claudine Zbinden@droit.unige.ch.

In addition, the Swiss Bar Association offers mediation training for lawyers, which qualifies participants for the title of 'Mediator of the Swiss Bar Association'. Apart from 80 hours of general mediation training, participants are required to attend a special class on the role of the lawyer as a mediator.

Appendix 1 – Checklist for Drafting Arbitration Clauses*

I. Key elements for all arbitration clauses

- ☐ intent to arbitrate
- ☐ exclusive jurisdiction of the arbitral tribunal
- ☐ seat of the arbitration (country and city)
- ☐ written clause
- ☐ broad scope ('any dispute arising out of or in connection with this contract')

II. Institutional arbitration

1. Strongly recommended elements

- ☐ model clause wherever possible; if not,
- ☐ unambiguous designation of the applicable set of arbitration rules
- ☐ language of the arbitration

2. Additional elements

- ☐ number of arbitrators
- ☐ procedure for the appointment of the arbitrators (if the parties wish to depart from procedures in the institutional rules)
- ☐ nationality of the arbitrators/specific qualifications (if the parties wish to depart from procedures in the institutional rules)

---

* The aim of the following recommendations is to assist in the drafting of arbitration clauses. These recommendations are in addition to various legal issues to be verified in any event (legal requirements as to form; arbitrability of the dispute; power of the persons signing the agreement; restrictions on the capacity of a party to arbitrate; etc.).

- ☐ version of the chosen arbitration rules in case of future changes
- ☐ power of the arbitrators to decide *ex aequo et bono*/as *amiable compositeurs*

III. Ad hoc arbitration

1. Strongly recommended elements

- ☐ number of arbitrators
- ☐ procedure for the appointment of the arbitrators
- ☐ procedure for the challenge/replacement of the arbitrators
- ☐ appointing authority
- ☐ rules governing the arbitral proceedings (e.g. UNCITRAL Rules)
- ☐ language of the arbitration

2. Additional elements

- ☐ nationality of the arbitrators/specific qualifications
- ☐ power of the arbitrators to decide *ex aequo et bono*/as *amiable compositeurs*
- ☐ determination and apportionment of costs

IV. Multi-party/multi-contracts arbitration

1. Multi-contract

- ☐ co-ordination of the arbitration clauses

2. Multi-party

- ☐ precise definition of the parties
- ☐ possibility to cause a third party to participate in the arbitration and enforcement of that clause
- ☐ waiver of the right to participate in or to challenge the formation of the arbitral tribunal

V. To be avoided

- ☐ naming the arbitrators

- ☐ having multiple dispute resolution mechanisms
- ☐ providing for pre-arbitration amicable settlement proceedings without precisely defining the condition(s) which must be satisfied before the parties may file for arbitration, including, possibly, time-limits
- ☐ in institutional arbitration, providing for procedures that differ from the institutional rules

Appendix 2 – Swiss Rules of International Arbitration

Swiss Rules of International Arbitration (Swiss Rules)

MODEL ARBITRATION CLAUSE

Any dispute, controversy or claim arising out of or in relation to this contract, including the validity, invalidity, breach or termination thereof, shall be resolved by arbitration in accordance with the Swiss Rules of International Arbitration of the Swiss Chambers of Commerce in force on the date when the Notice of Arbitration is submitted in accordance with these Rules.

The number of arbitrators[1] shall be ... (one or three);

The seat of the arbitration shall be ... (city in Switzerland);

The arbitral proceedings shall be conducted in … (insert desired language).

INTRODUCTION

(a) In the past, six Chambers of Commerce and Industry in Switzerland had their own different rules of arbitration for the resolution of international commercial disputes.

(b) In order to promote institutional arbitration in Switzerland and to harmonise the existing rules of arbitration, the Chambers of Commerce and Industry of Basel, Bern, Geneva, Ticino, Vaud and Zurich (hereinafter collectively "the Chambers") have adopted the present uniform rules, the Swiss Rules of International Arbitration (hereinafter the "Rules"), which replace the Chambers' former rules of international arbitration.

---

1 For the sake of convenience, only the masculine form is used within theses Rules.

These Rules are based on the UNCITRAL Arbitration Rules, to which two types of changes and additions have been made:

i. Changes and additions required to adapt the UNCITRAL Arbitration Rules to institutional arbitration;

ii. Changes and additions reflecting modern practice and comparative law in the field of international arbitration.

These changes and additions have been deliberately kept to a minimum. A comparative version of these Rules, in which the modifications to the UNCITRAL Arbitration Rules are italicised, is available on the website of the Chambers: www.swissarbitration.ch.

(c) When a Notice of Arbitration is submitted to one of the Chambers listed in Appendix A, an arbitral tribunal shall be constituted in accordance with these Rules.

(d) In order to ensure the administration of arbitrations under these Rules, the Chambers have appointed an Arbitration Committee (hereinafter the "Arbitration Committee"), which shall exercise the powers vested in the Chambers under these Rules, so that any reference to the Chambers in these Rules shall be deemed to refer to the Arbitration Committee.

(e) The Arbitration Committee is comprised of experienced practitioners of international arbitration. The Arbitration Committee shall designate from among its members the person or persons who will assist the Chambers in the administration and monitoring of the arbitral proceedings. In addition, the Arbitration Committee has designated from among its members a Special Committee (hereinafter the "Special Committee"), which shall render decisions under Articles 11 and 12 on the challenge and revocation of arbitrators and under Article 16 on the seat of arbitration, and advise the Chambers on other procedural matters that may arise in relation to the application of these Rules.

Section I. Introductory rules

SCOPE OF APPLICATION

Article 1

1. These Rules shall govern international arbitrations, where an agreement to arbitrate refers to these Rules, or to the arbitration rules of the Chambers of Commerce and Industry of Basel, Bern, Geneva, Ticino, Vaud, Zurich and any further Chamber of Commerce and Industry that may adhere to these Rules.

2. The parties are free to designate the seat of the arbitration anywhere in Switzerland.

3. These Rules shall come into force on January 1st, 2004 and, unless the parties have agreed otherwise, shall apply to all arbitral proceedings in which the Notice of Arbitration is submitted on or after that date.

NOTICE, CALCULATION OF PERIODS OF TIME

Article 2

1. For the purposes of these Rules, any notice, including a notification, communication or proposal, is deemed to have been received if it is physically delivered to the addressee or if it is delivered to its habitual residence, place of business or mailing address, or, if none of these can be found after making reasonable inquiry, then at the addressee's last-known residence or place of business. Notice shall be deemed to have been received on the day it is so delivered.

2. For the purposes of calculating a period of time under these Rules, such period shall begin to run on the day following the day when a notice, notification, communication or proposal is received. If the last day of such period is an official holiday or a non-business day at the residence or place of business of the addressee, the period is extended until the first business day which follows. Official holidays or non-business days occurring during the running of the period of time are included in calculating the period.

3. If the circumstances so justify, the Chambers may extend the time-limits provided in Section I (Introductory Rules) and Section II (Composition of the arbitral tribunal), as well as any time-limits that they have set.

NOTICE OF ARBITRATION AND ANSWER TO THE NOTICE OF ARBITRATION

Article 3

1. The party initiating recourse to arbitration (hereinafter called the "Claimant" or, where applicable, "Claimants") shall submit a Notice of Arbitration to the Chambers at any of the addresses listed in Appendix A.

2. Arbitral proceedings shall be deemed to commence on the date on which the Notice of Arbitration is received by the Chambers.

3. The Notice of Arbitration shall be submitted in as many copies as there are other parties (hereinafter called the "Respondent" or, where applicable, "Respondents"), together with an additional copy for each arbitrator and one copy for the Chambers, and shall include the following:

   (a) A demand that the dispute be referred to arbitration;

   (b) The names, addresses, telephone and fax numbers and e-mail addresses (if any) of the parties and of their counsel;

   (c) A copy of the arbitration clause or the separate arbitration agreement that is invoked;

   (d) A reference to the contract or other legal instrument(s) out of or in relation to which the dispute arises;

   (e) The general nature of the claim and an indication of the amount involved, if any;

   (f) The relief or remedy sought;

   (g) A proposal as to the number of arbitrators (i.e. one or three), if the parties have not previously agreed thereon;

   (h) The payment, by check or transfer to the account of the Chamber to which the Notice of Arbitration is submitted as listed in Appendix A, of the Registration Fee as required by Appendix B (Schedule of the Costs of Arbitration) in force on the date when the Notice of Arbitration is submitted.

4. The Notice of Arbitration may also include:

   (a) The Claimant's proposals for the appointment of a sole arbitrator referred to in Article 7;

   (b) The Claimant's designation of an arbitrator, for the purpose of constituting a three-member arbitral tribunal referred to in Article 8;

   (c) The Statement of Claim referred to in Article 18.

5. If the Notice of Arbitration is incomplete or if the copies or attachments are not submitted in the required number, or if the Registration Fee is not paid, the Chambers may request the Claimant to remedy the defect within an appropriate period of time. The Chambers may also request within such time-limit a translation of the Notice of Arbitration if it is not submitted in English, German, French or Italian. If the Claimant complies with such directions within the applicable time-limit, the Notice of Arbitration shall be deemed to have been validly filed on the date when the initial version was received by the Chambers.

6. The Chambers shall provide without delay a copy of the Notice of Arbitration and of any exhibits included therewith to the Respondent, unless the Chambers decide, after consultation with the Special Committee, that there is manifestly no agreement to arbitrate referring to these Rules.

7. Within thirty days from receipt of the Notice of Arbitration, the Respondent shall submit to the Chambers an Answer to the Notice of Arbitration. This Answer to the Notice of Arbitration shall be submitted in as many copies as there are other parties, together with an additional copy for each arbitrator and one copy for the Chambers, and shall, to the extent possible, include the following:

   (a) The name, address, telephone and fax numbers and e-mail address (if any) of the Respondent and of its counsel (if different from the description contained in the Notice of Arbitration);

   (b) Any plea that an arbitral tribunal constituted under these Rules lacks jurisdiction;

   (c) The Respondent's comments on the particulars set forth in the Notice of Arbitration, pursuant to Article 3, paragraph 3(e);

   (d) The Respondent's answer to the relief or remedy sought in the Notice of Arbitration, pursuant to Article 3, paragraph 3(f);

   (e) The Respondent's proposal as to the number of arbitrators (i.e. one or three), if the parties have not previously agreed thereon, pursuant to Article 3, paragraph 3(g).

8. The Answer to the Notice of Arbitration may also include:

   (a) The Respondent's proposals for the appointment of a sole arbitrator referred to in Article 7;

   (b) The Respondent's designation of an arbitrator for the purpose of constituting a three-member arbitral tribunal referred to in Article 8;

   (c) The Statement of Defence referred to in Article 19.

9. Any counterclaim or set-off defence shall in principle be raised with the Respondent's Answer to the Notice of Arbitration. The provisions of Article 3, paragraph 3 are applicable to the counterclaim or set-off defence.

10. If no counterclaim or set-off defence is raised with the Respondent's Answer to the Notice of Arbitration, or if there is no indication of the amount of the counterclaim or set-off defence, the Chambers may rely exclusively on paragraph 3(e) of the present Article 3 in order to determine the possible application of Article 42, paragraph 2 (Expedited Procedure).

11. The Chambers shall provide without delay a copy of the Answer to the Notice of Arbitration and of any exhibits included therewith to the Claimant.

12. Once the Registration Fee has been paid and all arbitrators have been confirmed, the Chambers shall transmit without delay the file to the sole arbitrator or to the arbitral tribunal.

13. The parties may be represented or assisted by persons of their choice. The names and addresses of such persons must be communicated in writing to the other party and the Chambers; such communication must specify whether the appointment is being made for purposes of representation or assistance.

CONSOLIDATION OF ARBITRAL PROCEEDINGS (JOINDER), PARTICIPATION OF THIRD PARTIES

Article 4

1. Where a Notice of Arbitration is submitted between parties already involved in other arbitral proceedings pending under these Rules, the Chambers may decide, after consulting with the parties to all proceedings and the Special Committee, that the new case shall be referred to the arbitral tribunal already constituted for the existing proceedings. The Chambers may proceed likewise where a Notice of Arbitration is submitted between parties that are not identical to the parties in the existing arbitral proceedings. When rendering their decision, the Chambers shall take into account all circumstances, including the links between the two cases and the progress already made in the existing proceedings. Where the Chambers decide to refer the new case to the existing arbitral tribunal, the parties to the new case shall be deemed to have waived their right to designate an arbitrator.

2. Where a third party requests to participate in arbitral proceedings already pending under these Rules or where a party to arbitral proceedings under these Rules intends to cause a third party to participate in the arbitration, the arbitral tribunal shall decide on such request, after consulting with all parties, taking into account all circumstances it deems relevant and applicable.

Section II. Composition of the arbitral tribunal

CONFIRMATION OF ARBITRATORS

Article 5

1. All designations of a sole arbitrator or of the arbitrators composing a three-member arbitral tribunal, made by the parties or the arbitrators, are subject to confirmation by the Chambers, upon which the appointments shall become effective. The Chambers have no obligation to give reasons when they do not confirm an arbitrator.

2. Where a designation is not confirmed, the Chambers may

   (a) either invite the party or parties concerned, or the arbitrators, as the case may be, to make a new designation within a reasonable time-limit; or

   (b) proceed directly with the appointment.

NUMBER OF ARBITRATORS

Article 6

1. If the parties have not agreed upon the number of arbitrators, the Chambers shall decide whether the case shall be referred to a sole arbitrator or to a three-member arbitral tribunal, taking into account all relevant circumstances.

2. As a rule, the Chambers shall refer the case to a sole arbitrator, unless the complexity of the subject matter and/or the amount in dispute justify that the case be referred to a three-member arbitral tribunal.

3. If the arbitration agreement provides for a three-member arbitral tribunal and if this appears inappropriate in view of the amount in dispute or of other circumstances, the Chambers shall advise the parties that they may wish to agree to refer the dispute to a sole arbitrator.

4. Where the amount in dispute does not exceed CHF 1,000,000 (one million Swiss francs), the provisions of Article 42, paragraph 2 (Expedited Procedure), shall apply.

APPOINTMENT OF A SOLE ARBITRATOR

Article 7

1. Where two or more parties have agreed that the dispute shall be referred to a sole arbitrator, they shall jointly designate the sole arbitrator within thirty days from the date when the Notice of Arbitration was received by the Respondent(s), unless the parties' agreement provides otherwise.
2. Where the parties have not agreed upon the number of arbitrators, they shall jointly designate the sole arbitrator within thirty days from the date when the Chambers' decision that the dispute shall be referred to a sole arbitrator was received by them.
3. If the parties fail to designate the sole arbitrator within the applicable time-limit, the Chambers shall proceed with the appointment.

APPOINTMENT OF ARBITRATORS IN BI-PARTY OR MULTY-PARTY PROCEEDINGS

Article 8

1. Where a dispute between two adverse parties is referred to a three-member arbitral tribunal, each party shall designate one arbitrator, unless the parties have agreed otherwise.
2. If a party fails to designate an arbitrator within the time-limit set by the Chambers or resulting from the arbitration agreement, the Chambers shall appoint the arbitrator. Unless the parties' agreement provides otherwise, the two arbitrators so appointed shall designate, within thirty days from the confirmation of the second arbitrator, a third arbitrator who shall act as the presiding arbitrator of the arbitral tribunal. Failing such designation, the Chambers shall appoint the presiding arbitrator.
3. In multi-party proceedings, the arbitral tribunal shall be constituted in accordance with the parties' agreement.
4. If the parties have not agreed upon a procedure for the constitution of the arbitral tribunal in multi-party proceedings, the Chambers shall set an initial thirty-day time-limit for the Claimant or group of Claimants to designate an arbitrator and set a subsequent thirty-day time-limit for the Respondent or group of Respondents to designate an arbitrator. If the group or groups of parties have each designated an arbitrator, Article 8, paragraph 2 shall apply by analogy to the designation of the presiding arbitrator.

5. Where a party or group of parties fail(s) to designate an arbitrator in multiparty proceedings, the Chambers may appoint all three arbitrators and shall specify the presiding arbitrator.

INDEPENDENCE AND CHALLENGE OF ARBITRATORS (ARTICLES 9 TO 12)

Article 9

1. All arbitrators conducting an arbitration under these Rules shall be and remain at all times impartial and independent of the parties.
2. A prospective arbitrator shall disclose to those who approach him in connection with his possible appointment any circumstances likely to give rise to justifiable doubts as to his impartiality or independence. An arbitrator, once appointed or chosen, shall disclose such circumstances to the parties unless they have already been informed by him of these circumstances.

Article 10

1. Any arbitrator may be challenged if circumstances exist that give rise to justifiable doubts as to the arbitrator's impartiality or independence.
2. A party may challenge the arbitrator appointed by it only for reasons of which it becomes aware after the appointment has been made.

Article 11

1. If the arbitrator being challenged does not withdraw, the Special Committee shall decide on the challenge.
2. The decision of the Special Committee is final. The Special Committee has no obligation to give reasons.

Article 12

1. If an arbitrator fails to perform his functions despite a written warning from the other arbitrators or from the Chambers, the Special Committee may revoke the appointment of that arbitrator.
2. The arbitrator shall have an opportunity to present his position to the Special Committee. The decision of the Special Committee is final. The Special Committee has no obligation to give reasons.

REPLACEMENT OF AN ARBITRATOR

Article 13

1. If an arbitrator designated by a party deceases or becomes unable to perform his functions due to any reasons beyond his control, the Chambers shall set a time-limit for the party having designated that arbitrator to designate a replacement arbitrator. This rule also applies if an arbitrator has been successfully challenged, has been otherwise removed or has resigned.
2. If the party concerned fails to designate a replacement arbitrator within the applicable time-limit, the Chambers shall appoint a replacement arbitrator.

CONSEQUENCES OF THE REPLACEMENT OF AN ARBITRATOR

Article 14

If an arbitrator is replaced, the proceedings shall as a rule resume at the stage where the arbitrator who was replaced ceased to perform his functions, unless the arbitral tribunal decides otherwise.

Section III. Arbitral proceedings

GENERAL PROVISIONS

Article 15

1. Subject to these Rules, the arbitral tribunal may conduct the arbitration in such manner as it considers appropriate, provided that it ensures equal treatment of the parties and their right to be heard.
2. At any stage of the proceedings, the arbitral tribunal may hold hearings for the presentation of evidence by witnesses, including expert witnesses, or for oral argument. After consulting with the parties, the arbitral tribunal may also decide to conduct the proceedings on the basis of documents and other materials.
3. At an early stage of the arbitral proceedings and in consultation with the parties, the arbitral tribunal shall prepare a provisional time-table for the arbitral proceedings, which shall be provided to the parties and, for information, to the Chambers.
4. All documents or information supplied to the arbitral tribunal by one party shall at the same time be communicated by that party to the other party.

5. The arbitral tribunal may, after consulting with the parties, appoint a secretary. Article 9 of these Rules shall apply by analogy to the secretary.
6. All participants in the arbitral proceedings shall act in accordance with the requirements of good faith.

SEAT OF THE ARBITRATION

Article 16

1. If the parties have not determined the seat of the arbitration, or if such designation is unclear or incomplete, the Special Committee shall determine the seat of the arbitration taking into account all relevant circumstances, or shall request the arbitral tribunal to determine the seat.
2. Without prejudice to the determination of the seat of the arbitration, the arbitral tribunal may decide where the proceedings shall be conducted. In particular, it may hear witnesses and hold meetings for consultation among its members at any place it deems appropriate, having regard to the circumstances of the arbitration.
3. The arbitral tribunal may meet at any place it deems appropriate for the inspection of goods, other property or documents. The parties shall be given sufficient notice to enable them to be present at such inspection.
4. The award shall be deemed to be made at the seat of the arbitration.

LANGUAGE

Article 17

1. Subject to an agreement by the parties, the arbitral tribunal shall, promptly after its appointment, determine the language or languages to be used in the proceedings. This determination shall apply to the Statement of Claim, the Statement of Defence, and any further written statements and, if oral hearings take place, to the language or languages to be used in such hearings.
2. The arbitral tribunal may order that any documents annexed to the Statement of Claim or Statement of Defence, and any supplementary documents or exhibits submitted in the course of the proceedings, delivered in their original language, shall be accompanied by a translation into the language or languages agreed upon by the parties or determined by the arbitral tribunal.

STATEMENT OF CLAIM

Article 18

1. Unless the Statement of Claim was contained in the Notice of Arbitration, within a period of time to be determined by the arbitral tribunal, the Claimant shall communicate its Statement of Claim in writing to the Respondent and to each of the arbitrators. A copy of the contract, and of the arbitration agreement if not contained in the contract, shall be annexed thereto.
2. The Statement of Claim shall include the following particulars:
   (a) The names and addresses of the parties;
   (b) A statement of the facts supporting the claim;
   (c) The points at issue;
   (d) The relief or remedy sought.
3. As a rule, the Claimant shall annex to its Statement of Claim all documents it deems relevant.

STATEMENT OF DEFENCE

Article 19

1. Within a period of time to be determined by the arbitral tribunal and unless the Statement of Defence was contained in the Answer to the Notice of Arbitration, the Respondent shall communicate its Statement of Defence in writing to the Claimant and to each of the arbitrators.
2. The Statement of Defence shall reply to the particulars (b), (c) and (d) of the Statement of Claim (Article 18, paragraph 2). If the Respondent has raised an objection to the jurisdiction or to the proper constitution of the arbitral tribunal, the Statement of Defence shall contain the factual and legal basis of such objection. As a rule, the Respondent shall annex to its Statement of Defence all documents on which it relies for its defence.
3. The provisions of Article 18, paragraphs 2 (b) – (d), shall apply to a counterclaim and a claim relied on for the purpose of a set-off.

AMENDMENTS TO THE CLAIM OR DEFENCE

Article 20

1. During the course of the arbitral proceedings either party may amend or supplement its claim or defence unless the arbitral tribunal considers it inappropriate to allow such amendment having regard to the delay in making it or prejudice to the other party or any other circumstances. However, a claim may not be amended in such a manner that the amended claim falls outside the scope of the arbitration clause or separate arbitration agreement.

2. The arbitral tribunal may adjust the costs of the arbitration if a party amends or supplements its claims, counterclaims or defences.

PLEAS AS TO THE JURISDICTION OF THE ARBITRAL TRIBUNAL

Article 21

1. The arbitral tribunal shall have the power to rule on objections that it has no jurisdiction, including any objections with respect to the existence or validity of the arbitration clause or of the separate arbitration agreement.

2. The arbitral tribunal shall have the power to determine the existence or the validity of the contract of which an arbitration clause forms a part. For the purposes of Article 21, an arbitration clause which forms part of a contract and which provides for arbitration under these Rules shall be treated as an agreement independent of the other terms of the contract. A decision by the arbitral tribunal that the contract is null and void shall not entail ipso jure the invalidity of the arbitration clause.

3. As a rule, a plea that the arbitral tribunal does not have jurisdiction shall be raised in the Answer to the Notice of Arbitration, but in no event later than in the Statement of Defence referred to in Article 19, or, with respect to a counterclaim, in the reply to the counterclaim.

4. In general, the arbitral tribunal should rule on a plea concerning its jurisdiction as a preliminary question. However, the arbitral tribunal may proceed with the arbitration and rule on such a plea in its final award.

5. The arbitral tribunal shall have jurisdiction to hear a set-off defence even when the relationship out of which this defence is said to arise is not within the scope of the arbitration clause or is the object of another arbitration agreement or forum-selection clause.

FURTHER WRITTEN STATEMENTS

Article 22

The arbitral tribunal shall decide which further written statements, in addition to the Statement of Claim and the Statement of Defence, shall be required from the parties or may be presented by them and shall set the periods of time for communicating such statements.

PERIODS OF TIME

Article 23

The periods of time set by the arbitral tribunal for the communication of written statements (including the Statement of Claim and Statement of Defence) should not exceed forty-five days. However, the arbitral tribunal may extend the time-limits if it concludes that an extension is justified.

EVIDENCE AND HEARINGS (ARTICLES 24 AND 25)

Article 24

1. Each party shall have the burden of proving the facts relied on to support its claim or defence.
2. The arbitral tribunal may, if it considers it appropriate, require a party to deliver to the tribunal and to the other party, within such a period of time as the arbitral tribunal shall decide, a summary of the documents and other evidence which that party intends to present in support of the facts in issue set out in its Statement of Claim or Statement of Defence.
3. At any time during the arbitral proceedings the arbitral tribunal may require the parties to produce documents, exhibits or other evidence within such a period of time as the tribunal shall determine.

Article 25

1. In the event of an oral hearing, the arbitral tribunal shall give the parties adequate advance notice of the date, time and place thereof.

2. Any person may be a witness or an expert witness. If witnesses or expert witnesses are to be heard, at least fifteen days before the hearing each party shall communicate to the arbitral tribunal and to the other party the names and addresses of the witnesses or expert witnesses it intends to present, the subject upon and the languages in which such witnesses or expert witnesses will give their testimony.
3. The arbitral tribunal shall make arrangements for the translation of oral statements made at a hearing and for a record of the hearing if either is deemed necessary by the tribunal under the circumstances of the case, or if the parties have agreed thereto and have communicated such agreement to the tribunal at least fifteen days before the hearing.
4. Hearings shall be held in camera unless the parties agree otherwise. The arbitral tribunal may require the retirement of any witness or witnesses or expert witnesses during the testimony of other witnesses or expert witnesses. The arbitral tribunal is free to determine the manner in which witnesses or expert witnesses are examined.
5. Evidence of witnesses or expert witnesses may also be presented in the form of written statements or reports signed by them.
6. It shall not be improper for a party, its officers, employees, legal advisors or counsel to interview witnesses, potential witnesses or expert witnesses.
7. The arbitral tribunal shall determine the admissibility, relevance, materiality and weight of the evidence offered.

INTERIM MEASURES OF PROTECTION

Article 26

1. At the request of either party, the arbitral tribunal may take any interim measures it deems necessary or appropriate.
2. Such interim measures may be established in the form of an interim award. The arbitral tribunal shall be entitled to order the provision of appropriate security.
3. A request for interim measures addressed by any party to a judicial authority shall not be deemed incompatible with the agreement to arbitrate, or as a waiver of that agreement.
4. The arbitral tribunal shall have discretion to apportion the costs relating to a request for interim measures in the interim award or in the final award.

TRIBUNAL-APPOINTED EXPERTS

Article 27

1. The arbitral tribunal, after consulting with the parties, may appoint one or more experts to report to it, in writing, on specific issues to be determined by the tribunal. A copy of the expert's terms of reference, established by the arbitral tribunal, shall be communicated to the parties.
2. The parties shall give the expert any relevant information or produce for his inspection any relevant documents or goods that he may require of them. Any dispute between a party and such expert as to the relevance of the required information or production shall be referred to the arbitral tribunal for decision.
3. Upon receipt of the expert's report, the arbitral tribunal shall communicate a copy of the report to the parties who shall be given the opportunity to express, in writing, their opinion on the report. A party shall be entitled to examine any document on which the expert has relied in his report.
4. At the request of either party the expert, after delivery of the report, may be heard at a hearing where the parties shall have the opportunity to be present and to interrogate the expert. At this hearing either party may present expert witnesses in order to testify on the points at issue. The provisions of Article 25 shall be applicable to such proceedings.
5. The provisions of Article 9 shall apply by analogy to any expert appointed by the arbitral tribunal.

DEFAULT

Article 28

1. If, within the period of time set by the arbitral tribunal, the Claimant has failed to communicate its claim without showing sufficient cause for such failure, the arbitral tribunal shall issue an order for the termination of the arbitral proceedings. If, within the period of time set by the arbitral tribunal, the Respondent has failed to communicate its Statement of Defence without showing sufficient cause for such failure, the arbitral tribunal shall order that the proceedings continue.
2. If one of the parties, duly notified under these Rules, fails to appear at a hearing, without showing sufficient cause for such failure, the arbitral tribunal may proceed with the arbitration.
3. If one of the parties, duly invited to produce documentary evidence, fails to do so within the established period of time, without showing sufficient cause for such failure, the arbitral tribunal may make the award on the evidence before it.

CLOSURE OF PROCEEDINGS

Article 29

1. The arbitral tribunal may inquire of the parties if they have any further proof to offer or witnesses to be heard or submissions to make and, if there are none, it may declare the proceedings closed.
2. The arbitral tribunal may, if it considers it necessary owing to exceptional circumstances, decide, on its own motion or upon application of a party, to reopen the proceedings at any time before the award is made.

WAIVER OF RULES

Article 30

A party who knows that any provision of, or requirement under, these Rules has not been complied with and yet proceeds with the arbitration without promptly stating its objection to such non-compliance, shall be deemed to have waived its right to object.

Section IV. The Award

DECISIONS

Article 31

1. When there are three arbitrators, any award or other decision of the arbitral tribunal shall be made by a majority of the arbitrators. If there is no majority, the award shall be made by the presiding arbitrator alone.
2. In the case of questions of procedure, when the arbitral tribunal so authorises, the presiding arbitrator may decide on his own, subject to revision, if any, by the arbitral tribunal.

FORM AND EFFECT OF THE AWARD

Article 32

1. In addition to making a final award, the arbitral tribunal shall be entitled to make interim, interlocutory, or partial awards. If appropriate, the arbitral tribunal may also award costs in awards that are not final.

2. The award shall be made in writing and shall be final and binding on the parties. The parties undertake to carry out the award without delay.
3. The arbitral tribunal shall state the reasons upon which the award is based, unless the parties have agreed that no reasons are to be given.
4. An award shall be signed by the arbitrators and it shall contain the date on which and the place where the award was made. Where there are three arbitrators and one or two of them fail(s) to sign, the award shall state the reason for the absence of the signature(s).
5. Publication of the award is governed by Article 43.
6. Originals of the award signed by the arbitrators shall be communicated to the parties and to the Chambers by the arbitral tribunal. The Chambers shall retain a copy of the award.

APPLICABLE LAW, AMIABLE COMPOSITEUR

Article 33

1. The arbitral tribunal shall decide the case in accordance with the rules of law agreed upon by the parties or, in the absence of a choice of law, by applying the rules of law with which the dispute has the closest connection.
2. The arbitral tribunal shall decide as amiable compositeur or ex aequo et bono only if the parties have expressly authorised the arbitral tribunal to do so.
3. In all cases, the arbitral tribunal shall decide in accordance with the terms of the contract and shall take into account the usages of the trade applicable to the transaction.

SETTLEMENT OR OTHER GROUNDS FOR TERMINATION

Article 34

1. If, before the award is made, the parties agree on a settlement of the dispute, the arbitral tribunal shall either issue an order for the termination of the arbitral proceedings or, if requested by both parties and accepted by the tribunal, record the settlement in the form of an arbitral award on agreed terms. The arbitral tribunal is not obliged to give reasons for such an award.

2. If, before the award is made, the continuation of the arbitral proceedings becomes unnecessary or impossible for any reason not mentioned in paragraph 1, the arbitral tribunal shall inform the parties of its intention to issue an order for the termination of the proceedings. The arbitral tribunal shall have the power to issue such an order unless a party raises justifiable grounds for objection.

3. Copies of the order for termination of the arbitral proceedings or of the arbitral award on agreed terms, signed by the arbitrators, shall be communicated by the arbitral tribunal to the parties and to the Chambers. Where an arbitral award on agreed terms is made, the provisions of Article 32, paragraphs 2 and 4 to 6, shall apply.

INTERPRETATION OF THE AWARD

Article 35

1. Within thirty days after the receipt of the award, either party, with notice to the other party, may request that the arbitral tribunal give an interpretation of the award. The arbitral tribunal may set a time-limit, normally not exceeding thirty days, for the other party to comment on such request.

2. The interpretation shall be given in writing within forty-five days after the receipt of the request. The interpretation shall form part of the award and the provisions of Article 32, paragraphs 2 to 6, shall apply.

CORRECTION OF THE AWARD

Article 36

1. Within thirty days after the receipt of the award, either party, with notice to the other party, may request the arbitral tribunal to correct in the award any errors in computation, any clerical or typographical errors, or any errors of similar nature. The arbitral tribunal may set a time-limit, normally not exceeding thirty days, for the other party to comment on such request.

2. The arbitral tribunal may within thirty days after the communication of the award make such corrections on its own initiative.

3. Such corrections shall be in writing, and the provisions of Article 32, paragraphs 2 to 6, shall apply.

ADDITIONAL AWARD

Article 37

1. Within thirty days after the receipt of the award, either party, with notice to the other party, may request the arbitral tribunal to make an additional award as to claims presented in the arbitral proceedings but omitted from the award. The arbitral tribunal may set a time-limit, normally not exceeding thirty days, for the other party to comment on such request.

2. If the arbitral tribunal considers the request for an additional award to be justified and considers that the omission can be rectified without any further hearings or evidence, it shall complete its award within sixty days after the receipt of the request.

3. When an additional award is made, the provisions of Article 32, paragraphs 2 to 6, shall apply.

COSTS (ARTICLES 38 TO 40)

Article 38

The arbitral tribunal shall determine the costs of arbitration in its award. The term "costs" includes only:

(a) The fees of the arbitral tribunal to be stated separately as to each arbitrator and to be determined by the tribunal itself in accordance with Article 39;

(b) The travel and other expenses incurred by the arbitrators;

(c) The costs of expert advice and of other assistance required by the arbitral tribunal;

(d) The travel and other expenses of witnesses to the extent such expenses are approved by the arbitral tribunal;

(e) The costs for legal representation and assistance of the successful party if such costs were claimed during the arbitral proceedings, and only to the extent that the arbitral tribunal determines that the amount of such costs is reasonable;

(f) The costs for the administration of the arbitration payable to the Chambers in accordance with Appendix B (Schedule of the Costs of Arbitration).

Article 39

1. The fees of the arbitral tribunal shall be reasonable in amount, taking into account the amount in dispute, the complexity of the subject-matter, the time spent by the arbitrators and any other relevant circumstances of the case, including, but not limited to, the discontinuation of the arbitral proceedings in case of settlement or other reasons. In the event of such discontinuation, the fees of the arbitral tribunal may be less than the minimum amount resulting from Appendix B (Schedule of the Costs of Arbitration).

2. The fees of the arbitral tribunal shall be determined in conformity with Appendix B (Schedule of the Costs of Arbitration).

3. The arbitral tribunal shall decide on the allocation of the fees among its members. As a rule, the Chairman shall receive between 40 % and 50 % and each co-arbitrator between 25 % and 30 % of the total fees, in view of the time and efforts spent by each arbitrator.

Article 40

1. Except as provided in paragraph 2, the costs of arbitration shall in principle be borne by the unsuccessful party. However, the arbitral tribunal may apportion each of such costs between the parties if it determines that apportionment is reasonable, taking into account the circumstances of the case.

2. With respect to the costs of legal representation and assistance referred to in Article 38, paragraph (e), the arbitral tribunal, taking into account the circumstances of the case, shall be free to determine which party shall bear such costs or may apportion such costs between the parties if it determines that apportionment is reasonable.

3. When the arbitral tribunal issues an order for the termination of the arbitral proceedings or makes an award on agreed terms, it shall determine the costs of arbitration referred to in Article 38 and Article 39, paragraph 1, in the text of that order or award.

4. Before rendering the award, the arbitral tribunal shall submit its draft award to the Chambers for consultation on the decision as to the assessment and apportionment of the costs.

5. No additional fees may be charged by an arbitral tribunal for interpretation or correction or completion of its award under Articles 35 to 37.

DEPOSIT OF COSTS

Article 41

1. The arbitral tribunal, on its establishment, shall request each party to deposit an equal amount as an advance for the costs referred to in Article 38, paragraphs (a), (b), (c) and (f). The arbitral tribunal shall provide a copy of such request for information to the Chambers.
2. Where a Respondent submits a counterclaim, or it otherwise appears appropriate in the circumstances, the arbitral tribunal may in its discretion establish separate deposits.
3. During the course of the arbitral proceedings the arbitral tribunal may request supplementary deposits from the parties. The arbitral tribunal shall provide a copy of such request for information to the Chambers.
4. If the required deposits are not paid in full within thirty days after the receipt of the request, the arbitral tribunal shall so inform the parties in order that one or another of them may make the required payment. If such payment is not made, the arbitral tribunal may order the suspension or termination of the arbitral proceedings.
5. In its final award, the arbitral tribunal shall render an accounting to the parties of the deposits received. Any unexpended balance shall be returned to the parties.

Section V. Expedited Procedure

Article 42

1. If the parties so agree, or if the provisions of Article 42, paragraph 2 are applicable, the arbitral proceedings shall be conducted in accordance with an Expedited Procedure based upon the foregoing provisions of these Rules, subject to the following changes:

   (a) The Chambers may shorten the time-limits for the appointment of arbitrators;

   (b) After the submission of the Answer to the Notice of Arbitration, the parties shall in principle be entitled to submit one Statement of Claim and one Statement of Defence (and Counterclaim) and, where applicable, one Statement of Defence in reply to the Counterclaim;

   (c) Unless the parties agree that the dispute shall be decided on the basis of documentary evidence only, the arbitral tribunal shall hold a single hearing for the examination of the witnesses and expert witnesses as well as for oral argument;

(d) The award shall be made within six months from the date when the Chambers transmitted the file to the arbitral tribunal. In exceptional circumstances, the Chambers may extend this time-limit;

(e) The arbitral tribunal shall state the reasons upon which the award is based in summary form, unless the parties have agreed that no reasons are to be given.

2. The following provisions shall apply to all cases in which the amount in dispute representing the aggregate of the claim and the counterclaim (or any set-off defence) does not exceed CHF 1,000,000 (one million Swiss francs), unless the Chambers decide otherwise taking into account all relevant circumstances:

   (a) The arbitral proceedings shall be conducted in accordance with the Expedited Procedure set forth in Article 42, paragraph 1;

   (b) The case shall be referred to a sole arbitrator, unless the arbitration agreement provides for a three-member arbitral tribunal;

   (c) If the arbitration agreement provides for a three-member arbitral tribunal, the Chambers shall invite the parties to agree to refer the case to a sole arbitrator. If the parties do not agree to refer the case to a sole arbitrator, the fees of the three arbitrators shall be determined in accordance with Appendix B (Schedule of the Costs of Arbitration), but shall in no event be less than the fees resulting from the hourly rate of Section 2.8 of Appendix B.

Section VI. Confidentiality and exclusion of liability

Article 43

1. Unless the parties expressly agree in writing to the contrary, the parties undertake as a general principle to keep confidential all awards and orders as well as all materials submitted by another party in the framework of the arbitral proceedings not otherwise in the public domain, save and to the extent that a disclosure may be required of a party by a legal duty, to protect or pursue a legal right or to enforce or challenge an award in legal proceedings before a judicial authority. This undertaking also applies to the arbitrators, the tribunal-appointed experts, the secretary of the arbitral tribunal and the Chambers.

2. The deliberations of the arbitral tribunal are confidential.

3. An award may be published, whether in its entirety or in the form of excerpts or a summary, only under the following conditions:

   (a) A request for publication is addressed to the Chambers;

(b) All references to the parties' names are deleted; and

(c) No party objects to such publication within the time–limit fixed for that purpose by the Chambers.

Article 44

1. None of the Chambers or their staff, arbitrators, tribunal-appointed experts or the secretary of the arbitral tribunal shall be liable for any act or omission in connection with an arbitration conducted under these Rules, save where the act or omission is shown to constitute deliberate wrongdoing or extremely serious negligence.

2. After the award has been made and the possibilities of correction, interpretation and additional awards referred to in Articles 35 to 37 have lapsed or been exhausted, neither the Chambers nor the arbitrators, the tribunal-appointed experts or the secretary of the arbitral tribunal shall be under an obligation to make statements to any person about any matter concerning the arbitration, nor shall a party seek to make any of these persons a witness in any legal or other proceedings arising out of the arbitration.

APPENDIX A:
Addresses of the Chambers of Commerce

Basel Chamber of Commerce
Aeschenvorstadt 67
P.O. Box
CH-4010 Basel
Telephone: +41 61 270 60 50
Fax: +41 61 270 60 05
E-mail: schiedsgericht@hkbb.ch
Bank details: UBS AG, CH-4002 Basel
Account No: 292 – 10157720.0
Clearing No: 292
Iban: CH98 0029 2292 10157720 0

Chamber of Commerce and Industry of Bern
Gutenbergstrasse 1
P.O. Box 5464
CH – 3001 Bern
Telephone: +41 31 388 87 87
Fax: +41 31 388 87 88
E-mail: info@bern-cci.ch
Bank details: BEKB
Account No: KK 16 166.151.0.44 HIV Kanton Bern
Clearing No: 790
Swift Code: KBBECH22
Iban: CH35 0079 0016 1661 5104 4

Chamber of Commerce and Industry of Geneva
4, Boulevard du Théâtre
P.O. Box 5039
CH - 1211 Geneva 11
Telephone: +41 22 819 91 11
Fax: +41 22 819 91 36
E-mail: arbitration@ccig.ch
Bank details: UBS SA, Rue du Rhône 8, 1204 Genève
Account No: 279-HU108533.1
Clearing No: 279
Swift code: UBSWCHZH12A
Iban: CH13 0027 9279 HU1085331

Chamber of Commerce and Industry of Ticino
Corso Elvezia 16
P.O. Box 2378
CH-6901 Lugano
Telephone: +41 91 911 51 11
Fax: +41 91 911 51 12
E-mail: cciati@cci.ch
Bank details: Banca della Svizzera Italiana (BSI), Via Magatti 2, CH-6901 Lugano
Clearing No: 8475
Account No: A201021A 8465
Iban: CH64 0846 5000 0A20 1021 A

Chamber of Commerce and Industry of Vaud
Avenue d'Ouchy 47
P.O. Box 205
CH - 1000 Lausanne 13
Telephone: +41 21 613 35 35
Fax: +41 21 613 35 05
E-mail: direction@cvci.ch
Bank details: Banque Cantonale Vaudoise, 1001 Lausanne
Account No: C. 308.53.47
Clearing No: 767
Swift Code: BCVLCH2 L
Iban: CH96 0076 7001 U030 8534 7

Zurich Chamber of Commerce
Bleicherweg 5
P.O. Box 3058
CH - 8022 Zurich
Telephone: +41 1 217 40 50
Fax: +41 1 217 40 51
E-mail: direktion@zurichcci.ch
Bank details: Credit Suisse, CH-8070 Zurich
Account No: 497380-01
Clearing No: 4835
Swift Code: CRES CH ZZ 80A
Iban: CH62 0483 5049 7380 0100 0

APPENDIX B:
Schedule of the Costs of Arbitration

(All amounts in this Appendix B are in Swiss francs, hereinafter "CHF")

1. Registration Fee

1.1 When submitting a Notice of Arbitration, the Claimant shall pay a Registration Fee of

- CHF 4,500 for arbitrations where the amount in dispute does not exceed CHF 2,000,000;
- CHF 6,000 for arbitrations where the amount in dispute is between CHF 2,000,001 and CHF 10,000,000;
- CHF 8,000 for arbitrations where the amount in dispute exceeds CHF 10,000,000.

1.2 If the amount in dispute is not quantified, the Claimant shall pay a Registration Fee of CHF 6,000.

1.3 If the Claimant fails to pay the Registration Fee, the Chambers shall not proceed with the arbitration.

1.4 The Registration Fee is not refundable.

1.5 The above provisions shall apply to any counterclaim.

2. Arbitrators' fees and the Chambers' Administrative Costs

2.1 The arbitrators' fees (Article 38, paragraph a) shall cover the activities of the arbitral tribunal from the moment the file is transmitted until the last award.

2.2 Where the amount in dispute exceeds the threshold specified in Section 2.3 of this Appendix B, Administrative Costs shall be payable to the Chambers, in addition to the Registration Fee.

2.3 As a rule, the arbitrators' fees and the Chambers' Administrative Costs shall be computed on the basis of the following scale, taking into account the criteria of Article 39, paragraph 1:

Amount in dispute (in Swiss francs)	Fee of Sole Arbitrator[1]		Fee of three-member Arbitral tribunal		Administrative Costs[2] fixed by the Chambers
	min.	max.	min.	max.	-
up to CHF 300'000	4%	12%	10%	30%	-
CHF 300'001 to CHF 600'000	2%	8%	5%	20%	-
CHF 600'001 to CHF 1'000'000	1.5%	6%	3.75%	15%	-
CHF 1'000'001 to CHF 2'000'000	0.6%	3.6%	1.5%	9%	-
CHF 2'000'001 to CHF 10'000'000	0.38%	1.5%	0.95%	3.75%	CHF 4'000 +0.2%
CHF 10'000'001 to CHF 20'000'000	0.3%	0.6%	0.75%	1.5%	0.1%
CHF 20'000'001 to CHF 50'000'000	0.1%	0.2%	0.25%	0.5%	0.05%
CHF 50'000'001 to CHF 100'000'000	0.06%	0.18%	0.15%	0.45%	0.01%
CHF 100'000'001 to CHF 250'000'000	0.02%	0.1%	0.05%	0.25%	CHF 50'000
over CHF 250'000'000	0.01%	0.06%	0.025%	0.15%	CHF 50'000

The fees and administrative costs payable for each successive range in this chart are **added together**.

The arbitrators' fees and the Chambers' Administrative Costs may exceed the amounts set out in the scale above only in exceptional circumstances and with prior approval by the Chambers.

1 The fees for a sole arbitrator represent 40% of the fees for a three-member arbitral tribunal.

2 This is a contribution, in the maximum amount of CHF 50'000, to the administrative costs of the Chambers, in addition to the Registration Fee. In the event of discontinuation of the arbitral proceedings (Article 39, paragraph 1), the Chambers may, in their discretion, reimburse all or part of the Administrative Costs.

2.4 Claims and counterclaims are added for the determination of the amount in dispute. The same rule applies to set-off defences, unless the arbitral tribunal, after consulting with the parties, concludes that such set-off claims will not require significant additional work.

2.5 Interest claims shall not be taken into account for the calculation of the amount in dispute. However, when the interest claims exceed the amounts claimed in principal, the interest claims alone shall be considered in calculating the amount in dispute.

2.6 Currencies other than the Swiss franc shall be converted into Swiss francs at the average rate of exchange between the date when the Notice of Arbitration is received by the Chambers and the date when the final award is made. For the purpose of determining the Registration Fee under Section 1 of this Appendix B, the rate of exchange shall be that of the date when the Notice of Arbitration is received by the Chambers.

2.7 If the amount in dispute is not quantified, the Arbitrators' fees and the Chambers' Administrative costs shall be fixed by the arbitral tribunal, taking into account all relevant circumstances.

2.8 Where the parties do not agree to refer the case to a Sole arbitrator as provided for by Article 42, paragraph 2 (Expedited Procedure), the fees of the three arbitrators shall be determined in accordance with the above Schedule of the Costs of Arbitration but shall in no event be less than the fees resulting from the application of an hourly rate of CHF 350 (three hundred fifty Swiss francs).

3. Arbitrators' expenses

The expenses of the arbitrators shall relate to the actual disbursements for the arbitration, such as expenses relating to: travel (first class airfare accepted only for distances exceeding 4000 kilometres), accommodation, meals (if in home city, only meals among arbitrators are taken into account), taxi, communications costs, and any other costs related to the conduct of the proceedings (such as rental of hearing rooms, court reporting services, interpreters, etc.). The Chambers may issue general guidelines to the arbitrators for the accounting of their expenses.

4. Income earned on deposits made by the parties

In consultation with the parties, the arbitral tribunal may invest the deposits made by the parties, taking into account market conditions and criteria of prudent and secure investment. When deciding whether to make such investments, the arbitral tribunal shall also have due regard to the possible need to make the deposited funds available immediately. Any income earned shall be included in the final computation of the costs of the arbitration in favour of the party or parties having made the deposit or deposits so invested.

APPENDIX C: Arbitrators' fees

Sole Arbitrator

Amount in dispute (in Swiss francs)		**Administrative costs**	**Sole Arbitrator** Minimum	Maximum
0-	300'000	-	12'000	36'000
300'001-	600'000	-	12'000 + 0.2% of amount over 300'000	36'000 + 8% of amount over 300'000
600'001-	1'000'000	-	18'000 + 1.5% of amount over 600'000	60'000 + 6% of amount over 600'000
1'000'001-	2'000'000	-	24'000 + 0.6% of amount over 1'000'000	84'000 + 3.6% of amount over 1'000'000
2'000'001-	10'000'000	4'000 + 0.2% of amount over 2'000'000	30'000 + 0.38% of amount over 2'000'000	120'000 + 1.5% of amount over 2'000'000
10'000'001-	20'000'000	20'000 + 0.1% of amount over 10'000'000	60'400 + 0.3% of amount over 10'000'000	240'000 + 0.6% of amount over 10'000'000
20'000'001-	50'000'000	30'000 + 0.05% of amount over 20'000'000	90'400 + 0.1% of amount over 20'000'000	300'000 + 0.2% of amount over 20'000'000
50'000'001-	100'000'000	45'000 + 0.01% of amount over 50'000'000	120'400 + 0.06% of amount over 50'000'000	360'000 + 0.18% of amount over 50'000'000
100'000'001-	250'000'000	50'000	150'400 + 0.02% of amount over 100'000'000	450'000 + 0.1% of amount over 100'000'000
> 250'000'000		50'000	180'400 + 0.01% of amount over 250'000'000	600'000 + 0.06% of amount over 250'000'000

APPENDIX C: Arbitrators' fees

Three Arbitrators

Amount in dispute (in Swiss francs)		**Administrative costs**	**Three-member arbitral tribunal**	
			Minimum	Maximum
0-	300'000	-	30'000	90'000
300'001-	600'000	-	30'000 + 5% of amount over 300'000	90'000 + 20% of amount over 300'000
600'001-	1'000'000	-	45'000 + 3.75% of amount over 600'000	150'000 + 15% of amount over 600'000
1'000'001-	2'000'000	-	60'000 + 1.5% of amount over 1'000'000	210'000 + 9% of amount over 1'000'000
2'000'001-	10'000'000	4'000 + 0.2% of amount over 2'000'000	75'000 + 0.95% of amount over 2'000'000	300'000 + 3.75% of amount over 2'000'000
10'000'001-	20'000'000	20'000 + 0.1% of amount over 10'000'000	151'000 + 0.75% of amount over 10'000'000	600'000 + 1.5% of amount over 10'000'000
20'000'001-	50'000'000	30'000 + 0.05% of amount over 20'000'000	226'000 + 0.25% of amount over 20'000'000	750'000 + 0.5% of amount over 20'000'000
50'000'001-	100'000'000	45'000 + 0.01% of amount over 50'000'000	301'000 + 0.15% of amount over 50'000'000	900'000 + 0.45% of amount over 50'000'000
100'000'001-	250'000'000	50'000	376'000 + 0.05% of amount over 100'000'000	1'125'000 + 0.25% of amount over 100'000'000
> 250'000'000		50'000	451'000 + 0.025% of amount over 250'000'000	1'500'000 + 0.15% of amount over 250'000'000

Appendix 3 - Translation of Chapter 12 of the Swiss Private International Law Act ('PILA')*

I. Scope of application. Seat of the arbitral tribunal

Article 176

[1] The provisions of this chapter apply to any arbitration if the seat of the arbitral tribunal is in Switzerland and if, at the time when the arbitration agreement was entered into, at least one of the parties had neither its domicile nor its habitual residence in Switzerland.

[2] The provisions of this chapter do not apply where the parties have in writing excluded its application and agreed to the exclusive application of the procedural provisions of cantonal law relating to arbitration.

[3] The seat of the arbitral tribunal is determined by the parties, or the arbitration institution designated by them, or, failing both, by the arbitrators.

II. Arbitrability

Article 177

[1] Any dispute involving an economic interest may be the subject-matter of an arbitration.

[2] If a party to the arbitration agreement is a state or an enterprise or organization controlled by it, it cannot rely on its own law in order to contest its capacity to be a party to an arbitration or the arbitrability of a dispute covered by the arbitration agreement.

---

* Translation taken from A. BUCHER/P.-Y. TSCHANZ (eds), *Switzerland, Private International Law and Arbitration, Basic documents*, Helbing & Lichtenhahn, Basle and Frankfurt on the Main 1996.

Article 178

III. Arbitration agreement

[1] As regards its form, an arbitration agreement is valid if made in writing, by telegram, telex, telecopier or any other means of communication which permits it to be evidenced by a text.
[2] As regards its substance, an arbitration agreement is valid if it conforms either to the law chosen by the parties, or to the law governing the subject-matter of the dispute, in particular the law governing the main contract, or if it conforms to Swiss law.
[3] The validity of an arbitration agreement cannot be contested on the ground that the main contract may not be valid or that the arbitration agreement concerns a dispute which has not yet arisen.

Article 179

IV. Arbitral tribunal

1. Constitution

[1] The arbitrators shall be appointed, removed or replaced in accordance with the agreement of the parties.
[2] In the absence of such an agreement, the matter shall be referred to the court where the arbitral tribunal has its seat; the court shall apply by analogy the provisions of cantonal law concerning the appointment, removal or replacement of arbitrators.
[3] Where a court is called upon to appoint an arbitrator, it shall make the appointment, unless a summary examination shows that no arbitration agreement exists between the parties.

Article 180

2. Challenge of arbitrators

[1] An arbitrator may be challenged:

a. if he or she does not meet the requirements agreed by the parties;
b. if the arbitration rules agreed by the parties provide a ground for challenge; or
c. if circumstances exist that give rise to justifiable doubts as to his or her independence.

[2] A party may challenge an arbitrator whom it has appointed or in whose appointment it has participated only on grounds of which it became aware after such appointment. The ground for challenge must be notified to the arbitral tribunal and the other party without delay.
[3] In the event of a dispute and to the extent that the parties have not determined the procedure for the challenge, the court having jurisdiction at the seat of the arbitral tribunal shall make the final decision.

Article 181

V. Lis pendens

The arbitral proceeding is pending as of the time when one of the parties submit its request to the arbitrator or arbitrators designated in the arbitration agreement or, in the absence of such designation, from the time when one of the parties initiates the procedure for the constitution of the arbitral tribunal.

VI. Procedure
1. Principle

Article 182

[1] The parties may, directly or by reference to arbitration rules, determine the arbitral procedure; they may also submit it to a procedural law of their choice.
[2] Where the parties have not determined the procedure, the arbitral tribunal shall determine it to the extent necessary, either directly or by reference to a law or to arbitration rules.
[3] Whatever procedure is chosen, the arbitral tribunal shall ensure equal treatment of the parties and their right to be heard in an adversary procedure.

2. Interim relief and conservatory measures

Article 183

[1] Unless the parties have agreed otherwise, the arbitral tribunal may, at the request of a party, grant interim relief and conservatory measures.
[2] If the party so ordered does not comply therewith voluntarily, the arbitral tribunal may request the assistance of the competent court. Such court shall apply its own law.
[3] The arbitral tribunal or the court may take the granting of interim relief or conservatory measures subject to the provision of appropriate security.

3. Taking of evidence

Article 184

[1] The arbitral tribunal shall itself take the evidence.
[2] Where the assistance of state authorities is needed for taking evidence, the arbitral tribunal, or a party with the consent of the arbitral tribunal may request the assistance of the court at the seat of the arbitral tribunal; such court shall apply its own law.

4. Other judicial assistance

Article 185

For any further judicial assistance the court at the seat of the arbitral tribunal has jurisdiction.

VII. Jurisdiction

Article 186

[1] The arbitral tribunal shall decide on its own jurisdiction.
[2] Any objection to its jurisdiction must be raised prior to any defense on the merits.

[3] The arbitral tribunal shall, in general, decide on its jurisdiction by a preliminary decision.

Article 187

VIII. Decision on the merits
1. Applicable law

[1] The arbitral tribunal shall decide the dispute according to the rules of law chosen by the parties or, in the absence of such a choice, according to the rules of law with which the case has the closest connection.

[2] The parties may authorize the arbitral tribunal to decide *ex aequo et bono*.

Article 188

2. Partial award

Unless the parties have agreed otherwise, the arbitral tribunal may make partial awards.

Article 189

3. Arbitral award

[1] The arbitral award shall be made in conformity with the procedure and form agreed by the parties.

[2] In the absence of such an agreement, the award shall be made by a majority decision or, in the absence of a majority, by the presiding arbitrator alone. It shall be in writing, reasoned, dated and signed. The signature of the presiding arbitrator is sufficient.

Article 190

IX. Finality

[1] The award is final from the time when it is communicated.

Setting aside
1. Principle

[2] Proceedings for setting aside the award may only be initiated:

a. where the sole arbitrator has been improperly appointed or where the arbitral tribunal has been improperly constituted;
b. where the arbitral tribunal has wrongly accepted or denied jurisdiction;
c. where the arbitral tribunal has ruled beyond the claims submitted to it, or failed to decide one of the claims;
d. where the principle of equal treatment of the parties or their right to be heard in an adversary procedure has not been observed;
e. where the award is incompatible with public policy.

[3] As regards preliminary decisions, setting aside proceedings can only be initiated on the grounds of the above paragraphs 2(a) and 2(b); the time-limit runs from the communication of the decision.

2. Competent court

Article 191

[1] Setting aside proceedings may only be brought before the Federal Supreme Court. The procedure is governed by the provisions of the Federal Judicial Organization Act relating to public law appeals.

[2] However, the parties may agree that the court at the seat of the arbitral tribunal shall decide in lieu of the Federal Supreme Court; its decision is final. For this purpose the cantons shall designate a sole cantonal court.

X. Exclusion agreements

Article 192

[1] Where none of the parties has its domicile, its habitual residence, or a place of business in Switzerland, they may, by an express statement in the arbitration agreement or by a subsequent agreement in writing, exclude all setting aside proceedings, or they may limit such proceedings to one or several of the grounds listed in Article 190(2).

[2] Where the parties have excluded all setting aside proceedings and where the awards are to be enforced in Switzerland, the New York Convention of June 10, 1958 on the Recognition and Enforcement of Foreign Arbitral Awards applies by analogy.

XI. Deposit and certificate of enforceability

Article 193

[1] Each party may at its own expense deposit a copy of the award with the Swiss court at the seat of the arbitral tribunal.

[2] At the request of a party, that court shall certify the enforceability of the award.

[3] At the request of a party, the arbitral tribunal shall certify that the award has been made in conformity with the provisions of this Act; such a certificate has the same effect as the deposit of the award.

XII. Foreign arbitral awards

Article 194

The recognition and enforcement of foreign arbitral awards is governed by the New York Convention of June 10, 1958 on the Recognition and Enforcement of Foreign Arbitral Awards.

Appendix 4 - Translations of Select Provisions of the Swiss Judicial Organization Act ('JOA')*

Art. 32

Time limits

a. Computation, observance

[1] In computing time limits, the day from which the time limit runs is not counted.

[2] When the last day falls on a Sunday or on a legal holiday under the law of the canton, the time limit expires on the next working day.

[3] The time limit is deemed to have been observed only if the act was accomplished before its expiry. Written briefs must reach the authority competent to receive them or have been remitted to their address at a Swiss postal office at the latest on the last day of the time limit. When a written brief reaches the Federal Tribunal before the expiry of a time limit, the latter is deemed to have been observed even if a cantonal authority was competent to receive the brief.

Art. 34

c. Suspension of time limits

[1] Time limits set by statute or by the judge do not run:

a. from the 7th day before Easter to the 7th day after Easter, inclusively;

b. from 15 July to 15 August inclusively;

c. from 18 December to 1st January inclusively.

[2] This rule applies neither in criminal matters nor in debt collection and bankruptcy matters.

---

* Free translation from the authors.

d. Granting of a new deadline

Art. 35

1 When a time limit has not been observed, a new deadline may be granted only if the moving party or its legal representative was prevented from acting within the deadline without any fault on its part. The request for a new deadline must specify the preventing factor to timely filing and be made within ten days following the lifting thereof. The act must be accomplished within that [new] time limit.

2 The decision is taken in the framework of written proceedings without any public deliberation; article 95 is applicable.

c. Other cases

Art. 85

1 The Federal Tribunal has jurisdiction to hear :

[...]

c. challenges of awards rendered by an arbitral tribunal in accordance with Articles 190 seq. of the Federal Acton on Private International Law of 18 December 1987.

Challenge of interim and interlocutory decisions

Art. 87

1 A public law appeal is admissible against interim and interlocutory decisions on jurisdiction and removal [of judges], each taken separately. These decisions may not be challenged subsequently.

2 A public law appeal is admissible against other interim and interlocutory decisions, taken separately, in case of potential irreparable harm.

3 If a public law appeal is not admissible under para. 2 or was not filed, interim and interlocutory decisions may be challenged with the final decision.

Entitlement to challenge

Art. 88

1 A person or an entity may challenge legislation or a decision that affect party personally or that are of general public interest.

Art. 89

Time limits

[1] The motion must be filed with the Federal Tribunal within 30 days from notification, according to cantonal law, of the legislation or decision being challenged.

[2] If the reasons of the decision being challenged are notified subsequently, the challenge may still be filed within 30 days from notification thereof.

[3] [...]

Art. 90

Motion

[1] In addition to the designation of the legislation or decision being challenged, the motion shall contain:

a. the appellant's prayers for relief;

b. a statement of the essential facts and a succinct statement of the violated constitutional rights or legal principles, specifying the elements which constitute such violation.

[2] If the appellant is able to obtain a copy of the decision being challenged, it must enclose it with the motion, failing which a short deadline is set for the appellant to act accordingly, with the consequence of inadmissibility in case of non-compliance.

Art. 91

Proceedings

[1] In general, the Tribunal decides on the public law disputes after a written procedure administered by the president or the judge in charge of the case.

[2] Upon request of one party, the tribunal may exceptionally order oral hearings for important reasons.

Art. 93

Exchange of briefs

[1] If the Tribunal orders an exchange of briefs, it transmits the motion to the authority having issued the legislation or decision being challenged, as well as to the opposite party or other possible interested persons, and grants an appropriate time limit for filing a response and to transmit the file.

[2] If the reasons for the legislation or decision being challenged are given for the first time in the response filed by the authority, a deadline may be granted to the appellant to file a supplemental brief.

[3] A second exchange of written pleadings may be ordered only exceptionally.

Provisional measures

Art. 94
[1] Upon request of a party, the president of the Tribunal may, after receipt of the motion, order provisional measures necessary to preserve the current situation or safeguard interests that are imperilled.

Evidentiary proceedings

Art. 95
[1] The judge entrusted with the evidentiary proceedings orders all evidentiary measures necessary to establish the facts. He may proceed with the taking of evidence himself or delegate this to the competent cantonal or federal authorities.

[2] The Tribunal weighs the evidence freely.

b. New facts

Art. 137
A motion for revision of a Federal Tribunal decision is also possible:[1]

a. when criminal proceedings establish that the decision was influenced to the detriment of the moving party by a felony or a crime, even if no conviction ensued. If criminal prosecution is not possible, proof can be brought in another manner;

b. when the moving party has subsequent knowledge of new and important facts or finds convincing evidence that it had not been able to invoke in the previous proceedings.

---

1 The French version of the statutory text uses the term '*recevable*', which should be translated into '*admissible*' and which pertains only to procedure as opposed to substance. However, this is a drafting error in the French text. The provision actually refers to the substantive conditions for a revision. We have therefore used the term '*possible*'.

Art. 140

Motion for revision

The motion must specify, with all supporting evidence, the ground for revision that is being invoked and that this ground has been invoked timely; it must also specify the modification to the decision and the restitution that are being sought.

Art. 141

Procedure

[1] The motion for revision must be filed before the Federal Tribunal, on pain of forfeiture:

a. Time limit

a. for the cases set out in art. 136, within thirty days at the latest from service of the written decision;

b. for the cases set out in art. 137, within ninety days at the latest from the discovery of the ground for revision, however at the earliest upon service of the written decision or upon completion of the criminal proceedings;

c. for the cases set out in art. 139*a*, within ninety days at the latest from the date on which the Federal Justice Department served the parties with the decision of the European authorities.

[2] After ten years, the motion for revision may be filed only in case of felony or crime.

Art. 142

b. Stay of enforcement

During the proceedings, the Tribunal or the president may, if necessary subject to the posting of security, order a stay of enforcement of the decision being revised and order other provisional measures.

Art. 143

c. Further rules

[1] If the Tribunal considers unanimously that the motion is inadmissible or without merit, it may render its decision without a public deliberation.

[2] Otherwise, the motion is communicated to the opposite party, who is invited to reply within a sufficient time limit and to file its own evidence.

[3] A further exchange of briefs or oral proceedings take place only exceptionally.

[4] If the admissibility of the motion depends on facts that are disputed, art. 95 is applicable by analogy.

d. Decision rendered on motion for revision

Art. 144

[1] When the Tribunal admits the ground for revision that was alleged, it annuls the challenged decision and rules anew. Il adjudicates at the same time on restitution on the merits and on the costs.

[2] The annulment of a decision remanding a case to a cantonal court entails the annulment of the final judgment rendered by that court.

Security for court costs and legal fees

Art. 150

[1] Any person seizing the Federal Tribunal must, upon order by the president, provide security to guarantee the expected court costs (art. 153 and 153*a*). Where particular reasons justify an exception, the Tribunal may refrain entirely or partially from demanding the provision of security.

[2] If a party has no fixed domicile in Switzerland or if it is established that it is insolvent, it may be invited by the president or by the judge in charge of the case, upon request by the opposite party, to provide security for the costs that may be incurred by the opposite party (art. 159 and 160).

[3] Security must be made by cash deposit at the Tribunal's cashier.

[4] If the security (under sub-section 1 or 2) is not posted within the time limit, the relevant party's prayers for relief are inadmissible.

Index